1

ISBN: 9781739474959

Imprint: HBM

First published 2023

Cover images – a hopping Jonathan Edwards, a stepping Yulimar Rojas and a jumping Józef Szmidt © Alamy

www.harveybennsmethod.com

TRIPLE JUMP
TRAILBLAZERS

By Andy Benns & Lawrence Harvey

Foreword by Willie Banks
Former Triple Jump World Record Holder

Dedication

Firstly, a huge thanks to Willie Banks and Jonathan Edwards – on behalf of both myself and Andy, we greatly appreciated your time, inspiration and support – it spurred us onto even deeper levels of research and insight in pursuit of writing the very best triple jump book we could.

To all those whom I have been fortunate enough to encounter throughout my time in athletics – from the coaches; Ted Hawkins, Trevor Bent, Mike Mein, Kevin Reeve, Colin Harris and Paddy O'Shea, to my training partners and friends; Paul Ralph, Steve Lake, Matt Morsia, Matt Hulyer, Farel Mepandy, Femi Akinsanya, Tom Bell and Navid Childs – to name but a few, thank you all for your support and encouragement over the years.

Last but not least, to yourself, the reader – Andy and I hope you are transported into the triple jump world with the same excitement and wonderment we felt putting our words onto the pages… may the steps of the past inspire you to take even bigger strides of your own into the future!

CONTENTS

FOREWORD BY WILLIE BANKS
FORMER TRIPLE JUMP WORLD RECORD HOLDER

I vividly recall the first time I set foot on the runway, ready to embark on a journey that would forever shape my life. The triple jump, a mesmerizing track and field event, has been my anchor, my passion, and my true calling. It is with utmost gratitude and admiration that I lend my voice to this remarkable book – a testament to the storied history of the triple jump.

As I turn the pages, I am transported through time, reliving the triumphs and tribulations of those who came before me. The authors have meticulously chronicled the evolution of this extraordinary event, delving deep into its roots and unearthing treasures that lay hidden within the annals of history. To Lawrence & Andy, I extend my sincerest appreciation for your unwavering dedication to capturing the essence of the triple jump.

Within these pages, a tapestry of stories unfolds – a tapestry woven with the threads of determination, perseverance, and unyielding spirit. From the pioneering leaps of its origins in Ireland to the modern-day innovations that push the boundaries of human potential, the journey of the triple jump unfolds like a symphony, captivating the hearts and minds of all who dare to dream.

It is through this book that we gain a newfound appreciation for the giants who have graced the sandpit – the legends who defied gravity and pushed the limits of what was thought possible. Their names echo through the ages, inspiring generations to pursue greatness. Their feats of athleticism, courage, and unwavering willpower serve as beacons of hope for every aspiring triple jumper.

But this book is not just a collection of remarkable stories; it is a testament to the relentless pursuit of excellence that permeates the world of track and field. It celebrates the unsung heroes – the coaches, the trainers, the officials – who have dedicated their lives to nurturing talent, shaping careers, and ensuring the integrity of the sport. It is a tribute to the camaraderie that thrives within the track and field community, a bond forged by shared passion and mutual respect.

The collective noun for a group of World Record holders... *greatness?*

From the private collection of Willie Banks, left to right – Willie Banks (17.97m, WR, 1985), Teruji Kogake (16.48m, low-altitude best, 1956), Mikio Oda (15.58m, WR, 1931), Adhemar da Silva (16.56m, WR#5, 1955) & Chūhei Nambu (15.72m, WR, 1932).

To the readers who hold this book in their hands, I invite you to embark on a journey — a journey that will illuminate the beauty and complexity of the triple jump. As you immerse yourself in the pages before you, may you be inspired by the triumphs and setbacks, the moments of elation and the lessons learned from defeat. Let this book be your guide, your source of knowledge, and your source of inspiration.

To Lawrence & Andy, I express my deepest gratitude for your tireless efforts in meticulously piecing together this magnificent tapestry of the triple jump's history. You have ensured that the legacy of this awe-inspiring event endures, shining a light on the immense talent and indomitable spirit that define the triple jump community. Your work will inspire generations to come, fostering a deep appreciation for this event and its remarkable athletes.

In closing, let us embrace the past, present, and future of the triple jump with reverence and awe. As we reflect on the triumphs of the past, let us pave the way for future athletes to soar to unimaginable heights. May this book serve as a reminder that the legacy of the triple jump is not confined to the sandpit — it lives within each of us, inspiring us to push beyond our limits and make our mark on the world.

With immense gratitude and boundless admiration,

Willie Banks, June 2023

GLOSSARY

IAAF/World Athletics – the International Amateur Athletic Federation (from 1912-2001), the International Association of Athletics Federations (from 2001-2019) and now World Athletics; the international governing body for the sport of athletics, including the recognition of World Records and the sanctioning of athletics competitions, including the World Athletics Championships.

IOC – the International Olympic Committee, the supreme authority of the Olympic Movement worldwide, including organization of the modern Olympic Games.

The Triple Jump – defined by World Athletics as:

> *One of the two horizontal jump events on the track and field programme, competitors sprint along a runway before taking off from a wooden board. The take-off foot absorbs the first landing, the hop. The next phase, the step, is finished on the opposite foot and then followed by a jump into a sandpit. The distance travelled, from the edge of the board to the closest indentation in the sand to it, is then measured. A foul is committed – and the jump is not measured – if an athlete steps beyond the board. The order of the field is determined by distance jumped. Most championship competitions involve six jumps per competitor, although usually a number of them, those with the shorter marks, are often eliminated after three jumps. If competitors are tied, the athlete with the next best distance is declared the winner. The event requires speed, explosive power, strength and flexibility. At major championships the format is usually a qualification session followed by a final.*
> [https://worldathletics.org/disciplines/jumps/triple-jump]

WR, World Record – the best athletics performances, ratified as official World Records by World Athletics. Various criteria for World Records are defined by World Athletics in their Competition Rules, including specific rules such as the landing mark in the sandpit not to be raked until the fully on-field electronic distance measurement has been made.
[https://worldathletics.org/about-iaaf/documents/book-of-rules]

OR, Olympic Record – records recorded in the Olympic Games since 1896; some have also been World Records. Variations include CR, Championship Record for the leading mark in the World Championships for example.

PB, Personal Best – an athlete's best performance in his or her life; variations include Season Best.

Wind-assisted or wind-assistance – the benefit an athlete receives from the wind in outdoor competition, as measured by a wind gauge at the time of the jump; a tailwind will increase the speed of the athlete whilst running and there is an allowable limit of 2 meters per second (displayed as +2.0m/s) in order for a performance to be established as a World Record by World Athletics.

[https://worldathletics.org/about-iaaf/documents/book-of-rules]

Altitude-assisted – performances above 1000m above sea-level are classified as altitude-assisted; they can be accepted as World Records, but are denoted as such by an '(A)' next to the mark in the record-books.

Junior – a category of athletics competition for athletes under the age of 20. World Athletics organise a World U20 Championships every two years, launched as the IAAF World Junior Championships in Athletics in 1986.

Youth – a category of athletics competition for athletes under the age of 18. World Athletics previously organised a World U18 Championships every two years until 2017, launched as the IAAF World Youth Championships in Athletics in 1999. Discontinued by the then IAAF as it was not felt to be the best pathway for athletes.

INTRODUCTION

This is not just the story of the greatest triple jumpers of all time. It is a telling of a sport, still considered by many in track and field to be one of the oddest – it is not a natural action to jump from the same leg twice, then switch to the other – through its greatest athletes and the greatest performances. The men's World Record has stood since 1995, testament to when Jonathan Edwards became the first man to legally leap beyond 18 metres, then bettered his own record a short while later, but the story of the sport is so much more than its greatest afternoon. Current triple jumpers have the chance to etch their name into the record-books, yet even if they cannot claim the World Record or match the accolades of the very best, they still have a responsibility to advance the sport in other ways, each a trailblazer or torchbearer for those jumpers still to come.

Many current leading sports stars are as focussed on wealth generation and fame as they are on sporting success, the prism of social media (with its totemic hierarchy of followers and likes) central to attracting sponsors, as much as on field performance. Track and field athletes contend with significant financial pressure, being paid much less than their peers in other professional sports, and the sport as a whole enjoys much less popularity than it did in its heyday in the 1990's; this is even more obvious in the United States than in Europe, where stadiums are packed, particularly for Diamond League meetings, but earnings (appearance money, win bonuses) are still low. The young adult generation ('Generation Z', born in about 1997-2012) are commonly defined by their aspiration and drive, with a perceived habit for nostalgia increasingly tapped into by marketeers. Those of this demographic cohort, now aged 11-26, may include future leading triple jumpers who elect to also look backwards when considering how to shape their own legacy and wanting to be famous – and wealthy – is certainly not the same as becoming *great*.

This is not a comprehensive history, more a journey that the authors from Great Britain have gone on in their own ways, Lawrence a triple jump World Masters Athletics Champion (M35) in 2016 and Andy with a keen interest in track and field from his childhood. The impetus for this book came to Lawrence as he drove home from a wet and cold evening's training on the track – there are few books on the triple jump, especially with any technical knowledge or serious research into the event's past – and a conversation with schoolfriend Andy led to this collaboration that we hope you enjoy reading. We have certainly enjoyed researching and writing it together, which we hope comes out on these pages.

We explore the stories of those that came before the current leading stars and it is important that these stories are re-told, without going into the depths of full biography. We consider how the technique has evolved, the progression of the men's and women's World Records, the landmark performances of its greatest athletes and consider those still working towards bettering the respective leading marks at the time of publication, with many of the record jumps taking place in Olympic Games through the ages, historically when interest in the event would peak amongst his leading proponents. We also made a commitment to exploring the legacy of the leading women's triple jumpers, so this is not a story of just the men's event, as many books on athletics can be. And after all that, we may even be able to decide for ourselves who are the *greatest* triple jumpers of all time...

WHY THE TRIPLE JUMP?

This is the question I have been asked the most over the last 25 years. In truth, you could ask the same question of many activities in life; as humans we can find our own passion in the most obscure places…think chess, snooker, acting, ballet, any form of 'collective' pursuits, and even kicking a ball around, as millions around the world do daily when playing football (soccer), regardless of their wealth or circumstance. In sport, different activities enjoy considerably different participation levels and occupy our minds to a greater or lesser extent – our natural instinct as humans is to be part of a tribe, so when coupled with the need for social identity and genuine enjoyment, this typically results in team sports being much more conscious in our minds. In truth, as an active child I was surrounded by sport, participating in all the main team sports and with a father in the military, we found ourselves moving around a lot on account of his job as a Physical Training Instructor (he was also an international water polo player and an excellent squash player, to this day despite his advancing years!).

My constant was sport and for me it was the *in* at every school I ever attended; I was generally the fastest kid in my class wherever we ended up, and that ability, which would flash in team sports, would see me truly come to life when the track and field season commenced. The annual 'sports day', a staple event in the calendar of British schools to this day, would provide that one moment when everyone would pause and watch to see who the fastest boy and girl in the school was – after the finish, there being no further debate about who would hold that status, at least until the next race! Athletes of all ability will share similar memories when track and field allowed them to stand out as the winner

– the best amongst their peers – and my own journey as an athlete would take me from being a decent schoolboy sprinter to an obsessive *triple jumper.*

The triple jump has been a part of my life from the age of 10 and I cannot imagine a future without it being so. I remember watching the Barcelona Olympics in 1992 on television with my father and by chance we found the men's triple jump final, in which Mike Conley of the United States would win Gold with a staggering jump of 18.17m; a would-be World Record were it not for the fact that the wind was marginally over the allowable limit at +2.1m/s (more on that later). The nature of the event fascinated me – a combination of speed, power, and technique, coupled with multiple attempts to improve your best distance. Furthermore, there was an immediacy about it, success being possible in such indiscriminate ways, a true diversity of height, weight, speed, nationality, race, strength, power and even technique on display to a then awestruck ten-year-old!

I was transfixed by this event in particular and since the 1992 Olympics athletics has been the ever-present thread in my life, the magazine *Athletics Weekly*[1] quickly becoming the medium in a pre-internet age that allowed me to read and dream about the sport in my every waking hour. The challenge I had in my teenage years was that we mostly did team sports at school, with no dedicated athletics event coaching, so anything I attempted in track and field came from reading, trial and error, and my own natural ability. However, 1995 would see my passion for the triple jump step out of the shadows, what was then a little-known event within athletics becoming a major news story in Great Britain on account of one man... Jonathan Edwards.

---

[1] English language track and field magazine, founded in 1945 and now called *AW*.

As an avid athletics fan, I knew of Jonathan Edwards, then a very good British athlete with podium claims in every major championship, but what he did in 1995 for the event, for athletics and for British sporting pride, was to make him a legend. British athletics had enjoyed its own heyday in the late 80's and early 90's, both in terms of international success and wider public interest, with the 1993 World Championships in Stuttgart the peak,[2] but Edwards was to take being a world-beating British athlete to a whole new level, his performance that evening being watched at home by a massive television audience who were to take him – and the event of the triple jump, unknown to many – to their hearts, in a way that has never truly been repeated in Great Britain. To watch Jonathan Edwards triple jump in 1995 was to see near sporting perfection and re-watching him glide over the runway in Gothenburg to this day makes me feel the same way. The speed, grace, the hitherto unknown strength, the effortless flowing technique, the smile, the raised hands, and in the end, the barrier-breaking achievement beyond first 18m and then 60ft, was breath-taking then and remains so even now.

The passion and excitement I experienced in the 1990's has not diminished and my hope is that this book is a worthy contribution to your own enjoyment of the sport. The women's event in particular has never seen an athlete like Yulimar Rojas and we do not yet know how far she will advance the discipline, already assured of legendary status with her peak years still to come; we do know that Edwards has reached near-fabled status as the men's World Record holder and to this day he is the standard by which all others are measured, be it a

---

[2] Linford Christie, Colin Jackson, and Sally Gunnell claimed Gold in the men's 100m, men's 110m hurdles and women's 400m hurdles respectively; each were household names in Great Britain at the time and their collective achievement was unprecedented for the country.

novice jumper marking out his record distance of 18.29m to compare to their own efforts or those leading jumpers working to write their own name in the record books.

I think I only really *got* the triple jump in 2000 – up until this point, on reflection I had been ignorant of the intricacies necessary to achieve world class performance. For context, in 1997 I jumped 12.70m (41ft $6\frac{1}{2}$in) as a 15-year-old with no specific triple jump training, but at Loughborough University a couple of years later I was fortunate and privileged to train alongside a wonderful French international named Farel Mepandy,[3] with a later personal best of 15.88m. Farel taught me the *art* of the triple jump – many coaches had explained it to me, I had of course watched it many times on television, but he *showed* it to me. I did not have a full-time jumps coach at Loughborough University, despite its athletics pedigree within Great Britain and listening to my body and how things *felt*, became very important, in addition to being coached from afar.

I graduated from university in 2003 aged 21, with a personal best of 14.87m, placed fourth in the national U23 rankings. I then had to learn to balance a business career with training, since being in-and-out of the sport many times and even 'retiring' from competition in 2012, until the overwhelming need to pick up the spikes returned a few years later! It was not until my late twenties that I surpassed 15m for the first time and a year later (2011), I jumped what remains my best to this day – 15.22m (49ft $11\frac{3}{4}$in). Ironically, my late introduction to proper athletics training and the long periods of time I have spent out of the sport due to work commitments has (by luck rather than judgement) helped preserve my body.

---

[3] Farel Mepandy, Congo-born, with a career best fourth place in the 2004 African Championships [1979-].

And so, when 2015 arrived, by now mostly training alone and accepting I would not reach the levels I expected as a younger jumper, I felt at peace with my athletics, work and life. With the support of my wife, I decided to shoot for the World Masters Athletics Championships in 2016. An early season fractured heel stopped me from jumping for many months, but I arrived in Perth, Australia in good form, despite a lack of practice. On 31 October 2016, I won Gold for Great Britain with a distance of 15.09m and was an extremely proud Masters World Champion (M35)! It was, and remains, my greatest achievement in athletics and it marked the culmination of my own journey as a triple jumper, which started way back in 1992 watching the great Mike Conley in Barcelona...

The final page of the history of the triple jump will never be written, but our narrative is both a tribute to the trailblazers of the sport, men and women who have advanced the discipline and a snapshot of where it is at *the moment*. The current crop of extremely talented triple jumpers are creating their own history in real-time and we fully expect that new chapters in this story will need to be written in the near future. As fans of athletics, that continues to excite us for the future of the triple jump, which remains so close to my heart. Growth and progress in sport is crucial and it will be our privilege to reflect upon and write about their feats when the time comes, but in the meantime, we can enjoy this great sport as it has been, and is now...

Lawrence Harvey, July 2023

PREFACE

The earliest 19th century exponents of the sport now called the triple jump – previously the hop, skip and jump, then the hop, step and jump – would have made a standing start from the board and some competitions allowed two hops and a jump until the current sequence was codified before the 1900 Olympics. James Connolly[4] of the United States was the inaugural men's triple jump Olympic Champion in Athens in 1896, yet even a casual observer would struggle to align the event on display in that final with what followed at subsequent Games. Connolly was a twenty-seven-year-old mature student at Harvard University, when he quit after one semester to undertake a 16,000-mile journey to the first Olympic Games in modern history and he would win by over a metre with a technique he had not used since he was a boy...

Robbed of his wallet in Naples, Italy when he reached Europe, forced to jump on a moving train to flee local police and partying hard in Athens the night before the final – believing he had nearly two weeks to rest before his competition started – he became the first Olympic Champion in the event in over 1500 years (also the very first champion of those Games). Yet he did this with a jump sequence that included two hops, both accepted styles used in that final and with Connolly awarded a medal that was *silver* in colour, athletes forbidden from marking out their run-up, only seven entrants and no distances revealed until the end of the competition, this was not the *triple jump* as we know it. Connolly has his place in the record-books as the first modern-day

---

[4] James 'Jamie' B. Connolly, the first modern Olympic Champion in the triple jump in 1896, taking Silver in Paris 1900 amongst a total of four Olympic medals in his three Games; also a journalist and respected maritime author [1868-1957].

Olympic Champion in any event, fellow American Myer Prinstein[5] would claim back-to-back Olympic Golds in 1900-04, but we have chosen to start our narrative in the period that the IAAF finally ratified a World Record, focussing on those athletes who left their mark on the triple jump as it *is*, not how it *was*.

We will tell our narrative through the men's and women's World Records and the greatest performances. We do not profess to tell the story of every triple jumper nor will we give full biographies, and we hope to take the reader on a journey through the evolution of a sport that deserves its history to be better known. The triple jump was long thought of as the poor relation to the long jump, seen as a secondary event to those athletes without the necessary speed for the long jump, but it is as technically challenging as any discipline in track and field. The men's World Record has stood since 1995 yet it *will* be broken one day... the women's World Record stood for nearly 26 years until it was smashed in the re-arranged 2020 Olympics and that had been seen as untouchable for many years. The story of the triple jump is not finished, but join us for a telling of this great sport as we see it...

---

[5] Myer (or Meyer) Prinstein, Polish American horizontal jumper, with Olympic Gold in the triple jump in 1900 & 1904, along with the long jump title in 1904 and Silver in 1900 [1878-1925].

PROLOGUE

18 July 1995, Pistas del Helmántico, Salamanca, Spain

Now a crumbling municipal stadium, the *Pistas del Helmántico* was widely thought of in the 1980's and 1990's as *the* place for jumpers. Set in the ancient city of Salamanca in Castile and León, north-western Spain, the stadium is just below the benchmark for performances that could be considered altitude-assisted and was then the location for an annual international meeting that attracted many top athletes looking for their own landmark best. Nowadays the mini stadium is officially named *Javier Sotomayor* after the great Cuban,[6] the dominant high jumper of the 1990's, the 1992 Olympic Champion and the World Record holder since 8 September 1988, the first of two occasions in which he set the World Record in this stadium, latterly in 1993.

The men's triple jump World Record has been set only 27 times since it was first ratified by the IAAF in 1912 and one athlete was confident the record was going to fall that day in the *Gran Premio Diputación de Salamanca* meeting. As Great Britain's Jonathan Edwards began his second jump of the evening in a golden summer for the World Record, he knew that he was in the form of his life. He began the season with a 17.58m personal best in the Loughborough International Match, England on 11 June 1995, a triumphant return to the sport after the preceding year had been heavily disrupted by the Epstein-Barr virus. He could have been forgiven if he had retired in the winter of 1994-95 as he struggled to recover his health and make a return to form, then a very good triple jumper with a World Athletics

---

[6] Javier Sotomayor Sanabria, Olympic high jump champion in 1992 and Silver medallist in 2000; two-time World Champion in 1993 & 1997 amongst a host of major championship victories and still the only man to high jump 8ft (2.44m) [1967-].

Championships Bronze and two Commonwealth Games Silver medals. Instead, he came back in 1995 on the verge of the most triumphant season the sport has ever seen. That day in Salamanca, Edwards jumped 17.98m (+1.8m/s), extending Willie Banks' 10-year-old World Record by only 1cm, a record he had been chasing for the past month. It was a beautiful jump into the history books from an athlete on the verge of greatness, a world landmark that he himself would gloriously surpass only 20 days later in Gothenburg... twice, within the space of 20 minutes.

18.07.1995 **WR 17.98m** (58ft 11$\frac{3}{4}$in) Jonathan Edwards (GBR) Salamanca, Spain (+1.8m/s)

Part 1 – Approach

In its simplest terms, the triple jump is an athletic event within the track and field programme that entails sprinting down a runway (typically on an all-weather track surface), taking off from either leg (on the take-off board, not over it), to land on the same leg again (i.e. the *hop*) using the velocity built up on the runway, then bounding onto your other leg (i.e. the *step*), and then leaping as far as you can into the sandpit at the end of the runway (i.e. the *jump*). The distance from the take-off board (rectangular in shape and made of rigid material, normally wood) and the mark left by the athlete in the sand from where they land (closest mark to the take-off board) is then measured – the athlete who performs this discipline to achieve the furthest distance is then the winner. In most triple jump competitions, each athlete has six attempts; the furthest of these six attempts is then taken as their best mark and is the comparison against which all athletes are then placed in the final positions for medals and such like.

Athletic track surfaces, including the triple jump runaway, have evolved significantly over the past century. Historically, surfaces have ranged from grass, to dirt, crushed stone, cinders (volcanic rock), and then in more recent times 'all-weather' artificial surfaces as the science has developed – cinder tracks are generally considered slower than the synthetic tracks athletes race on today and this is of benefit to modern athletes, along with the advances in shoes – or 'spikes' – and clothing. The first synthetic track to be used in an Olympic Games was in 1968 and they have become standard ever since, creating a surfacing industry with numerous competitors, such as Mondo (Mondotrack), California Sports Surfaces (Plexitrac) and 3M (Tartan).

The first stage of the triple jump is the run or **Approach**. Being a good sprinter is key to contesting the triple jump and talented jumpers without speed will likely end up being steered by coaches to another discipline. Novice jumpers will attempt the triple jump from a shorter approach until their technique is sufficiently developed to handle the speed of a longer run up and the leading men now use around an 18-stride approach. Historically some competitions provided sloping runways to aid the jumps, but by the 1900 Olympics, the rules had been codified to include the hop, skip and jump, or hop, step and jump in the manner we now know it and as the sport has evolved, the *run* has become an integral part of the triple jump.

Some triple jumpers will accelerate to their maximum speed from the start – see Jonathan Edwards who redefined sprinting speed in the triple jump – and others will seek to hit peak velocity in the final strides before the board – such as Yulimar Rojas – but speed is now considered key to gaining overall distance in a triple jump, the application of correct technique allowing the athlete to maintain that optimal speed through take-off and into the subsequent phases. Although the Scandinavians who dominated the event in the Olympic Games either side of the First World War and kept up interest in it in Europe in the 1930's, made up for a perceived lack of speed with their elasticity and bounce, commonly called *spänst* in Swedish,[7] reflecting the diversity of approaches throughout the sport's history.

Athletes may also display idiosyncrasies on the runway, many speaking to themselves as they prepare, some almost exaggeratedly (again Rojas is worth watching in particular, especially her hand movements in miming the jump sequence) and the now ubiquitous rhythmic hand-clapping with the crowd has become an important part of the overall jump (more on this later with Willie Banks). The Cubans even introduced an extended stride or slight leap into their run-ups, which has been subsequently adopted by many leading jumpers of all

---

[7] *A World History of Track and Field Athletics 1864-1964*, p.264, Roberto L. Quercetani, 1964.

nationalities, such as Americans Christian Taylor and Will Claye, a noticeable skip, series of shorter paces, stutter-step or an elongated stride assisting an athlete with finding the correct stride length and frequency in their approach. The distance from the take-off board to the landing area is also different for each sex, at least 13m for men and at least 11m for the women, so there are many variations shown in the number of strides an athlete takes.

Athletes waiting to jump will need to consider weather conditions before they start their approach and also factor in the variances of the surface itself, a 'fast' or 'springy' surface requiring changes in their usual run up length, oftentimes even more important when indoors. An athlete can usually be seen watching the wind indicator on particularly blustery days – a gauge in elite competition, or a basic windsock further down the athletics pyramid – to try and ensure that any jump they make is within the allowable limit (up to 2.0m/s) for record purposes, although a wind measurement above that limit will not stop them registering a valid jump in competition. A tailwind is usually considered to be of benefit, but excess wind can make it difficult for a triple jumper to maintain horizontal velocity through the first two (hop and step) phases, the all-important control being lost in particularly windy conditions.

Horizontal jumpers also have to factor in the effect of rain on the runway or other extremes such as heat or humidity; a 'hot' surface may mean that an athlete runs faster than normal and this could adversely affect the speed of their approach, any inconsistencies in that regard causing them to over-step the plasticine on the take-off board and the attempt be ruled a foul. A technician could write an entire book on the approach to either a triple or long jump run-up and take-off, both similar in composition and there is much more to the approach than simply running at full speed and making sure you do not over-step the board. Modern athletes should also find themselves thankful they do not have the challenges of their predecessors, with Józef Szmidt's World Record leap in 1960 having to factor in frogs running across the rain-soaked runway built on peaty ground!

IRISH TRAILBLAZERS

"Long-jumping as a theatre of [Irish] national excellence"[8]

[9]Our triple jump record journey starts in New York City, USA, in May 1911, with Irish-born Dan Ahearn competing in a singlet bearing the 'Winged-Fist' of the Irish American Athletic Club at Celtic Park, Long Island. Born on 12 April 1887

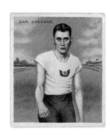

in Dirreen, Athea, County Limerick, **Daniel Francis Ahearne**[10] and elder brother Timothy Joseph Ahearne were famed Irish athletes of the day and it is fitting that Irishmen open our account of the story of the triple jump. It is commonly believed that the sport that has become the 'triple jump' of track and field originated from the ancient Irish game of the same name, the *geal-ruith*, which originally involved two hops and a jump to clear a distant puddle or river.

The triple jump was part of the inaugural modern Olympics in 1896, although it still allowed two hops of the same foot and was not widely competitive across the globe; in addition, the standing events, including a triple jump, were a feature of the early Olympic Games, particularly Paris 1900, St. Louis 1904 and London 1908, dominated by eight-time Gold medallist Raymond Ewry[11] of the United States. He

---

[8] 'Great leaps forward – An Irishman's Diary about our supposed national talent for long-jumping', Frank McNally, *Irish Times*, 12 April 2018

[9] Hassan Cigarettes collectible card of Dan Ahearne, 1910, from their 'Champion Athlete and Prize Fighter Collection'.

[10] Baptism records suggest this year of birth is correct, but elsewhere he went by 1888 and some records show middle name as William or Francis. The final 'e' of Ahearne was dropped when he migrated to the United States, although references continued to be made to Ahearne in some publications.

[11] Raymond 'Ray' C. Ewry, eight-time Olympic Champion in the standing high, long, and triple jump from 1900-1908 and holder of the record for the most Olympic medals with a 100% record [1873-1937].

is amongst the most successful Olympians of all time, with his record of three Gold medals in two events in consecutive Games not matched until 2012, by the great swimmer Michael Phelps[12] of the United States. Ewry was confined to a wheelchair as a boy due to polio and for him to even walk again was some achievement, let alone what he later achieved as an Olympian!

The *geal-ruith* is believed in Irish mythology to have been contested in the ancient Irish Tailtean Games as far back as 1829 BC, giving the sport a history of sorts over a couple of thousand years. Indeed, Irish literature includes the God-like figure of *Cú Chulainn*, one of Ireland's greatest mythological warriors and a hero of folklore tales, battling vast armies of men and mythological creatures, a common feature of bedtime stories for many an Irish child and a favoured character because he was said to be human, despite his feats and supernatural encounters. In *The Wooing of Emer*[13], the hero had to perform a 'salmon-leap' across three ramparts to reach his future wife and secure her hand, fighting off a company of warriors and her own three brothers at the same time as part of this great feat. In other stories, we find a 7th century figure, *Mongán* jumping across the three ramparts of a fort and the concept of a 'triple jump' was not uncommon for a great warrior in the medieval tales of a country from where the modern sport very likely emanated.

Hopping forward from motif to actual jumping, the earliest unofficial World Record for a 'triple jump' appears to be Hanmer Webb[14] at 12.19m (1in shy of 40ft) on 30 April 1856 in Cheltenham,

---

[12] Michael F. Phelps II, the most successful and decorated Olympian of all time, with an incredible 23 Gold medals; he surpassed Ewry in 2016 with three Gold medals in three events in three Games [1985-].

[13] An 11th century hero-tale, unknown author but attributed to Cú Chulainn himself.

[14] Later the Rev. Prebendary Webb-Peploe, notable preacher in the Church of England and a leader of Evangelical thought [1837-1923].

England. He made a reputation for himself as a champion gymnast and jumper at Cheltenham College and then Cambridge University, although a serious spinal injury at the latter meant he had to spend three years in bed, from where he completed all of his ordination examinations! The unofficial record changed hands between a couple of British athletes until the 1870's, when the Irish took over and made the record in particular their own until the 1920's, whether competing in Ireland, representing Great Britain or the United States.

[15]Tim Ahearne and younger brother Dan were at the pinnacle of this golden period in Irish athletics which culminated in two decades at the start of the 20th century, the preeminent athletes of the jumping sports alongside the group of Irish-born or émigré athletes that dominated the weight-throwing field events and became known as the 'Irish Whales'.[16] They were born and raised on the family farm in County Limerick, working the land alongside brothers William and Mick, and trained for their athletic events by jumping the River Awbeg near the family homestead.[17] Both Tim and Dan were natural athletes though, excelling at various sports including Gaelic Football at the local club in Athea and their talents were to take them far from Limerick. The elder Tim first came to prominence as an eighteen-year-old in 1904, winning two competitive jumping events in Listowel, County Kerry and going on to dominate jumping sport in Ireland in 1907, culminating with victory at the All-Round Championship of Munster

---

[15] Dan Ahearn competing for the IAAC in the triple jump © unknown

[16] Known by this nickname due to their sporting prowess, prodigious appetites, and obvious physical size; six athletes were commonly known as 'The Whales' and between them they won 12 Olympic Gold medals between Paris 1900 and Antwerp 1920.

[17] 'Ahearne men leapt to glory on world stage', Tom Aherne, *Limerick Leader*, 10 September 2016

in Fermoy, County Cork and the GAA[18] long jump title. From that magnificent run of events – said to include 16 other first place finishes – he was selected for the Great Britain and Ireland team at London 1908, the only option for an Irishman then to compete in the Olympic Games, a choice that rankled with many even if they did accept the invitation.

At this stage, athletes in the 'triple jump' were still competing in events of that name where there was a standing start, two hops and a jump, and a hop, step and jump, although each event was consistent, even if competitions varied widely, including sloping runways! The World Record in the sport had yet to be ratified at this stage and from the various claims to be the holder, it is likely that as the Olympics opened in 1908, the best mark stood at 15.34m (50ft 4in), set by Irishman John Bresnihan[19] at Bandon, County Cork, on 26 August 1906 in the hop, step and jump, with the previous record likely having stood for sixteen years.

[20]The Olympic triple jump final took place on Saturday 15 July 1908 in White City Stadium, London, with a wide-open field and no obvious favourite, with the event rarely competed at national track and field meetings of that time, although the jump format was codified in line with the present-day rules, including a runway for the first time at the Games. Twenty athletes from twelve countries (five being Irish-

---

[18] Gaelic Athletic Association, founded in 1884, Irish international sporting association, promoting both sporting and cultural recognition of indigenous Gaelic games and pastimes.
[19] John J. Bresnihan, a great Limerick athlete whose feats are little known [1882-believed 1962].
[20] Tim Ahearne completing in the triple jump at the 1908 Olympics © unknown

born) took part across two rounds, similar to the modern divided final but with the top 3 athletes only progressing to the 'medal-round'. Tim had been disappointed to finish eighth in the long jump final three days earlier and with both the standing long jump and the 110m hurdles having also yielded no medal for him, the triple jump took on extra importance. He was not to disappoint on the grandest stage despite being a rank outsider, competing fiercely with Canadian Garfield MacDonald[21] in their own private competition, setting a new Olympic Record in qualifying at 14.72m (48ft $3\frac{1}{2}$in), this then being eclipsed by his opponent in the medal-round by 4cm, before Ahearne set a new mark of 14.92m (48ft $11\frac{1}{4}$in) that MacDonald could not match, winning the Gold medal by only 6in. He never competed internationally again and his Gold remained the last to be won by Great Britain in a field event until Lynn Davies[22] in the long jump at Tokyo 1964.

In 1909 Tim won Irish titles in the high jump, long jump and the hurdles, crossing to England to also win the AAA[23] long jump competition. He then left his homeland for the United States, arriving in New York on 30 September 1909 and subsequently joined the Irish American Athletic Club, based in Queen's and the top US athletics club of the day. Most accounts have Dan following his elder brother to the United States, a route taken by many Irish seeking a better life or increased economic opportunity, and although his *hop* across the Atlantic cost him the final 'e' in his surname, almost certainly as a result

---

[21] James 'Garfield' MacDonald, Silver medallist in the triple jump in London 1908 [1881-1951].

[22] Lynn Davies, one of Great Britain's greatest athletes, Olympic long jump champion in 1964, European Champion in 1966 and two-time Commonwealth Champion in 1966 & 1970; later a coach, technical director, and elected official [1942-].

[23] The Amateur Athletic Association (AAA), the oldest national athletics governing body in the world, being established in 1880 and now absorbed into England Athletics.

of rushed immigration paperwork at Ellis Island on landing, he was to eclipse the achievements of his elder brother.

Contrary to the consensus in modern accounts, it is more likely that Tim followed Dan to the United States, with newspaper accounts recording Dan competing for the Irish American Athletic Club at Celtic Park on 5 June 1909 (*Sporting Life*, 16 June 1909) and in Boston on 3 July 1909 (*Sporting Life*, 2 December 1909). These dates are important as the story of Dan Ahearn in the United States is of a fight to achieve recognition for his record-breaking jumps when he was the greatest triple jumper in the world, seemingly at odds with the AAU[24] and later the American Olympic Committee, resulting in an unsatisfactory performance in Antwerp 1920 when past his prime, an Olympic Games more memorable for United States athletes due to off-field turbulence.

The IAAF was not formed until 1912 to govern international athletics and until then the AAU tended to consider American records set at their own meetings as the benchmark for performance, although not being widely recognised or known of overseas. Edward Bloss[25] set a mark of 14.78m (48ft 6in) in the AAU Championship in Chicago on 16 September 1893, with even olympics.com, the official website of the IOC, still stating that Tim Ahearne's winning jump in 1908 was a new World Record, despite the best global mark at the time that we can find being the Bresnihan record (15.34m) from 1906. The triple jump was not even on the AAU program from 1893-1908, so there was little or no opportunity for United States-based athletes to better any marks considered to be the best and James Connolly's Olympic Gold medal

---

[24] Amateur Athletic Union, founded in 1888 and the organizer of most youth athletics national championships in the United States since then.
[25] Edward B. Bloss, triple and long jumper, considered the first American national champion in the former [1870-1941].

winning triple jump in 1896 was made with a then acceptable two hops on the same foot, with other leading efforts of his that season also questionable as to whether he followed the soon-to-be internationally established jump sequence.

In the summer of 1909 Dan Ahearn established himself as the best jumper in the United States, despite a plethora of existing stars, many Irish-born or with Irish heritage. According to various accounts, he set several 'best' marks for the triple jump but the AAU would not recognise them or threw them out on technicalities, possibly because he was a migrant; at the Bricklayers' Union meeting, Celtic Park, on 5 June 1909, he was said to have bettered the Bloss record by $16\frac{2}{3}$in but it did not stand due to the wind behind him[26] and another record jump that month was denied when the linen measuring tape was found to be too stretchy.[27]

It was at Celtic Park, New York, home of his Irish American Athletic Club that the World Record did fall to Dan, a stadium known for the number of world bests in track and field being set and quickly bettered. Newspaper accounts of the time can be confusing to follow, but on 4 July 1909, he established an American record of 50ft $1\frac{3}{4}$in (abt. 15.28m) for the hop, step and jump at Celtic Park, with a standard steel tape used for the measuring, to ensure it would be ratified by the AAU committee! The *Boston Globe*, 5 July 1909 stated the World Record was set at 50ft 2in (15.29m) by Dan Shanahan[28] in Limerick 21 years previously, although we think this was bettered by Bresnihan in 1906. Thereafter, Dan Ahearn made the unofficial triple jump record his

---

[26] *Sporting Life* 16 June 1909
[27] *Boston Globe*, 30 June 1909; there was no official measure of an 'illegal wind' in this era and the umpiring could be very subjective.
[28] Dan Shanahan, said to be the earliest Irish champion of the hop, step and jump under organized rules, his distances all the more remarkable as he was on a grass runway or on 'the sod' as they would say in Ireland [1866-1913].

own, as claimed in various newspaper accounts and online records, sometimes contradictory:

- 3 July 1909, 50ft $2\frac{7}{10}$in (15.31m), Boston[29]

- 31 July 1909, 50ft 6in (15.39m), Boston[30]

- 1 August 1909, 50ft $6\frac{1}{2}$in (15.40m), New York[31]

- 1 August 1910, 51ft $1\frac{1}{8}$in (15.57m), New York[32]

- ? August 1910, 51ft $2\frac{7}{8}$in (15.62m), New York[33]

- 30 May 1911, 50ft 11in (15.52m), New York[34]

- 4 June 1911, 51ft $4\frac{1}{2}$in (15.66m), New York[35]

In the winter of 1911, focus turned to Stockholm 1912 and whilst it was expected that Dan would claim Olympic Gold as the World Record holder and Tim was the defending champion from London, the question of nationality had to be resolved for the two top triple jumpers in the world. The following spring it came to light that Tim had not been in the United States for the required period of time to file the papers to become naturalised and Dan's failure to do so was down to carelessness... "Dan Ahearne is sure to score points for whatever country he competes for, for there is no competitor in the United States who can hold his own with him in the three standing jumps nor in the hop, step and jump. His brother, Tim Ahearne, also takes up these events and the Ahearne family is likely to prove the bête noire[36] of whatever country it competes against."[37]

---

[29] *Sporting Life*, 2 December 1909
[30] Online sources
[31] *Charlotte Daily Observer*, 2 August 1909
[32] *The Washington Post*, 2 August 1910
[33] *New York Tribune*, 15 August 1910
[34] Online sources
[35] *Evening World*, 5 June 1911
[36] Bête noire, a person or thing that is particularly disliked.
[37] *Hawaiian Star*, 19 March 1912

But in the end, they did not compete for any country at the 1912 Olympics. Some have claimed that Tim would not represent Great Britain again as an Irishman and there was a story that he had become *persona non grata* in British athletics circles after replacing the British Union Flag with an Irish flag at the medal ceremony in 1908, which could explain why he emigrated to the United States the following year. Some accounts stated that Dan had returned to Great Britain after his failure to become an American citizen in time for selection,[38] but whatever the truth, it was unlikely that a proud Irishman of the Irish American Athletic Club would elect to jump for Britain. The winning jump in that summer's Games was only 14.76m (48ft 5in) from Gustaf Lindblom[39] of Sweden, a distance that Dan was regularly surpassing at that time and with no 1916 Olympics due to the First World War, his peak years sadly did not include a statement victory on the global stage like his elder brother in 1908.

[40]Between 1910 and 1918, Dan Ahearn won 8 AAU triple jump titles and was undoubtedly the world's best in that period (Tim was runner up 4 times). By 1920 he was on the decline as an athlete and the challenges he had faced from the AAU in having his first record jumps acknowledged, manifested themselves once again in petty decision-making by an athletics committee. He was suspended for breaking a curfew in Antwerp, Belgium and it looked like he would miss the 1920 Games, although his argument was that the United States team accommodation was sub-standard and he was forced to make his own arrangements for

---

[38] *Atlanta Constitution*, 7 April 1912
[39] Gustaf Lindblom, Gold medallist on home soil in Stockholm 1912, the nation's first medal in the triple jump [1891-1960].
[40] Dan Ahearn in the colours of the Illinois Athletic Club, Chicago © unknown

lodgings. The entire United States team threatened to resign if he was not reinstated and with a 'them and us' situation once more holding back his career, he held firm and was subsequently reinstated by the committee. He performed nowhere near his expected standard, more than 4ft off his best mark and finished a disappointing sixth in his only Olympics.

[41]Dan had moved to Chicago in the summer of 1911 with his wife Helen, representing the Illinois Athletic Club with distinction and it was in this city that he worked at a meatpacking company and then later as a Policeman, having at least three children, before he passed away on 20 December 1942. His brother returned to  farming in Upstate New York after his athletics career, breeding prize-winning cattle and died on 12 December 1968. The achievements of neither brother have been forgotten, certainly not in Athea where a simple bronze statue of 'winged feet' celebrates the feats of these famous sons of Limerick.

For Dan, his defining moment came in 1912, when his jump of 15.52m (50ft 11in) at Celtic Park on 30 May 1911 was ratified by the IAAF as the first official triple jump World Record, reserving his place in the record books as the first man to officially jump over 50ft. Quite possibly it was a bittersweet moment for him in the year he was unable to compete for the Olympic Gold medal he so deserved, but a man that was said to often take only one jump and sit out the rest of the competition as he was so far ahead of his peers, always knew he was the greatest jumper of his time whether he had the official record or

---

[41] A brooding Dan Ahearn © unknown

not. It has been said that the hop, step and jump was an 'Irish pastime' with their success in the early 20th century under various flags and it is fitting that our journey through the sport begins with these Irish trailblazers, with Dan having the distinction of "being the last of the 'old glory' line."[42] The World Record was to last for 13 years, one month and 12 days until the 1924 Olympics, and with that later winning distance of Nick Winter amended downwards to match Ahearn after the Second World War, his 1911 mark was technically not bettered until 1931, giving Ahearn on paper the second-longest period as a triple jump World Record holder after Jonathan Edwards (1995 to date).

30.05.1911 WR 15.52m (50ft 11in) Daniel Ahearn (USA) New York, USA (NWI)

---

[42] 'Great Limerick Athletes, (No. 11) – DAN AHEARNE of Athea', Séamus Ó Ceallaigh, *Limerick Leader*, believed to be 1950's but available online.

FROM THE BUSH TO PARIS

"Any team without Winter is a farce"[43]

Largely unheralded in life and death, which probably suited an Australian country boy down to the ground, Nick Winter seemingly came from nowhere to take triple jump Olympic Gold on a swelteringly hot Paris day in July 1924. Defending champion Vilho Tuulos[44] of Finland was heavily favoured to retain the title, having recently recorded the second furthest jump of all time at 15.48m (50ft $9\frac{1}{2}$in), only 4cm behind Dan Ahearn's thirteen-year-old World Record. After the early 20th century domination of the Irish jumpers, Stockholm 1912 and Antwerp 1920 were dominated by Scandinavian athletes, Sweden in particular claiming 5 of the 6 triple jump medals available in those Games. The sport appeared to have lost its lustre in Western Europe/North America[45] and the popular 'standing' jumping events had ceased to be on the Olympic program after 1912, which makes it even more intriguing how it came to be that a near 30-year-old Fireman from New South Wales (NSW), the first Australian to compete in an Olympic field event, stood *barefoot* only minutes before his final jump, needing to break the new Olympic Record in Colombes, Paris, to achieve his life's ambition...

---

[43] Article detailing Nick Winter's Olympic victory and referencing his almost non-selection for the team; *The Sun*, 15 July 1924

[44] Vilho I. Tuulos, three-time Olympic medallist in triple jump from 1920-28 and known for his reliable jumping, being close to the World Record in 1923 and then having a jump of 51ft $1\frac{1}{2}$in (15.58m) disallowed in 1928 due to wind, although there was still no specific rule in international sport on tailwinds at that time [1895-1967].

[45] The American record set by Dan Ahearn in May 1911 would not fall until June 1941, when Billy Brown bettered it by only 1cm in Philadelphia.

Born **Anthony William Winter** on 25 August 1894 in Brocklesby, NSW, but always known as 'William' or 'Billy' in his youth and 'Nick' in later life, probably to differentiate him from his father Anthony, he grew up in a tiny country town, with a population now of less than 200 and where the local Public School was not even constructed until 1898. It was once a main railway centre for the transportation of grain and Nick's father was originally a fettler, working on the maintenance of the all-important railway lines in the region, but the area is now more characterised by its many sheep. His father later moved the family to the slightly larger town of Marrar, NSW, where he ran a snooker saloon, a sport central to Nick's life along with billiards and to which we will return. His father went on to run at least two further saloons in Sydney in later years, but by the time Nick enlisted for service in the First World War, he was recorded as a labourer and his family lived in Marrar.

[46]His military enlistment papers from 24 July 1915 survive,[47] enabling us to visualise the young athlete he clearly was before he became an Olympian. He was nearly 23 when he enlisted for service abroad in the Australian Imperial Force (AIF), 5ft 11in (1.80m) tall, 11st 11lbs (75kg) in weight and with a chest measurement of 36-38" (91-96cm); the average  British soldier in the war was commonly held to be around 5ft 5in and 8st, so the champion wood-cutter who presented himself for enlistment in Cootamundra was a rare sight at the time, towering over almost everyone he came into contact with and with the physique of a

[46] A youthful looking Nick Winter in his Australian Imperial Force uniform © unknown
[47] Available online courtesy of the National Archives of Australia; Barcode: 8846587, Series: B2455.

Strongman in comparison to regular Australians. There was no conscription in Australia during the war, so his enlistment was entirely voluntary and the country boy joined the mounted infantry of the 7th Light Horse Regiment, recruited from his home State, perhaps seeking some adventure away from the bush, but choosing to serve with those with a similar upbringing amongst the wattle trees (acacia) of rural NSW.

Nick embarked for the war in Sydney in October 1915 and served first in Egypt upon arrival in the Middle East. He transferred to the Army Service Corps in January 1916 as a Driver, so his time as a Lighthorseman was short, and served in France from June 1916 to the end of the war. He was never promoted and seemed to spend the majority of his service in depot duties bouncing between units, before being discharged in Sydney on 25 July 1919, but it is likely that his time in the military was a pivotal period in his life, as it was for so many servicemen and he performed whilst at the 'front', including a "hop, step and jump of over 48ft"[48] and "won numerous championships in France and Belgium at hurdling, high, broad jump and hop, step and jump."[49]

Within five months of his return to Australia, he commenced employment as a fireman, stationed in the Sydney beachside suburb of Manly and began to rise to athletics prominence in Sydney with his first national triple jump record in December 1919, a journey that would peak in Paris at the 1924 Olympics. Nick was a natural athlete, later said to have been proficient at twelve sports,[50] muscular, tall and slender, almost certainly ambidextrous and quite possibly double-

---

[48] *The Sun*, 14 October 1919
[49] *The Sun*, 15 July 1924
[50] *ABC Weekly*, 12 June 1946

jointed, using left and right hand at equal ease.[51]   He excelled at mainstream sports like rugby, football (Australian Rules[52]), cricket and tennis, competed in the javelin, discus, hurdles and pole vault, enjoyed boxing, wrestling and ju-jitsu, won local events as a bike rider, as well as niche, challenge-style events, such as the single tug-of-war, roller-skating and cycling backwards, but it was jumping events that he enjoyed most of all and in which he truly shone.

A. W. Winter,
A returned member of Botany Harriers, and one of the discoveries of the present track season. While at the front he put up many fine performances, including a hop, step, and jump of over 48ft. In the challenge match against Maitland, he won the hop, step, at 45ft. 7in. He is also a hurdler, high jumper, and pole vaulter of ability.

Competing for the Botany[53] Harriers Athletics Club in the annual Dunn Challenge Shield contest in December 1919 at the Sydney Sports Ground, Moore Park, this was the prominent amateur athletics event in the State at the time, organised by the New South Wales Amateur Athletics Association (NSWAAA) and always with large crowds.   A contemporary newspaper report[54] (see picture) recorded him as a "returned member of the Botany Harriers", the returned part referring to his being an ex-serviceman now home from the war, rather than a returning member of the club.[55] Having been discharged from the Army in July 1919, at 26 he was older than most other athletes, often recruited from local colleges and universities to improve the club performance in these competitions, and by October 1919 he was described as "one of the discoveries of the present track season", seemingly eager to make up for lost time.   The 1919 Dunn Shield contest is the first recorded State-wide competition

---

[51] *Referee*, 16 July 1924
[52] First played in 1859, contact sport most predominant in Australia, based on football (soccer) but resembling a form of rugby and played on a cricket field!
[53] Southern Sydney suburb, the Botany Harriers were founded in 1907 and are now the Randwick-Botany Harriers.
[54] *The Sun*, 14 October 1919
[55] Botany Harriers was his first recognized club; *The Sun*, 15 July 1924

in which Nick appeared and he was to compete in the 120yd hurdles (110m), high jump, pole vault and the triple jump, making his name in the latter with an Australasian[56] record.

The week-long contests for the Dunn Shield concluded on 13 December 1919 and in the 'running hop, step and jump', Nick was to better the National Record set in the 1911 Dunn Shield, with victory in the event already seen as a foregone conclusion in reports of the time. The previous mark of 47ft 3in (14.40m) was increased by 4in to 47ft 7in (14.50m), a jump described as a "beautiful effort"[57] which cleared the sandpit on his first attempt[58] and was good enough to have claimed Olympic Bronze in Stockholm 1912 by some way, only a metre away from the World Record. The 1920 Olympics were due the following August and whilst Nick was only just coming to prominence in Sydney, he must have felt he had a chance of selection with his prodigious leap in the Dunn Shield demonstrating his exceptional ability in the event. On 10 January 1920, he competed in the club championship of the Botany Harriers, again at the Sydney Sports Ground, where he broke the Australasian record for the *standing* hop, step and jump with a mark of 30ft 10in (9.40m)[59] and for good measure showcased his all-round strength and athleticism, by carrying off the 120yd hurdles, high jump and the discus throw!

On 24 April 1920, Nick took part in a match in Sydney between NSWAAA members – former AIF servicemen and The Rest – in order to raise funds for the Olympic representation fund. There was some debate about which of the star athletes for the Diggers[60] such

---

[56] Region covering Australia, New Zealand and now some neighbouring islands.
[57] *Evening News*, 16 December 1919
[58] *The Queanbeyan Age*, 9 January 1920
[59] *The Sun*, 11 January 1920; previous record beaten in three successive jumps.
[60] Affectionate term for Australian servicemen used by their countrymen and Allied soldiers during the war.

as sprinter Edwin Carr[61] were in training or were even going to compete and Nick is listed amongst other athletes who would be "good men on the field... but look like being overwhelmed."[62] He was to comfortably win his event despite the newspaper pessimism of his team's overall chances against the top amateurs in the State, but this period is crucial in explaining why his Olympic dream was to go on hold for four more years, despite already jumping distances that would have won him a medal in the 1912 Olympics.

Whilst the NSWAAA was very active in raising funds in the stated aim of having Australia well represented at the first Olympics since 1912, both Australia and the 'home country' of Great Britain found that sport was yet to be sufficiently re-established following the First World War, with enthusiasm for international competition not as remarked as it previously was; *The Herald* reported that "the matter of expense is uppermost in the minds of... officials who argue... that it would be inadvisable to send to contests of such high standard men who appeared to have little prospect of success."[63] It should be noted the article was arguing that Australians produce their best when faced with the sternest of challenges, alluding to the military feats of their men during the war, but it was in that prevailing mood that Nick was battling for selection along with more recognised athletes.

In Australia at that time, the States – dominated in sporting terms by the 'Mother State' NSW and Victoria – would put forward athletes for selection by the Australian Olympic Council.[64] Contemporary newspaper reports carried stories of the success of

---

[61] Edwin 'Slip' Carr, competed for Australia in the 1924 Olympics in the 100m & 200m; also capped 4 times for the 'Wallabies' in rugby union in 1921 [1899-1971].

[62] *Referee*, 14 April 1920

[63] *The Herald*, 28 February 1920

[64] Became the Australian Olympic Federation officially in 1923 and the Australian Olympic Committee in 1990.

NSW star sprinter William 'Walton' Hunt[65] and race-walker George Parker[66] in their respective events in the Australasian Championships in February 1920, but Nick was essentially barred from competition on a national stage as the triple jump did not form part of the championships programme until 1927! Against this, there were voices calling for his selection for the Olympics – a correspondent to *Referee*, calling himself 'Fair Go'[67] wrote that his record jump was only 5in worse than the winning jump of the last Olympic Games and "...gives him as good a chance as Hunt or Parker, if not better!"[68] – but by the time the selections from NSW were submitted in time for departure to Europe in May 1920, it was only those two athletes who were to go and Nick was omitted.[69] No reliable source can be found to confirm why he was not sent to Antwerp, but it was likely that the 'bean-counters' in NSW decided that his chances were not sufficient to merit the extra cost involved beyond supporting the established stars in Hunt and Parker,[70] or a cap on total places for financial reasons meant he was merely unfortunate.

Whatever the reason behind his non-selection, for the 1920 season he went on to compete for the South Sydney Amateur Athletics Club having left Botany Harriers. His 1919 Australasian record was only marginally less than the Gold medal distance in Antwerp by Vilho Tuulos of Finland at 47ft 7in (14.50m), but he went on to break his own record a number of times in the 1920 season, exceeding that

---

[65] William 'Walton' Hunt, competed in the 100m in the 1920 Olympics, departing in the quarterfinals [1898-1977].
[66] George R. Parker, Silver medallist in the 3,000m walk in Antwerp 1920 [1897-1974].
[67] Common Australian phrase, normally an egalitarian appeal for fairness to all.
[68] *Referee*, 21 April 1920
[69] NSW nominated five swimmers, two athletes and one cyclist – *The Mildura Cultivator*, 8 May 1920. Four athletes in total competed for Australia in that Olympics.
[70] Parker won Silver in the 3,000m walk in the Antwerp Olympics, whilst Hunt did not progress beyond the quarterfinals of the sprints. Australia claimed two Silver and one Bronze in total.

44

winning jump of Tuulos – on 6 November 1920 in the South Sydney Harriers meeting, with a leap of 47ft $7\frac{3}{4}$in (14.52m), 47ft 11in (14.60m) in a meeting the weekend prior[71] and then on 4 December 1920 he jumped 48ft 2in (14.68m)[72] in the Dunn Shield, having earlier tied and beaten the record with 48ft (14.63m) at that meeting; he also won the discus throw in the same meeting, again showing just how versatile he was as an athlete!

In July 1921 Nick married Minnie Josland in Helensburgh, NSW, later having two children and perhaps determined to prove his doubters wrong, he drove himself on as a jumper, having also broken the national standing high jump record in May 1921.[73] On 5 November 1921 at the Sydney Sports Ground once more, he broke the Australasian record twice in one meeting in his club competition, taking the distance to 48ft $7\frac{1}{2}$in (14.82m) and then 48ft $10\frac{1}{4}$in (14.89m), in front of invited officials to ensure the jump of this "marvellous fireman would receive the recognition of the association."[74] One newspaper account of the time made reference to the World Record of 'D. F. Ahearn (USA)' at 50ft 11in and with Nick possessing the possibility to yet reach those figures.[75] In the Dunn Shield, he made further progress, winning the event again in extending his record to 49ft $8\frac{1}{2}$in (15.15m),[76] finally going over 15m in a properly observed event and continuing to make a mockery of his non-selection for the 1920 Olympics.

---

[71] *The Sun*, 7 November 1920 & *Western Argus*, 9 November 1920
[72] *Queensland Times*, 7 December 1920
[73] *Observer*, 7 May 1921
[74] *The Sun*, 6 November 1921
[75] *Young Witness*, 10 November 1921
[76] *The Sun*, 10 December 1921

In the 1922 season, Nick bettered his standing hop, step and jump record to 31ft 9in (9.68m), an increase of 11in from the previous best[77] and was again victorious in the Dunn Shield in December, 2ft ahead of second place but nearly 3ft down on his own record best. A report at the time stated the competitors had pushed for a longer, uninterrupted run up, but performances were down across the board, with the commentator recording that the jumpers tended to "run too far and the old arrangement kept them down more to correct distance – against their will."[78] The following year he improved his distance from the previous Dunn Shield, but again was unchallenged by his competitors, second place being over 3ft behind and remained unbeaten at the triple jump in all other events that season, including the 1923 South Sydney AAC Championships in November where he took three first places and two seconds in total![79] Thereafter, attention was turned towards Paris 1924 and a presumed straightforward selection to Olympic team as the dominant Australasian jumper of his generation.

[80]However, this time round there was still to be a debate and he remained underrated by athletics officials, despite his many achievements. *The Herald* recorded that Nick had been selected for the Olympic team on 11 February 1924, amongst others, but the *Northern Star* two weeks later stated his nomination had been lost, "on the casting vote of the chairman".[81] On 29 March 1924, he won the NSW State

---

[77] Record broken on Easter Sunday 17 April 1922; *The Sun*, 28 December 1922
[78] *Referee*, 13 December 1922
[79] *Referee*, 28 November 1923
[80] Photograph shows Nick Winter mid-jump on a sports oval, New South Wales, c. 1924 © Out of Copyright
[81] *Northern Star*, 25 February 1924

Championship by 4ft 10in, reaching 48ft $1\frac{1}{2}$in (14.67m) and described as "with his early departure in view, Winter is within sight of his best efforts, and he will leave Australia possessing the confidence of all athletic supporters,"[82] so his place was seemingly settled by that stage. His jump in March was $7\frac{1}{2}$in better than Tuulos' winning distance in Antwerp, but it seems that his final place selection came only "after much persuasion,"[83] with Victorian members opposing his nomination on the grounds that the event was not popular, little practiced in Victoria and "it would be a waste of money sending him,"[84] but the support of the Mother State secured his inclusion. He was finally heading off to the Olympics, to chase "his life's ambition in winning the event"[85] and to also prove his father wrong...

Anthony Winter senior was an adept jumper in his younger days, said by some sources to have been National Champion and it was inevitable that his daredevil son would seek to emulate his sporting prowess, particularly in the triple jump. Nick began to jump at the age of 8 and claimed to have been undefeated from 13 to 30,[86] with the post First World War period certainly not in question. In an article from the *Daily Advertiser* in 1942 when he was discussing a return to Dunn Shield competition at the age of 47, he stated that at 15 his best leap was 44ft (13.41m) and he had not been below that distance since. At either 16 or 17 – depending on newspaper reports – he beat his father for the first time, which was also the first time he in turn had actually lost a hop, step and jump competition; his father was said to

[82] *The Sydney Morning Herald*, 31 March 1924
[83] *The Herald*, 14 July 1924
[84] *Ibid.*
[85] *Geelong Advertiser*, 14 July 1924
[86] *Daily Advertiser*, 7 February 1942

have been "compelled to 'sky the towel' as a signal of defeat."[87] As a child his father is believed to have told him he would not go far as an athlete and the young boy is said to have resolutely told him he would "make the Olympics one day".

The Australian Olympians from Antwerp 1920, in particular race-walker George Parker who claimed a Silver medal in the 3,000m event, reported on their return home that they had been at a major disadvantage to the other nations in that they did not arrive sufficiently early enough to become accustomed to the food, acclimate to local conditions and regain their physical fitness after a near 5-week voyage, with only 5 weeks in Europe to prepare for the pinnacle of sporting competition.[88] The same mistake was to be repeated in 1924, particularly with Nick being such a late selection and with funds still a major issue, thereby limiting the travelling party size – he was later prevented from joining the post-Olympiad celebrations in Paris of the successful athletes for financial reasons – and whilst he was unable to take part in any warm-up meetings, he managed to prepare himself by jumping in trial events in late June, in London (48ft, 14.63m) where was he "rapidly striking form"[89] and then Paris (48ft 5in, 14.76m) where he exceeded the French record.[90]

Our story about Nick and his World Record began by saying he seemingly came from nowhere and whilst his performance in the Olympic final was a surprise to the rest, he had come from the other side of the world with high expectation from Australian sports fans that he could claim Gold after his many athletic feats. His 1921 Australasian record far exceeded the winning distance from Antwerp

---

[87] Phrase is the Australian version of 'throwing in the towel'; *The Queanbeyan Age*, 9 January 1920
[88] *National Advocate*, 2 September 1920
[89] *The Sun*, 19 June 1924
[90] *Sunday Times* (AUS), 29 June 1924

in 1920 and whilst he was not to be the National Champion until 1930 with the event only included from 1927, incidentally when he did not take part as it was held in Wellington, New Zealand, that jump in the 1921 Dunn Shield made him the number one ranked jumper in that year, so what followed in Paris was no David slaying Goliath.[91]

The Olympic triple jump final was held on 12 July 1924 in swelteringly hot, Australian-like weather, with 20 competitors from 12 nations, although some modern accounts incorrectly mention 37 athletes. The Gold and Silver medallists from Antwerp returned and Vilho Tuulos of Finland was favoured to repeat his victory, recently jumping close to the World Record, with Luis Brunetto[92] from Argentina tipped to also compete for a medal having jumped 49ft $8\frac{1}{2}$in (15.15m) in 1923,[93] the same as Nick's Australasian record. The athletes were split into two pools and whilst the jumping order has not survived, Nick experienced early difficulty against Brunetto in his side of the draw, the latter setting a new Olympic Record of 50ft $7\frac{1}{4}$in (15.42m) on his first jump, beating that set by Tim Ahearne of Great Britain in London 1908.

Each athlete was allowed three jumps in his 'round' or pool – in reality more similar to the modern divided final – and the top six advanced to the final, where they had three further jumps in which to improve their best score before the medals were decided. Nick fouled on his very first jump in international competition when over-stepping the board, perhaps affected by Brunetto's record leap, but on his second he reached 49ft $9\frac{2}{3}$in (15.18m), beating his personal best and

[91] Biblical reference, in modern terms that has taken on a secular meaning where an underdog is victorious in a contest.
[92] Luis A. Brunetto, Silver medallist in triple jump in Paris 1924 [1901-68].
[93] https://olympics.com/en/athletes/luis-bruneto

likely giving him the confidence that he could compete against international standard athletes, having been untried against competition outside of Sydney to that point, the stick that had been used against him for years by partisan athletics officials in Australia. He fouled on his third jump but his new Australasian best secured him a place in the final, second only to Brunetto's new Olympic Record.

The two jumpers from Finland were to improve their best jumps in the final round and 5 athletes in total exceeded the former competition record set by Ahearne in 1908, but the fifth and sixth placed qualifiers could not improve their initial round jumps. The final essentially came down to whether Nick could beat Brunetto and the omens did not look good. He scored on his fourth jump but did not better his second and then fouled for the third time in the competition on his fifth. That fifth jump was said to be well over 52ft[94] and in making that attempt he bruised his heals, an injury that was to give him great pain for the next two weeks when he put weight on them and he was said to have cried with pain when he landed.[95]

At this time, he felt his Olympic dream had ended, as he said in interviews afterwards and before his final leap, he was sitting in third place. An Olympic Bronze medal would have been good enough for many athletes, but not Nick Winter. He had started life in the bush, survived three years of war, possibly been mustard-gassed,[96] had synovitis in both knees trouble him during his military service[97] and throughout his athletics career and until he came to Europe he had only ever competed on grass, but the man who would "have a fly at"[98]

---

[94] *Singleton Argus*, 15 July 1924

[95] *Saturday Evening Express*, 20 September 1924

[96] 'UNIQUE "NICK" WINTER The AMAZING ALL-ROUNDER', *Pix*. Vol. 1 No. 10, 2 April 1938

[97] Confirmed in medical history in AIF service record.

[98] *The News, 19 July 1924*

any challenge that required nerve, skill, speed and stamina, and had a terrific natural spring, was not going to give up on his life's ambition without a fight.

Removing his shoes, he had his sore heels massaged and contemplated his sixth jump, which is believed to have also been the final one in the competition. He was nearly 30 years old and at his athletic peak, competing on the grandest stage of all in the grandest city in Europe and now with a chance to give his critics the perfect riposte, an Olympic title in track and field for Australia, their first ever and the first Gold medal for the country at that Games, from the last athlete selected for the team. All he had to do was to make sure he did not over-step for the fourth time...

Nick Winter commenced his triple jump into the record books 'some inches' short of the board. No reliable evidence exists as to how short he was, but he himself said afterwards that he was not taking any chances that he would over-step and it must have been some jump to still break Dan Ahearn's record from 1911. His winning jump was measured at 15.525m,[99] 4in ahead of Brunetto's now previous Olympic Record and *half a centimetre* ahead of Ahearn, giving Nick the new World Record when registered with the IAAF as 15.53m. He was mobbed by reporters at trackside and the photograph of him above taken post-victory shows him in all

---

[99] It should be noted most Australian newspaper reports shortly after his victory stated the record to be 51ft $1\frac{1}{4}$in, but it was initially recorded as 15.525m, registered as 15.53m and has been corrected since the Second World War by the IAAF (now World Athletics) to 50ft $11\frac{1}{4}$in (15.52m). Tim and Dan Ahearn(e) both departed from the record books in the same competition, although Dan later returned as a shared World Record holder in the history books.

his muscled glory,[100] without his shoes on for obvious reasons, but this laid-back, "regular, devil-may-care Australian"[101] born on the Murray River, who always worked full time to support his family, had made history. And that was that, as far as he was concerned.

[102]Australia's Olympic team returned as heroes, having won three Gold, one Silver and two Bronze medals and the Gold medallists all had ties to Manly. Nick remarked in an letter to his hometown newspaper that they had enjoyed themselves most of all in Ireland on their journey home, taking part in the modern iteration of the Tailtean Games, a nod to the 'Irish Trailblazers' of the previous chapter, but he was quoted as saying "there is no place in the wide world like dear old Aussie."[103] He was to continue his athletics career until the age of 37, competing in the 1928 Olympics only having secured his selection in a specially organised trial with officialdom against him yet again, but his preparation let him down and he finished twelfth, jumping well below expectations, even at the age of 33. He moved to the Western Suburbs Athletic Club in late 1925 to combine coaching with competition, later competed for Kensington Athletic Club and in 1932 he unsuccessfully sought a position as a masseur with the Olympic team.

He left the Fire Service in December 1927 and thereafter ran a tobacconist's shop, hairdressing saloon and finally billiards halls in Sydney. He gave few interviews about the Olympics and his World Record jump, seemingly happy to disappear from view as an athlete

---

[100] Famous portrait of Nick Winter taken shortly after winning Gold in 1924 and used on a commemorative postcard in Australia © Out of Copyright
[101] Attributed to Frederick A. M. Webster, famous British athletics coach and writer of over 30 books on athletics and the Olympic Games [1886-1949].
[102] Portrait of 'Olympic player' Nick Winter taken in c.1930 in NSW © Out of Copyright
[103] *The Murrumbidgee Irrigator*, 11 November 1924

and to seek new challenges in his life. He made tentative returns to jumping at various stages, by then only competing for a podium place, but it was to billiards that he put his main focus after his jumping career ended and which may well have given him the most pleasure in his sporting life. He had perfected his skills at the fire station and he revelled in trick shots, more interested in an exhibition of skill than winning a match and he was said to be the greatest trick shot player in Australia, with a shot that even the great billiards player Walter Lindrum[104] could not execute.

On the evening of 6-7 May 1955 and by now a heavy drinker for several years and with his wife dying of cancer, he was overcome by gas asphyxiation in his bathroom at home, likely to have occurred when he fell and hit his head on a pipe, allowing the gas to escape. An extremely tragic end to the extraordinary life of one of Australia's most gifted sportsmen, who once told a newspaper reporter that "he got a greater thrill out of winning the hop, step and jump championship at Marrar than he did when he won the Olympic title... the first time his father had been beaten."[105] His World Record would remain the Australian best until 1960 and was good enough to have still claimed Gold in London 1948. The sporting feats of Nick Winter transcended NSW where he spent the majority of his life, but in death he was remembered more modestly, as he would have chosen – as a Digger rather than a World Record holder and Olympian, with a military headstone commemorating '1134 Driver A. W. Winter'.

12.07.1924 WR 15.52m (50ft 11¼in) Nick Winter (AUS) Paris, France (NWI)[106]

---

[104] Walter 'Wally' Lindrum, Australian holder of the World Professional Billiards Championship from 1933-1950, with 57 World Records to his name, some of which stand to this day [1898-1960].
[105] *Daily Advertiser*, 7 February 1942
[106] According to World Athletics, his distance of 15.525m was initially registered as 15.53m and corrected after the Second World War to 15.52m.

THE JUMPING SONS OF JAPAN

"I'll try until I break the world record"[107]

We begin our story of the Japanese dominance of the triple jump through to the last Olympics (Berlin 1936) before the Second World War, with Mikio Oda, sixth in the 1924 Olympic final at only nineteen years of age. Oda was a rival of Nick Winter, with whom he later exchanged gifts as a mark of friendship and was described as a 'boy' in his first Games,[108] at 5ft 6in (1.67m) in height, a marked contrast to the sporting Hercules[109] from Australia. Winter's World Record lasted for seven years, three months and 15 days before he was supplanted in 1931 by this fine all-round athletics star from Japan, who claimed Gold in 1928 Amsterdam in his second Games, when the Australian was a disappointing twelfth attempting to defend his title.

Oda's victory in 1928 was the first Olympic Gold medal for a Japanese athlete and the first for an Asian, securing his place in the history books aged only 23. With the same format as Paris 1924, Oda came into the event as one of the favourites, with the best jumps of the preceding years and he quickly asserted his dominance, in a final high on overall quality, but with youthful athletes in abundance and the other favourites Vilho Tuulos and Nick Winter fouled on their first jumps. His winning jump was measured at 49ft $10\frac{4}{5}$in (15.21m), which would not have even given him a medal in Paris and was below his

---

[107] Diary entry made by Mikio Oda on the day he won Olympic Gold in 1928; noted in the transcript of an interview he gave in 1998 shortly before his death and shared by World Athletics online. The content of that interview has been relied upon heavily here.

[108] He competed in three Olympic Games, in the triple, high and long jump, medalling once.

[109] Roman divine hero, famous for his feats and strength and many adventures.

personal best at the time, but it was the foundation for Oda's journey to becoming a hallowed figure in Japanese athletics and a great Olympian, a long-time coach, official, administrator, journalist and a central figure in the rehabilitation of Japan in international sport after the Second World War.[110]

[111]**Mikio Oda** was born on 30 March 1905 in the town of Kaita, Hiroshima Prefecture. He first came to prominence as a teenager in winning both the long and triple jump in the 1923 Far Eastern Championship Games[112] in Osaka, Japan, setting a new National Record of 46ft $9\frac{4}{5}$in (14.27m) in the latter, having set the national best marks for

the long and high jump in the championship trials.[113] This was his first international competition and as an 18-year-old his performances really stood out, although the Games only included Japan, China and the Philippines until 1930. The following year he was selected for the 1924 Olympics in Paris and having undertaken a two-week journey by train with no chance to train himself until he reached Europe, he took every opportunity to learn from his international competitors in France and returned home convinced he could better the new National Record he set in Paris.

Oda went on to win seven Golds in the Far Eastern Championship Games from 1923-30, in the long, triple and high jump and the decathlon, but his finest hour in competition came in the Olympic triple jump in Amsterdam 1928. He was by now a student at

---

[110] Japan's first international sporting event after the Second World War was the 1951 Asian Games in Delhi, India; Oda was the team manager.
[111] A young Mikio Oda in national colours, year and location unknown © unknown
[112] The precursor to the modern Asian Games.
[113] In his career he set at least 20 National Records.

Waseda University's School of Commerce in Tokyo and remarked in later life that when he returned to Japan after Paris, there was no official reception for the new star, with limited public interest in the Olympics and his achievement given little celebration beyond a special edition newspaper and a local party in his hometown. Interest would grow after Los Angeles 1932, where he finished twelfth as the defending champion whilst carrying an injury that had put his participation in doubt, and it would peak in Berlin 1936, but his finest hour had come outside of the Olympics on 27 October 1931, when he broke the World Record in Tokyo that he had set his sights on despite winning Gold back in 1928.

[114]The 1964 Olympics were held in Tokyo and proved to be the culmination of Japan's sporting reintegration after the Second World War. Oda fully embraced the 'Olympic Spirit'[115] and his own efforts were fundamental in returning his country to its place in the international sporting community. Beyond the Olympic Movement, he realised that Japanese athletes at that time were easily intimidated by foreign competitors, even at the mention of their name and the psychological damage of the two-decade rebuilding of the country led to a hesitancy when competing abroad.[116] As an athlete himself, he had no such problems and starting with his record jump in 1931, Oda, Chūhei Nambu and Naoto Tajima were to own the triple jump World Record for one month shy of twenty years, with only a brief seven

---

[114] Mikio Oda's winning leap in Amsterdam 1928 © IOC
[115] Defined by the IOC as requiring "mutual understanding with a spirit of friendship, solidarity and fair play."
[116] 'A different era: Oda wins Japan's first Olympic gold in 1928', Stephen Wade & Kaori Hitomi, *Associated Press*, 19 July 2019

month hiatus in 1935 when Australian Jack Metcalfe 'borrowed' it for a short period. This was *the* golden period for Japanese track and field and these 'Jumping Sons of Japan' were the main stars in the jumping events.

[117]For all that has been written about Oda as both a great athlete and Olympian, posthumously voted the male Asian athlete of the century in 2000, we return to where he made his most notable addition to the record books in what has been loosely described in modern accounts as the 'Physical Education'

competition held at *Meiji Jingu Gaien Stadium*, Shinjuku, Tokyo on 27 October 1931. Both Oda and Nambu were to set the World Record in the triple and long jump respectively on that day, and whilst no account of the actual competition or description of the record jump survives, we know that Nambu went on to set his own mark in the long jump after Oda's triple jump, indicative of the friendly rivalry that drove these close friends on to their own jumping successes, more so with both having been members of the same university track and field club before their recent graduation.[118]   Oda's World Record was measured at 51ft $1\frac{1}{4}$in (15.58m) and was to stand for only nine months and 18 days, until the Los Angeles Olympics in 1932.

This competition in October 1931 is believed to have been a "national athletics meet,"[119] a match between Japanese amateurs and students, and it is a sign of the high standard of jumping in the country that a World Record would be set in a domestic event, with Oda still

---

[117] Portrait of Mikio Oda, date unknown © IOC
[118] 9 of the 16 members of Japan's track and field team in 1928 were students from Waseda University; https://yab.yomiuri.co.jp/adv/wol/dy/culture/140326.html
[119] *San Pedro News-Pilot* (USA), 27 October 1931

working full-time as a reporter at the time. He had already taken his chance to prove his ability at the Olympics in 1924 and more notably in 1928, and whilst the Olympic flag in Tokyo 1964 was raised to an exact height of 15.21m in recognition of his Gold medal winning jump in 1928, his advancing of the World Record is truly the pinnacle of his athletics career.

The Olympics is said to have only become a global 'show' from the 1960's[120] and for Oda, participation in the Games was primarily seen as the promulgation of his daily regime.[121] He did not wait to collect his Gold medal in 1928, having already departed for another international meet, highlighting the lack of stature for the Games in those days, but his motivation was always to jump 1cm further and run 1sec faster, adopting a logical approach to his research into jumping technique and his practice routines. It is telling that his diary entry from the evening of his Gold medal triumph in 1928 focuses on his motivation to beat the World Record and whilst this remarkable athlete who wanted the record left Amsterdam with an Olympic Gold medal, he was to claim that record in 1931 on home soil, putting paid to the lie that Japanese could not be great jumpers like the Western athletes. Oda himself said in a speech in later years, "the short legs of the Japanese physical constitution were believed to be a big handicap in jumping... [later] Japanese jumpers came forward one after another"[122] and this is his legacy, to be the first of a golden age of triple jumping amongst Japanese athletes. He enjoyed a long life, becoming a Professor of his old university, awarded the Olympic

---

[120] See Wade & Hitoma article from 2019.
[121] 1998 interview shared by World Athletics.
[122] https://www.insidethegames.biz/articles/1107749/japans-first-olympic-champion-blog

Order[123] in 1976 and later recognised by his own government for his outstanding cultural contributions, before dying aged 93 on 2 December 1998.

[124]The Gold medallist in Los Angeles 1932 was Oda's close friend and student training partner **Chūhei Nambu**, the next Japanese athlete to hold the triple jump World Record in this golden age for the nation's jumpers. Born on 27 May 1904 in Sapporo, Hokkaido, he also attended Waseda University and later became a sports journalist like Oda. It is said that Nambu kept a picture of Oda in his room for encouragement, despite being slightly older and whilst their motivation may have differed, the rivalry they enjoyed as friends spurred them both on to their notable accomplishments, not least in the triple jump.

Nambu was not the fine all-round athlete that Oda was, with only one victory in the Far Eastern Championship Games in the long jump in Tokyo in 1930, but he did claim six medals in total, including Silver (1925) and Bronze (1927) in the triple jump and Bronze in the 100m (1930). Where he differed, was that he was a fine long jumper and whilst he went on to set a World Record in both the horizontal jumps – still being the only male athlete to hold both at the same time – his Gold medal in triple jump in Los Angeles 1932 means he is more frequently recalled as a triple rather than long jumper.

---

[123] Established in 1975, awarded by the IOC for particularly distinguished contributions to the Olympic Movement.
[124] Portrait of Chūhei Nambi, date unknown © Hawaii Times Photo Archives Foundation

Jumping after club-mate Oda had himself broken the triple jump World Record in Tokyo on 27 October 1931, Nambu is said to have been inspired to go on and break the record in the long jump. His distance was measured at 26ft 2in (7.98m), extending the mark of 1928 Olympic Silver medallist Sylvio Cator[125] of Haiti by 5cm, a final in which Nambu was 9th and lasting until it was broken by the great 'Jesse' Owens of the United States in May 1935.[126] In October 1931, international press coverage focussed on the record in the more popularly known 'broad' or long jump and despite Nambu going on to medal in both events in 1932, it has never been a given that being a good long jumper would translate to the technically more difficult triple jump, which is what makes his accomplishments all the more fascinating.

[127]The meticulous preparation and logical approach to training of Mikio Oda for the 1928 Olympics was borne out of his experience in Paris 1924. Having observed international athletes up close in Europe, his idea was to tailor his methods to suit the Japanese physique, deciding that further study of Western methods from secondary sources  was no longer effective and he deduced that the national habit of squatting had developed muscles to a degree none of his competitors could match.[128] This new style was based on the exceptional strength

---

125 Sylvio P. Cator, three time Olympian 1924-32 in the long jump, Silver medallist in 1928 and World Record holder from 1928-31 [1900-52].
126 The leap was the Asian record until 1970 when beaten by Japanese Hiroomi Yamada [1942-81], the first Asian athlete to go over 8m and a two-time Olympian in 1964-68.
127 Vintage collectible card of Chūhei Nambu issued by Mühlen Franck in a series entitled 'Olympia 1936'
128 'AROUND THE MULBERRY BUSH', Herbert W. Wind, *Sports Illustrated*, 3 March 1958

of his knees and ankle joints and whereas Nick Winter was said to have had ankles almost twice the normal size,[129] he was a physical one-off, but Oda's techniques were able to be adopted by Chūhei Nambu to great effect for the Los Angeles Olympics in 1932.

[130]The men's long jump final at the 1932 Olympics took place on 2 August. There were 12 participants from 9 countries and Cator of Haiti along with Nambu were the favourites, the Japanese as the World Record holder. He had disappointed in his three events in Amsterdam 1928 and with his revised training and jumping style having paid dividends with the World Record in late 1931, he must have been confident of Gold in Los Angeles. In 1964 he was said to have told a Bulgarian athlete arriving for the Tokyo Olympics without her luggage that he had made his first jump in Los Angeles barefoot for the same reason[131] and his first jump in 1932 was 24ft $5\frac{1}{3}$in (7.45m), placing him second, whether he was barefoot or not. He is commonly said to have been bothered by a bad back or leg injury in the competition and could not improve on that distance, finishing in what for him was a disappointing third place. If he could manage his injury, he had the triple jump to contest to make up for his failure in the long jump, but it was in only two days...

Returning to his training, Nambu had some interesting methods of his own, possibly apocryphal but nonetheless worth repeating. It was said that he would practice indoors during the winter and part of this involved doing his workouts in local department stores,

[129] 'UNIQUE "NICK" WINTER The AMAZING ALL-ROUNDER', *Pix.* Vol. 1 No. 10, 2 April 1938
[130] A smiling Chūhei Nambu competing in the 1932 Olympics © IOC
[131] https://theolympians.co/2020/02/14/an-olympic-wedding-at-the-1964-tokyo-olympics-the-fairy-tale-of-diana-yorgova-and-nikola-prodanov/#more-16253

weaving through the customers in his routines and leading to him being banned! In addition, he sought to hone his technique by taking a keen interest in the world around him – paraphrasing the IOC website, he learnt to run from watching horses, to leap from observing frogs and monkeys and to see how his arms should move correctly he watched the wheels of trains.[132]

The 1932 Olympics marked a huge upturn in Japanese Olympic interest and despite the worldwide economic depression, they sent the second largest delegation and finished ahead of sporting powerhouses of the time like Great Britain and Hungary. The success of its athletes was a measure of the progress of 'foreign' sports in a historically insular country and echoed the rising expansionist militarism of its politicians and generals, with areas of culture even imbued with an Olympic nationalism. The Japanese press embraced the event for the first time and a great many reporters were sent to cover the Games, in contrast to the near media blackout of Amsterdam. But Nambu was not thinking about the ambitions of his country to host an Olympic Games or increase their international influence and he had to now do something he had not yet done to even have a chance of a medal – beat defending champion Mikio Oda in a triple jump competition!

[133]In the Los Angeles Memorial Coliseum on 4 August 1932, the men's triple jump competition was stood on its head by Nambu's first jump, although the jumping order has not survived. He reached 49ft 5$\frac{1}{3}$in (15.07m) and in the event this would prove enough

132 https://olympics.com/en/athletes/chuhei-nambu
133 Chūhei Nambu in action during the 1932 Olympics triple jump final © IOC

to have claimed Bronze. Oda had brought a leg injury into the competition and was certainly restricted, not even reaching 14m in what would prove to be his final Olympics as an athlete, when his form that year had promised so much more, so Nambu was assured of beating his compatriot for the first time in this event. His only real challenge came from Sweden's Erik Svensson,[134] the long-time National Record holder was in his second Olympics and was another dual long and triple jumper. He jumped 50ft $3\frac{1}{8}$in (15.32m) in the second round to move into the lead and Nambu could not respond on his next three leaps, although he had improved to 49ft $11\frac{4}{5}$in (15.22m) on his third.

With "wings on his ankles and springs in his knees,"[135] Nambu was to make history on his fifth jump, pushing the World Record to 51ft $6\frac{3}{4}$in (15.72m) and winning Gold by 40cm from Svensson, the best possible response to his close friend Oda's misfortune. The man who some had expected to miss the triple jump to focus on the long jump due to the emergence of Kenkichi Oshima[136] in the former – some sources have him setting an unofficial World Record as a student and was one of the favourites, but a bathing accident before the Olympics hampered his form and he finished third – made history with his World Record and carved out a place for himself as another legendary Japanese jumper. His record in the latter was to stand for three years and four months and he is still the only man to hold both the long and triple jump record at the same time. He remained in athletics after retirement, marrying in his 1932 Olympic uniform shortly after his

---

[134] Karl 'Erik' Svensson, two time Olympian 1928-32 and Silver medallist in the triple jump in 1932 [1903-86].

[135] *The Sun* (AUS), 10 September 1932

[136] Kenkichi Oshima, two time Olympian 1932-36 triple jump and Bronze medallist in 1932; later member of IOC and author of numerous books [1908-85].

triumphant return,[137] managing the team at the 1964 Olympics and died on 23 July 1997, aged 93, the same age as his great friend Mikio Oda.

Some sources, including the Official Report of the 1932 Olympics, put the superior performances down to a number of factors, including the introduction of an Olympic Village for the first time, although construction was on the cheapest side of 'pre-fabrication' due to the Great Depression,[138] rent was charged to athletes to stay in the village and it emptied very quickly after competition ended! The 1932 Olympics was characterised as a Japanese 'Gold Rush', with five Gold, five Silver and two Bronze medals placing the country in fifth overall and one soon to be notable athlete of the 131-strong delegation was Naoto Tajima. He had finished sixth in the long jump final in Los Angeles and in 1936 he would go on to etch his own name in the record books for the triple jump.

[139]Oda may have been the pioneer of the Japanese dominance of the triple jump in the late 1920's and early 1930's, and also its most celebrated exponent, but it was **Naoto Tajima** who would be the first athlete to reach 16m in the event when completing the 'hat-trick' of  victories for his nation in Berlin 1936. Metaphorical storm clouds hung over Europe at this time, with Nazi Germany using their Olympics as a show of propaganda and the inclusion of 49 nations to legitimize their regime, despite some lukewarm calls for a boycott beforehand, but as with the Olympism of Oda and the fine long jumping of Nambu

---

[137] *The Tribune* (Philippines), 29 October 1932

[138] The Great Depression, the worst economic crisis in modern times (1929-39) and impacted most countries around the world; first evident after a shock fall in stock prices in the United States.

[139] Portrait of Naoto Tajimi taken in 1932 © Kingendai Photo Library/Nippon News

overshadowing their respective triple jump feats, Tajima was to see his own record-breaking exploit overshadowed.

Born on 15 August 1912 in Osaka Prefecture, he grew up in his father's hometown of Iwakuni, Yamaguchi Prefecture. His interest in athletics came from elder brother Moto Tajima, a champion athlete who was said to have trained with Mikio Oda in Hiroshima and it is likely that the younger Tajima was of the generation inspired by the success of Oda in Amsterdam 1928. Naoto excelled at the jumping disciplines himself, taking medals in the long and triple jump in the national championships in 1930[140] and by the 1932 Olympics, he was a student at Kyoto Imperial University and budding athletics star ready for his first international competition in Los Angeles in the long jump. In a field of only 12, featuring the World Record holder Chūhei Nambu and strong favourites from the home nation, he did well to finish sixth with a best jump of 7.15m and would have gained valuable international experience ahead of the next Olympics in Berlin.

In the 1934 Far Eastern Championship Games in Manila, Philippines, the last to be held following Japan's territorial aggression in Manchuria, now Northeast China, Tajima claimed Gold in the long jump and Bronze in the triple jump, the latter behind 1932 Olympic Bronze medallist Kenkichi Oshima, and it is said that he won the national triple jump title in 1932 and 1935. He was developing into a fine jumper and in 1935, he had been one of three Japanese to claim victories in track and field in the International University Games in Budapest, Hungary, further demonstrating their dominance in jumping events in this era. Japan won the high jump, pole vault and long jump,

---

[140] http://www.athleticsasia.org/legends-of-asia-naoto-tajima/?fbclid=IwAR2XEYZaX_q8VEQexc6JRH5ISxm-VAAtmqmenoCSb0tEKZ_-jRFNLBIXiZc; also relied on for further biographical information later in this chapter.

with Tajima claiming the honours in the latter event, 0.2cm ahead of German 'Luz' Long,[141] favoured to compete for a medal in his home Olympics the following summer.

Tajima entered Berlin 1936 with his confidence having been boosted by the victory in Budapest, but he was to run into the unstoppable force that was Jesse Owens of the United States,[142] one of the Americans conspicuous by their absence in Budapest the previous year. Owens would go on to  dominate the track and field events of the Berlin Games, winning the 100m, 200m, 4x100m relay and the long jump, arguably the greatest Olympic performance of all time. As an African American, his performances in front of a global audience were a powerful rebuttal of the Aryan supremacy propagandized by Nazi Germany and whilst modern accounts have corrected the myth that he was directly snubbed by Adolf Hitler,[143] the leader of Nazi Germany, Tajima found himself on centre stage for the most memorable image of protest from these politically charged Games.

[144]Tajima was the only returning long jumper from the previous Olympics and from the qualifying round on 4 August 1936 it was clear that Owens was in a class of his own, having already broken the World Record in May 1935. He was to improve the Olympic

[141] Carl L. 'Luz' Long, long jumper known for his Olympic Silver in 1936 and association with Jesse Owens, which continued via letter after Berlin; died of wounds in Italy during the Second World War [1913-43].

[142] James 'Jesse' C. Owens, four-time Gold medallist in track and field in Berlin 1936, an iconic figure in Olympic history as the most successful athlete in those Games and a powerful symbol of the struggle for racial equality [1913-80].

[143] Adolf Hitler, dictator of Nazi Germany and one of the most reviled figures in human history [1889-1945].

[144] Famous photograph of the long jump medal ceremony in the 1936 Olympics © unknown

Record in securing Gold and in a tight final round, Tajima emerged with the Bronze medal with a best jump of 7.74m, equalling his personal best. The 100,000 Germans said to be inside the Olympic Stadium during the Games took to Owens immediately when he claimed the 100m on 2 August, but it was the long jump medal ceremony that has proven iconic. Foreign athletes were expected to give the Nazi salute – see Luz Long on the right of the photograph on page 66 – but both Owens and Tajima were to refuse, the Japanese later commenting along the lines of the Games leaving an unpleasant taste, since they were too cleverly exploited by the Nazis.[145]

[146]After the disappointment of a Bronze in the long jump, Tajima belatedly entered the triple jump on 6 August 1936. He was little fancied, with both Oshima and Masao Harada[147] heavily favoured to be the leading Japanese and extend the nation's dominance of the event. The World Record holder was Australian Jack Metcalfe and the story of the 1936 triple jump final is that of two record holders, of the young Australian that had seemingly been on an inexorable rise from 1932 towards the record once held by compatriot Nick Winter for seven years and the unexpected excellence of the Japanese to reclaim the record for his country only seven months after it had been lost, in the final of an event that he valued less than the long jump...

John Patrick Metcalfe, known as 'Jack', was born on 3 February 1912 in Bellingen, New South Wales and died on 16 January 1994, aged 81, having been one of Australia's premier athletes in the 1930's and the nation's only medallist at the 1936

---

[145] https://theolympians.co/2017/02/23/naoto-tajima-part-2-the-last-japanese-star-at-the-end-of-japans-track-and-field-golden-age/
[146] Jack Metcalfe in athletic uniform, New South Wales, Australia, c. 1930's © Out of Copyright
[147] Masao Harada, Olympic Silver medallist in the triple jump in 1936 [1912-2000].

Olympics. He was another all-rounder, world class in high and long jump, competitive in the javelin and shot put, but truly excelling in triple jump. He came to international attention in winning the triple jump at the 1934 British Empire Games[148] in London with a leap of 51ft $3\frac{1}{3}$in (15.63m), taking third in the long jump and fourth in the high jump. He was to retain his crown in the triple jump in the 1938 Games, but it was his leap in London that brought him wider recognition, despite a drop off in performance on his return home.[149] Metcalfe was already the National Record holder when he extended it further in January 1935 by $1\frac{1}{4}$in and on 14 December 1935 he enjoyed his finest moment, breaking the World Record at the Sydney Sports Ground by reaching 51ft $9\frac{1}{4}$in (15.78m) in the State Championships. Nambu is said to have written to him to offer congratulations on breaking his record and it is in this spirit of friendly rivalry that we return to the final of the triple jump in Berlin 1936.

In Berlin it is commonly accepted that Metcalfe, Tajima, Harada and Oshima trained together. Metcalfe was self-coached and was quick to offer the Japanese pointers on style, with some in the Australian track and field team feeling his coaching had improved the technique of Tajima in particular, to the point that he was then able to out-perform all expectations and break Metcalfe's World Record.[150] It was very much in the spirt of the Olympics at the time that he would assist his rivals and he does not seem to have let it publicly get to him; after all, he had etched his name in the history books with the World Record in 1935 and whilst he posted a distance of 50ft $10\frac{1}{4}$in (15.50m)

---

[148] First held in 1930 and the event has evolved into the ongoing Commonwealth Games.
[149] *The Labor Daily*, 21 January 1935
[150] https://sahof.org.au/hall-of-fame-member/jack-metcalfe/

on his first and best jump in the final, he could not compete with what Tajima went on to do, namely what no man had done before, in reaching 16m with a hop, step and a jump.

Jack Metcalfe would go on to win a second triple jump Gold in the 1938 British Empire Games in Sydney, where he had gone to both school and university (studying law and latterly having his own law practice), and in addition he took Bronze in the javelin, with a 5th place in the long jump and 7th in the high jump! He has long remained an underrated Australian athlete, being world class in all three of his jumping events and it was only the Second World War that prevented him from likely adding to his Olympic medal record. He continued to compete at club-level into the 1950's, even placing third in the shot put in the 1947 National Championships and he was able to return to the Olympics in 1948 as the manager of the Australian athletics team. He later helped to organise the Melbourne Olympics in 1956, also being appointed chief jumps referee and he was to remain involved in athletics as coach, administrator and selector for many years. He died aged 81 in 1994 and should certainly be better remembered beyond the shores of his native Australia that he represented so proudly.

Tajima would jump 51ft $8\frac{1}{2}$in (15.76m) on his first attempt in Berlin, smashing his personal best of 15.40m and setting a new Olympic Record. It was to everyone's surprise that it was this Japanese athlete leading the way in the competition, when he was ranked nationally behind Harada, but Metcalfe would readily acknowledge the superiority of the Japanese jumpers, particularly on a cinder track and he had seen them up close in training. The format of the competition followed the standard two-round format we see in modern events, albeit with a pre-qualifying round where jumpers had to reach 14m but Tajima had seemingly blown his rivals away. All three Japanese went over 15m on their first jump, but whilst the number one ranked jumper Oshima was to foul on his next five attempts, Masada landed all six, almost reaching Nambu's previous Olympic Record on his final leap. Tajima fouled on his second jump, made 15.44m on his third and in the form of his life, he then reached 16m, or 52ft 5$\frac{3}{4}$in[151], the first man in history to achieve this mark and give him the World Record, 22cm beyond Metcalfe's mark in 1935. Masada took the Silver medal and Oshima finished a disappointing sixth, but the nation had once again dominated the event.

[152]Tajima's World Record was the first since Ahearn's 1911 jump was ratified, to extend the world best by a significant amount. He was nearly 24 years old and a recent graduate, an unprecedented triple jumper in terms of distance and the third Japanese in a row to claim triple jump Olympic Gold. As he stood on the podium

and watched the 'Rising Sun' flag of his nation being raised, patriotic tears ran down his cheeks as he contemplated having "made cheap"[153] the previous best figure in an event that he did not particularly favour. It was said that he valued the long jump Bronze as much as this Gold, seeing the latter event as an extra skill to his specialism in the former and it was for his place in the iconic image of the long jump podium alongside Jesse Owens, for which he is best remembered.

---

[151] Commonly recorded as 52ft 5$\frac{3}{4}$in but 52ft 5$\frac{9}{10}$in is more accurate.
[152] Naoto Tajima competes in the men's triple jump during the Berlin Olympics on 6 August 1936 © unknown
[153] *The Telegraph* (AUS), 7 August 1936

[154]He married on his return home to another Japanese athlete he had met in Los Angeles, but his athletics career was to enjoy no further highlights, retiring in 1938 when the Far Eastern Championship Games had been cancelled due to regional conflict. The outbreak of the Second World War in 1939 meant that the dominance of the great Japanese jumpers was to come to a premature end,[155] with no Olympic Games again until London 1948 and Japan not readmitted until Helsinki 1952. A sport that had been advanced so much in the country by Oda and successive athletes faded considerably, with no Japanese winning a medal in any major international triple jump competition since and the *next* track and field Gold medallist in any athletic event being Naoko Takahashi[156] in the women's marathon in Sydney 2000. Tajima went on to coach the Japan athletics teams in the 1956 and 1964 Olympics, worked for a coal mine, became a university lecturer, was a member of the Japanese Olympic Committee and the managing director of the Japan Association of Athletics Federations, before he died aged 78 in 1990.

27.10.1931 WR 15.58m (51ft $1\frac{1}{4}$in) Mikio Oda (JPN) Tokyo, Japan (NWI)

14.08.1932 WR 15.72m (51ft $6\frac{3}{4}$in) Chūhei Nambu (JPN) Los Angeles, USA (NWI)

14.12.1935 WR 15.78m (51ft $9\frac{1}{4}$in) Jack Metcalfe (AUS) Sydney, Australia (NWI)

06.08.1936 WR 16.00m (52ft $5\frac{3}{4}$in) Naoto Tajima (JPN) Berlin, Germany (+0.6m/s)

---

154 Vintage collectible card of Naoto Tajima issued by Mühlen Franck in a series entitled 'Olympia 1936'

155 The nation that dominated the jumping events in the pre-war era, also boasted pole vault Silver in 1932 and 1936 for Shuhei Nishida [1910-97] and Bronze for Sueo Ōe in 1936 [1914-41].

156 Naoko Takahashi, long-distance runner who won Gold in Sydney 2000 in the women's marathon and for a short period in 2001 held the World Record [1972-].

DEATH FROM BRAZIL

"A solitary genius"[157]

[158]The 1959 Brazilian musical film *Orfeu Negro*, or Black Orpheus, is not where you would expect to find a double Olympic Gold medallist and one of *the* great triple jumpers. A film particularly noted for its *bossa nova*[159] soundtrack which has gone on to become a classic in itself, this retelling of the Greek

legend of star-crossed lovers Orpheus and Eurydice in the Rio de Janeiro *favela*[160] during the Carnival, became a major international hit, winning the *Palme d'Or* at the Cannes Film Festival in 1959 and the Academy Award for Best Foreign Language Film in 1960, amongst others.[161] The female lead Eurydice is pursued across Rio by the murderous spectral apparition of Death itself, the actor clad in a skeletal leotard, in an ancient tale made fresh by its French director,[162] the bewitching samba-style music giving a vivid intensity that has continued to make this romantic tragedy culturally significant.

The actor playing Death was Adhemar da Silva, the two-time triple jump Olympic Gold medallist from 1952 and 1956, a

---

[157] *A World History of Track and Field Athletics 1864-1964*, p.264, Roberto L. Quercetani, 1964.

[158] 1959 poster for the film Black Orpheus, or Orfeu Negro, likely from Italy due to the spelling of 'Orfeo' © unknown

[159] A style of samba developed in Rio de Janeiro, Brazil in the 1950's and 60's.

[160] Portuguese word used for a type of slum or shantytown in Brazil, normally located on the outskirts of a major city and populated by a suburban underclass, unduly impacted by historic governmental neglect.

[161] Also awarded the Golden Glove Award for Best Foreign Film in 1960 and nominated for the 1961 Best Film BAFTA Award.

[162] Marcel Camus, French director of nearly a dozen films, best known for his work on Black Orpheus using mostly amateur actors [1912-82].

phenomenal jumper who showed the world that a balancing of the three phases could lead to longer distances, breaking the World Record five times! Once described by the prolific French athletics writer Alain Billouin[163] as, "...displaying the poise and finesse of a samba dancer," his athletics career started late aged nineteen, but reached unprecedented heights over four Olympic Games. Samba would come naturally to a Brazilian and the charismatic 'Hero of Helsinki' who invented the 'Victory Lap' in the 1952 Olympics brought a whole new rhythm and vividness to the triple jump.

[164]Born on 29 September 1927 in Casa Verde, a suburb of São Paulo, **Adhemar Ferreira da Silva** dreamed of musical fame as a teenager. His mother had ensured he was educated well, despite their lack of money, latterly attending a São Paulo Technical School, but the guitar-playing singer Adhemar had ambitions in music and if that was not going to happen he wanted to be a footballer (soccer) for his home club, Santos FC, forever associated with the great Brazilian forward, 'Pelé'.[165] The teenage Adhemar entered every musical radio competition he could find, winning them all and was the star of his neighbourhood football team,[166] but it was to be in an open trial at *São Paulo Futebol Clube*, a nearby multi-sports club, that he came across the man who would change his life, turning a lanky teenager without either extraordinary

[163] Alain Billouin, author of over twenty books on athletics and wrote for leading French newspaper L'Equipe for 33 years; quote commonly shared online and likely from his 2003 work, 'The Fabulous History of Athletics' [1940-].
[164] A young Adhemar da Silva in São Paulo FC colours © unknown
[165] Edson Arantes do Nascimento, or Pelé, arguably the greatest footballer of all time and an iconic figure in Brazil, having won the World Cup three times [1940-2023].
[166] 'THE TRIPLE JUMPER FROM BRAZIL', George de Carvalho, *Sports Illustrated*, 31 August 1959

73

speed or long jumping ability as we saw with previous elite triple jumpers, into the greatest athlete in South American history and a revered character in Brazil to this day, his record-breaking achievements continuing to be recognised by two gold stars on the club badge of Santos FC.

It was in 1947 that Adhemar is believed to have met German coach Dietrich Gerner,[167] having been invited to an evening training session by his friend, a footballing member of the São Paulo club. His parents had encouraged him to find another sport to focus his efforts on, football not being the success he hoped it would be in failing that trial in 1947 and by chance he was to find his niche in the triple jump, commencing a lifelong friendship with Gerner that would transpose that of athlete and coach, Adhemar coming to call him his 'little uncle', *titio* in Portuguese, or his 'German dad'.

Gerner had emigrated to Brazil in 1929 for a career in timber exports, his own amateur athletics career as a runner and hurdler peaking when narrowly missing qualification for the 1928 Olympics in the 400m hurdles, having been ranked 9th in the world.[168]   He continued as an athlete for a period in Brazil, setting the South American decathlon record in October 1931, shortly before he became a sports teacher and gave up on any chance of competing in Los Angeles 1932 for his adoptive country. By 1944 he was a track coach for São Paulo and despite Adhemar failing his football trial aged eighteen, he impressed Gerner, or at least his long legs did – said to be 3ft $6\frac{1}{2}$in of his 5ft 10in (1.78m) frame.[169] Adhemar had the physique

---

[167] Dietrich Gerner, German-born coach of two-time Olympic Gold medallist Adhemar da Silva and the first coach from South America to receive a World Athletics Heritage Plaque [1902-n/k].

[168] 'Adhemar da Silva and the "little uncle", Volker Kluge, *Rio Special*, Journal of Olympic History – Vol. 24/No. 2 - 2016.

[169] de Carvalho, *op. cit.*

of a track and field athlete, but he did not shine in any of the sprints, distance events, or jumping disciplines that the German tried him in, his motivation for continuing to train to maintain his elegant body shape, despite the lack of success. His coach later remarked that, "I'd just about lost hope... then he tried the hop, step and jump and went 11.40m... and I couldn't believe it. But I remeasured it myself and, by God, it was 11.40. From then on, he just leaped to glory."[170]

His first triple jump competition may well have quickly followed in mid-1947 in Mexico City,[171] jumping 13.05m (42ft $9\frac{4}{5}$in), followed by a Brazilian beginners record of 13.56m (44ft $5\frac{9}{10}$in) on 1 June 1947.[172] It is clear that the 19-year-old novice took to the technique straightaway and with daily practice sessions his distances rose markedly in a short period of time, Adhemar noting for himself, "after trying so long, it was wonderful to be good at something,"[173] confounding expectations in qualifying for London 1948 as the third ranked Brazilian jumper.

The Olympics returned after the Second World War to London in 1948, a gap of twelve years from Berlin in 1936 and unsurprisingly there were no returning jumpers in the triple jump, with Japan also yet to be reintegrated to international sport. The World Record was still held by Naoto Tajima who had retired in 1938 and in the intervening years interest in the event in Europe had only been kept alive by the Scandinavians, with the European Record being set at 50ft

---

[170] de Carvalho, *op. cit.*; 11.40m is 37ft $4\frac{4}{5}$in.
[171] From the International Society of Olympic Historians (ISOH); other sources such as de Carvalho have his first trip outside of São Paulo, let alone Brazil, being the 1948 Olympics.
[172] Kluge, *op. cit.*
[173] de Carvalho, *op. cit.*

11in (15.52m) on 16 July 1939 by Onni Rajasaari[174] of Finland, only a few weeks before Central Europe would experience war. Sweden had dominated in Stockholm 1912 and Antwerp 1920 claiming both Golds, and were to repeat that success with Arne Åhman[175] in 1948, narrowly claiming victory with 50ft $6\frac{1}{3}$in (15.40m) ahead of Australian George Avery.[176] In 5th, 8th (Adhemar) and 11th places were Brazilians, a sign of the domestic competition that was to inspire the first phenomenon of the post-Japanese era to come to prominence and give rise to the triple jump being a "Brazilian domain,"[177] mostly through the feats of its "solitary genius."[178]

Åhman was another example of a champion triple jumper to have initially been proficient in one of the other jumping disciplines, good enough to claim a medal in the high jump in the European Championships in 1950, but Adhemar marked the first elite triple jumper to have been an event specialist. He was just not a natural high or long jumper,[179] despite his obvious physical assets and with his 'little uncle' Gerner by his side overseeing his methodical training, he brought an elegant style and balance to the triple jump, introducing the world to the idea that distribution between speed and jumping action would lead to ever longer distances, the event second only to the pole vault in becoming the technically demanding discipline it remains to this day and not just an 'extra skill' for committed long jumpers like Naoto Tajima in the 1930's.

---

[174] Onni R. Rajasaari, 11th in triple jump in the 1932 and 1936 Olympics, European Championships Gold in 1938 and seven-time national champion from 1933-39 [1910-94].
[175] Per A. Åhman, Olympic triple jump Gold in 1948 and a good high jumper, with Silver in the 1950 European Championships [1925-2022].
[176] Gordon G. Avery, Silver medallist in the triple jump in London 1948 [1925-2006].
[177] Kluge, *op. cit.*
[178] Quercetani, *op. cit.*, p.264.
[179] Although he did place fourth in the long jump in the 1951 Pan American Games.

Adhemar returned from London 1948 as one of three Brazilian jumpers who would continue to dominate the event in South America for the next decade. He had jumped 47ft $6\frac{1}{2}$in (14.49m) when finishing eighth in his first Olympic Games, with the best placed Brazilian being Geraldo de Oliveira,[180] ranked second in the world in 1947 and disappointing in finishing fifth in London, when favoured to take a medal. De Oliveira was the first of this wave of Brazilian triple jumpers to make a mark in the 1940's, but it was the third, Hélio da Silva,[181] 11th in London, who would prove to be the biggest threat to Adhemar's rise. In the next major championship for the Brazilians following the London Olympics, Hélio claimed victory in April 1949 in the South American Championships in Lima, Peru, setting a Championship Record of 50ft $\frac{4}{5}$in (15.26m), with de Oliveira second and Adhemar in third, with a jump of 48ft $6\frac{1}{4}$in (14.79m). Adhemar was said to have reached 15m in 1948, ranking in the world top 10 for the first time and in 1949 twice jumped 50ft $10\frac{3}{5}$in (15.51m),[182] incredibly making him the number one ranked triple jumper.

The tough domestic competition must have quickened his development from such a late start in athletics, a phenomenal progression culminating in him setting his first World Record a little over three years from being introduced to the event. On 3 December 1950 at the *C. R. Tietê Stadium*, São Paulo, Adhemar leaped to 52ft $5\frac{3}{4}$in (16.00m), tying Tajima's World Record that had stood for 14 years,

[180] Geraldo de Oliveira, two-time Olympian in 1948 and 1952 and three-time South American Championships triple jump Gold medallist 1945-47; also won Gold in long jump in the 1946 South American Championships [1919-n/k].
[181] Hélio C. da Silva, competed for Brazil in the 100m in London 1948 and South American triple jump champion in 1949 [1923-n/k].
[182] 'Brazil's two-time Olympic champion Adhemar Ferreira da Silva passes away', Benedito Turco, World Athletics website, 15 January 2001.

three months and 27 days and been little threatened, other than wind-assisted efforts like the 51ft 10$\frac{4}{6}$in (15.82m) jump from Norway's Kaare Strøm[183] in September 1939, ruled illegal with a tailwind of +8.0m/s! This World Record signalled Adhemar's arrival as an elite triple jumper, yet he was also inspiring Hélio onto greater distances himself, the largest threat to a potential Olympic crown in 1952 being from his own countryman, a 10.4sec 100m sprinter turned triple jumper,[184] who placed second to him at the 1951 Pan American Games.

The World Record holder continued his own relentless improvement and on 30 September 1951 he extended the record by 1cm to 16.01m at a Brazilian national meeting in Rio, making the mark his own. His rival Hélio had reached 15.90m on 2 September 1951 and had a foul measured at 16.03m in the same competition. On 18 November 1951 in Rio, he reached his own landmark when recording a jump of 52ft 5$\frac{1}{2}$in (15.99m),[185] the third furthest of all time and over 0.50m beyond the third ranked athlete that year. Unfortunately, he was seriously injured in landing that jump – some say he broke his leg – and he was never the same athlete on his return, missing the 1952 Olympics and not going over 15m in the triple jump ever again.

Thereafter, Adhemar was forced to look overseas for strong competition and he became known as an athlete for the major occasions, particularly in the Olympic Games. He went to Helsinki 1952 as the co-favourite with Leonid Shcherbakov of the Soviet Union, the second ranked triple jumper behind Adhemar in 1949 and 1950, and the 1950 European Champion (we will cover him in more detail in the next chapter). Shcherbakov would go on to become a formidable

---

[183] Kaare Strøm, Norwegian long and triple jumper, national champion in the latter in 1938 and 1939, also the National Record holder from 1939 to 1962 [1915-82].
[184] Quercetani, *op. cit.*, p.264.
[185] Quercetani, *op. cit.*, p.264.

rival in the next few seasons and cause the Brazilian to continue to improve his technique even after the events of 23 July 1952 in Helsinki, when he made his most famous contribution to the history of the sport.

[186]On one of the most remarkable days in Olympic track and field history, Adhemar went on to break the World Record twice, landing jumps in excess of his previous best mark  four times, giving him an average distance of 15.995m from six legal attempts and his first Olympic Gold medal, only five years after discovering the sport. Continuing the two-round format introduced in 1936, with 35 athletes from 23 nations competing, the Brazilian blew an elite field away with an opening final jump of 52ft $3\frac{9}{10}$in (15.95m), nearly 1m ahead of his competitors, including the defending Olympic Champion in Arne Åhman and three others to have placed in the top six in 1948. It was not unexpected that Adhemar would reach such heights in this final as the World Record holder, but despite his successes in the intervening years since London, what followed next was still truly remarkable.

His second jump measured 52ft $10\frac{1}{2}$in (16.12m),[187] giving him his third World Record at the age of 24 and in all probability secured him the Gold medal, when only two men had been over 16m in history and he was one of them. He had jumped within himself in the qualifying round at 50ft $3\frac{3}{20}$in (15.32m) then showed in the final that he could raise his game on the biggest stage, with the superior control

---

[186] Adhemar da Silva competing in the Helsinki Olympics in 1952 © unknown

[187] Recorded as such when the record was ratified, but more correctly 52ft $10\frac{3}{5}$in.

of his body – his "formidable sense of equilibrium"[188] according to his coach – evident in the perfect combination of balance, flexibility and thrust on display that day in the Olympic Stadium. It was said the wind was well under the allowed limit[189] (no records exist of the exact windspeed) and it was the performance of a master of his art, rather than a world class athlete just having a 'career day'.

Accounts of that day in Helsinki always remark that Adhemar thrilled the knowledgeable Finnish crowd and how the 70,000 people in attendance would be thrilled by what was still to come, having already witnessed a World Record. Shcherbakov improved to 52ft $5\frac{1}{10}$in (15.98m) on his fourth attempt, a new European Record, spurring the Brazilian to ever greater feats. On his fourth jump he made 52ft $9\frac{1}{2}$in (16.09m), then set the second World Record of the day on his fifth, reaching 53ft $2\frac{1}{2}$in (16.22m),[190] before ending the final with a distance of 52ft $7\frac{9}{10}$in (16.05m), the fourth jump in the series in excess of 16m for this 'bigtime' jumper, even more impressive when we consider the distance had only previously been achieved three times in history!

[191]He received a standing ovation on the podium during his medal ceremony, the crowd chanting "da Silva, da Silva" and, supposedly at the urging of an official, he took off with the Brazilian flag and completed what is commonly accepted as the first 'victory lap'

---

[188] de Carvalho, *op. cit.*
[189] Quercetani, *op. cit.*, p.265.
[190] Recorded as such when the record was ratified, but more correctly 53ft $2\frac{3}{5}$in.
[191] Adhemar da Silva on the medal podium waving to the crowd in Helsinki 1952, Leonid Shcherbakov to the left © unknown

of the stadium track, habitually completed by Gold medallists to this day. The Finnish people completely took this outgoing and warm-hearted Brazilian to their own hearts, impressed by his fluency in their language that he had picked up in 1949 when following Finnish officials around at a competition in Brazil and thereafter he was known as a 'Hero of Helsinki', an honorific title that was later formalised by the government of Finland in 1993 on a return visit to the country for a track meeting.

[192]Having broken the World Record twice in less than two hours and become the 'story' of the Games alongside the other 'Hero of Helsinki', three-time Gold medallist Emil Zátopek[193] who would go on to be a good friend for almost 50 years, Adhemar returned home having comfortably claimed Gold in reaching the pinnacle of his sport.

His career had been on an ever-rising trajectory to that point and whilst it is easy to attribute his achievements as those of "a solitary genius"[194] – natural talent fully exploited by the training methods of his coach – his rise came despite fundamental impediments. His record-breaking and Olympic successes had been trumpeted by the Brazilian press, the story of an individual's dedication to his sport projecting the name of his country onto the world scene, a dedication to his nation that he readily espoused himself in interviews, once stating, "and, thinking of Brazil, only of Brazil, I went to the sandpit where I achieved the

---

[192] A colourised image of Adhemar da Silva jumping in the 1952 Olympics, reproduced in a 1972 Panini sticker album © Public Domain

[193] Emil Zátopek, Czech long-distance runner who won the 5,000m, 10,000m and marathon in Helsinki; considered one of the greatest runners of the 20th century and the only athlete to win those three events in the same Games [1922-2000].

[194] Quercetani, *op. cit.*, p.264.

greatest result of my entire career."[195]   Adhemar was very patriotic, spreading joy through his sport and his charisma, so beloved by fans, is clear in every photograph of him, but his valorisation as a proud Brazilian projecting a positive image of his country is most noticeable because it was achieved despite crippling employment and financial issues.

Adhemar graduated as a sculptor in São Paulo in 1948, having first studied the trade at Technical School, but an early job mass-producing ornamental statues for cemeteries and gardens paid very little. He tried office work and sales in attempts to reconcile his status as an amateur athlete with the obvious burden on his time and expense of training and travel, the latter mostly international as his star rose. He then obtained a job in the São Paulo City Hall, but despite being the Olympic Champion and feted as a national hero after his exploits in Helsinki, he was fined for attending the 1953 South American Championships in Santiago, Chile and later lost his job in a municipal crackdown, despite members of the public publicly protesting the move.

[196]It was this disconnect between the "national martyr"[197] who belonged to Brazil, expressing nationalistic sentiments in all his victory speeches and the fact that he struggled to make ends meet throughout his athletics career that makes his commitment to his amateur status even more profound.   He loved his country, his countrymen loved him, but his country did very little for him in terms

[195] *Olimpismo: The Olympic Movement in the Making of Latin America and the Caribbean*, p.100, Antonio Sotomayor & Cesar R. Torres.
[196] Photograph of Adhemar da Silva competing in the colours of second club, Vasco de Gama © unknown
[197] Sotomayor & Torres, *op. cit.*, p.99.

of supporting his sporting preparation and even once retired he never enjoyed the riches that came to the other Brazilian icon of this period, Pelé, the iconic footballer. As an athlete he had to transfer to the more affluent *Club de Regatas Vasco de Gama* of Rio in 1955 to improve his employment opportunities, with Gerner taking a job coaching the club rowing team, his own income also very modest and heavily dependent on bonuses, despite their successes. Adhemar eventually settled on employment as an instructor at a recreation centre in 1956 after two years of training, supplementing his income by writing stories for a Rio tabloid newspaper, *Última Hora*, but he never lived more than modestly.

In 1953 Adhemar toured Europe and then Japan, his coach accompanying him to the latter as a reward for the Olympic victory and there he was to meet former World Record holder Naoto Tajima. On 13 August he was victorious in the Summer International University Sports Week in Dortmund, West Germany, still a sports student himself, with a jump of 52ft $2\frac{3}{4}$in (15.92m), nearly 1m ahead of the next best, but news arriving from Moscow only 6 days later showed that the maestro who had celebrated a lot after Helsinki and practiced very little,[198] had to re-commit to his craft to stay at the top.

Leonid Shcherbakov set a new world best on 19 July 1953 in Moscow of 53ft $2\frac{3}{4}$in (16.23m),[199] increasing the previous World Record which had stood for 11 months and 26 days by only 1cm. He had worked tirelessly to improve after Helsinki, strengthening his leg muscles with the aid of weights in training jumps and honing his own technique. Similar to Adhemar, he was of moderate speed on the approach, but Russian technicians had focussed on the 'step' more than any other country, making it Shcherbakov's strong point and taking full

---

[198] Kluge, *op. cit.*

[199] 16.23m is just shy of 53ft 3in, being more accurately 53ft $2\frac{98}{100}$in.

advantage of "his hyper-strong ankles for a low and long step."[200] He had experienced an incremental increase in his jumping distances since 1948 as he overcame his lack of elite speed and his new World Record forced the Brazilian and his coach to renew their focus on the 'step', long considered his weakest phase, despite his lanky frame and elasticity.

Adhemar equalled his former World Record in São Paulo on 21 April 1954, but could not improve the mark that season. The gauntlet had been laid down by the Russian and the Brazilian was quick to take it up, despite his previous successes, but he had to wait for the following year for the perfect conditions in which to respond to Shcherbakov, at high altitude in Mexico City. Since the 1936 Congress, the IAAF (now World Athletics) required that *assisting* windspeed must be 2.0m/s or less for a performance to be accepted for official recognition, but the effects of altitude have never been formally mitigated against, beyond being denoted that the ratified record was achieved at altitude. A whole book can be written about the effects on altitude in sports, particular explosive events, with performances achieved at 1000m or greater classed as *altitude-assisted*, but it is commonly accepted that the long and triple jump along with the sprinting events see the most significant benefit in performance from altitude, with the forward propulsion of the body through the air via technique and momentum key to achieving distance.

It had long been known that altitude gave benefits to explosive athletes, the reduced wind resistance, or drag, permitting them to perform with greater efficiency, although athletes competing over distance or when swimming would find that having less oxygen to breathe would conversely affect their performances.   The 1968

Olympics in Mexico City were the pinnacle for elite international athletes gaining a benefit on performance at high altitude, with numerous records being broken (we will return to this in a later chapter), but over a decade before, Adhemar went to the 1955 Pan American Games in that city full of expectation that he could regain the World Record in favourable conditions. Despite the decline in oxygen delivery in Mexico City at a height of 7,350ft (2,240m), on 16 March 1955, he landed a mighty leap of 54ft $3\frac{3}{4}$in (16.56m),[201] beating Shcherbakov's mark by 33cm in the rarefied air of the *Estadio Olímpico Universitario* and with Venezuela's 1952 Olympic Bronze medallist, Asnoldo Devonish,[202] second with his own fine leap of 52ft 11in (16.13m). Adhemar had now broken the World Record five times, the last coming on the occasion of his 100th competition and he had truly re-written the history of his event.

The 1956 Olympics were in Melbourne, Australia and the Brazilian was the overwhelming pre-competition favourite. In the intervening period since Helsinki, he had gained considerable prestige in Brazil and was commonly held to be the nation's greatest sportsman of the time, notwithstanding the popularity of the football (soccer) players, with the Belo Horizonte track and field stadium named in his honour.[203] He had come to embody the cultural identity of his country, his qualities being endlessly highlighted in Brazilian newspapers and whilst he may have only witnessed segregation as a *black* man when competing and travelling in the United States, his being a person of colour in a country that essentially characterised itself as 'mixed-race'

---

[201] 16.56m is just shy of 54ft 4in, being more accurately 54ft $3\frac{97}{100}$in.

[202] Asnoldo V. Devonish Romero, third in the triple jump in Helsinki and Venezuela's first Olympic medallist, being awarded the Olympic Order in 1990; also adopted Gerner's training methods having started out in football [1932-97].

[203] Sotomayor & Torres, *op. cit.*, p.106.

85

was only ever a positive, with none of the terms of colour evident in press coverage of him used pejoratively, still then in much evidence overseas, particularly in Europe and the United States. It is debatable that the country was as comfortable in terms of racial equality as it would seek to portray via its hero in Adhemar, but he was the very model of 'Brazilian-ness' to the rest of the world, most obviously as the flag-bearer for his country in the 1956 Olympics opening ceremony.

Melbourne offered him the chance to achieve what no Brazilian had yet done, in successfully defending an Olympic title. As he approached the age of 30 and with little financial compensation for his sporting successes – he had declined the gift of a house from the Brazilian people in 1953 so he would not risk his amateur status and forfeit the chance to go to the 1956 Olympics – he had spent the two years preceding the 1956 Games in training for a physical instructor's degree to enhance his employment prospects, whilst still managing to be an elite athlete jumping distances many had felt humanly impossible up to that point! He said himself in 1959 that despite being in top physical shape before Melbourne because of his degree, he had amazingly not completed any technical training for the triple jump itself, saying "I hadn't done it even once for weeks,"[204] so any success he might enjoy at the forthcoming Games was going to come in spite of his own lack of preparation and the absence of any tangible support from the government of the country he so embodied.

In the days leading up to the Olympic triple jump final on 27 November 1956 (qualifying was held in the morning), Adhemar's preparation had been further impeded, spending three days laid up with a tooth infection, eating little solid food and groggy from antibiotics.

---

[204] de Carvalho, *op. cit.*

On the day of the final, he roused himself with a steak and egg breakfast, loosened his body and mind and qualified well within himself. He ate more steak for lunch and woke from a nap seemingly feeling great, ahead of the final that afternoon. His wife Elza, to whom he was devoted, was known for leaving him notes in his socks and shoes that he would find as he prepared for competition and that day was no different, a "perfectly timed pep letter"[205] sending him excitedly on his way to attempt to make further history at the Melbourne Cricket Ground stadium.

Morning qualifying had been led by Teruji Kogake[206] of Japan, holder of the low-altitude world best[207] of 16.48m set the preceding month in the Japanese National Championships, although an ankle injury sustained when setting that mark would greatly impede him in Melbourne. He was also a graduate of Waseda University like Mikio Oda and Naoto Tajima, yet would finish eighth in his only Olympics and represented the last hurrah of the Japanese triple jumpers that followed in the wake of the great Oda, the conclusion of a truly golden era for their proud nation. He ended the year ranked number one in the world, the last Japanese to do so and was to retire after the 1957 season through injury, remaining heavily involved in athletics throughout his life. In correspondence with the authors, Willie Banks, who broke the World Record in 1985 and later lived and worked in Japan, commented that he had been fortunate to meet all of the great Japanese jumpers, with the exception of Naoto Tajima who was unwell,

---

[205] de Carvalho, *op. cit.*

[206] Teruji Kogake, retired early due to injury and became a longtime administrator and coach, leading Japanese teams to the Olympics from 1964-92 [1932-2010].

[207] Low-altitude mark is now 17.65m (+0.1m/s) by Alexis Copello of Cuba (Azerbaijan since 2017), set on 30 May 2009 in Havana, Cuba.

yet it was Teruji Kogake who was his *sensei*, or teacher, and he had a hand in Banks' success.[208]

[209]The 1956 final went on to be full of unexpected performances. Bill Sharpe[210] of the United States was the surprise leader with a National Record after the first round of jumps in the final, consisting of the 22 athletes who had made the qualifying mark. In the second round, Vilhjálmur Einarsson[211] of Iceland came to unexpected

attention with an Olympic Record of 53ft $4\frac{2}{5}$in (16.26m), stunning the crowd in resting the record away from the defending champion and pre-tournament favourite from Brazil, giving some belief that the 22-year-old Games debutant could achieve the unthinkable and take the Gold. Some sources claim that Einarsson's jump may have been wind-assisted, but it was not ruled as such and it was up to Adhemar to respond if he was going to claim a second Gold and emulate early triple jump pioneer Myer Prinstein[212] of the United States, Gold medallist in both 1900 and 1904.

Despite having only qualified in 11th place and with as poor an injury-free preparation as you could imagine, the man who supposedly never exceeded 50ft 4in in training[213] once more proved himself to be a competition animal, saving his best for when pressure

[208] Email correspondence between Willie Banks and Lawrence Harvey, 20 June 2023.
[209] Adhemar da Silva jumping in the Melbourne 1956 triple jump final © unknown
[210] William 'Bill' J. Sharpe, later the Gold medallist in the triple jump in the 1963 Pan American Games in São Paulo and a three-time Olympian, 1956-64 [1932-95].
[211] Vilhjálmur Einarsson, Iceland's first ever Olympic medallist in 1956 [1934-2019].
[212] Myer (or Meyer) Prinstein, Polish American horizontal jumper, with Olympic Gold in the triple jump in 1900 & 1904, along with the long jump title in 1904 and Silver in 1900 [1878-1925].
[213] de Carvalho, *op. cit.*

was highest and a big performance was required. On his second jump he had gone over 16m himself, faded slightly on his third and then reclaimed the Olympic Record on his fourth, landing a prodigious leap of 53ft $7\frac{7}{10}$in (16.35m); for good measure, on his fifth and sixth attempts he demonstrated that he had found his groove, with jumps of 16.26m and 16.21m respectively. Einarsson could not respond and so finished second, great rival Shcherbakov was disappointing in only finishing a distant sixth and further surprises came with Vitold Kreyer[214] of the Soviet Union in Bronze and first-round leader Sharpe in an excellent fourth.

Adhemar was now a two-time Olympic Champion and despite the humble Brazilian dedicating his latest victory to all sportsman of his country and acknowledging the debt owed to his coaches, including his 'little uncle' Gerner,[215] his achievement was stunning, accomplished despite all his adversities, seemingly overcome by the inherent devotion to country he always he attributed his successes to. He was now 28 and coming to the back end of a storied career, but with the support of his wife Elza he committed to continuing in competitive sport, until at least the 1960 Olympics in Rome, saying "with a different wife I would have dropped out years ago... for a family with no money, international amateur athletics is too much of a sacrifice."[216]

In the following years, he defended his title at the 6th World Festival of Youth and Students, or World Student Games, in Moscow in 1957, the South American Championships in Santiago, Chile in 1958 and completed a hat-trick of Pan American Games titles in Chicago in

---

[214] Vitold A. Kreyer, Olympic Bronze medallist in the triple jump in 1956 and 1960, three-time Olympian (1956-64), later coach of three-time Olympic triple jump champion Viktor Saneyev and head of the Soviet athletics team (1967-80) and the Russian team in the 2000 Olympics [1932-2020].
[215] Sotomayor & Torres, *op. cit.*, p.109.
[216] de Carvalho, *op. cit.*

1959, the latter his final title at an international competition.[217] Rome 1960 was to prove his fourth and final Olympic appearance and despite being close to 33 years old, the long unbeaten run in major international competition was going to come to an end, having seen his World Record broken three times since Melbourne, by different Soviet jumpers in 1958 and 1959 (more on them in the following chapter) and then Józef Szmidt of Poland who would exceed 17m only one month before the Games.

Adhemar was still capable of jumping 16m+, but fell ill in Rome ahead of his competition and some have speculated that this contributed to a disappointing 14th place in the final, his last international outing. It was not the farewell he had hoped for when coming to Rome as his country's flag-bearer for the second time, but the event had moved on from his pinnacle in 1956 and stronger competition meant that an athlete who would never start to worry until the finals could no longer get by on just his physical traits and natural balance. He had been a technical jumper *sine pari*[218] throughout the 1950's and younger jumpers were taking the discipline to new heights, yet still, he enraptured the Italian crowd, who chanted "Orfeo, Orfeo" in homage to his popular film role, despite his sub-par performance on the day.

Following retirement, a man who embodied the argument that sport is a social tool was determined not to rest on his laurels. At 31 he had taken pre-law classes at night and would continue to seek learning opportunities throughout his life, graduating with a law degree from the Federal University of Rio de Janeiro in 1968 and a public relations degree from a private university in 1990. He retained a

---

[217] He did also claim Gold at the 1960 Ibero-American Games, the first iteration of the competition which was not ratified by the IAAF until 1983.
[218] Latin phrase for 'without equal'.

concern for the lives of his countrymen, particularly those in the lowest social classes like himself and his popularity, or celebrity, allowed him to follow a specific post-athletics trajectory. He was the cultural attaché at the Brazilian Embassy in Nigeria from 1964-67, worked as a newspaper columnist, sports commentator, lawyer, mentor to various sporting administrators and launched programs connected to sports to help children from the deprived favelas seen in *Orfeu Negro* to escape from a life of drugs and crime. He also worked as a lobbyist for a foundation seeking government and private support for his country's Olympic athletes, the type of assistance that he never enjoyed himself.

Life always remained a struggle in financial terms and he never left the family house that he had grown up in. The man with a heart even bigger than his enormous smile touched all of those he came into contact with and yet his legacy is *rich*, being posthumously inducted into the IAAF (now World Athletics) Hall of Fame in 2012, as one of the inaugural twelve athletes, some honour! He was an icon for the Brazilian people, an equal in his lifetime to the great Pelé himself, and brought joy to fans across the world, whether with his sporting exploits, charismatic interviews or even through his music, having sung and played guitar as an athlete "over radio stations and at nightclubs, from Finland to Fresno."[219]

However, whilst he conquered his sport, winning every major competition he entered from 1951-59 and still the only South American athlete to retain an Olympic track and field title, the political powers of his country never fully embraced him beyond trumpeting his success as one of the nation over the individual, a rhetoric he was happy to follow as a patriot. The 2016 Olympics were held in Rio, but the greatest athlete in Brazilian track and field history, who was carried on

---

[219] de Carvalho, *op. cit.*

a 6-mile funeral procession after his death on 12 January 2001, was essentially forgotten by the organisers of the Games, with little acknowledgement of his famous achievements drawing sharp criticism from fans, critics and family members.[220]

Adhemar da Silva always went by the maxim that "glory is temporary"[221] and his true legacy is the achievements in the record books that mark him out as a great Olympian, a five-time World Record holder who added 56cm to the record in total and an athlete remembered fondly across the world, from Helsinki to Melbourne. His celebrity helped to popularise the discipline and his true legacy is to have been the first triple jumper to define an era through his prowess. He considered himself to have been born lucky, but he really was an athletic genius, and in the way of his sole film credit refreshing an ancient tale, he was able to make fresh the ancient sport derived 'hop, step and jump' into the 'triple jump' that modern sporting audiences have come to love, introducing a new level of technical proficiency that subsequent athletes and coaches took even further in the following years.

03.12.1950 WR 16.00m (52ft 5$\frac{3}{4}$in) Adhemar da Silva (BRA) São Paulo, Brazil (+1.6m/s)

30.09.1951 WR 16.01m (52ft 6$\frac{1}{4}$in) Adhemar da Silva (BRA) Rio de Janeiro, Brazil (+1.2m/s)

23.07.1952 WR 16.12m (52ft 10$\frac{1}{2}$in) Adhemar da Silva (BRA) Helsinki, Finland (NWI)

23.07.1952 WR 16.22m (53ft 2$\frac{1}{2}$in) Adhemar da Silva (BRA) Helsinki, Finland (NWI)

19.07.1953 WR 16.23m (53ft 2$\frac{3}{4}$in) Leonid Shcherbakov (URS) Moscow, Soviet Union (+1.5m/s)

16.03.1955 WR(A) 16.56m (54ft 3$\frac{1}{4}$in) Adhemar da Silva (BRA) Mexico City, Mexico (+0.2m/s)

---

[220] https://www.insidethegames.biz/articles/1040623/adhemar-ferreira-da-silva-the-brazilian-sporting-legend-forgotten-by-rio-2016
[221] de Carvalho, *op. cit.*

Part 2 – Hop

The triple jumper should reach the take-off board at optimal speed, regardless of the length of their approach and it is fundamental that the athlete runs *through* the board. A novice triple jumper may hesitate as the board approaches or seek to take-off at the highest angle possible to gain height, but each is a common mistake amongst those new to the sport. Vertical height gained does not equate to horizontal distance covered in the triple jump and the athlete motions to run past the foot they plant on the board, emphasising horizontal movement; Yulimar Rojas has put considerable work into improving her speed in the final strides before the board and that has helped her to conserve horizontal momentum through the step in recent seasons, particular in her two (to date) World Record leaps.

The take-off and landing in the triple jump are on the same foot and it is common that an athlete leads with their strongest leg, so that only one phase (the step) is completed on the 'weaker' leg, although Christian Taylor was forced to change take-off leg due to injury and has since won an Olympic Gold medal when leading with each leg, but this is extremely rare! The **Hop** follows the take-off and has commonly been the longest of the three phases throughout the history of the sport. Many athletes have favoured the hop (notable the Japanese jumpers of the 1930's) and it is the phase that lends itself most readily to overall triple jump distance, but the world-class jumpers in the modern era have shown that conserving momentum through the hop can allow for even greater distances in the final jump phase, leading to a number of World Records as the later narrative in this book will show.

As the athlete strikes the board on take-off – in *running through* it – he or she will apply some downward force (or vertical push) with a straight leg as they jump and must ensure their foot does not touch the plasticine strip on the board, or the attempt will be ruled a foul by the judges. The legs will be cycled through the air as the athlete's momentum carries them to the hop, in which they will use the same leg from take-off to plant the foot on the ground. The foot will land flat and the athlete will look to roll forwards from heel to toe to conserve velocity into the step, a technique popularised by Australians such as Jack Metcalfe in the 1930's, more easily utilised on the turf they competed on at home rather than the cinders then more common in the rest of the world.[222] The arms will be free as the athlete moves through the air from the board to the hop, either utilising the single or double-arm method and broadly speaking, competent coaching will ensure that these arms move as if the athlete is still running.

---

[222] *The Telegraph* (AUS), 7 August 1936

THE EASTERN BLOC ARRIVES

"We must set every world record!"[223]

Despite not competing in an Olympic Games until Helsinki 1952, the Union of Soviet Socialist Republics, USSR or more succinctly the Soviet Union, finished second in the final medal

rankings in its first appearance, with 22 Gold and 71 total medals.[224] Before the Second World War, the Soviet Union did not take part in international sporting events on ideological grounds, competitive sports being seen as a tool of capitalism, but post-war, with Cold War[225] tensions ever rising around the globe, Soviet leaders viewed the Olympics in particular as an ideal arena to express their dominance over the West without entering outright conflict. One of the medallists in Helsinki was triple jumper Leonid Shcherbakov, the great rival of Adhemar da Silva throughout the 1950's, voted one of the top ten triple jumpers of all time by the IAAF in 1987 and the earliest prominent exponent of the 'Russian Style' on the world stage, "the *chef de file* of a

---

[223] Tagline from Soviet sports propaganda poster shown above, believed to have been designed by Victor Govorkov in 1935. Variously translated as "We should hold all the world's records!" and "All world records must be ours!".

[224] The Russian Empire competed previously in the 1900 Games, then in 1908 & 1912.

[225] Term commonly used for the period 1947-1991 for the global geo-political tension between the United States and Soviet Union and their allies, respectively the Western and Eastern Blocs. No large-scale conflict broke out between these two superpowers in this period, despite periods of extreme tension and where they supported regional proxy conflicts, they each used sport as a means of broadening their influence on the global stage.

new dynasty,"[226] the Eastern Bloc jumpers who would raise the event to new heights of technical proficiency and jump ever further distances.

It is commonly held that the Soviet Union did not compete in London 1948 over fears that they could not sufficiently challenge the Western athletes for medals of any colour. Russian athletics standards at that time have been described as "pathetically low for many years",[227] but with tensions in a post-war world triggering pseudo-conflict in other areas where global influence could still be projected, the Soviet leaders placed a high focus on the supremacy of elite sport, an arena in which their people could glorify in the achievements of their athletes as a whole and with an importance engendered in everyday life that was unparalleled.

The Soviets had unleashed a vast program of co-operative *physical culture* in the years before the Second World War, figuratively through the symbolism of statues of sporting heroes in many parks, popular visual media across all walks of life – see the sports propaganda poster on the preceding page – and formally endorsed in industry and professions through the pre-eminence of trade unions, an ideal of physical fitness for all Soviet people promulgated by the state, with the whole structure overseen by Moscow via various committees down to a local level. The Soviet Union provided sporting and physical cultural opportunities to the vast majority of its citizens, with the most memorable embodiment of these facilities being the famous sports clubs of the day, named Dynamo, Torpedo and Spartak, the names still in use to this day by the most prolific football clubs of the post-Soviet Union nations, including Spartak Moscow (of Russia) and Dynamo Kyiv (of Ukraine).

---

[226] Quercetani, *op. cit.*, p. 265; *chef de file* means figurehead or exponent.
[227] Quercetani, *op. cit.*, p. 265

In 1947-48, the Soviet Union did not have a triple jumper ranked in the world top 10, yet by 1949, the systemic programme of sports science funded by the government after London 1948 would lead to Leonid Shcherbakov being world number two, commencing a rivalry with Brazilian great Adhemar da Silva that would see them dominate the sport in the 1950's, with Shcherbakov breaking the World Record in 1953 and ranked in the top 10 through to 1958, by which time the Soviet Union had succeeded in proliferating the event to such an extent, that their style of jumping dominated by the hop phase became known as the 'Russian Style'.

[228]**Leonid Mikhailovich Shcherbakov** was born on 7 April 1927 in Olebino, Yaroslavi Oblast, Russian Soviet Federative Socialist Republic, now modern-day Russia and was by all accounts a man of *quite ordinary* physical attributes. Similar in height to his later great rival Adhemar da Silva, the physical comparisons would end there and he was not blessed with the long legs the Brazilian used to great effect, nor the perfect balance that aided his career-long pursuit of major titles and the World Record. Instead, the Russian was to become one of the early manifestations on the global stage of this universal system of physical education and sports, that continued to great effect until the end of the Soviet Union in 1991. It is not known how he came to the attention of the sporting authorities, nor for certain which Voluntary Sports Society (VSS) – the main structural parts of the Soviet sports and physical education system, predominated by trade unions – he came through, but he would have been identified as an athlete with potential at an early age,

---

[228] An undated photograph of Leonid Shcherbakov competing in the triple jump © unknown

in spite of his modest physical gifts, particularly having only "mediocre speed."[229]

For a man who was later voted one of the top ten triple jumpers of all time in 1987 by the IAAF, he often appears in athletics histories as little more than a footnote to the Adhemar da Silva story and the Soviet Union was a closed society to the rest of the world for much of his life, contributing to the mystery of a man who still managed to make such a vivid and memorable mark in the history of the event, despite not becoming Olympic Champion like many of the other most notable triple jumpers.

He was only 22 years old when he first came to international notice, at the 2nd World Festival of Youth and Students in Budapest, Hungary in mid-August 1949. Jumping for the first time in international competition, although mainly against Eastern European athletes, he claimed triple jump Gold with a leap of 47ft $9\frac{1}{4}$in (14.56m), in a bi-annual competition he would dominate until bested by his great Brazilian rival in 1957, when attempting to win the title for the fifth time in succession. The following month in September 1949 he was to win his first Soviet Athletics Championship at the Central Dynamo Stadium[230] in Moscow, the central venue of the All-Soviet Dynamo Sports Club of which he was a member. He would go on to claim the Soviet title eight times in a row, but it was only when he jumped 50ft $7\frac{1}{2}$in (15.43m) in October 1949 in a competition in Tbilisi, now modern-day Georgia, that this top Soviet athlete showed he could threaten the best of the international athletes, ending that year as the second ranked triple jumper in the world.

---

[229] Quercetani, *op. cit.*, p. 265
[230] Now replaced by the VTB Arena – Dynamo Central Stadium, having been reopened in 2019.

The new world number one in 1949 was Adhemar da Silva and whilst the Brazilian had exploded on the scene as a late comer to the sport being blessed with extremely beneficial physical gifts harnessed by a perfect coach-athlete synergy, the Soviet athlete was the product of a nationalised approach to sports success, an intensive training regime allied with what could be described as a *talent* for hard work, possessed with a character that led him to train like every session was his last and extract every ounce of improvement from his body that he possible could, so that by Helsinki 1952 he was co-favourite for Gold.

The triple jump had been highlighted by Soviet sporting authorities as one of the weakest events of the major European countries and the United States in particular, being dominated by 'lesser' nations in the 1930's and 1940's, athletes from Japan, Australia and Scandinavia to the fore as we have seen in previous chapters of this book. The Soviet technicians sought to gain an advantage by emphasising the training of power, which could be specifically developed more easily than speed or spring, harking back to Nick Winter and later Chūhei Nambu, the former renowned as a power jumper and the latter setting his own World Record with a very long hop, almost to the detriment of his own step and jump phases.

The Olympic rules of the mid 20th century stipulated that only amateur athletes could compete in the Games. Whereas Adhemar da Silva struggled for any kind of practical support from the Brazilian government and made great personal sacrifices to retain his amateur status, Soviet athletes were state-funded and essentially trained as full-time athletes, disbursed through various VSS to protect their amateur status, but enabled by their government to "live well, eat well and... not [be] too much exposed to political pressures,"[231] creating a disbalance

---

[231] 'SPORTS IN THE U.S.S.R.', Jerry Cooke, *Sports Illustrated*, 2 December 1957

in international competition that would only be rectified when the regulations were abandoned in the 1990's. Purportedly amateur, whilst claiming a job of sorts outside of sports, Shcherbakov would have spent most of his time training in world class facilities, in a training system that from the 1952 Olympics showed the rest of the globe how far ahead the Soviets were of their competition, with a much broader view of how training could affect athletic performance than Western coaches, that in time would revolutionise sports training throughout the world.

Soviet sports scientists had looked at the triple jump in particular as an event with an underdeveloped technique – even the great Japanese jumpers covered earlier in this book varied their jumping style with no one true 'method' for the triple jump – and they conducted experiments to calculate the best exercises to prepare an athlete's body for the specific demands of the discipline. The result was a high volume of jumping exercises combined with intensive weight training, a precursor to the depth jumps and Shock Method publicised by Professor Yuri Verkhoshansky in the 1960's, that later gained widespread attention when formally established in the United States as *plyometrics* (more on both in later chapters). These exercises were designed to develop explosive strength and it was Shcherbakov's improving power that took him to a European title at the Heysel Stadium in Brussels, Belgium on 23 August 1950, a leap of 50ft $5\frac{9}{10}$in (15.39m) setting a new Championship Record, having broken the European Record in Moscow on 20 July 1950, with a jump of 51ft $6\frac{1}{10}$in (15.70m).[232]

---

[232] On 16 July 1950, Shcherbakov had jumped 51ft $1\frac{3}{4}$in (15.59m) in Moscow but it was not ratified as a European Record. A later record distance in 1953 was also not ratified, but some record him as having set the European Record six times.

The European Record had been held for eleven years by Norwegian Kaare Strøm and Shcherbakov would extend it four times in the following eight years, until the record was claimed by another Soviet jumper, Oleg Ryakhovskiy. His new record was good enough for him to remain the number two ranked jumper in the world in 1950 and despite registering a best of only 15.23m in 1951, he went to Helsinki 1952 with strong expectations of claiming a medal, his only real challenge being World Record holder Adhemar da Silva who was regularly jumping around 16m, a distance that Shcherbakov could not yet get close to...

In Helsinki on 23 July 1952 the Brazilian would go on to have a day for the ages in the final, setting the World Record twice and dominating a high-level field. Shcherbakov would have his own notable success in that elite company, with a fourth-round jump of 52ft 5$\frac{1}{10}$in (15.98m), nearly 30cm further than he had ever jumped before and good enough to secure him Silver, his contribution to the collective achievement of the Soviet Union finishing those Olympics in second place overall. His second-place jump was a new European Record and at 25 years old he was approaching his peak as an athlete, his reputation as a top triple jumper of the day to be cemented the following July.

In the 1930's, the Soviets had created a number of bodies to oversee their vast co-operative program of sports for all citizens, the *physical culture* of the masses with casual sports for everybody beyond just elite athletes. This was to change in the Cold War as mass participation sport and general social provision were overlooked in order to devote resources to elite sport and whilst the names of some of the organisations that oversaw sport in the Soviet Union have evolved over time, by the time Shcherbakov came into contact with his influential coach Nikolay Ozolin,[233] who only retired from competition himself in 1950 and who also represented Dynamo Moscow, the latter was in charge of the athletics department of the State Centre for Physical and Physical Culture (from 1937), before later becoming the Director of the All-Russian Research Institute of Physical Culture (1952-62). He had been a successful pole vaulter in the 1930's and 1940's, Silver medallist in the 1946 European Championships and was treading a common path for Soviet athletes by continuing in the sport as coaches and trainers. He specialised in the theory and methodology of sports, and under his tutelage Shcherbakov was able to maximise his power and steadily improve on his mediocre ground speed.

After enjoying such success in Helsinki, Shcherbakov went back behind the strong 'Iron Curtain' of the time, the term used to describe the physical boundary of the Cold War in Europe and began to work even harder. He strengthened his leg muscles using weights around his waist in training jumps and was able to exploit "hyper-strong ankles for a low and long step,"[234] in much the same way as Australian Nick Winter, whose ankles were said to be twice normal size. In being able to reach maximum height in his hop, the power in his lower body allowed him to regain additional height in the jump phase and land greater distances, the high-flying characteristics of what was becoming known to the rest of the world as the 'Russian Style'.

One of the most powerful strength-speed exercises utilised by Shcherbakov and other Soviet triple jumpers in the 1950's was the depth jump. Being faced with no suitable indoor facilities to specifically train the triple jump in the winter, athletes came up with

---

[233] Nikolay G. Ozolin won pole vault Silver in the 1946 European Championships aged nearly forty and would go on to have a long career as an athletics coach, honoured many times in the Soviet Union and author of over 200 works on the theory and practice of sports [1906-2000].
[234] Quercetani, *op. cit.*, p. 265

depth jumps in order to train their strength-speed, or explosive strength, which remains fundamental to the triple jumper to this day. Variations of these exercises remained a crucial part of a triple jumper's warm-up throughout the season, but in rooms small by necessity, they would jump from high boxes seeking to emulate the gravitational forces of a triple jump – the forces experienced during the ground contact – and gain some relevant strength training. These exercises were designed to create the necessary contractions in the leg muscles required to overcome the impact on the ground when landing, the so-called 'shock' of the general strength training of the Shock Method of which depth jumps formed a major part.

On 19 July 1953 in Moscow, Shcherbakov was to enjoy his finest moment as a triple jumper, breaking Adhemar da Silva's World Record by 1cm. No detailed description exists of the jump itself, at least in the West, and the record would only stand for just over 18 months before the Brazilian would wrest it back at altitude in Mexico City, but the mark of 53ft $2\frac{3}{4}$in (16.23m)[235] meant his place in the record books was assured. Shcherbakov continued to improve as an athlete, his overall progression slower than others because of his lack of top-end speed, yet despite retaining his European Championships title in Bern, Switzerland on 26 August 1954 with another Championship Record and having set a personal best of 54ft (16.46m) in Moscow on 4 July 1954, he was disappointing on the grandest stage in Melbourne 1956, forced to be content with sixth-place as his great rival retained his Olympic title in emphatic style. He continued to hold the Soviet title through 1956 and competed until 1959, but other Soviet athletes had now overtaken him.

---

[235] Recorded as such when the record was ratified, but more correctly 53ft $2\frac{49}{50}$in.

[236]Having retired from competition, his desire for learning and improvement did not end. He became a coach and trainer himself, initially working as a teacher at the Central Institute of Physical Education,[237] obtained a PhD and went on to become a renowned coach, particularly for his work in Cuba as Pedro Pérez's coach when he broke the World Record in August 1971 (more on him later). A man who trained assiduously to make himself an elite triple jumper when not blessed with specific natural gifts like many others who reached the pinnacle of the sport, he worked just as tirelessly in passing on his experience to others and he embodied the work of countless scientists and athletes to meet the Soviet demand for supremacy in the Olympic sports. He is believed to have died in 2004, but as with much about Leonid Shcherbakov, the truth lies somewhere still behind the Iron Curtain...

In his long career, Shcherbakov would extend the European Record four times in six years and hold it for eight, until the record was claimed by another Soviet jumper, Oleg Ryakhovskiy, in setting his own World Record in July 1958. Ryakhovskiy's star would shine for only four years and include no major championship honours or Olympic Games participation, but in re-claiming the World Record for the Soviet Union from Adhemar da Silva in the first international meeting between the USA and the USSR, his major achievement was so voluminous that he is remembered to this day when many of his competitors are not.

---

[236] Leonid Shcherbakov competing in the triple jump in the 1954 European Championships in Bern, Switzerland © unknown
[237] Now the Russian State University of Physical Education, Sport, Youth and Tourism.

[238]**Oleg Anatolevitch Ryakhovskiy**  was born on 19 October 1933 in Tashkent, Uzbek Soviet Socialist Republic, now modern-day Uzbekistan in Central Asia. Ryakhovskiy rose to elite status in November 1955, breaking into the world top twenty with a jump of 50ft $6\frac{3}{10}$in (15.40m) in Tbilisi and followed that up with 52ft $3\frac{2}{5}$in (15.93m) in his home city in October 1956, a distance that pushed him to number seven in the world. 1957-58 would prove to be his *annus mirabilis*,[239] claiming the Soviet triple jump title in Moscow by dethroning eight-time champion Shcherbakov with a winning jump of 53ft $5\frac{3}{10}$in (16.29m) and ending that season as world number one.

Despite now being a triple jumper at the elite level and new Soviet Champion, the similarities with Shcherbakov went no further. Ryakhovskiy was not tall, nor did he have the explosive power of the former champion, but he had a unique style for the time based on superior speed like the stocky Japanese great, Chūhei Nambu. It is said that he was a 10.6sec 100m sprinter and he was to develop his own style for the triple jump, keeping his trajectory low to the ground and relying on the speed gained in his approach to make distance, regaining height as he made his jump, rather than in the hop and step phases as was common at the time. He still benefited from the intensive sports science behind the Soviet successes post-war, but his own

---

238 An undated photograph of Oleg Ryakhovskiy competing, possibly in the inaugural USA-USSR athletics match in 1958 © unknown
239 Latin for 'marvelous year', often used to denote years where events of great importance occur.

achievements almost came in spite of technique rather than because of it – with him raw speed was everything!

The peak of Ryakhovskiy's competitive career was to come on 28 July 1958. The Cold War tensions between the United States and the Soviet Union were still to come to a head with the Cuban Missile Crisis[240] in 1962, but despite a smaller crisis unfolding that July with the Superpowers supporting opposing belligerents in the Lebanese Civil War of 1958, the planned inaugural athletics meeting between them was still able to go ahead in Moscow. This was to be the first of nineteen meetings through to 1985 and whilst pseudo-conflict between them was frequently occurring around the world, these meetings were intended to allow representatives of both nations to meet under the umbrella of sporting diplomacy without the threat of overt conflict. But despite the exhibitions of mutual friendship between athletes and welcoming noises made by the Soviet hierarchy, the inherent patriotism of both teams meant that the result of the competition was all-important...

The United States got off to the better start on day one of what became colloquially known as the 'Cold War Track Meet Series',[241] but Ryakhovskiy's victory in the triple jump sparked a run of Soviet wins that gave them hope of overall victory, ultimately only being secured by the superior performance of the Soviet women's team of this dual meet. His victory in the Lenin Stadium[242] in front of a partisan crowd on 28 July 1958 was most notable for securing the World Record with a leap of 54ft 5in (16.59m)[243] and it was to be the peak of his career in

---

[240] A 35-day confrontation between the United States and the USSR in October-November 1962 that escalated into an international crisis and became a defining moment in world history as the closest the planet has come to nuclear war.
[241] More correctly the 'USA-USSR Track and Field Dual Meet Series'.
[242] Now the Luzhniki Stadium.
[243] Ratified as such, but more correctly 54ft $5\frac{3}{20}$in.

bettering Adhemar da Silva's three-year-old record by 3cm, but it should not be forgotten that it was achieved under extreme presume in what was billed as a 'stubborn' struggle with the Americans, the so-called 'Match of the Century' that the Soviets edged by a combined score of 172-170.

The following year Ryakhovskiy's star would begin to burn out and injury would bring a premature end to his all too fleeting time at the top. In August 1958 he had been outperformed by Poland's Józef Szmidt in the European Championships in Stockholm, placing second by some way and missing out on what would prove to be his only opportunity for an international title, never going to an Olympic Games himself. In those European Championships on 23 August 1958, he had become the first European to go over 16m but was easily surpassed by Szmidt who broke the Championship Record,[244] a portent of the superstar he was to become (see following chapter), although Ryakhovskiy finished the 1958 season with his second successive victory in the Soviet Athletics Championships.

He finished 1959 ranked fifth in the world, having landed the second-best jump of his career in Moscow in August, with a distance of 53ft $8\frac{9}{10}$in (16.38m), but his countrymen in particular were edging ahead of him, Oleg Fedoseyev breaking the World Record that May and two other Soviets in Vladimir Goryayev[245] and Vitold Kreyer finishing ahead of him in the end of season rankings. Ryakhovskiy had enjoyed great success as a student-athlete in his brief period at the top, winning Gold in the 1957 World University Games, the 1959 World

---

[244] Third was Vilhjálmur Einarsson of Iceland, one of three Europeans that day to reach the 16m.
[245] Vladimir Goryayev, or Goryaev, Olympic Silver medallist in Rome 1960, world number one in 1962 and Soviet triple jump champion in 1962-63 [1939-].

Festival of Youth and Students and the first Universiade[246] the same year, but the 1960 season was affected by a leg injury and despite returning to fifth in the world rankings in 1961 – Vitold Kreyer of the Soviet Union was number one that year – that was to prove his final year of competition at the elite level.

[247]He retired thereafter to focus on his academic career, later becoming a Professor at Moscow State Technical University having specialized in the mechanics of athletics and served on the IAAF Technical Committee for twelve years. At the time of writing, he is believed to be alive at the ripe age of 89, the first World Record holder featured here to remain with us. For a man whose technique was said to be like 'creeping' along the track when remaining so low, he burst on the top-level scene in his own inimitable fashion, before being overtaken by a cabal of technically proficient Soviets and the great Pole, Józef Szmidt, a brief appearance at the top of his sport as the Soviet Bloc athletes truly arrived *en masse*.[248]

The final Soviet triple jump World Record holder of the 1950's was **Oleg Georgiyevich Fedoseyev**,[249] a member of an armed forces sports society, or VSS and the CSKA Moscow club, but seemingly never a professional soldier. He was born on 4 June 1936 in Moscow, Russia  and would commit to the triple jump as a two-time Soviet long jump champion (1956 and 1958), having finished eighth in both the 1956 Olympics and 1958 European Championships, the former whilst aged

---

[246] An international multi-sport event for university students that continues to this day as the World University Games, with both winter and summer editions.

[247] Oleg Fedoseyev competing in the Olympic triple jump final in 1964 © Out of Copyright

[248] Verb attributed to the French language, but commonly used in England to mean 'as a whole'.

[249] Surname elsewhere spelt as Fedoseev.

only twenty. His raw speed was good enough to be a Soviet champion in the 4x100m relay in 1962 and at 6ft 1in (1.85m) he was noticeably taller than both Shcherbakov and Ryakhovskiy. He abandoned the long jump when he began to be overshadowed by the younger Igor Ter-Ovanesyan,[250] yet within a year of changing discipline full-time he was Soviet champion and even more impressively the World Record holder!

Fedoseyev was a good enough triple jumper to be ranked 7th in the world in 1955 with a distance of 51ft $5\frac{3}{4}$in (15.69m), but that was his only top ten ranking before he broke the World Record. He was not a novice when he committed to the triple jump when faced with Ter-Ovanesyan's overwhelming talent, but his progression from middling long jumper to the best triple jumper in the world during one season in 1959 is quite astonishing. The intensive Soviet elite athletics programme – then beginning to be noticed after their success in Melbourne 1956 and later described in 1961 as a "simple combination of studious development of technique and unceasing diligence"[251] would see further fruit borne in the exploits of Fedoseyev.

Regardless of attempting to measure technique or results in an objective manner, Oleg Fedoseyev had the physique of a natural athlete, the raw speed of a borderline elite sprinter and with his long jumping pedigree and the commitment to hard work expected of all Soviet athletes, he was able to coalesce those 'intangibles' into a good international career as a triple jumper, emboldened by one perfect jump on 3 May 1959 in Nalchik, Soviet Union. He was a 25ft+ long jumper

[250] Igor A. Ter-Ovanesyan, the first European to long jump 8m, twice the World Record holder, five-time Olympian with two Olympic Bronze medals in 1960 & 1964, three-time European Champion in 1958, 1962 & 1969 and European Silver in 1966 & 1971 [1938-].
[251] 'POWER VERSUS PERFECTION: THE U.S.-EUROPE TRACK MEETS', Tex Maule, *Sports Illustrated*, 17 July 1961

110

and whilst that was some way off the elite jumpers in his former discipline, his jump phase in Nalchik was measured at 5.49m, a *long* jump indeed when compared to the 5.16m of Ryakhovskiy in 1958 and demonstrating how he was able to extend the World Record that day to 54ft $9\frac{1}{4}$in (16.70m), [252] despite comparable hop and step phases to the former record holder.

And as quickly as he rose to the top of the triple jump rankings with that magnificent jump in the foothills of the Caucasus Mountains in 1959, the following season he could not make the world top ten, Goryayev and Kreyer being third and fourth respectively. Fedoseyev, who had also beaten Ryakhovskiy into second place at the Spartakiad[253] in Moscow in August 1959 when the latter made the second-best jump of his career, would not return to the world top ten until 1962 when he placed fifth, reaching third in 1964 and not returning to the rankings after that, his final competition being in 1966. It is possible that he missed the 1960 season (and the Rome Olympics where fellow Soviet Goryayev claimed Silver) due to injury, the season where Józef Szmidt of Poland broke his short-lived World Record, but as with much about Soviet athletes of this period it is difficult to be precise, with biographical information sparse.

His form had returned in time to claim Bronze in the 1962 European Championships in Belgrade, Yugoslavia, 1960 Olympic Champion and World Record holder Szmidt claiming the title ahead of Goryayev with a Championship Record of 16.55m. In October 1964 he participated in the Tokyo Olympics and with defending champion Szmidt having had knee surgery only a few months before, he had an

---

[252] Ratified as such, but more correctly 54ft $9\frac{1}{2}$in.

[253] The Spartakiad of the Peoples of the USSR was a mass multi-sport event in the Soviet Union from 1956-1991, comprising athletes from the constituent Republics of the Soviet Union.

outside chance of challenging for the title. Szmidt quickly found his form though and with a new Olympic Record of 16.85m, Fedoseyev had to settle for a still impressive Silver, having jumped the second-furthest distance of his career in round five. After the Rome Olympics his elite level career was to fade once more, even though he was only 28 years old, and whilst it is not known what he turned to post-athletics, he died on 14 June 2001, aged only 65.

Fedoseyev was the last of the Soviet athletes of the 1950's to break the triple jump World Record in such unexpected fashion, but thereafter the rest of the world knew of the threat posed by the triple jumpers from behind the Iron Curtain. Soviet triple jumpers arrived in such numbers that they began to proliferate the world rankings, in 1957 seven of the top eight being from the Soviet Union for example. The Soviet Union and Poland popularised the event in the 1950's in the same way Australia and Japan had done so previously, by taking a mass programme of *physical culture* designed to prepare a society for probable warfare, into an intensive and resource-heavy training scheme for elite athletes, with the sole purpose of using sport as a proxy for the ideological conflict raging between the United States and the Soviet Union in the Cold War. The Soviet leaders demanded that their athletes "set every record"[254] and in Shcherbakov, Ryakhovskiy and Fedoseyev they found the right candidates.

19.07.1953 WR 16.23m (53ft $2\frac{3}{4}$in) Leonid Shcherbakov (URS) Moscow, Soviet Union (+1.5m/s)

16.03.1955 WR(A) 16.56m (54ft $3\frac{1}{4}$in) Adhemar da Silva (BRA) Mexico City, Mexico (+0.2m/s)

28.07.1958 WR 16.59m (54ft 5in) Oleg Ryakhovskiy (URS) Moscow, Soviet Union (+1.0m/s)

03.05.1959 WR 16.70m (54ft $9\frac{1}{4}$in) Oleg Fedoseyev (URS) Nalchik, Soviet Union (0.0m/s)

---

[254] Common sports propaganda tagline, see opening of this chapter.

17 METRE JÓZEF

The Silesian Kangaroo

By the late 1950's, the Soviet Union was the most prolific producer of world class triple jumpers on the planet. The United States had yet to take a serious interest in the event as a nation, with only fleeting appearances in the world top ten rankings in the 1950's for Olympians Ira Davis[255] and Bill Sharpe. Soviet athletes had broken the World Record three times in the 1950's on home soil and as the decade ended, the world best stood at 54ft $9\frac{1}{4}$in (16.70m), with the idea a man could yet triple jump 55ft as far away as ever. Between Naoto Tajima in 1936 and Oleg Fedoseyev in 1959, the World Record had only advanced 0.7m, but a Polish athlete who had worked assiduously on his speed and power, would utilise a flat technique more akin to Adhemar da Silva than the then common Soviet steep trajectory in breaking the 17m barrier, going on to dominate the triple jump for nearly ten years and then disappearing from public view.

[256]Born on 28 March 1935 in Miechowitz, Germany, now Miechowice[257] in Bytom, Poland, **Józef Szmidt**[258] was a natural sportsman, who despite some initial reticence to take up athletics seriously, would focus on becoming the

---

[255] Ira S. Davis, three-time Olympic triple jump finalist in 1956-64 and 2cm from a Bronze medal in 1960, when he finished fourth [1936-].

[256] Portrait of Józef Szmidt, date unknown © unknown

[257] Part of Upper Silesia, predominated by Polish speakers but in the 1930's still part of Germany.

[258] The original spelling of his name was Josef Schmidt, but this was changed when the borders changed after the Second World War and the family took Polish nationality.

phenomenal triple jumper who led the sport in the early 1960's, setting technical trends observed to this day. Elder brother Edward Szmidt[259] was a sprinter who would go on to represent Poland at the 200m and the 4x100m relay in Melbourne 1956, and it was his encouragement that eventually brought Józef into athletics at the age of 20, first as a sprinter and soon by chance a triple jumper, needing to fill a gap when the *Górnik Zabrze*[260] team was short. Górnik was the sports club that both brothers would represent for the majority of their respective careers, Józef spending a period with the military sports club of *Śląsk Wrocław* in his military service in 1956-57, Edward's influence as a leading Polish athlete enabling this transfer so his younger brother could continue with his nascent specialist training as a promising triple jumper.

Józef was a mechanic by profession and as an athlete would be given a favourable job in a large repair workshop after his military service finished, the expected hours of work from him much less than regular co-workers. He was said to be a 10.4sec sprinter in the 100m like his brother and would be fast enough to be part of Polish champion 4x100m relay teams in 1959 and 1960, even after winning his first national championship in the triple jump in 1958 and would be Polish triple jump champion ten times through to 1971. His build was described as slender, but with his track speed and height at 6ft (1.84m) he quickly proved himself to be very adept at the triple jump, reaching national standard with a season best of 14.40m in 1955 in the year that he took up athletics, 15.61m by 1957 and then jumping

---

[259] Edward J. Szmidt, or Eberhard Schmidt, five-time Polish champion in relay races [1931-2018].

[260] Founded after the Second World War to support the promotion of sports participation amongst young Poles, the club had traditions in mining in Zabrze and the football club remains a top-flight team in the Polish top league, the Poland Ekstraklasa.

16.06m the following season when he became Polish champion and record holder for the first time.

On 23 August 1958 in Stockholm, he would mark himself out as an athlete of international quality in winning his first European Championship with a jump of 53ft $10\frac{17}{20}$in (16.43m). He decisively beat new World Record holder Oleg Ryakhovskiy of the Soviet Union in difficult conditions, dealing with both adverse weather and a poor runway, and would end that season as the new number two in the world, ahead of the likes of Vitold Kreyer, Leonid Shcherbakov and Adhemar da Silva. The 1959 season would be disrupted by a tendon injury – the first of a number of joint and muscle injuries and ailments that would plague his career – and Soviet Oleg Fedoseyev would break the World Record in May of that year, but his training would see his own performances peak the following season, all the more important with it being an Olympic year.

[261]His form in the early part of the 1960 season was strong, with career bests of 16.53m in June and then 16.69m in July, yet despite being recognised as an athlete of vast potential, none would have

expected what came in August of that year. In the Polish Championships held in the *Leśny Stadium* (Forest Stadium), Olsztyn on 5 August 1960, Józef would become the World Record holder with an astonishing jump of 55ft $10\frac{1}{4}$in (17.03m)[262] in the final. This was a truly startling result, the first man over 17m in breaking the 55ft barrier,

---

[261] Józef Szmidt having landed his World Record jump of 17.03m on 5 August 1960; remarkably video footage of the jump survives © unknown
[262] Ratified as such, but closer to $10\frac{1}{2}$in than $10\frac{1}{4}$in.

taking himself to a level above his competition and achieving what was then considered to be the triple jump equivalent of the 4-minute mile,[263] whilst extending the world best mark by 33cm! The wind assistance was negligible and he may have lost several centimetres due to an imperfect landing,[264] but he had made history with his jump, second placed Jan Jaskólski[265] recording a best of only 15.78m. Jaskólski later recalled that the judges measured, checked and took pictures for half an hour after his jump, the packed stadium in a frenzy of joy and other coaches and athletes rushed to congratulate Józef, with the most famous Polish sports daily, *Przegląd Sportowy*,[266] the next day carrying a headline referencing the "atomic jump of a world record",[267] extremely appropriate for the Cold War tensions of the time!

[268]Józef went to the Rome Olympics that September as the outright favourite, despite a veteran field featuring the returning  two-time Olympic Champion in Adhemar da Silva, Silver and Bronze medallists from Melbourne in Vilhjálmur Einarsson and Vitold Kreyer respectively, as well as the majority of the finalists from 1956. The Pole was a newcomer to the Olympics, but was European Champion and then the only man in history to go over 17m. He would not disappoint, breaking Adhemar's Olympic Record on his first jump of the two-

---

[263] First achieved in 1954 by British runner Roger Bannister, now the standard of professional middle distance runners around the world. The record for the mile has since been lowered by 17sec.

[264] Quercetani, *op. cit.*, p. 266

[265] Jan Jaskólski, three-time Olympian 1960-68 [1939-2013].

[266] Translated as 'Sports Review'.

[267] '60 years have passed since Józef Szmidt's world record. He was the first to cover 17 metres in a triple jump', Piotr Platek, *Wyborcza.pl*, 5 August 2020.

[268] The 1960 Olympics triple jump medallists, Kreyer (L) and Goryayev (R) either side of Józef Szmidt © unknown

round format, then improving it twice more in the final, winning Gold with a best jump of 55ft $1\frac{4}{5}$in (16.81m), the three furthest jumps of all time now belonging to the 25-year-old, with the Silver and Bronze medals going to the Soviet Union (Goryayev and Kreyer), who each exceeded the former Olympic Record.

Now dubbed the 'Silesian Kangaroo' by *Przegląd Sportowy*, a nod to his roots and jumping exploits, he had replaced Adhemar da Silva as the pre-eminent triple jumper in the world and it was the Brazilian's balanced technique that he had further developed to such an extent that it became known as the 'Polish Style'. The Brazilian never had the ground speed of the Pole and whilst the kangaroo moniker was catching, Józef certainly was not a high-hopping jumper like the majority of the Soviet athletes, more an exponent of the flat technique of the Icelandic Einarsson and continuing with the low, skimming trajectory of former World Record holder Oleg Ryakhovskiy.

Józef was a good long jumper, being Polish champion in 1961 and trusted his wise coach Tadeusz Starzyński,[269] together pioneering the running or 'Polish Style' technique. They had a falling out that meant that the individualistic Józef would strike out on his own in the 1959 season, losing his national title despite being European Champion and returning to his coach the following year having seen his average results fade significantly, the 1960 season then seeing history made with an astonishing World Record and his first Olympic Gold. Starzyński had become a renowned coach after his own middling triple jump career ended, training other Polish triple jumpers including Jaskólski

---

[269] Tadeusz Starzyński [1923-2001].

and Ryszard Malcherczyk[270] and notably later working with long jumper Irena Szewińska,[271] recognised by the IAAF in 2018 as one of the 12 most outstanding figures in the history of athletics.

[272]In the 1962 European Championships held in Belgrade, Yugoslavia[273] on 13 September 1962, Józef defended his title with a Championship Record of 16.55m, easily seeing off the challenge of the Soviet Union once more, in Goryayev (Silver) and Oleg Fedoseyev (Bronze), compatriot Jaskólski placing fourth, but Goryayev would end the season ranked number one in the world. Poland had become part of the Eastern Bloc after the Second World War, renamed as the Polish People's Republic and was the second most-populous communist country in Europe, but it was only ever regarded as a satellite state of the Soviet Union and the relationship of the common people with their communist leaders was at best uneasy, with periods of social unrest in each decade before independence in 1989. And the German-speaking 'Silesian Kangaroo' was never fully at ease in his adoptive country either.

---

[270] Ryszard Malcherczyk, domestic rival to Józef Szmidt in his early career, two-time Olympian 1956-60, and Polish champion in 1961 and 1964, improving the National Record 9 times [1934-].

[271] Irena Szewińska, one of Poland's greatest female athletes; medallist in four consecutive Olympic Games, 1964-76, seven-time Olympic medallist with three Golds and 16-time medallist in the European Championships, including indoor competition [1946-2018].

[272] Józef Szmidt jumping in the Rome Olympics, 1960 © Alamy

[273] Belgrade is now the capital of Serbia.

His parents were native German speakers, his father having died in the war serving in the Wehrmacht[274] and the change from Schmidt to Szmidt was government policy, rather than any desire of the family to feel Polish. They were forced to learn the language they did not speak and whilst he was trumpeted as a national hero, being voted the Polish athlete of the year in 1960 and 1964, he never felt like he belonged in the country he now found himself living in after national boundaries were re-aligned. He had been shy and reserved as a boy, literally being forced by his brother to take up athletics and as quickly as he rose to the top of his sport, he found that opportunities for him were limited, never being rewarded for his World Record by the Polish government, promises broken and other prizes for athletic success halved or mysteriously reduced. He had a use to his communist masters whilst he was an elite sportsman winning international medals, but the man who had never sought the spotlight and might well have been happier remaining as a mechanic or miner would see his unease at his altered circumstances culminate in October 1975, when he fled to Amsterdam.

First, we must go back to the 1964 season and the scene of what Józef himself later deemed his greatest success in a rare 2020 interview.[275] Poland had again one of the most powerful track and field teams in the 1964 Tokyo Olympics and in Józef Szmidt they had the clear favourite for the triple jump, still "the *bête noire*"[276] of the leading Soviet jumpers. The Soviet athletes were again under extreme pressure to win – Adhemar da Silva had remarked about Vitold Kreyer in the 1956 Olympics, "poor guy, he had orders to win... he just fell apart"[277]

---

[274] The armed forces of Nazi Germany from 1935-45.
[275] Platek, *op. cit.*
[276] Quercetani, *op. cit.*, p. 267; *bête noire* means a person or thing strongly detested or avoided, essentially a nightmare to his opponents!
[277] de Carvalho, *op. cit.*

– but Józef differed in that the only pressure he felt was from himself, with the events of 1964 showing how much victory in the Olympics that year meant to him.

In the spring of 1964, a duodenal ulcer began to trouble Józef, a minor ailment compared to the knee injury that flared up in June and which threatened to derail his Olympic dream. With only 100 days until the Tokyo Olympics would begin, he had his synovial bursa drained, leaving precious time for rehabilitation and sufficient training. Matters got even worse for him in July when a torn ligament was diagnosed, with swelling at the back of the knee, namely a Baker's cyst. He left hospital on 1 August and at the age of 29 with recent knee surgery, he was advised by specialists not to participate in the Games, but those doctors had not reckoned on the personal bravery of this man who was already a great athlete and would go on to cement his iconic status even further.

It is said that he struggled to climb the stairs in the Olympic Village and he had to remove his bandage on the morning of competition, seemingly inappropriate to jump with such an obvious sign of injury and he had not yet been able to return to full training. As news of his knee injury spread in the summer of 1964, Soviets Fedoseyev and Victor Kravchenko[278] had replaced Józef as co-favourites for the title and his own claims for victory were now widely seen as questionable, his struggles becoming a national problem in Poland. In the first jump of qualifying on 16 October 1964, he cleared 16.18m to secure his place in the final round and demonstrate that he was still in contention for a medal, then made 16.58m on his second jump in the final to take the lead, allowing him to skip the next jump on the advice of his coach with the pain in his knee increasing, the

---

[278] Viktor P. Kravchenko, Olympic Bronze medallist in 1964 and two-time Soviet champion in 1964 & 1966 [1941-].

fierce resentment he held against his doctors for the state of his leg driving him on. In rounds four and five, his rivals Kravchenko and Fedoseyev landed jumps of 16.57m and 16.58m respectively, forcing him to need to go again if he was to become the third man to repeat as Olympic triple jump champion after Myer Prinstein and Adhemar da Silva...

[279]His final jump in the 1964 Olympics was massive and all the more impressive considering he was carrying a partially rehabilitated knee injury in an event where the ability to absorb force in that joint is everything. The sixth and final jump for him was measured at 55ft $3\frac{2}{5}$in (16.85m), a new Olympic Record and remarkably it was further than he had jumped in Rome when fully fit and in the form of his life! The pain in his knee must have been immense, but he had achieved what many felt was unthinkable, in going from his hospital bed to defending his Olympic title. On his return to Poland, he was honoured by the government and voted Polish athlete of the year for the second time by his countrymen and the press, but this was a victory for himself, remarking cynically in a 2020 interview that "there were many fathers of success."[280]

Józef Szmidt remained world number one for the following season, but thereafter injuries, time and the progression of younger rivals began to take its toll on this great athlete, who remained competitive in spirit but gradually lost the ability to truly challenge. He was fifth at the 1966 European Championships in Budapest, one place

---

[279] Józef Szmidt jumping in the 1964 Olympics in Tokyo © Out of Copyright
[280] Platek, *op. cit.*

behind fellow Pole Jaskólski, with the title claimed by Georgi Stoykovski[281] of Bulgaria and would still win the sixth of his ten Polish triple jump titles that season, but the slide had begun. Three months before the Mexico City Olympics in 1968 – his third Games – he tore an Achilles tendon, but would brave a painful and debilitating injury to participate, struggling with his injury and as he had so often done before, pulling off a great jump with his final attempt, finishing a respectable 7th having reached 16.89m, in a final for the ages at high altitude, where the top six all cleared 17m and *FIVE* World and Olympic Records were set in the same competition, with a new star of the sport named Viktor Saneyev of the Soviet Union claiming Gold.

Józef's own World Record had lasted for eight years, a tribute in itself to the size of his achievement in being the first man over 17m and it would not be until 1985 that the record would be brought back down to sea-level by Willie Banks of the United States. His last major competition was the European Championships in August 1971 in Helsinki. He had been omitted from the team for the 1969 European Championships, subsequently retiring from the national team before a change of heart led him to compete in Helsinki. His body was now slowed by frequent injury and he was 36 years old, but this brave athlete still wished to challenge the best despite the inevitable passage of time. He finished a disappointing 11th with a best distance of only 15.62m, being defeated by athletes only a few years before he would have beaten easily and he was now a minor actor on the international stage, Saneyev the dominant jumper and World Record holder after his exploits at Mexico City 1968.

After Helsinki he found that the mood of the Polish authorities towards him had changed now his results were getting

---

[281] Georgi I. Stoykovski, 1966 European Champion and two-time Olympian in 1964 & 1968 [1941-].

weaker and influential voices in the press were saying he was no longer needed in Polish sport. 1970 was the last season he was ranked in the world top 25 and he found in the next few years before final retirement in 1974 that he was being overtly forgotten in his country, his final medal being a Bronze in the 1972 Polish Championships. He had put Polish track and field on the world stage with his victories, but he was no longer appreciated nor supported when he wished to train the next generation in his retirement. Most Polish accounts of his life mention a reluctance to get involved in politics, despite his wide popularity, as contributing to his problems in that period, with others mentioning unfortunate comments to a journalist about the election as the cause of his ostracism, being then blacklisted and unable to find a job. In the early 1970's he had sought permission from the communists to emigrate to Germany and this longing for his old homeland was not to be forgotten, his name censored and mentions of him removed from memoirs and histories.

On 15 October 1975 he took matters into his own hands and using the visit of the national football team to Amsterdam as official cover to leave the country, he essentially defected to West Germany. His two sons followed a few months later, but his wife Łucja was not able to join them for another year, suffering from official persecution from the authorities and with little money to subsist on, selling all their possessions to survive and then to escape. The family were able to start over in West Germany and they both found employment in a hospital near Dortmund, resident in the country of his mother tongue yet still never feeling completely at ease, continuing to use the Polish spelling of his surname and with his wife's parents still in Poland. Józef never completely turned his back on the country he had represented with such distinction despite the insults visited on him by their authorities, and following encouragement from their sons and the fall of the Berlin Wall in 1989, Józef and Łucja unexpectedly returned to north-western Poland in 1992, bought land in Drawsko Pomorskie close to where her parents lived, breeding goats on his farm and living there to this day as a virtual recluse.

Józef was always an individual when he competed, in terms of developing his own training methods and jumping style, and he remains a great individualist to this day, now aged 88. He has never fully regained his trust in journalists, for good reason, has little interest in speaking about his sporting career and has agreed to very few interview requests since his return to Poland. Whilst he was living in West Germany, a number of Polish leaders invited him home to speak with them, but he would not forget how he was censored and cast aside by the authorities when his career waned and he would not be their puppet at election time. He receives a German rather than Polish pension and still refuses invitations from the Polish Olympic Committee and Polish Athletic Association,[282] his sense of betrayal unyielding.

The last word on the great Józef Szmidt should come from one of the few interviews he has given in recent years. In 2010 he returned to the scene of his moment in history in the remains of the Forest Stadium in Olsztyn, where he became the first man to break the 17m barrier and where he insisted in an interview marking that anniversary visit that he was unaware he had broken the World Record in 1960 until he was back in the dressing room.[283] In that same interview he said that instead of talking, he would still rather jump and that is the mark of the man who singlehandedly showed the Soviet Union that Polish athletes could compete with them in sporting quality,

---

[282] Platek, *op. cit.*

[283] https://www.olsztyn24.com/news/10300-jak-bdquoslaski-kangurrdquo-honorowe-obywatelstwo-olsztyna-odbieral.html

if not quantity. The secret to the success of the 'Silesian Kangaroo' was his dynamic start and undoubted speed, enabling him to fully exploit a technique where he kept fast and flat in the first two phases. He was then able to regain height for the jump, making that last leap almost a technically proficient long jump, using a side, or American, landing in the sandpit to prevent him from falling backwards and ceding distance as many others did. He may not have made any money in his sporting career, but he mastered an approach to triple jumping that is still used to this day and he will always remain the first man to cover 17m in a triple jump, regardless of whether he truly felt German, Polish, Silesian or just *European*.

05.08.1960 WR 17.03m (55ft $10\frac{1}{4}$in) Józef Szmidt (POL) Olsztyn, Poland (+1.0m/s)

MILESTONES IN MEXICO CITY

'Beamonesque'[284]

The 1968 Olympics in Mexico City would take place against a backdrop of protest, the raised fist, Black Power[285] salute of United States sprinters Tommie Smith[286] and John Carlos[287] on the 200m podium the iconic image of those Games and a symbol of the fight against racism and injustice to this day. In the days before the opening ceremony, more than 200 student demonstrators were killed and one thousand injured by the Mexican Army, when protesting the government's funding of the Olympics over the needs of the people and it seemed that the first Games in Latin America would be remembered for the wrong reasons, repression the message rather than the core values of Olympism, being excellence, friendship and respect. Yet these Games were the first to use an all-weather track rather than the traditional cinders and also the first to be at high altitude, the perfect conditions for a *Mexican Revolution* in track and field, in more than one event.

The track and field star of the 1968 Olympics would be long jumper Bob Beamon[288] of the United States. On 19 October 1968, he

---

[284] Commonly held to mean an overwhelming sporting feat or exploit.

[285] A political movement for the advancement of self-determination for black people.

[286] Tommie C. Smith, one-time Olympic Gold medallist, the first man to officially run the 200m sub-20sec and later a track coach and college teacher, with an interlude as a professional American footballer. Both Smith and Carlos were banned from the Olympic Village and sent home, their protest deemed contrary to the ideals of the Olympics by the IOC and the United States Olympic Committee [1944-].

[287] John W. Carlos, Bronze medallist in the 200m in 1968, later involved in the United States Olympic Committee, coach and an organiser of the 1984 Olympics [1945-].

[288] Robert 'Bob' Beamon, Olympic long jump Gold medallist in 1968 and his former World Record is still, astonishingly, the second-best mark in the event and remains the Olympic Record; later a track coach and now involved with the promotion of youth athletics [1946-].

soared into the thin air of Mexico City, extending the long jump mark by nearly 2ft to 29ft $2\frac{1}{2}$in (8.90m), a World Record that would stand for almost 23 years until compatriot Mike Powell[289] broke it in the 1991 World Championships in Tokyo. He was literally overwhelmed by the gravity of his feat – having seemingly defied gravity in making the leap – the effort it took resulting in a brief episode of cataplexy, a sudden muscular weakness seeing his legs give way and he collapsed on the track. His feat was astonishing to spectators and competitors alike, redefining what was thought possible in the long jump and making such a mark on sport in general, that his name was taken for the phrase *Beamonesque*, a once in a generation sporting feat, so spectacular it is scarcely believable. But the day before that long jump, metaphorically into "somewhere in the next century,"[290] the triple jump final would witness its own collective *Beamonesque* exploits, four men exceeding a formerly venerated distance in one day, the fourth athlete not even making the podium and each of them bettering a world best only set the day before in qualification...

[291]The first actor in this heady company of record-breakers at altitude is **Guiseppe Gentile**. Born on 4 September 1943 in Latina, Lazio region, central Italy, he would be haunted for many years by what happened in the 1968 Olympics, having broken the World Record on consecutive days yet gone home with *only* a Bronze medal. He

[289] Michael 'Mike' A. Powell, long jump World Record holder since 1991, two-time World Champion in 1991 & 1993 and two-time Olympic Silver medallist in 1988 & 1992 [1963-].
[290] 'THE UNBELIEVABLE MOMENT', Coles Phinizy, *Sports Illustrated*, 23 December 1968
[291] A portrait of Guiseppe Gentile taken in 1968, reproduced in a 1969-70 Panini sticker album © Public Domain

had been a middling competitor on the international stage until the 1968 season, a best distance in 1967 of 53ft $6\frac{1}{2}$in (16.32m) and was never ranked higher than 11th in the world at season's end, until his exploits in Mexico City. He was larger than most jumpers at 6ft 3in (1.90m) in height and just under 14st (83kg) in weight, but this bear of a man would be able to *walk on the moon* of his sport a year ahead of the Apollo 11 Moon landing,[292] but find the zenith of his sporting career to be fleeting and all too quickly eclipsed.

'Peppe' Gentile was a great-grandson of the famous Italian philosopher, Giovanni Gentile, an idealist, educator, politician from the 1920's and an enthusiastic embracer of Fascism, latterly serving as the fifth President of the Royal Academy of Italy, until his death at the hands of anti-Fascist fighters in July 1944, during the Second World War. Peppe grew up in Rome, representing the *Centro Universitario Sportivo di Roma* club – not the *Gruppo Sportivo Fiamme Oro*, the sports section of the Italian police force as some sources state[293] – and quickly proved to be a talented sportsman, competing internationally from 1962 aged only nineteen, when he finished 19th in the European Championships in Belgrade and claimed his first National Record in the triple jump in 1965, with a jump of 16.17m.

Gentile ended the 1967 season ranked 22nd in the world, had a best distance of 16.32m and won his second successive Silver medal in the Mediterranean Games[294] in Tunis, Tunisia in September of that year, with a jump of 16.04m; he had also been a Bronze medallist in the 1967 Summer Universiade in Tokyo, Japan in early September, but it

---

[292] Reference to Americans Neil Armstrong and 'Buzz' Aldrin becoming the first people to walk on the moon on 20 July 1969.

[293] Gentile is not listed in the club's roll of Olympic medallists on their website, which now includes double Gold winning sprinter Marcell Jacobs from Tokyo 2020 – https://www.poliziadistato.it/articolo/26525

[294] First held in 1951 and continuing to this day, including countries from Africa, Asia and Europe that border the Mediterranean Sea.

128

had been a weak field. He would turn 25 in the 1968 season and was also a law student, suggesting that vast improvement was not to be expected, but from August he would begin to surprise athletics watchers in an inexorable rise to the Mexico City podium. Peppe was in good form that season and on 17 August 1968, he would have what many thought would prove to be his career day. In the Italy versus Poland International Match in Chorzów, Poland, Gentile would break both the triple and long jump National Records, reaching 54ft 11in (16.74m) in the former and 7.91m in the latter. This meant he was only 1in away from joining the '55 footers' as the elite triple jumpers of the time were known and would go to Mexico City in October of that year in the form of his life, although a thigh injury when indulging his passion for the high jump would mean that he would compete with a rather incongruous white thigh band on his right leg!

[295]The qualification round for the Olympic triple jump final took place on the morning of 16 October 1968, in the *Estadio Olímpico Universitario*. The time of day is important as the statistical chaos that followed the succeeding day meant that Peppe's period as the World Record holder was brief, being able to enjoy only one *full day* as the then greatest exponent of his sport. He fouled on his first jump in qualification, then to the surprise of all, not least his competitors, he bounded to a new World Record of 56ft 1in[296] (17.10m), with no wind assistance recorded. Józef Szmidt's World Record had stood for eight

---

[295] Guiseppe Gentile being interviewed on the evening of 16 October 1968 whilst watching other Olympic competitions and by then the new triple jump World Record holder © Public Domain

[296] Ratified as such, but more correctly 56ft $1\frac{1}{4}$in.

years, two months and 11 days, but that of Peppe Gentile would only last for one day…

The following afternoon the scraggy bearded Italian returned to the stadium as the World and Olympic Record holder, but even then, he was not expected to become the Olympic Champion. Prior to the 1957 season, only Szmidt and Aleksandr Zolotarev of the Soviet Union[297] had ever exceeded 55ft, with the 1958 season the first time that two athletes were able to make that distance in the same meet[298] and the 1968 season best mark being the 55ft $9\frac{1}{3}$in (17.00m) jumped by Finland's Pertti Pousi[299] in Kuortane, Finland on 23 June, the second furthest in history at that time. But what followed on the afternoon of 17 October 1968 was essentially an assault on the World Record, a shocking sequence of jumps that would see Peppe extend the record by a further 12cm, only for two other athletes to then break his world best mark with a barely legal wind assistance that had been absent when he jumped, taking full advantage of the favourable track and air conditions to electrify the triple jump.

In an April 2019 interview,[300] Gentile would say that his sporting life began on 16 October 1968 and ended the day after, an indication of the torment that followed him for the majority of his life after Mexico City, a story of a broken dream and a broken medal. He had promised his long-time coach Gigi Rosati[301] that he would win Gold that morning and they would have half of the medal each, a

---

[297] Aleksandr Zolotarev, or Zolotaryev, world number one in 1967 with a distance of 16.92m in Chorzów, then competed in the triple jump in the 1968 Olympics but did not reach the final [1940-].

[298] Viktor Saneyev and compatriot Nikolay Dudkin in Leningrad, Soviet Union on 21 July 1968.

[299] Pertti Pousi, competed in the long and triple jump in the 1968 Olympics [1946-].

[300] 'Olimpiadi Città del Messico 1968 Gentile e la medaglia spezzata', Gaetano Campione, *La Gazzetta del Mezzogiorno*, 5 April 2019

[301] Luigi 'Gigi' Rosati, renowned Italian athletics at the *CUS Roma* club, an innovator in several sports from swimming to Paralympic events [1935-2019].

'shared medal' reflecting the affectionate bond that existed between them, similar to that enjoyed by the great Brazilian Adhemar da Silva and his coach. Rosati had come from a military background and his was a coaching method at odds with the Italian Federation, focussed on first gaining power and correcting technical defects, before relentless practice of the 'perfect jump' by way of multi-event training, including working on his *elevation* through the high jump so enjoyed by Peppe, *thrust* when working over the 400m hurdles and *flat speed* through sprinting.[302]

The stadium at the 1968 Olympics was the first in the history of the Games to utilise a smooth, all-weather track and it has become the standard since. The track at the *Estadio Olímpico Universitario* was a Tartan, a trademarked synthetic surface made of polyurethane that has become the generic name for all-weather tracks and the Mexico City Tartan quickly gained a reputation amongst athletes as being both fast and springy. The decision to award the Games to Mexico City had not been without controversy due to the well-known effects of altitude on the explosive events (to the positive) and debilitative effect on the middle-distance and endurance events, and even after Peppe had broken the World Record in qualification, rival Art Walker[303] of the United States remarked, "he'll never do that again... but others will be able to beat that."[304]

---

[302]
http://www.sportolimpico.it/index.php?option=com_content&view=article&id=25
53:saro-greve-luigi-rosati-maestro-amico-e-fratello&catid=1:focus
[303] Arthur 'Art' F. Walker, the best American triple jumper in the late 1960's, 4th in the 1968 Olympics and 29th in 1972; three-time US champion in the triple jump and three-time National Record holder [1941-].
[304] 'Saneyev Wins Toughest Test', Dick Drake, *Track & Field News*, Olympic Games issue, Oct./Nov. 1968

[305]The following day Peppe went 56ft 5$\frac{3}{4}$in[306] (17.22m) on his first-round jump in the final, jumping 11th and surprising onlookers once more in breaking the World Record on consecutive days! The overall conditions had proven very much to his liking and we know from an October 2018 interview[307] that he thought the Gold medal to be within his grasp, but that first-round jump would prove to be 'cursed' – the

Italian word *maledetto* is best used to describe his feelings when confronting the memory of that day in later years and it has a phonetic resonance even to an English speaker – the final being both the zenith and nadir of his athletics career, devastatingly within only a few hours.

The story of what followed Gentile's second World Record is an interweaving of progressively more shocking events, at least to contemporary observers, best described in some form of chronological order. Thirteen athletes advanced to the 1968 final and after three jumps the top eight contested the three medal rounds. Distances had been reset after qualifying, so the new World Record became the benchmark for the final rather than the minimum standard required for Gold and the opening round was collectively disappointing until Peppe sparked the competition into life. No athlete was within 0.5m of him after the first round, but two had gone over 54ft and the next actor in our story is the undoubted star, the man who would give the final its

---

[305] Guiseppe Gentile competing in the 1968 Olympic triple jump final, with the flashy bandage on his thigh on show © Public Domain

[306] Ratified as such, but more correctly 56ft 5$\frac{19}{20}$in.

[307] https://www.gazzetta.it/Atletica/17-10-2018/messico1968-olimpiadi-300740440534.shtml

dramatic suspense and go on to dominate the event for the next ten years.

[308]**Viktor Danilovich Saneyev** was born on 3 October 1945 in Sokhumi, Georgian Soviet Socialist Republic, now part of the Republic of Abkhazia, but considered  internationally part of Georgia, in the ethnically diverse Caucasus region. He was the epitome of a Soviet athlete, handsome, close-cropped hair and a dominant all-round athlete who exuberated power married with technical proficiency, yet he was not ethnically Russian and in Moscow 1980 he was almost denied the chance to carry the Olympic Torch as he was deemed not Russian enough. He had recently turned 23 before the Games commenced and had only been competing internationally since the 1967 season, ending the year ranked sixth in the world, but came to Mexico as one of the favourites, in a final yet still expected to be an open affair.

Saneyev had made the 1968 season his own and came to the Games as the second ranked jumper in the world, with a season best of 55ft $4\frac{1}{2}$in (16.88m) and newly crowned as the USSR champion, the first of eight Soviet titles he would win in 1968-71, 1973-75 and 1978. We will cover his career in more detail in the following chapter – he really was 'Golden Viktor' – but having been one of two jumpers over 54ft in the first round of the final, he had the surprise leader Gentile in his sights in such favourable conditions, whose pre-Games best was good enough for 7th only in the world that season and the wind assistance had markedly picked up since the second World Record

---

[308] A later career portrait of Viktor Saneyev © unknown

jump. The Italian was said to have the longest step of the leading jumpers – around 18ft or 5.50m – and in perfect form he had landed that record leap standing up.[309]

Third after the first jump, the Soviet improved his distance by over 1ft in the second round, but still trailed Gentile's new World Record and Brazilian Nelson Prudêncio, who had gone to 17.05m with his second-round effort. In near perfect conditions for triple jumping – a fast, springy runway surface, the thinner air density at altitude reducing resistance, the wind reading now increasing and a competitive field which included two-time Olympic Champion Szmidt – Saneyev sought to take over the competition. Only around 50 minutes had passed since Gentile's second World Record, when the Soviet began his own assault on the record books, soaring through the air to land the third World Record in two days, a distance of 56ft $6\frac{1}{4}$in[310] (17.23m) achieved with a tailwind just on the allowable limit of 2.0m/s. Saneyev had improved the record by only 1cm or $\frac{1}{2}$in, but it was enough to shatter the hopes of the Italian, fouling his own second and third-round jumps, registering a lowly 16.54m in the fifth round after fouling on his fourth attempt and completing the competition with yet another foul. Gentile had landed two great jumps, but after his first-round record, his technique collapsed as he chased a fading dream.

Saneyev was now the World Record holder and followed up in the fourth-round with another strong jump of 17.02m, demonstrating that he had not finished. Phil May[311] of Australia matched that distance in the same round, one of seven athletes who

---

[309] Drake, *op. cit.*

[310] Ratified as such, but more accurately it was 56ft $5\frac{7}{20}$in.

[311] Philip J. May, triple and long jumper who was good enough to be ranked in the top ten for both in 1970; 1970 Commonwealth Games Champion in the former and Silver medallist in the latter, and later a successful businessman in Australia [1944-2014].

would exceed Szmidt's previous Olympic Record in the final and the sixth who would reach 17m in an increasingly high calibre competition. Fellow Soviet, Nikolay Dudkin[312] jumped 17.09m in the fifth round, with the wind exceeding the allowable limit and it was clear that the athletes were taking every advantage of the conditions on offer. It was now time for our final actor to enter the stage and have his own career day.

[313]Born on 4 April 1944 in Lins, São Paulo, Brazilian **Nelson Prudêncio** was destined to become a footnote in the history of the triple jump and a regular on lists of the shortest athletics World Records. Yet he was a great triple jumper himself and working in the shadow of Viktor Saneyev, he would become a two-time Olympic medallist who had the uncanny ability to time his best performances for major championships. He had ended the 1967 season ranked only 23rd in the world and despite claiming Silver in the 1967 Pan American Games in Winnipeg, Canada in August with a wind-assisted distance of 16.45m, he was largely unheralded when the Olympics came round and was not expected to medal. Described as having a "high-bounding but smooth style,"[314] the twenty-four-year-old Prudêncio had soared to 17.05m in the second-round, around 75cm further than he had ever jumped before and a distance in excess of Szmidt's former World Record. The Brazilian had announced himself in bold fashion and had a strong

---

[312] Nikolay Dudkin, 1968 Olympian [1947-].
[313] Nelson Prudêncio jumping in 1968, reproduced in a 1969-70 Panini sticker album © Public Domain
[314] Drake, *op. cit.*

chance of a surprise medal, achieving what would be South America's only podium in track and field in those Games.

In the fourth round he fouled, before his own moment of destiny was to come in the fifth. Saneyev had broken the new World Record in the third round and was still jumping magnificently, not to foul on any of his six attempts in the final. Prudêncio had broken fellow Brazilian Adhemar da Silva's thirteen-year-old South American Record with his second-round jump and was maturing fast as an athlete on the grandest stage, proving himself to be an exceptional talent. The jumping order in the final has not survived, but Nikolay Dudkin jumped before the Brazilian in the fifth round, reaching 17.09m and pushing him out of the medals, so Prudêncio had to go again to re-secure a medal. And go he did.

His fifth jump was unexpected when considering his pre-Games distances, but should not be surprising in light of the shattering of expectations and records in that competition. Prudêncio was a remarkably fast sprinter and video footage of his record jump shows him to be firmly in the 'Polish Style', reliant on his speed like the great Józef Szmidt and his face a picture of determination in willing his body through the phases, all arms and legs as he reaches for the sandpit, but graceful enough to land on his feet. His jump was a new World Record at 56ft $7\frac{3}{4}$in[315] (17.27m), besting Saneyev's former mark by 4cm which had incredibly only stood for an hour that afternoon, yet the expectant crowd knew that this drama could yet have further twists and turns before the competition ended.

---

[315] Ratified as such, but more accurately it was 56ft $7\frac{9}{10}$in.

[316]And twists it had. Saneyev had been the World Record holder for a passing moment, but in contrast to Gentile and Prudêncio, this was not to be the peak of his career and an athlete on the verge of greatness now demonstrated that he could perform under immense pressure. Entering the final round, all eyes were on whether the Georgian could respond and the near-perfect conditions had continued, the wind reading still around the allowable limit. Saneyev did not look like an athlete under pressure when he jumped for the final time that day and the leap itself was close to perfection, bounding out to an incredible 57ft $\frac{1}{2}$in[317] (17.39m) to secure a last-gasp win, twisting on landing to secure the maximum distance. The twenty-three-year-old was the Olympic Champion and had his second World Record of the day, the winner of the most pulsating competition in the history of the triple jump and the youngest protagonist of our three record-breakers had become the eventual victor.

In an astonishing afternoon of triple jumping, the World Record had been broken by three athletes on four occasions. Prudêncio's record had only lasted for around five minutes and after this onslaught over thirty hours, that of Saneyev would itself stand for nearly three years. Six men had gone over 17m in the final, five of them exceeding Szmidt's World Record distance from 1960, although Dudkin's best was wind-aided and Phil May who was 6th and Szmidt who was 7th, both bettered the previous Olympic Record of 16.85m

---

[316] Viktor Saneyev jumping in the 1968 Olympic Games final © unknown

[317] More accurately 57ft $\frac{13}{20}$in.

from 1964. Prudêncio had exceeded the 1960 record three times and ended up with a Silver medal, Gentile had broken the record twice in claiming Bronze and Art Walker is really the forgotten man, landing 17.12m on his final jump and only finishing 4th.

Saneyev would go on to have a storied career with two further Olympic Gold medals, two-time European Champion, an Olympic and European Silver in addition to one final World Record in 1972, cementing his place as one of the leading jumpers of all time. We will pick up his career in full in the next chapter, but for now we return to Gentile and Prudêncio, now former World Record holders whose respective careers would take different trajectories after the heady heights of Mexico City. The latter was ecstatic to claim a Silver medal, despite his brush with the Gold and was now considered a world class jumper, with increasing similarities being drawn to fellow black Brazilian Adhemar da Silva, although they had yet to meet at this stage and Prudêncio was quick to point out they had very different styles.[318]

[319]The Brazilian had gone to Mexico City having split his time between his studies and his athletics training. His first competition was in 1964 and by 1968 he was still only training a couple of times a week, it being rare for a black Brazilian to be able to attend higher education and he would not waste the opportunity. He had gone to the Olympics with the aim of beating Adhemar da Silva's South American Record and achieved so much more, but on his return, he decided to focus on his studies at the Physical Education School in São Carlos, later becoming a Professor at the *Universidade Federal de São*

[318] Drake, *op. cit.*
[319] A clearly ecstatic Nelson Prudêncio with his 1968 Olympic Silver medal © unknown

Carlos, a public research university in his home-state of São Paulo and when studying in the United States, forgoing many competitions. He was still talented enough to be ranked fifth in the world in 1971-72, having claimed a Silver in the 1971 Pan American Games in Cali, Colombia and most impressively when again showing his major championship pedigree in Munich 1972, claiming a most unexpected Bronze. He returned for one final Olympic Games in Montreal 1976, but did not make the final and was later Vice President of the Brazilian Athletics Confederation, before dying at the age of only sixty-eight from lung cancer, on 23 November 2012.

Peppe Gentile returned from Mexico City as one of only two Italian medallists in track and field, the other being Eddy Ottoz,[320] and it should have been a moment of triumph. However, the second World Record meant nothing to him, "everyone thought it was enough to win... except me."[321] The disappointment led him to forgo his promise to halve the medal with coach Gigi Rosati, a decision that haunted him for 25 years until he looked for some form of personal redemption in honouring that worthy promise, no longer denying Gigi the joy of a goal they achieved together. The peace he wanted did not come and it was only with the publication of his autobiography in 2012, *La medaglia (con)divisa*,[322] that he could retrace the steps of his life and the emotions he had repressed for many years, a story that did not end in Mexico City.

---

[320] Eddy Ottoz, Bronze medallist in the 110m hurdles in 1968, two-time European Champion in 1966 & 1969 and three-time European Indoor Champion; retired at only 25 and now a board member of the Italian National Olympic Committee [1944-].
[321] Campione, *op. cit.*
[322] Loosely translated as 'The medal (with)divided', or 'The shared medal'.

[323]Gentile was an elegant and powerful jumper, continuing to compete in international competition until Munich 1972, but winning no further major medals and not qualifying for the final in his last Olympics. He was Italian triple jump champion twice more in 1970-71, giving

him six career national titles in both the triple and long jump, and was the first Italian to win an Olympic medal in his event. His Bronze medal was an achievement in itself and he was only defeated by two athletes that set new World Records with the wind assistance on the limit of legality, chance denying him any recorded wind at all on his own attempts. In 1969, he appeared in the role of Jason in the film *Medea*, opposite the great soprano Maria Callas,[324] but declined future roles as they were deemed of lesser quality. He remains a sporting purist to this day and having overcome his own bitterness – never directed at his opponents and more the circumstances that befell him – he has adopted a more philosophical view of that day, befitting the great-grandson of a famous thinker. In the October 2018 interview referred to previously, he said that what went wrong in that final, was, "the end of the first jump and the beginning of the second," to him, that World Record jump being quite *cursed*!

16.10.1968 WR(A) 17.10m (56ft 1in) Guiseppe Gentile (ITA) Mexico City, Mexico (0.0m/s)

17.10.1968 WR(A) 17.22m (56ft $5\frac{3}{4}$in) Guiseppe Gentile (ITA) Mexico City, Mexico (0.0m/s)

17.10.1968 WR(A) 17.23m (56ft $6\frac{1}{4}$in) Viktor Saneyev (URS) Mexico City, Mexico (+2.0m/s)

17.10.1968 WR(A) 17.27m (56ft $7\frac{3}{4}$in) Nelson Prudêncio (BRA) Mexico City, Mexico (+2.0m/s)

17.10.1968 WR(A) 17.39m (57ft $\frac{1}{2}$in) Viktor Saneyev (URS) Mexico City, Mexico (+2.0m/s)

---

[323] Guiseppe Gentile on the set of the 1969 Italian film, *Medea* © unknown
[324] Sophie C. Kalos, 'Maria Callas', an American-born Greek soprano and renowned as one of the most influential opera singers of the 20th century [1923-1977].

GOLDEN VIKTOR

'He came down the runway like a madman'[325]

The 1968 Olympics had seen the World Record improved to such an extent, that 56ft had been essentially bypassed in the record books! The pre-Mexico City Olympic Record of 16.85m had been thought to be a creditable standard for world class athletes, but Saneyev's final round jump to claim Gold had seen him become the first man to cover 57ft and change what was thought *humanly* possible in the event. At only twenty-three-years-old, he had the triple jump world at his feet and it was expected that he would claim further major championships in the coming years. The Soviet Union finally had their champion in the much-coveted event and in Saneyev they appeared to have the perfect exponent of the 'Russian Style'. He would eventually retire after the 1980 Games as the most decorated Olympic triple jumper in history, the only athlete of either sex to win three Gold medals and with a total haul of four medals. He would have to cope with his own disappointments over his storied career, his success by no means unopposed and his dominance in the 1970's would see him come to define the end of the era of the hop-dominated jumpers, the 1980's seeing a balanced approach come to the fore.

Saneyev's family were descended from Kuban Cossacks, now a distinct Russian sub-ethnical group, but by the late 1920's when his parents moved to Sokhumi, Georgia, their people had suffered heavily from a Soviet policy aimed at eliminating their separate cultural and economic identity. He grew up in poverty with a father that had been

[325] 'NOT QUITE AS HIGH, BUT A BIT MIGHTIER', Joe Marshall, *Sports Illustrated*, 17 July 1978

bed-ridden for as long as young Viktor could remember, his mother's plight leading him to go to a state-sponsored boarding school aged twelve, three years before his father finally died and where he would spend the next nine years. His school was in the Abkhazian town of Gantiadi, on the Black Sea coast of Georgia and close to the training camp then used by star Soviet athletes each spring, including high jumper Valeriy Brumel[326] and long jumper Igor Ter-Ovanesyan.[327]

The young Saneyev would first take up the high jump at the Gantiadi boarding school, initially enthusiastic about developing his power through self-created methods having watched the Soviet stars in training. However, in his teens he began to grow considerably, and his interest switched to the higher profile sport of basketball, being offered a place on the Georgian national squad, before a local Sokhumi coach and friend of the Saneyev family, Akop Kerselyan,[328] convinced the "long-legged adolescent"[329] to commit to track and field, telling him that he could be a champion if he did. They would forge a career-long bond and Saneyev would have so much faith in Kerselyan, he would in time call him his second father.[330]

In 1964, he was to compete internationally for the first time, in the unsanctioned European Junior (U20) Games in Warsaw, Poland, the first edition of what would become the official European Junior Athletics Championships in 1970. The nearly nineteen-year-old

---

[326] Valeriy N. Brumel, Olympic Champion in 1964, Silver medallist in 1960 and European Champion in 1962; a multiple World Record holder between 1961-63, a motorcycle accident ended his career in 1965 but his record lasted until 1971. He turned to acting and writing in his enforced retirement [1942-2003].

[327] Igor A. Ter-Ovanesyan, the first European to long jump 8m, twice the World Record holder, five-time Olympian with two Olympic Bronze medals in 1960 & 1964, three-time European Champion in 1958, 1962 & 1969 and European Silver in 1966 & 1971 [1938-].

[328] Akop S. Kerselyan, famous as Saneyev's coach, working within the Dynamo Sports Society system for over thirty years [1918-2004].

[329] 'VICTOR SANEYEV APPROACHES THE 60-FOOT MARK', Alexei Srebnitsky, *Soviet Life*, No. 6, June 1973

[330] *Ibid.*

Saneyev won Silver in both the triple and long jump, in the former losing by only 1cm and he chose to focus on this event at the conclusion of the championship. Saneyev was by this time a student in citrus fruit cultivation, going on to graduate from the Georgian Institute of Subtropical Crops in his hometown as a trained agronomist, a passion for growing the likes of tangerines and lemons that became a lifelong interest.

[331]The 1967 season ended with Saneyev ranked the sixth triple jumper in the world and he came to international prominence that September with victory in the European Cup with a jump of 16.67m, a team competition between European countries consisting of 31 events and held that year in Kyiv, then in the Soviet Union. The field contained some quality opponents, second being Hans-Jürgen Rückborn[332] of East Germany, a 1964 Olympian and a notable veteran was in third place, the great Józef Szmidt of Poland, now at the back end of a famous career and three years removed from his second Olympic Gold. The following season would see him claim his first USSR Championship and then become the central protagonist in the electrifying drama of the triple jump final in Mexico City, ending that season as Olympic Champion and World Record holder. The 1968 Olympic final is covered in detail in the preceding chapter and we continue Saneyev's growing hegemony at the 1969 European Championships.

Saneyev returned from Mexico City as the leading triple jumper in the world and he would go on to dominate the 1969 season,

---

[331] Viktor Saneyev jumping during the 1968 Olympic final © unknown
[332] Hans-Jürgen Rückborn, 1964 Olympian in the triple jump [1940-].

seemingly yet to find a true rival. Three men had broken the World Record in the 1968 Olympics, but both Guiseppe Gentile and Nelson Prudêncio would fail to rank in the top 10 the following year, the Italian slowed by injury and the Brazilian focussing on his academic studies. The highlight of that season for Saneyev would come on 17 September 1969 in Athens, Greece as he became European Champion for the first time, competing against the best athletes in the region, who were then amongst the best in the world, including East Germans Klaus Neumann[333] and Jörg Drehmel,[334] Soviet Nikolay Dudkin who had also exceeded the 1960 World Record in the Olympic final in Mexico City, albeit wind-assisted and an injury-hampered Peppe Gentile.

[335]In qualifying on the preceding day, Neumann was to set a new Championship Record at 16.78m, but could not re-produce that form in the final, taking Bronze with a distance of 16.68m. Drehmel had a career best jump of 16.64m that June, but he could not challenge for the European crown either and it was Saneyev who was left to seemingly compete against himself in winning the title, a wind-assisted effort of 56ft $10\frac{7}{10}$in (17.34m) nearly 0.5m ahead of second-placed Zoltán Cziffra[336] of Hungary and close to the mark he set at altitude when winning Olympic Gold. He remained the leading triple jumper in the world, a European Championships victory in the 1970's viewed as so

---

[333] Klaus Neumann, competed in triple jump qualifying in the 1968 Olympics [1942-].
[334] Jörg Drehmel, European Indoor Silver medallist in 1970, European Championship Gold in 1971 and Olympic Silver medallist in 1972 [1945-].
[335] Viktor Saneyev competing in the 1969 European Championships in Athens, reproduced in a 1970 Panini sticker album © Public Domain
[336] Zoltán Cziffra, multiple National Champion, with 1969 being his career year, claiming Silver in both the European Championships and the European Indoor Games [1942-].

much more important than today due to the high overall standard of competition, but he had not seen the last of Drehmel.

The 1970 season would see Saneyev victorious in the European Athletics Indoor Championships, held in Vienna, Austria in March, a new early season competition that replaced the European Indoor Games which itself had only been conceived in 1966. Soviet athletics authorities had quickly realised the importance of indoor events, especially for training purposes in the off-season with the harsh winters in Eastern Europe preventing any real prospect of outdoor sessions. Indoor athletics in the Soviet Union had featured at national level since the 1940's, with an annual competition in some degree held since 1949 and was seen as an integral part of the national training programme in supplementing the summer outdoor Soviet Athletics Championships. Saneyev had spent his winters training indoors in specialist facilities and the advent of the indoor track and field events at an international level, offered further opportunity for him to dominate his sport in major events.

Between 1970 and 1977, Saneyev would become six-time European Indoor Champion, missing the competition in 1973 and only 10th in 1974. He claimed his first European indoor crown on 15 March 1970 in the *Wiener Stadhalle*, Vienna, aged 24 and setting what was to be the first of four world indoor bests in reaching 55ft $7\frac{3}{10}$in (16.95m). The IAAF did not ratify indoor World Records until 1 January 1987, but his dominance of the indoor scene in the 1970's is unquestioned and despite indoor competition being known for slower track surfaces and less subject to the variances in heat or wind conditions that could produce noticeable improvements outdoors, he still posted distances indoors that were comparable to some of the marks of the leading outdoor athletes of the day.

In Grenoble, France in March 1972, he would extend his world best to 16.97m in claiming a hat-trick of European indoor titles, then go to 17.10m and finally to 17.16m, or 56ft $3\frac{6}{10}$in, the latter two in Moscow at opposite ends of the 1976 season. He won his final indoor title in San Sebastián, Spain in March 1977, aged 31, finishing just ahead of Soviet compatriot Jaak Uudmäe who would feature so strongly in Saneyev's final Olympic appearance in 1980 and who we will return to later in this book. The athlete who finished second to Saneyev in that first European Athletics Indoor Championship in 1970 was the East German, Jörg Drehmel. Saneyev had been dubbed the 'Sokhumi Kangaroo' after his first major victory in 1968,[337] but the beginnings of a rivalry started in that first indoor championship and would peak so memorably the following year, a rivalry that was ephemeral rather than enduring, yet contributed to a moment of failure for the Georgian that would precipitate much subsequent success.

Drehmel had only switched to the triple jump from the decathlon in 1966 and training within the Soviet system as an East German, the country then being the German Democratic Republic within the Eastern Bloc, he quickly progressed to international competition, ranking eighth in the world in 1969. The following season saw him claim his first major success in winning the European Cup in Stockholm, Sweden, in August 1970, a Championship Record of 56ft $2\frac{4}{10}$in (17.13m) beating Saneyev into second at 17.01m, with a thirty-five-year-old and by then legendary Józef Szmidt in third. They were to meet for the first time in a major competition in the 1971 European Championships in Helsinki, Finland and the unthinkable was about to happen...

---

[337] Srebnitsky, *op. cit.*

Already considered a great jumper at a young age, Saneyev had yet to be defeated in a major championship final. He had lost the 1970 European Cup to Drehmel, but still ended that season the world number one, a distance of 56ft $10\frac{7}{10}$in (17.34m) in his hometown that October being 21cm further than Drehmel's career best in Stockholm. He went to Finland fully expecting to retain his European title and in Drehmel was to come up against an athlete in the midst of his *annus mirabilis*, the years 1970-72 being the absolute peak of his career. The first German to have gone over 17m, the gusty conditions in the Helsinki Olympic Stadium on 15 August 1971 saw him claim an unexpected victory over the mighty Soviet, a distance of 56ft $3\frac{6}{10}$in (17.16m) aided by a wind rating of +3.7m/s edging out Saneyev's best of 17.10m, the latter jump made with a recorded wind of +3.0m/s. The Olympic Champion had been defeated in major competition for the first time and this came hard on the heels of an even greater setback that month, his World Record having been claimed by Pedro Pérez of Cuba, only ten days before that loss in Helsinki.

[338]**Pedro Damián Pérez Dueñas** was born in the tobacco-growing province of Pinar del Río, Cuba, on 23 February 1952 and his sporting prowess stood out at a young age, a keen basketball and volleyball player in particular. He represented his province in the National School Games in

1967, mostly just to be with his friends who were also competing and having been enrolled in both the high and triple jump, only because there were vacancies, the hand of fate pushed him towards the event

---

[338] An undated photograph of Pedro Pérez triple jumping © unknown

in which he would excel, second place in that competition encouraging further specialized training, especially as he never really had the height for basketball. Subsequently he entered a Higher School for Athletic Improvement (ESPA), one of three types of government created sports academies instituted after the culmination of the Cuban Revolution in 1959,[339] and whilst the ESPA coaches favoured him for the high jump, he elected to focus on the triple jump, noticing his physique to be more like that of the leading athletes in the event. He was 5ft 11in (1.80m) and only 11st 5lbs (72kg), smaller and noticeably less muscular than the powerful Saneyev, but with his background in gymnastics, volleyball, basketball, hurdling and high jump, he had a latent technique willing to be refined, although in what was probably his last interview before his death, he remarked that if he had managed to be 1.85m or 1.90m tall, he would still have been a basketball player![340]

In much the same way that the Soviet government utilized their sports societies, these academies in Cuba were part of a policy intended to develop athletes for both national and international competition, supported financially by the politically aligned USSR. As part of this support, Pérez came under the auspices of Leonid Shcherbakov, the 1953 World Record holder, two-time European Champion and 1952 Olympic Silver medallist (see earlier chapter on the first Soviet athletes to reach the top of the sport). The Cuban government were fanatical about international sporting success in order to enhance their global reputation and the concept of proletarian internationalism[341] enabled them to harness leading coaches from the

---

[339] The others were EIDE and CEAR.
[340] http://www.cubadebate.cu/noticias/2018/07/19/pedro-perez-duenas-reivindicacion-de-un-hombre-record/
[341] The idea that all Communist revolutions were part of a concerted global struggle against capitalism and not just local events.

Soviet Union and other Eastern European nations, with Shcherbakov coaching Cuban triple jumpers until 1976. Pérez is commonly held to have greatly benefitted from the expertise of his renowned athlete turned coach and he was to jump in the style of the leading Soviet of the day, Viktor Saneyev.

In January 1970, Pérez was to set the first of three Junior World Records, reaching 16.38m in Havana and good enough to break the National Record aged only seventeen, an able demonstration of the burgeoning talents of this tyro. Later that season he made his international debut at the Central American and Caribbean Games in Panama City, Panama, winning Gold with a distance of 16.33m against a limited standard of opposition, the rest of the podium being taken by fellow Cubans. His major international breakthrough was to come the following August in Cali, Colombia, competing in the 1971 Pan American Games, a traditional springboard for the Olympics typically held the subsequent season.

The favourite for the title in Cali was Brazilian Nelson Prudêncio, the 1968 Olympic Silver medallist and one of the World Record breakers from that pulsating final, if only for the few minutes it took for Saneyev to wrest the record back. Prudêncio was in the midst of a career defined by peaks in performance at major championships and despite falling out of the world top twenty in the 1970 season as he pursued his academic studies, he came to Cali full of confidence, aiming to improve on the Silver medal he claimed in the event in 1967. The United States dominated the Pan American Games and had high hopes of adding the triple jump against Latin American rivals such as the improving Cuba, opponents in both the sporting and political environments. American hopes rested with John Craft,[342] later

---

[342] John M. Craft, 1972 Olympian and five-time AAU champion in the triple jump, later a coach [1947-].

fifth placed in the 1972 Olympics and an AAU star both indoors and outdoors, but the duel for the Pan American title in 1971 would be between the novice Cuban and the Brazilian with the major championship pedigree, Craft finishing some way behind in claiming Bronze.

The full jumping order on 5 August 1971 has not survived, yet we know that the Cuban landed a jump of 55ft $6\frac{3}{20}$in (16.92m) on his first attempt, despite a slip causing him to fall on his backside when landing, breaking the great Adhemar da Silva's 1955 Championship Record that had stood since he set his final World Record at high altitude in Mexico City. The *Estadio Olímpico Pascual Guerrero* in Cali is around 1,036m above sea-level, enough to ensure all best marks are qualified as altitude-assisted like Mexico City and in a stadium since commonly dubbed the 'Sports Capital of America' due to its prominence amongst stadia in Latin countries, Pedro Pérez was to achieve a quite unexpected World Record before he had even turned twenty.

[343]Against a backdrop of Cuban athletes choosing to defect whilst in Colombia before the competition, Pérez achieved a result that many had thought unthinkable of a youth athlete from this small island nation and he carved out a unique position in revolutionary sporting history. He had no real major championship experience, yet had a flawless technique for the time and utilising the double-arm take-off method first demonstrated to a global audience by Saneyev to great

---

[343] Pedro Pérez jumping in Cali on 5 August 1971 © unknown

effect in 1968, the Soviet-coached Cuban was able to add over 1m to his career best in the competition, landing four of six jumps over 17m (his five best averaged 17.13m) and finishing 0.5m ahead of Prudêncio.

Pérez's second jump that day went to 57ft 1in (17.40m), 1cm ahead of Saneyev's best mark in Mexico City, with a minimal tailwind of only +0.4m/s and the effects of altitude in Cali barely on the threshold of performance enhancement. It is hard to quantify how astonishing this set of jumps really was from an athlete who was still so young, yet Prudêncio commented how his rival truly deserved the Gold medal and despite his career being in the nascent stages, he was extremely talented, so much so that his leap in Cali stood as the North and Central American U20 mark until 2018.[344] The communist leader of Cuba, Fidel Castro,[345] would later laud his victory as an ideological one over the United States and whilst sporting success was an important part of reshaping the nation's image on the world stage, this was a victory of effort, discipline and perseverance in favourable conditions, when a talented young athlete's body had yet to be slowed by the merciless series of injuries, particularly to his knees, that plagued his later career.

[346]Because as quickly as Pérez would reach the pinnacle of his event with that World Record, the decline in sporting terms would begin. He would *never* land another legal jump over 17m after the 1971 season – a distance of 17.01m when successfully

---

[344] Record broken by a then seventeen-year-old Cuban, Jordan A. Díaz Fortun; he defected to Spain in 2021 but missed the re-scheduled Tokyo Olympics of that year as he did not acquire Spanish citizenship until 2022 [2001-].
[345] Fidel A. Castro Ruz, revolutionary and politician, Cuban leader from 1959-2008 [1926-2016].
[346] Pérez competing in the 1972 Olympics in Munich, West Germany © unknown

defending his Central American and Caribbean Games title in 1974 being over the allowable wind speed – and his World Record would last for just one year, two months and ten days. He went to Munich 1972 in September with only an outside chance of challenging for the podium in a highly competitive field, after an injury suffered in June, when competing in Poland. He had prepared assiduously for the Olympics over the 1972 season and a medal was his dream, but the leg injury hampered him in the qualifying rounds and he failed to progress to the final, finishing a lowly 24th in jumping only 15.72m.

The following season was marred by that injury before a return to form in 1974 when taking a comfortable victory in the Central American and Caribbean Games in the Dominican Republic. He finished that season fourth in the world courtesy of his 16.83m jump in those championships, a wind-assisted distance of 17.01m in the same final, his only leap over 17m since the 1972 season when he broke the World Record. Yet the injury curse was to remain with this talented jumper, missing the Pan American Games in Mexico City in October 1975, when Brazilian João Carlos de Oliveira broke the World Record that Saneyev had reclaimed from Pérez three years previously. Seemingly fully fit once more, the still only twenty-four-year-old Cuban went to the 1976 Olympics in Montreal, Canada, led the final for two rounds after an opening effort of 16.81m, before the agony of another leg injury in the Olympic Games put paid to his hopes of a medal, finishing fourth having not been able to improve on that distance.

[347]Pérez's competitive, top-level career essentially ended in Montreal, with retirement coming in 1978, following chronic knee problems and a failure to regain form and fitness for the Moscow Olympics that year. He had taken up medicine in the mid-1970's and his student obligations influenced his decision to walk away from competition aged only 26. But he was not to walk away from athletics entirely, graduating as a doctor in 1980 and electing to specialise in Sports Science. He worked for the *Instituto Nacional de Deportes, Educación Física y Recreación,* or INDER, the organisation responsible for the development of sports, physical education and recreation in Cuba, before becoming the doctor of the Cuban athletics team for nearly 30 years. In 1986 his achievements and enduring commitment to athletics were recognised with the award of the Olympic Order of Merit and he was later inducted in the regional Athletics Hall of Fame in 2013, before he died in Havana aged only 66, on 18 July 2018.

The first great Cuban triple jumper secured a lifetime position in the revolutionary sporting history of his country by virtue of a phenomenal performance one August day in 1971. In modern sporting parlance he 'had a day', yet by the time of his death he had witnessed his small Caribbean nation become arguably the number one triple jumping country in the world, a great tradition that continues in both the men's and women's events to this day. The real legacy of his World Record performance was to inspire others from an island with no history of triple jumping to follow in his footsteps and amongst a high number of Olympic medals since his retirement, there have been three

---

[347] Dr Pérez in later years © unknown

Cuban born World champions, Yoelbi Quesada[348] in 1997 and Pedro Pichardo[349] in 2022 for the men and two-time women's champion, Yargelis Savigne[350] (2007 & 2009). Pérez's jumping that day in Cali occurred whilst he was in the shape of his life and injuries thereafter prevented him from recapturing that form, but it truly had come out of nowhere for an international audience. His World Record was no fluke, despite never reaching similar distances again and when Saneyev was asked what made the ideal man for the triple jump, he answered with the ultimate compliment to the Cuban, saying, whoever has my strength, Butts'[351] speed and Pérez's technique.[352]

Returning to August 1971 and Viktor Saneyev's *mensis horribilis*,[353] when he lost his World Record to Pérez and was defeated in a major championship for the first time by now-rival Drehmel, we find a great athlete in search of sporting redemption. He had been world number one since the 1968 season, but now had to respond to the setback of being dethroned so crushingly in just one month of competition, despite not being far off his best himself. The 1972 season offered him the chance to defend his Olympic title in Munich, West Germany and the showdown between Saneyev, Drehmel and Pérez was to be much anticipated, although the latter would not figure

---

[348] Yoelbi L. Quesada Fernández, Olympic Bronze medallist in Atlanta 1996, three-time Pan American Games Champion (1991-99) and World Champion in 1997 with a personal best of 17.85m; the most decorated Cuban triple jumper of all time [1973-].
[349] Pedro P. Pichardo Peralta, represented Portugal since August 2019 and holder of the current Olympic, World and European titles; still the Cuban National Record holder with a distance of 18.08m in 2015 [1993-].
[350] Yargelis S. Herrera, two-time World Champion in 2007 & 2009, Olympic Bronze medallist in Beijing 2008 and the Cuban National Record holder since 2007, with a distance of 15.28m. Also World Indoor Champion in 2008, amongst many other major championship medals [1984-].
[351] James A. Butts, Olympic Silver medallist in 1976 and renowned for his ground speed [1950-].
[352] http://www.cubadebate.cu/noticias/2018/07/19/pedro-perez-duenas-reivindicacion-de-un-hombre-record/
[353] Literal Latin translation of 'horrible month', similar to annus mirabilis and annus horribilis, but much less used.

154

in the final itself due to injury. Kept apart in qualifying, lots were drawn to determine the jumping order in the final and the Soviet was fortunate to gain an advantage in jumping ahead of his East German rival.

[354]The Munich 1972 triple jump final took place on 4 September in the Olympic Stadium and whilst Pérez's World Record would prove to be safe, there were big performances from the co-favourites for the title. Saneyev powerfully bounded to a first-round distance of 56ft $11\frac{1}{10}$in (17.35m), said to have kept well inside of the board and with

only a marginally illegal wind of +2.2m/s. Drehmel fouled on his first attempt and only made 17.02m on his second, having taking care to ensure his take-off was legal. He then fouled two further times, the second of which was said to be a record distance, before registering his best jump of the day on his fifth attempt, measured at 17.31m and good enough for an East German record, but only Silver in this final. Saneyev would not improve on his first attempt and had become the fourth man to repeat an Olympic title in the event, Bronze being taken by Brazilian Nelson Prudêncio, another of the record breakers in Mexico City in 1968. Drehmel never regained the form he showed in the two years up to the 1972 Olympics and the rivalry ended in Munich, Saneyev making history as the only track and field champion from Mexico City to repeat.

---

[354] Viktor Saneyev jumping in the 1972 Olympic final © unknown

[355]And the Soviet had further history to make that 1972 season, capping it off in the best possible way. Saneyev was the prototypical Soviet, or Russian, triple jumper, not blessed with great speed but a picture of strength, no description of the great man complete, without mention of his *muscular* figure. He was a strong man in the truest sense and his triple jumping style was based around this attribute, a loping running style in his approach that built to a crescendo as he reached the board, a long and powerful hop, seemingly to the detriment of his final jump with the speed that was lost, yet with an extraordinarily elegant step phase propelled by the technique pioneered by the Soviet jumpers. Saneyev's jumps were characterised by the double-arm rotation of his take-off and the corresponding impact on the step in maintaining speed, now the common method for male triple jumpers, female athletes favouring the single arm technique that values balance over power. Saneyev may not have had the technique of Pedro Pérez, but he had a superior overall strength and balance, allowing him to generate more distance per phase through his three levers (the two arms and one leg that touch the ground, being his *levers*), nowhere more so than on 17 October 1972.

Competing in his hometown of Sokhumi and on the four-year anniversary of his two World Records in Mexico City, the long-legged Saneyev was able to combine all his power and elegance into a jump of

---

[355] Saneyev photographed in c.1972, reproduced in a 1973 Panini sticker album © Public Domain

57ft $2\frac{1}{2}$in (17.44m),[356] a 4cm improvement on Pérez's distance in Cali in August 1971 and a return of the World Record to sea-level, with the last six having been at altitude. It was no surprise to the rest of the world that the leading jumper of his generation had regained the record and even with a headwind of -0.5m/s, the 'Sokhumi Kangaroo' had gone further than any triple jumper in history and was widely considered a habitual winner, on an afternoon where Soviet sources recorded all six of his efforts exceeding 17m and the record coming on his last attempt of the competition.

Further international success followed in September 1974, when he regained the European title in Rome, Italy with a Championship Record of 17.23m, some way in front of Romanian Carol Corbu[357] in second, former rival Drehmel only a distant fourth, despite having the leading jump of the season before Rome. In both 1975 and 1976 he was European Indoor Champion (to be repeated also in 1977) and this chapter titled 'Golden Viktor' is to close with the 1976 Olympics, the end of his career in 1980 and later life picked up in the subsequent chapter. The World Record had been wrested away from Saneyev in October 1975 by João Carlos de Oliveira of Brazil (more on him next too), but his sporting hegemony of the triple jump was to peak as a three-time Olympic Champion in Montreal, Canada, finding the strength necessary to claim what was looking like an unlikely Gold so late in the final.

Only two men had ever been champion in the same track and field event in three consecutive Olympics up to 1976 and Saneyev

---

[356] Ratified as such, but more correctly 57ft $2\frac{6}{10}$in.

[357] Carol Corbu, European indoor champion in 1973 and competed in the 1972 Olympics in both the long and triple jump [1946-].

entered competition bidding to emulate John Flanagan[358] (hammer) and Al Oerter[359] (discus) of the United States, the latter having been victorious in four consecutive Games. The Soviet had lost his status as the World Record holder the preceding October and this Olympic final was being billed as a showdown between him and de Oliveira, Saneyev the last World Record holder with a hop-dominated style and the twenty-two-year-old Brazilian the first with a true jump-dominated technique. Saneyev had enjoyed near total supremacy in the event since the 1968 Olympic final, but the budding superstar from South America was the favourite for Gold, having improved the record by nearly 0.5m, to this day still the largest single improvement in the event's best mark.

The twelve athletes that qualified for the Olympic triple jump final on 30 July 1976, included three past or current World Record holders in Saneyev, Pérez and de Oliveira, the 1973 European Indoor Champion Carol Corbu of Romania and James Butts of the United States, already renowned for his runway speed and a sign that this sporting powerhouse of a nation was now beginning to take the event seriously. Pérez was determined to make up for the disappointment he suffered when injured in 1972 and he was to lead the final after the first two rounds, a distance of 16.81m comfortably ahead of his two main rivals, Butts then being in second.

The co-favourites had both fouled on their opening jumps in the final and despite being the leading jumper in qualifying the day before, de Oliveira was clearly hampered from the stomach surgery he had required just before the Games. This was his first Olympics and

---

[358] John J. Flanagan, Irish American champion of the hammer throw in three Olympics, 1900, 1904 & 1908 and one of the Irish Whales referred to in the 'Irish Trailblazers' chapter [1868-1938].
[359] Alfred 'Al' Oerter Jr., four-time Olympic Champion in the discus, 1956-68; one of only six Olympians to win Gold in the same individual event at four consecutive Games, with fellow American Carl Lewis the only other from athletics; an inductee to the IAAF Hall of Fame [1936-2007].

he later admitted to being nervous, but his physical condition would mean that he was a long way from being in peak fitness, as he had been when setting the World Record in the 1975 Pan American Games. Pérez would sadly pick up his own second injury in an Olympic final to see his challenge fade after taking that early lead and with de Oliveira lacklustre, the Soviet star seemingly had a clear run to a third Gold medal and a place in Olympic history...

[360]Saneyev moved into the lead with a third-round attempt of 17.06m, the first man over that threshold in the final and de Oliveira followed him with a respectable 16.85m to go second. In the fourth round, Butts of the United States threw down the gauntlet to the Soviet with a then career best distance of 17.18m and he admitted later that he started to dream of victory, wistfully saying in a 1978 interview that, "I had the Gold in my pocket".[361] What the American had not accounted for though, was the grit and determination so inherent in the character of this great Soviet athlete and particularly evident in his major championship record. So, on his fifth attempt, Saneyev, in the words of a rueful Butts in that interview, "came down the runway like a madman... even I had to applaud."

That fifth jump reached 56ft $8\frac{7}{10}$in (17.29m) and would claim a famous third Gold medal for Saneyev, elevating him into exalted company in the Olympic track and field pantheon. The athletics 'three-peat' at the Olympics has been achieved a number of times since, most

---

[360] Viktor Saneyev jumping in the 1976 Olympic final, his face a picture of determination © unknown
[361] Marshall, *op. cit.*

notably by Jamaican Usain Bolt[362] who did it in both the 100m and the 200m, but in 1976 it was much rarer still and gave him legendary status in his sport. He had edged the American by 11cm and with de Oliveira no better than 16.90m on his final jump in finishing third, the record books make his third Gold look a straightforward affair, yet to do so he had been forced to find strength beyond that which even he was by then renowned for. Saneyev was the leading star of the Soviet athletics system, a symbol throughout the world of the supremacy of their political and social ideologies, and his status would grow further as the extension of the Cold War into international sports reached a nadir in the 1980 Olympics, where he was *expected* by his political masters to win them a fourth consecutive Gold in Moscow.

05.08.1971 WR(A) 17.40m (57ft 1in) Pedro Pérez (CUB) Cali, Colombia (+0.4m/s)

17.10.1972 WR 17.44m (57ft $2\frac{1}{2}$in) Viktor Saneyev (URS) Sokhumi, Soviet Union (-0.5m/s)

---

[362] Usain St.L. Bolt, eleven-time World Champion, eight-time Olympic Gold medallist from 2008-16, widely considered the greatest sprinter of all time and still the World Record holder in the 100m, 200m and 4x100m relay [1986-].

Part 3 – Step

The *Step* phase is the one that differentiates the elite athletes from the rest and is the most difficult to master. A novice or inexperienced jumper will use the step as a *link* phase and this will reduce the distance covered in a triple jump, overall length a result of three balanced phases or two balanced and one long, whether that be hop-dominated or jump-dominated. An athlete who over-emphasises the hop will be fighting against the effects of that predominance in the step, with a corresponding loss of velocity and they will have to propel themselves forward again, rather than have the forward momentum from the hop do that for them. The fundamental part of a successful step is to get off the ground as quickly as possible and this is what the great Willie Banks has called pawing the ground like a horse (more on this later).

This pawing of the ground is best described as an *active* landing and is necessary in both the hop and step phases to optimise distance by mitigating the impact of your foot with the ground. In essence, the trick is to rake the landing foot backwards upon impact, not only to break the gravitational pull of the impact (c.20 times bodyweight!), but to actually make it work for you and propel you into the next phase of your jump, hence the term 'active'. As the athlete lifts off the ground in the step, the leading knee is high, being almost parallel to the hips and the trailing leg is swung assertively to maximise distance. There can be no waste of movement in the step phase and both arms and posture have to be correct, to achieve the greater distances. It also helps to be powerful and some triple jumpers from the early days of the event, such as Nick Winter, have been noted for the size of their ankles in particular (his commonly said to be almost twice normal size), which help to absorb of the impact of the force that occurs on landing; he was such a powerful jumper, that he was said to bound or spring through each phase,[363] very different from the evolved techniques on display from the 1950's. A good step phase will see the athlete gain height once again – the body held in shape to achieve a 'hang' effect in mid-air – and its effectiveness is measured by how successfully it sets up the jump phase, primarily the *flight* into the jump.

---

[363] *Sporting Globe*, 1 January 1941

MISCHIEF IN MOSCOW

'Let people only have rivalry in sports arenas'[364]

We return to 15 October 1975 and the Pan American Games in Mexico City, when young Brazilian João Carlos de Oliveira broke Viktor Saneyev's near three-year-old World Record. The Soviet athlete had returned the record to sea-level in October 1972 in his hometown of Sokhumi, competing for the 'Saneyev Prize', a tangerine wreath named in his honour and awarded to the winner of this local competition, the fruit motif a nod to his academic studies in the cultivation of sub-tropical crops.[365] De Oliveira was a twenty-one-year-old, 55ft jumper before those Pan American Games, but in the same rarefied air that had propelled Adhemar da Silva to a world best in 1955, then seen five new marks achieved in that storied 1968 Olympics, he astonished the world. He set an absolute figure that would not be beaten for nearly ten years, a period in which Cold War tensions would pervade the sport of athletics in particular and in which the Brazilian would remain an increasingly tragic but central figure, before the United States established a superiority over the Soviet/Russian athletes in the triple jump that has never been lifted.

[366]**João Carlos de Oliveira** was born on 28 May 1954 in Pindamonhangaba, São Paulo state, one of at least eight boys, orphaned young and washing cars to make a living as a youngster, before later becoming a mechanic in

---

[364] Part of a greeting from Soviet cosmonauts at the opening ceremony of the Moscow Games.

[365] Srebnitsky, *op. cit.*

[366] A young João Carlos de Oliveira © unknown

a Volkswagen car dealership. His was a humble background and he remained grounded throughout his short life, even when later twice elected a state, or parliamentary, deputy in São Paulo. He began to make a name for himself on the school sports court as a tall and thin boy, exceeding all the sandpits laid out for his jumping training, graduating to specialist training at the local Army barracks under the auspices of his first coach. He gained regional prominence in a championship held in Cruzeiro, winning the 100m, long jump and high jump,[367] then being identified through his physical power as perfect for the specialty of Brazilian athletics, the triple jump, and not the long jump that he had favoured as a boy. He was to now follow in the footsteps of two World Record holders, Brazilian athletics royalty in Adhemar da Silva and Nelson Prudêncio, the later then still competing.

De Oliveira had caught the attention of an Army Colonel, Quirino Carneiro Rennó, in those regional championships and being also involved in athletics in São Paulo, he encouraged the talented boy to leave the countryside and follow his dream. At 18 he moved to São Paulo, joining the Army in the state capital, with the goal to continue his training as an athlete. He initially joined the *São Paulo Futebol Clube* of the great triple jumper Adhemar da Silva, soon moving to *Esporte Clube Pinheiros*, or EPC, where he met the coach who would remain alongside him throughout his career, Pedro Henrique de Toledo,[368] known as Pedrão ('Big Pedro') or more recently in Brazil, the 'King of Athletics'. At the traditional EPC he experienced oblique racism, in much the way that fellow black Brazilian Adhemar da Silva had also suffered from hypocritical behaviours and disguised attitudes, but his

---

[367] https://www.uol.com.br/esporte/reportagens-especiais/a-morte-tripla-de-joao-do-pulo/#page7
[368] Professor Pedro Henrique C. de Toledo, coach of the Brazil athletics team at four Olympic Games, amongst various other positions within Brazilian sport [n/k-n/k].

was a talent that could not be ignored and with his irrepressible character he soon won over the conservative members of the club.

He is commonly said to have broken the World Junior Record in 1973 in a South American Championship with a jump of 14.75m,[369] but it is known for sure that he reached 14.67m in October 1972, aged eighteen, when winning the South American Junior Championships in Asunción, Paraguay. His first notable regional victory in adult competition came at the 1974 South American Championships in Athletics in Chile, ahead of countryman Nelson Prudêncio, Silver medallist and a brief World Record holder in the 1968 Olympics, then third in the 1972 Olympics. De Oliveira broke the Championship Record with a leap of 16.34m and in a feature of his career, also finished third in the long jump. By the start of the 1975 season, he was already well known in Brazil as both a triple and long jumper, but the rest of the world had yet to know what 'João do Pulo', or 'Jumping John', as he had become known at home, was fully capable of.

That 1974 South American Championships in Chile had established him a competitor of weight in the region and he had a personal best of 16.74m before the 1975 season. He had been mentored in these early years by Prudêncio, who at 31 was approaching the end of his career, but it was the elder Brazilian who went to the 1975 Pan American Games in Mexico City, with the goal of breaking Saneyev's World Record whilst at high-altitude. De Oliveira was by now a Corporal in the Army, long-legged and similar in height to Saneyev at 6ft 1 in (1.86m), but always described as slender or agile, in being noticeably lither than the well-muscled Soviet. He was a naturally talented jumper which gave rise to the 'João do Pulo' moniker by which

---

[369] No record of this jump or championship of that name in 1973 can be found; see record claimed in https://www.geledes.org.br/a-historia-de-joao-do-pulo-um-icones-do-esporte-brasileiro/

he was forever known, in contrast to the Soviet who was an impressive athlete who through dedicated training became a master triple jumper and it was the young Brazilian who was about to announce himself in some style on the world stage as a growing rival to the Soviet.

[370]De Oliveira entered both the long and triple jump in the 1975 Pan American Games, winning the former on 13 October with a distance of 8.19m and came to the triple jump final two days later full of confidence. Prudêncio was the favourite for Gold with his Olympic pedigree and had been second in both the 1967 and 1971 Pan American Games, but this time he

really wanted the World Record, in such favourable conditions at altitude. The main challengers were expected to be Tommy Haynes[371] and Milan Tiff[372] of the United States, the nation fielding an increasing number of elite-level competitors in the discipline and it was Tiff who took a first-round lead, before Haynes broke the National Record on his second attempt in reaching 17.20m. Prudêncio was disappointing in registering a best effort of only 16.85m to finish behind the Americans and just as he had witnessed Pedro Pérez break the World Record in August 1971, he was to be a bystander to another astonishing moment in triple jump history, 'João do Pulo' setting a new landmark with a leap of 58ft $8\frac{1}{4}$in (17.89m),[373] the older Brazilian remarking later

[370] João Carlos de Oliveira breaking the World Record on 15 October 1975 © unknown
[371] Thomas 'Tommy' Z. Haynes, Silver medallist in the 1975 Pan American Games and fifth in the 1976 Olympics [1952-].
[372] Milan Tiff, also sometime known as Caleb A. Rahman, Bronze in the 1975 Pan American Games, five-time National Champion in the triple jump and later competed in Masters athletics into his 60's [1949-].
[373] Recorded as such when the record was ratified, but more correctly 58ft $8\frac{3}{10}$in.

he "was travelling at 900km per hour and João Carlos was travelling at the speed of light."[374]

[375]This distance was the greatest single improvement in the men's triple jump World Record and remains as such today. The twenty-one-year-old was at the pinnacle of his sport and the achievement was to raise him to iconic status in Brazilian sport, the charismatic young athlete proudly showing off his two Golds on his return home as soon as he got off the plane and the 'Jumping John' moniker was permanently attributed to him. He had truly made his name with just one jump into the record books and reinforced his nation's reputation for first-rate triple jumping, the country's musical heritage and sense of rhythm inherent in any self-respecting young Brazilian, metaphorically represented in the vitality of their jumping.

The now World Record holder was the favourite for the 1976 Olympics the following summer in Montreal, but his personal choice to compete in both the triple and long jumps – the latter final was the day before the triple jump – and surgery on his stomach in the run-up to the Games hampered him. He finished fifth in the long jump and third in the triple jump, a combination of the injury and nerves leading to an inhibited performance in the event he was expected to win, as we saw in the preceding chapter, but he still ended the year as the world number one, courtesy of a jump of 17.38m in Rio de Janeiro in late August. The following season would be a down year for both Saneyev

---

[374] https://www.cbat.org.br/atletas/nelson.asp
[375] João do Pulo proudly shows off the medals he won in the 1975 Pan American Games on his triumphant return to Brazil © unknown

and de Oliveira, the former struggling with ankle injuries that required surgery, the first time in his career that the incredibly durable athlete had been out of action for long periods and his final European indoor title that March was to be his last major competition victory, this season also being the first since 1967 that he failed to reach 17m. 'Father Time' was catching up with the three-time Olympic triple jump champion and in de Oliveira, he had a much younger and dangerous rival, world number one in both 1978 and 1979.

Despite being thirty-four-years-old as the 1980 season opened, Saneyev would reach the summer knowing he had a strong chance of winning his fourth consecutive Gold medal in that year's Olympics on Soviet soil. His gritty victory in Montreal in 1976 had reinforced his reputation as a fearsome competitor and despite the 1977 season seeing him struggle with injury, he had reclaimed the USSR title in 1978 for the eighth and final time, although by the end of the 1979 season he was only ranked 9th in the world and had been disappointing when placing second to Miloš Srejović[376] of Yugoslavia in the 1978 European Championships in Prague. Politicians had always used sport to further their own ends and in early 1980 with the Cold War at its peak, Saneyev would see many of the main challengers fall by the wayside and improve his own medal prospects, before the Games had even begun.

'João do Pulo' was now the leading jumper in the world and in July 1979 had retained both of his horizontal jumping titles at the Pan American Games in San Juan, Puerto Rico, but second and third on the triple jump podium were Americans and this heralded a renewed interest in the event from the sporting superpower of the West. The United States had claimed the first three Olympic titles in the event up to 1904, then since been ambivalent about it at best, with James Butts'

---

[376] Miloš Srejović, European Champion in 1978 and the Serbian National Record holder from 1981 [1956-].

Silver in Montreal their first Olympic medal in the discipline since 1928 and the long jump regularly favoured by their leading athletes. By the late 1970's they had a number of elite-level jumpers, with Willie Banks (Silver) and Butts (Bronze) on the podium in the 1979 Pan American Games, Ron Livers[377] the leading jumper in the world in 1977 as a student and Milan Tiff heavily favoured to challenge for Gold in Moscow 1980, but for all these athletes from the United States, the chance to participate was denied by their own government.

Western governments had faced calls for an Olympic boycott from activists from the 1970's in response to Soviet human rights abuses, yet there had been little support in the proposal. This changed with the Soviet intervention, more correctly an invasion, of Afghanistan in December 1979 and with the Western world horrified that Soviet ambitions could extend further if left unchecked, the United States proposed a series of sanctions, including an international boycott of the Games if the Soviet Union did not withdraw its forces. The deadline in mid-January 1980 came and went, and with attempts to mediate by the IOC unsuccessful, no United States athletes were ultimately able to participate. Many other Western nations joined the boycott in varying degrees, Great Britain putting the decision down to sporting associations and individual athletes, but the reality was that a great many athletes would not be able to realise their Olympic dream and the sporting integrity of that year's competition would be adversely affected.

The United States and Soviet Union had been engaged in a proxy war since the 1950's and the boycott of the 1980 Olympics is the

---

[377] Ronald W. Livers, world number one in 1977 as a student athlete, and winner of three NCAA Championships; in the Gill Athletics podcast quoted here and hosted by Mike Cunningham, Banks thought the 5ft 8in Livers, who had longer legs than Banks, could have been the greatest triple jumper in the world, if he had not had the diving accident that ended his career [1955-2020].

most notorious example of Cold War tensions pervading the sporting world. The Olympics had always been politicised, despite its stated ideals, most demonstrably with the allocation of each Games host and in hindsight it was clear that the decision of President Jimmy Carter[378] of the United States achieved very little impact on the global stage. Triple jumpers Wille Banks and Milan Tiff were widely expected to be selected and challenge for a medal, but once President Carter announced on 21 March 1980 that the team would not be going to Moscow, their Olympic opportunity was denied, the later United States Olympic Trials in June poorly represented, with the triple jumpers officially 'selected' for the *paper* 1980 team being Banks, Greg Caldwell[379] and Paul Jordan.[380] An opportunity had been denied to a generation of leading athletes from the United States, but for the aging Soviet star in Viktor Saneyev, this was an opportunity he did not want to spurn.

The 1980 Olympic triple jump final took place on 24 July and would see only two returning athletes from the 1976 final, in Saneyev and de Oliveira. The former came into the competition with a season best of 16.78m and with five of the finalists already exceeding 17m that year, a fourth Gold medal did not seem likely, at least on paper. He came to the final having suffered repeated injuries in training and his legs ached so much he could not make a single jump in his warm-up. He wore a bandage below his right knee and visibly limped after each effort, but on Soviet soil, with 80,000 partisan fans vociferously supporting both him and the largely unknown Estonian Jaak

---

[378] James 'Jimmy' E. Carter Jr., the 39th President of the United States, from 1977-81 [1924-].
[379] Greg Caldwell, later finished sixth in the 1984 Olympic Trials [1957-].
[380] Paul Jordan, 1980 AAU champion [1956-].

Uudmäe,[381] the hopes of the Soviet Union rested on his shoulders, and whilst he would demonstrably summon every sinew of his famous strength in making his best jump of the day in the last round, this was the "triple jump-gate"[382] final and all was not as it seemed...

Against the backdrop of the Western boycott of the Games, the Soviets were determined that their athletes would represent the nation *well*. The stories of what this determination amounted to in Moscow are legion – de Oliveira being booed vociferously on each of his attempts through to the stadium gates being opened when Soviet athletes were competing in the javelin in order to benefit from the draft – but it is commonly held now that at best the officiating in the triple jump final was poor and at worst, the triple jump competition was fixed so Saneyev would win his fourth Gold and match the great American Olympian Al Oerter. Ours is a narrative rather than investigatory account, yet what transpired in the Lenin Stadium in that final suggests that 'João do Pulo' was denied the opportunity to win the Gold his performance that day deserved and the wrong Soviet athlete ironically ended up as the victor.

With the IAAF allowing their judges to be pulled in favour of local judges for the triple jump competition, a preposterous situation that continued into other events for at least a week, the favourite from Brazil was in the lead after the first two rounds with a best effort of 16.96m. Much action took place in the third round which was to set up a grandstand finish where Saneyev was the central figure. Uudmäe surprised all with a jump of 56ft 11in (17.35m) in the third-round – his career best – to take the lead and the Brazilian could only respond that

---

[381] Jaak Uudmäe, triple jump Olympic Gold medallist in 1980, European Cup winner in 1981 and still the Estonian record holder [1954-].
[382] 'Cheating the only conclusion you can jump to', Tim Lane, *Sydney Morning Herald*, 18 August 2013

round with a leap of 17.22m. Ian Campbell[383] of Australia had preceded Uudmäe in the third-round and landed beyond the Olympic Record marker in the sandpit, but his effort was quickly ruled a foul for scraping his foot in the step phase, an unlikely occurrence at the speed an elite triple jumper moves, with the sandpit too quickly smoothed over before he could fully appeal. In that final, Campbell and de Oliveira had a combined nine of twelve jumps ruled as fouls and despite the Estonian Uudmäe later suggesting the fouls could have been because of rapidly changing wind conditions,[384] both athletes were to see jumps beyond the winning distance discarded by the judges for no obvious reason.

[385]The stage was thus set for Saneyev to win the title with the final jump of the sixth round. De Oliveira, derided as nervy, as he admittedly had been in 1976, but more likely the victim of what he was later convinced was a Soviet conspiracy, could never improve on the third-round 17.22m and sat in second place. A visibly stricken Saneyev was to call on all of his

competitive spirit and grit for that last ever jump in competition, and despite edging past the Brazilian with a distance of 17.24m, itself a remarkable effort and against all the odds, it was only good enough for Silver, Uudmäe taking an unexpected victory for the Soviet Union. The Estonian disappeared from the top level of his sport as quickly as he reached it and to this day Ian Campbell is more well known for *not*

[383] Ian B. Campbell, fifth in the 1980 Olympic triple jump final and Silver medallist in the 1978 Commonwealth Games [1957-].
[384] https://uk.sports.yahoo.com/news/robbed-at-the-1980-olympics-123321307.html
[385] Viktor Saneyev competing in his fourth and final Olympics in 1980 © unknown

winning a medal in that final when coming fifth, the most maligned of all the competitors, with only one jump allowed to stand.

Saneyev retired after Moscow as the then greatest triple jumper of all time and the still the only one in his event, male or female, to have won four Olympic medals. In a post-competition interview, he commented that "the 1980 Olympics were the most difficult of the Games... perhaps my Silver medal would be as good as a Gold some other time."[386] He was correct to reference the challenge he had faced as a near thirty-five-year-old, literally on his last competitive legs, so whilst he was denied a fairy-tale ending, it was still a fine way to end his magnificent career. In his sporting twilight, he had been honoured with carrying the Olympic Torch into the stadium, despite being Georgian-born rather than Russian and on 'home' soil he was the most visible symbol of Soviet sporting superiority to the rest of the world. The Soviet Union had now claimed the Olympic triple jump title for four Games in a row and even allowing for the 'what-ifs' about the United States stars absent from Moscow, this was to prove the high point in the sport for the country, particularly poignant as the prototypical Soviet jumper Saneyev went into retirement.

[387]This had been expected to be the *great* Olympics for 'Jumping John' and he went home bitterly disappointed with a Bronze. He had put on a brave face on the podium – Uudmäe invited the other medallists to share the top step with him as a mark of respect – and Saneyev referenced him behaving with great dignity in that October 1980 article, but his coach, 'Big Pedro', in interviews

[386] 'UNFORGETTABLE MOMENTS', *Soviet Life*, No. 10, October 1980
[387] João do Pulo competing in Moscow 1980 © unknown

subsequent to the staggering tragedy that would shortly befall the still young athlete, would always tell of him being in tears on the bus leaving the stadium, saying repeatedly that he had been cheated. His had been a stubborn performance in that final and he showed all the qualities of a great champion, yet he never got another chance to claim the major international title he so craved and he was to be truly cheated on the night of 21 December 1981.

On that night, de Oliveira left his Army barracks with a brother and a friend, and in the dark his car was tragically hit head on by a car travelling in the opposite direction that had veered into his lane, killing the other (drunk) driver instantly. News of his accident shocked Brazil and his life was initially in the balance, his countrymen on tenterhooks as his accident dominated the news headlines. He was a national hero, four-time Pan American Games Gold medallist, two-time Olympic medallist and the incumbent World Record holder. He was still only twenty-seven-years-old at the time of the crash and despite attempts to save his badly injured right leg, it was eventually amputated nine months after his accident. The once-brilliant jumper was physically no longer 'Jumping John' and the coming years would prove yet further how that sporting adversity in Moscow was only half the real tragedy, being 'cheated' of an Olympic medal in a life he never imagined and then cheated out of that life altogether.

In December 1981, de Oliveira had been a triple jumper in the peak of his career and we will never know what he would have still achieved if he had not had the misfortune to come across a drunk driver that night. His career had been brilliant and in winning the first three IAAF World Cup events in 1977, 1979 and 1981 – the latter in September of that year, only three months before the car crash – he was considered the best triple jumper on the planet (the World Championships were only inaugurated in 1983). He was to win the fight for his life in surviving the accident and subsequent complications, but life itself would eventually prove too much for this once bright and charismatic man. Being so famous in a country where retired sportsmen have always turned to politics, he was twice elected a state deputy, but a defeat at a third election in 1998 and a series of failed businesses sent him into a depression that continued until the end of his life. He died on 29 May 1999 in hospital in São Paulo and whether it was pneumonia, liver disease, contaminated blood (said to be from a transfusion at the time of his accident) or just his avowed depression, he left two children from different marriages who sadly had no common ground or relationship between them beyond sharing a famous father, a fracture that has never healed.

'Jumping John' was a great athlete befallen by sporting tragedy, leading to a personal crisis that curtailed his life, aged only 45. To watch videos of him is to see him in all his elastic glory, agile and flexible when transitioning through the phases of his jump and it is easy to see why his coach would say he was physically close to perfection. 'Big Pedro' commented that he was a freak, someone that the technician (or coach) could "...even teach wrong that he ends up doing the right thing."[388] His sporting legacy is that his World Record would survive for nine years, eight months and one day, and his South American and Brazilian record would not be beaten until 2007,[389] then by 1cm only and still to be improved further at the time of writing.

To end this chapter, we must return to the pre-eminent jumper of the period, who had missed out on a fourth consecutive Gold by only 11cm in Moscow. Viktor Saneyev coached the Soviet jumping

---

[388] https://www.uol.com.br/esporte/reportagens-especiais/a-morte-tripla-de-joao-do-pulo/#page10
[389] Broken by Jadel A. G. Gregório, sixth in the 2008 Olympic final, Silver medallist in the 2007 World Championships and 2007 Pan American Games Champion; also coached by Pedro Henrique de Toledo [1980-].

team following his retirement and later returned to his formative club, Dynamo Tbilisi. He was to find that life as a retired athlete in the Soviet Union was not as favourable as it had been when he was on a pedestal and in the early 1990's the breakup of the USSR led to a civil war in Georgia. Offered a contract to coach at a university in Sydney, he left his home on the Black Sea and found a new one on Australian shores. His wife Tatiana (Yana) and son Alex went with him, and whilst the following years were not easy – his first contract came to an end so he worked odd jobs, including delivering pizzas and he briefly considered selling his Olympic medals for what would have been a pittance – he found happiness coaching at the New South Wales Institute of Sport. He passed away in his sleep on 3 January 2022 aged 76 and following his death, the huge number of articles that announced his passing demonstrated the depth of feeling about this legendary athlete, even 40 years after he had retired.

Leonid Shcherbakov had started a tradition of Soviet triple jumping that Viktor Saneyev took to the highest heights, his Silver in Moscow 1980 the eighth consecutive Games that a Soviet athlete was on the podium. In 1972 he had been awarded the Order of Lenin, the highest civilian decoration in the Soviet Union and he was later honoured by the IAAF when he was inducted into their Hall of Fame in 2013, the criteria at that time requiring at least two Olympic or World titles and at least one World Record, benchmarks he easily surpassed. And *surpassed* is the best word to describe the impact of Saneyev. He made over 60 career jumps beyond 17m and remarkably dominated a 'golden generation' of triple jumpers for over a decade. He has long been part of the conversation about who is the greatest triple jumper of all time and any determination of *greatness* that considers how an athlete fared against the best competition of the time, must always have him as the finest example. He beat everyone and did so repeatedly, over many years and avenged all his major defeats, with only the inevitability of age and injury eventually knocking him off his pedestal.

15.10.1975 WR(A) 17.89m (58ft 8$\frac{1}{4}$in) João Carlos de Oliveira (BRA) Mexico City, Mexico (0.0m/s)

HAND-CLAPPING WILLIE

"Why are they so quiet? I need noise!"[390]

The decade after the Moscow Olympics would see the triple jump enter the mainstream, both in terms of the number of superior athletes dedicating themselves to the event and the wider interest of the sporting public. Repeat champions – and medallists – in major competitions had been frequent in the sport until the 1980's, but as the United States awoke to the triple jump being a discipline in its own right and not just an extra competition for long jumpers, the most *obscure* of the field events would finally come to prominence, with American athletes front and centre, including Al Joyner[391] and Mike Conley,[392] Olympic Champions in 1984 and 1992 respectively, amongst a number of other major accolades for the latter. This chapter is named after one American athlete, but the story of this period is of the *other* sporting superpower taking on the mantle of the leading triple jumping nation in the world and the collective riposte to the hegemony of the Soviet Union, their wider geo-political Cold War nemesis.

The biggest personality of this era was Willie Banks of the United States, the man who would return the World Record to sea-

---

[390] 'THE BOUNDING BARRISTER', Anita Verschoth, *Sports Illustrated*, 17 May 1982
[391] Alfrederick 'Al' Joyner, Gold medallist in the triple jump at Los Angeles 1984 and latterly a track coach [1960-]; husband of Florence Griffith Joyner, notable American sprinter with three Olympic Golds in 1984 & 1988 and World Records in the 100m & 200m who died of an epileptic seizure aged only 38, and brother of Jackie Joyner-Kersee, winner of three Golds, one Silver and two Bronze medals in the heptathlon and long jump across four Olympic Games (1984-96).
[392] Michael A. Conley Sr., Olympic triple jump champion in 1992, Silver medallist in 1984 and World Champion in 1993, amongst a host of other victories; nine-time NCAA Champion whilst at the University of Arkansas and six-time world number one in the triple jump. Inducted into the United States National Track and Field Hall of Fame in 1994 and now an agent for a number of basketball stars, including his son Mike Conley Jr. [1962-].

level in June 1985 and impact his sport more figuratively than those whose sporting laurels far outweighed what chance and circumstance allowed him to achieve in his own period in the sporting spotlight. In 1980, the then twenty-four-year-old Willie Banks had been one of the leading jumpers in the world, ranked second before the Olympic final in Moscow with a season best of 17.13m. He had beaten all of the other big-name jumpers and had a strong chance of claiming Gold, hoping to become the first Olympic triple jump champion from the United States since 1904.

Then came the most politically charged Olympics in modern history, with the United States-led boycott depriving him of the chance to compete, forced to watch from afar as his early season best would have been enough to place fourth in that final, without even considering how he could have improved further in an Olympic final, the most fertile of surroundings throughout the sport's history. His athletic peak had been seemingly robbed of its signature moment, but the man who would later be widely known as 'The Bounding Barrister' and invent the rhythmic hand-clapping, or 'Jumpers Clap', now commonplace at athletics events worldwide, would still cement his place in triple jump history in some style, and perhaps even be responsible for saving the sport...

[393]**William Augustus Banks III** was born on 11 March 1956 at Travis Air Force Base, Northern California and would grow up near Carlsbad, Southern California. Growing up in a military family with a disciplinarian but fair father with whom he shared his name, his mother Georgia was the constant figure in his

---

[393] Willie Banks competing indoor in the Ostseehalle, Kiel, West Germany in 1984 © Society for Kiel City History

life, his father even after retirement from the United States Marine Corps in 1973 free at weekends only, due to the busy civilian job he then had working for the Air Force. His father set high standards for Willie and his four brothers and sisters, yet with work requiring his complete weekday focus, it was their mother who was the prime educator of the children and from her he gained his *direction*, sensing that opportunities can be limited and to grab each one with both hands, saying later himself that he "didn't want to miss out on anything... I was probably the luckiest kid in the family."[394]

And it was this sense of being open to learning that was to serve the young Willie Banks so well, as both a student-athlete and then throughout a career on the world athletics stage that continues to this day. At Oceanside High School in California, he was first a prominent long jumper before he excelled in the horizontal jump in which he would become famous and as we have seen before in this narrative, the triple jump was to *find* him. As a talented athlete who had tried the high jump, hurdles and the long jump, in 1973 his school included the triple jump in their programme for the first time and the energetic Banks was open to something new, already good enough to have competed in the state championships in the long jump. The school's cross-country and track coach had never coached the event before, but learning from a combination of books and film, he had to double the length of the school's sandpit, with Banks "popping 44-foot triples straight off the bat".[395]

Banks quickly proved himself to be a talented triple jumper as a high school junior and seeking knowledge wherever and whenever the opportunity arose, he improved his technique from such diverse sources as rival athletes in competition and most importantly a middle-

---

[394] Verschoth, *op. cit.*
[395] Verschoth, *op. cit.*

aged Oceanside High history teacher, named Bill Christopher.[396] The teacher had competed in the then rarely contested hop, step and jump in his home-state of Louisiana in the 1940's, before being a star athlete at Rice University in Texas and from him Banks learnt of the need for a consistent rhythm, being "tom, tom, tom, not tom, tatom."[397] In Banks' words, the teacher taught him "to go hop and then a long step, rather than a hop, skip, jump,"[398] improving from a 36-39ft to 45-46ft triple jumper and he felt lucky to have come into contact with the older man, who he said in a 2020 interview would have been an Olympian if not for the Second World War.[399] Banks had struggled with the step, in common with many novice jumpers and improvement of the middle phase is often seen as crucial in increasing the overall distance in a triple jump. There followed state titles in the triple jump in 1973 and 1974, in the latter setting a new meet record when exceeding 50ft 7in (15.42m)[400] and he only lost once in high school.[401]

After Oceanside High, Banks went to the illustrious University of California, Los Angeles (UCLA), the college he had set his heart on at elementary school yet still allowed famed UCLA track coach Jim Bush[402] to heavily recruit him for two years, even then aware of his own rising value as an athlete. At Oceanside High he was involved in student politics and had attained various positions of responsibility, latterly being vice-president of the student body in his junior and senior

---

[396] Willard 'Bill' N. Christopher, NCAA long jump champion in 1943, two-time All-American at Rice University and United States Marine Corps veteran of three wars; later inducted into the Rice University Athletic Hall of Fame [1921-2004].
[397] Verschoth, *op. cit.*
[398] '#63: Willie Banks-world record holder, Olympian, Triple Jump KING', *The Gill Athletics Track and Field Connections Podcast*, host Mike Cunningham, 10 August 2020
[399] Cunningham, *op. cit.*
[400] Verschoth, *op. cit.*
[401] Cunningham, *op. cit.*
[402] James 'Jim' S. Bush, long-time collegiate track coach, inducted into the USA Track and Field Hall of Fame in 1987; coached nearly 30 Olympians during his career [1926-2017].

years. It should be no surprise then that he went to UCLA more for its leading political science department than for athletics, but it happened to be more than coincidence that the man eager to learn in all facets of his life would choose to attend the college that turned out some of the best triple jumpers in the United States, including Milan Tiff and James Butts.

In 1975 the rising star began to make a name for himself on a national basis. On 3 May in Drake Stadium, Westwood, California, UCLA took on local rivals USC (University of Southern California) in what was always a fiercely contested match in front of 15,000 spectators and Banks was favoured to podium in the triple jump, but no better. He first competed in the long jump that day and found himself a surprise winner; the triple jump competition then ran on longer than scheduled and in a quirk of fate, the entire meeting was to be decided on this final event... and on Banks' last attempt. The UCLA tyro was roared down the runway by the home crowd – having been heckled by famous USC alumnus O. J. Simpson[403] who shouted "you'll never make it"[404] – and in landing a jump 2ft further than he had ever gone before, he emerged as the hero of the day, the UCLA team claiming overall victory with Banks triumphantly carried off the field by his teammates. His jump of 55ft 1in (16.79m) was enough for him to be ranked 11th in the world at season's end and he was emerging as an elite level triple jumper.

---

[403] Orenthal 'O. J.' J. Simpson, former American football running back, 1967 national champion at USC, the 1st overall draft pick in 1969 in the National Football League (NFL, American football) and had a storied career in the NFL, capped off with the 1973 Most Valuable Player award and inducted to the Pro Football Hall of Fame in 1983; later an actor and broadcaster, before a notorious court case in 1994 where has was acquitted of murdering his ex-wife and her friend derailed his career. Later imprisoned in 2008 for armed robbery and imprisonment, being released in 2017 [1947-].
[404] Cunningham, *op. cit.*

To this day, some still consider Banks' performance in that unofficial national title deciding UCLA-USC dual-meet to be his greatest moment. His winning jump was to prove the national outdoor best that season for the triple jump and his victory in the long jump came against supreme odds in upsetting 1972 Olympic Champion, Randy Williams[405] of USC, who the following year was to claim Olympic Silver in Montreal. The nineteen-year-old freshman who stood on the triple jump runway waiting to decide the outcome of the meet was under enormous pressure, yet UCLA coach Jim Bush later recalled him saying to himself "55 feet, 55 feet" over and over, and Banks himself said that he was so focussed, "all I could see was the end of the pit... I never saw the board."[406] Thereafter Banks was to command the attention of fans and with his constant smile he only endeared himself to them further. He was full of energy and joy, an athlete of promise but that was not enough to propel him to the top of his sport, third on his international debut at the 1977 Universiade, only ever a runner-up in the NCAA[407] Championships in 1977 and 1978, and missing out on selection for the 1976 Olympics by one place whilst still at college, finishing fourth in the trials. He was to be ranked amongst the world's best jumpers for the next fifteen years, but he had some significant steps still to take as the 1970's drew to a close.

In the chapter on Leonid Shcherbakov ('The Eastern Bloc Arrives') we introduced the jumping exercises publicised by some-time Soviet track coach and then researcher, Professor Yuri

---

[405] Randy L. Williams, Olympic long jump Gold in 1972 and Silver in 1976; denied a third Olympic appearance by the 1980 boycott and inducted in the United States National Track and Field Hall of Fame in 2009 [1953-].
[406] 'LEAP OF FAITH', Lonnie White, Los Angeles Times, 26 April 2005
[407] National Collegiate Athletic Association, the non-profit organization that regulates student athletics in the United States; formed in 1906.

Verkhoshansky.[408]   As a sports scientist, he pioneered the training methods that were first defined as the Shock Method in the 1960's and which athletes and coaches from the United States were to intently observe Soviet rivals using in their warm-up at international events. Sport has always involved imitation and depth jumps – in which the athlete would jump off a high box and experience the 'shock' of landing, followed by another jump upwards, in order to condition their lower leg muscles and increase explosive performance – were quickly seen as the reason behind improved Soviet performances in the sprinting and jumping events. These training activities became known simply as 'jump training', but by the 1980's had been formally established in the United States as *plyometrics*, an important part of a track and field athlete's training to this day. And it was this increasing use of *plyo* training, such as bounding drills designed to build leg power, that helped a wave of talented athletes from the United States come to the fore, led by Willie Banks.

The United States had dominated the long jump for extended periods through luminaries Jesse Owens, Ralph Boston[409] and Bob Beamon, but had always treated the triple jump as a secondary event that did not attract the best of their athletes, often being long jumpers without elite speed. This began to change from the mid 1970's with James Butts claiming Silver at Montreal 1976, their first medal in the event since 1928 and by the end of the decade Willie Banks and Milan Tiff were fully expected to challenge for the Olympic title in Moscow 1980. Banks had cleared 17m for the first time in May 1978 on home soil in Westwood, California and ended that season fifth in the world,

[408] Professor Yuri Verkhoshansky, Russian scientist widely known as the 'Father of Plyometrics' [1926-2010].
[409] Ralph H. Boston, long jump Olympic Champion in 1960, Silver medallist in 1964 and Bronze in 1968; also two-time Pan American Games Champion in 1963 & 1967 [1939-2023].

following up in 1979 with Silver in the Pan American Games (behind World Record holder João Carlos de Oliveira of Brazil) and his first notable international victory came at the 1979 Universiade in Mexico City, jumping 56ft $6\frac{3}{10}$in (17.23m) for a career best. He entered the 1980 season second in the world, with the Moscow Olympics firmly in his sights, having beaten all his rivals in recent competition.

We know from the previous chapter that the United States-led boycott of the 1980 Olympics would cheat Banks and many others of their chance to press their claims on the greatest sporting stage, but he had yet to fully exploit his potential, despite his status as a leading international jumper. He had been coached by Jim Bush, Tom Tellez[410] and Jim Kiefer[411] amongst others whilst at UCLA and was to increasingly rely on his own curiosity to seek out new training methods and technical help, even reaching out to rivals, a somewhat unusual approach at the global level. By the spring of 1982 he was working out on his own or alongside athletes from his alma mater, by now a second-year student himself at the UCLA law school, having majored in political science and known as 'The Bounding Barrister', such was his commitment to both his studies and his sport. Banks was so curious that he could not restrict himself to just sporting improvement, he had to be open to all that life would offer him, even by then having a stated aim to be the first to the 60ft mark in his event.[412]

---

[410] Thomas K. Tellez, field events coach at ULCA in the early 1970's, then head coach at the University of Houston until the late 1990's; coached long jumper and sprinter Carl Lewis most notably; from Tellez, Banks improved his technique and was introduced to bounding drills [1933-].

[411] Jim Kiefer, assistant track and field coach at UCLA from 1976-79 and worked to improve Banks' strength, fundamental to his later success, but Willie was initially hesitant having worked with Tellez primarily on his technique; long-time coach in the state of California, mostly at Fullerton College [c.1947-].

[412] Verschoth, *op. cit.*

Returning to the 1980 season, Banks had begun to work with UCLA alumni Milan Tiff that spring, the elder statesman telling the young star that, "you just don't know how to triple jump".[413] From Tiff he explored the idea of triple jumping as an art rather than a science, despite the success the Soviets with their research-led approach had enjoyed for many years. Just as the leading Brazilians like Adhemar da Silva and 'Jumping John' had always been attributed by observers with an innate sense of dance, or *samba*, in their jumping style, Banks would come to philosophize that the triple jump was to be considered as one movement, saying, "I'm swinging... it's not like I'm touching down at all."[414] He would soon fall out with Tiff and Ron Livers, who both wanted to skip the Olympic trials in June 1980 believing them to be futile after the boycott, and having disagreed with their gesture, he went on to win in style.

Banks would end the 1980 season with only two defeats, winning that Olympic Trials event and the prominent TAC[415] in June, the latter securing the first of his four national titles (1980-81, 1983 and 1985), with a wind-assisted distance of 17.36m. It must have been galling to watch as the unheralded Soviet Jaak Uudmäe won the Olympic title that July, having bested him in the 1979 Universiade, but having recovered from recurring back trouble that ended his 1978 season and a brief dalliance with retirement to focus on his studies, he was competing with a new-found vigour. He returned from that injury layoff in the form of his life and in 1980 the then twenty-four-year-old athlete was on a journey of athletic self-discovery.[416]

---

[413] Verschoth, *op. cit.*
[414] Verschoth, *op. cit.*
[415] The Athletics Congress, formerly the AAU and now USA Track & Field; the national championship in the United States.
[416] 'WILLIE BANKS', David Gleason, *Track & Field News*, November 1980

He had hoped to break the World Record in the 1980 season, rain in particular at the United States Olympic Trials preventing him from going as far as he felt he could that day and trouble with fouls hindering him at the UCLA/Pepsi Invitational in May when it felt within his reach. Whereas the young Banks had jumped on energy alone in that remarkable victory in the 1975 UCLA-USC meet, he had dedicated himself to his sport in 1979-80, having realised how important track and field was to him. He told a *Track & Field News*[417] interview in November 1980 that he was previously resistant to defining himself as an *athlete*, when he had interests in politics and was intent on going to law school, but a maturing Banks would come to realise that athletics was a "part of being Willie Banks,"[418] having missed it considerably when he was injured in 1978 and increasingly comfortable in himself.

The following seasons would see his drive and determination turned towards harnessing his undoubted athletic talent into some notable milestones. On 19 February 1982 in San Diego, California, he became the unofficial World Indoor Record holder with a leap of 57ft $1\frac{4}{10}$in (17.41m), having set his latest outdoor National Record on 21 June 1981 in Sacramento, California, with a career best of 57ft $7\frac{3}{10}$in (17.56m) making him world number one at season's end. He would be ranked first in the world only once more in 1985, so the 1981 season should not be easily dismissed when remembering his career highlights and having re-committed to his sport and making some technical enhancements – from Milan Tiff he learnt to stretch both legs out as straight he could in reaching for the hop, instead of cocking his lead leg as was the classic position – he was at the top of his sport, the fun-

---

[417] American monthly magazine, focussing on track and field, founded in 1948.
[418] Gleason, *op. cit.*

loving UCLA law student now afforded a place at the triple jump top table.

It was at the TAC championships in Sacramento in June 1981 that Banks made a footnote in the triple jump record books and an idea that became an indelible part of his own history began to formulate. His jump of 17.56m was the second-best distance of all time, with de Oliveira's 1975 World Record set at altitude in Mexico City, but he had found the Hughes Stadium crowd as flat as the low-lying city of Sacramento, later remarking that he needed an exuberant crowd to give him his own energy. In a 1982 interview he provided the comment that opens this chapter – "why are they so quiet? I need noise" – and in the form of his life, Banks went campaigning in Europe in the summer of 1981, intent on making some money and instead changing the perception of his sport permanently.

Triple jump competitions in the United States in particular were often buried in an athletics schedule at the end of the day and would attract only the hardcore jumping fans, with little crowd support or fanfare. Banks had taken to listening to funk[419] music through a tape-player as he waited to jump, a particular song he had first heard when roller skating in Los Angeles with Milan Tiff in the spring of 1980 having an electrifying effect on him. He would listen to music from the band Funkadelic who were active in the late 1960's through to the early 1980's and his adrenaline would rise as he listened to their songs until he reached the runway, the iconic image of him on page two of this chapter showing an effortlessly cool looking Banks, with the headphones almost incongruous yet an integral part of who he was.

The first stop of his trip to Europe in the spring of 1981 was Stockholm, Sweden. On 8 July he competed in the DN-Galan event

---

[419] A danceable form of music originating in the 1960's and characterized by a strong rhythmic or percussive groove.

in the Olympic Stadium, an invitational meeting featuring a number of leading American athletes in order to boost the crowd numbers. Having recently set the National Record, his jumping form was so good that the following week he was to record a long jump of 8.11m in Lausanne, Switzerland, good enough for 11th in the world that season, but the reason he was competing in that event at all is fundamental to the phenomenon that Banks gave rise to in Stockholm, the slow hand-clap which is now such a common part of athletics meetings, particularly for jumping athletes.

Banks and his agent arrived in Stockholm to find that the triple jump was not to be featured in the main European events of the summer, except the DN-Galan and the only opportunity for him to earn some appearance money was a place in that long jump competition in Lausanne. This was the dying days of the era of 'shamateurism', the sport rife with illegal payments to agents or third parties and promoter Andy Norman[420] of Great Britain was to prove an important figure in ending the strict amateurism that had hindered athletics for many years, despite being no saint himself with later legal troubles. For all his role in seeing a new definition of amateurism being passed by the IAAF, that day, according to Banks, he bore the American's ire for saying that the triple jump did not put bums on seats and was boring.[421] So an angry Willie Banks went off to do something about making it more fun...

Asking the other competitors to help him make the event less boring, which was in all their own commercial interest, the first nine jumpers proceeded to foul, seemingly unsure of the finer points of

---

[420] Andrew 'Andy' J. Norman, sports administrator and part responsible for pushing through rule amendments to allow athletes to accept compensation for their participation in international competitions [1943-2007].
[421] https://ca.milesplit.com/articles/244151/legends-of-the-sport-the-impact-of-willie-banks

Public Relations! Banks recalled that "it *was* boring"[422] and decided to take matters into his own hands. He began his 'performance' that day with an elaborate stretch, almost dancing to the funk music loudly playing on his tape-player and he was determined to prove the promoters who had cut his European season short (and impacted his earnings) that they were wrong to push him into the shadows, at least in the track and field sense. This would prove to be another 'lucky' moment in the life of Willie Banks (as far as he now commonly considers his success to be down to luck) and in a 2023 interview he said it would be this day that he would choose to re-live, out of all of his later milestones.[423]

His runway routine had long included him clapping his hands three times before shaking his fists the same number and the now probably slightly apocryphal story goes that five drunk Swedes began to mimic his clapping. He took the lead after his first jump and on his second attempt a few more in the crowd reacted to his rhythmic clapping. This increased on each attempt, one section slowly growing to include another, then one side of the stadium and having bettered the stadium record on his fifth jump, the whole crowd were in thrall to his *orchestration*. He fouled on what would have been a World Record distance on his fifth jump (Banks recalled the official nervously raising the red flag, such was the booing from the crowd[424]) and on his final attempt, energised by 25,000 spectators watching *him* and not the track races as was normal practice, he flew to within $\frac{1}{2}$ in of the American record he had recently set, landing the third furthest jump of all time

---

[422] https://ca.milesplit.com/articles/244151/legends-of-the-sport-the-impact-of-willie-banks
[423] Zoom interview with Willie Banks by author Lawrence Harvey, 8 March 2023.
[424] Harvey, *op. cit.*

at 57ft 7in (17.55m), over 1m ahead of the second placed athlete in the competition.

Banks was carried on the shoulders of boisterous fans in Stockholm and for one day at least he had made the triple jump an exciting experience for the spectators, bridging the gap between them and the athlete in a way never seen before. He had sought chaos and got it, 25,000 people in thrall to one man, yet it was likely to be ephemeral, Banks having no expectation that it would take off elsewhere, although the triple jump was reinstated to a number of promotions that season due to his efforts in Sweden and a now convinced Andy Norman would get him into many promotions in future trips to Europe.[425]

On 14 July he was in Lausanne to collect his second appearance fee, this time for the long rather than triple jump, never his event but when one is caught up in a storm like Banks had created in Stockholm anything can happen. After his fourth attempt, he turned to the crowd who had been urging on the increasingly popular American, when he made a gesture to them with his open palms showing he could do little more, when he recalled hearing "whomp, whomp, whomp" and the crowd erupted in a slow clap like they had in Stockholm.[426] Newly energized, he set a personal best on his next attempt, breaking the Swiss record and from then on, he clapped with the crowd at every meet, the slow-clap phenomenon taking a life beyond him and continuing to this day, no promoter from then able to say that the triple jump was too boring to feature in their event.

His 1981 season ended in September with disappointment, when placing third in the IAAF World Cup in Rome. He had missed

---

[425] Harvey, *op. cit.*
[426] https://ca.milesplit.com/articles/244151/legends-of-the-sport-the-impact-of-willie-banks

too much training after an injury the week after Lausanne and despite de Oliveira claiming his third World Cup title, it was Banks who was making an indelible impression on every crowd, bringing a somewhat sudden spotlight on the triple jump, despite the then superior exploits of the record-breaking Brazilian. Returning to the beginning of the 1982 season and that indoor record in San Diego, wider attention was turning towards the 1984 Olympics in Los Angeles, but Banks was also focussed on surpassing the World Record he felt was within reach, training 6-8 hours per day at his peak such was his commitment and utilising a jacuzzi in his apartment complex to aid the recovery process between sessions.[427]

As he had progressed to the top of his sport, Banks was to find that the pressure he was putting himself under was taking the fun out of life. In later years he would say that choosing to go through such a demanding experience as law school had a detrimental effect on his athletics career and this was a man with a myriad of interests, the restless and hyperactive child whose parents had initially sought professional help for, now a man in love with life and open to all that it could offer. He remained the American Record holder through to the 1984 Olympics, but in his wake were coming other talented jumpers like Al Joyner and Mike Conley, and the overall standard was rising inexorably. Banks was to struggle in this period with the pressure to remain at the head of his sport, manifested in a feeling that athletics had become a job, a 9-5 existence it had never been before and the formerly free-wheeling athlete was increasingly inhibited, at least in his own mind.

The inaugural World Championships in Athletics (World Athletics Championships since 2019) took place in Helsinki in August

---

427 Harvey, *op. cit.*

1983 and Banks was expected to win, the crowd firmly behind the very popular American. There had been a growing discontent amongst international athletes that they only had an opportunity to compete for a global title every four years at the Olympics and responding to the controversy of Mexico 1968 being at high altitude, Munich 1972 overshadowed by the massacre of Israeli athletes by terrorists and Montreal 1976 affected to a limited degree by a boycott of mostly African nations, the IAAF voted in 1978 to stage a World Championship in 1983, particularly prescient when Moscow 1980 was then cruelly taken away from the likes of Banks. World Record holder João Carlos de Oliveira had seen his career tragically cut short in 1981, shortly after his third World Cup title, but this event was to see the greatest gathering of track and field stars since Munich 1972 and Banks was favoured. Yet he was to come up short in the clutch, finishing an unexpected second to a largely unheralded Zdzisław Hoffmann[428] of Poland, a fifth-round leap of 17.42m securing the only major international title for the man who had failed to qualify for the 1980 Olympic final. That pressure Banks was under, was now only going to increase...

Hoffmann was never ranked in the world top twenty-five before the 1983 World Championships and it would prove to be the highpoint of his career. The IAAF claimed that one billion people watched each day of the televised competition and the lasting impression of Banks was the touching embrace he gave to the victorious Pole, rather than the major international title he craved to book-end his career as a leading jumper. He ended the season a lowly twelfth in the world and had it all to do in 1984, with competition for the three places on the United States Olympic team for the triple jump

---

[428] Zdzisław Hoffmann, 1983 World Champion, four-time National Champion in the triple jump and later twelfth at the 1987 World Championships [1959-].

expected to be fiercely contested, younger Americans Al Joyner and Mike Conley very much the coming men.

The Soviet Union returned the favour to their Cold War rival and boycotted the 1984 Olympics, citing concerns over commercialisation and the security of their athletes, but it was really in retaliation for the United States-led boycott in 1980. A total of 14 Eastern Bloc nations would be part of the boycott, leaving the field in Los Angeles wide open, World Champion Hoffmann of Poland absent, along with Bulgaria's Khristo Markov[429] and the Soviet Oleg Protsenko,[430] who had the leading mark of the season at 17.52m. Banks had been troubled by a knee injury in the 1984 season and struggled in the Olympic Trial in June, finishing third behind Mike Conley and Al Joyner respectively, Conley in the form of his life and from then favourite for the Olympic title that August.

Conley led the Olympic qualifying, but fell behind to Joyner in the first round, whose wind-assisted distance of 17.26m would prove good enough for Gold in a final short of quality without the Eastern Europeans, the paucity of competition in Los Angeles shown by three of the absentees clearing 17.29m in Moscow three weeks later. Banks was a disappointing sixth and never became a factor in the fight for the medals, Keith Connor[431] of Great Britain finishing third, some way behind Conley. He recalled in 2023 that being forbidden by officials from using his headphones to listen to his warm-up music and prevented from his usual entertaining of the crowd hampered him

---

[429] Khristo G. Markov, European Champion in 1986, World Champion in 1987, Olympic Champion in 1988 and indoor champion in both the World and European Championships in 1985; later coached compatriot Tereza Marinova to Olympic Gold in 2000 [1965-].

[430] Oleg V. Protsenko, fourth in the 1988 Olympics and Silver medallist in the 1987 World Indoor Championships, his most significant medal [1963-].

[431] Keith L. Connor, Bronze medallist at Los Angeles 1984, European Champion (and record holder) in 1982 and Commonwealth Gold medallist 1978 & 1982 [1957-].

significantly in that final. Banks has attributed mental capacity to 80-90% of his overall performance, and in that final he allowed himself to focus on what he was not allowed to do rather than what he wanted to do, saying he was "down and could not get up."[432] He was hurt which certainly hampered his jumping, but he *needed* the crowd to get into the competition with him to perform at his best and in the 1984 Olympics that was denied to him by the officials.

That night Banks was to cry for some time in his hotel room, his goal in life seemingly gone, having publicly flopped in his home Olympics and a reputation for failing to perform in major competitions growing. He had been the premier jumper in the United States for four years and the *job* he had fallen into was to win an Olympic title, but that was never the real Willie Banks. Having an epiphany of sorts in that hotel room, he vowed to find the joy in jumping once again, knowing other ambitions remained elsewhere in his life (to become an attorney for one) and his newly decided goal was making him smile once more. Failing at the Olympic Games, he had now decided to go even further and break the World Record, later recalling thinking, "this is going to be fun."[433]

The 1985 season would prove to be Willie Banks at his best as an athlete. The knee injury in 1984 had restricted his training in the run up to the Olympics and in the final itself, the Southern California native with the Coliseum crowd wholeheartedly behind him, kept mistiming his jumps, leading to Joyner claiming Gold in one of the most unexpected results of those Games. In 1985 Willie was different in mind, body and soul, and on no day was that more evident than on 16 June, at The Athletics Congress (TAC) championships in

---

[432] Harvey, *op. cit.*
[433] 'After the Tears, Banks Aimed for World Record', Robert Fachet, *The Washington Post*, 18 June 1985

Indianapolis, Indiana, USA. And it was to be a moment when the exuberant personality of Banks was at the fore, finally free from injury and the crushing pressure of being the top ranked American year on year, an athlete full of joy, who when he had climbed his personal mountain, still rushed to support another athlete attempting to climb her own, knowing he had made significant history at last.

Whereas his flop at the Los Angeles Olympics gave credence to a reputation of failing in the major events, the triple jump final in the TAC championships on the evening of 16 June 1985 showed the great bounder could *rebound* from crushing disappointment. Just as the 1981 season had seen Banks ranked first in the world after missing the Moscow Olympics in 1980, in 1985 he would return to form with five of the top ten jumps that season. The previous week he had bettered his National Record and having fouled beyond the World Record mark on his first jump in the Indiana University Michael A. Carroll Stadium in Indianapolis, he told those around him he had the record in him. He was noticeably faster that year on the runway, although still not close to the world-class speed of other jumpers and it helped that the stadium in Indianapolis was known as being 'fast', a firm surface conducive to gaining the horizontal velocity required to reach the furthest distances in a triple jump.

As the women's 800m race got underway, the 6ft 3in (1.90m), 12st 3lbs (78kg) Banks stood on the runway seeking to make history, as he had wanted to on many occasions previously when he felt the record was in his reach. He needed the right weather, favourable wind and track conditions, a favourite sandpit and to be injury free – finally he had these elements together, along with his Funkadelic songs on his tape-player! The attention of the crowd was off the great showman as the vast majority tracked the 800m race and perhaps it was in that moment that he finally escaped from the pressure that had been such burden to him. Mental strength is often suggested as one of the tenets of a World Record performance in any sport, particularly athletics and clear from injury at last, his mind was truly free and able to fully focus on his upcoming attempt, recalling later that he knew it was going to break the record, even before he started his run up for his second attempt that evening.

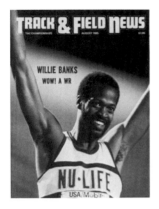

[434]His jump was measured at 58ft $11\frac{1}{4}$in[435] (17.97m) and in the words of television co-commentator Marty Liquori,[436] "much like [Bob] Beamon, it's taken a while to sink in, he's demolished the World Record." He had done his own personal clap routine before his jump, but this time he had not been orchestrating the crowd, attention elsewhere for once and it was apt that Liquori mentioned Beamon when describing the record performance that night. Beamon's long jump World Record from 1968 still stood in 1985 (being broken by Mike Powell in 1991) and in commentating on the 1984 Olympic triple jump final, he had remarked that Banks put too much focus on the crowd, being flat in his second phase in the Los Angeles competition. The overhead hand-clapping is a fundamental part of Banks' legacy, but in becoming the first American since Dan Ahearn in 1911 to hold the triple jump World Record and in returning the world mark to sea-level from the high-altitude of Mexico City, perhaps his concentration was fully on his jump rather than putting on

---

[434] *Track & Field News* cover following the World Record jump, August 1985 © Track & Field News

[435] Ratified as such, but 17.97m is more accurately 58ft $11\frac{1}{2}$in.

[436] Martin 'Marty' W. Liquori, middle distance runner who won Gold at the 1971 Pan American Games in the 1500m and a 1968 Olympian in the same event; later a successful businessman and commentator at six Olympic Games [1949-].

a show for the crowd for once, contemporary reports describing him as "subdued" in that competition[437] and he has often spoken about how he jumped better when he was not thinking, his sub-conscious taking over.[438]

When interviewed afterwards, the new World Record holder commented that triple jumping was "no longer a life and death situation" and he attributed his success to being injury and worry free. He hugged both his coach Chuck Debus[439] who had been an important figure in improving Banks' speed to the board and club-mate Louise Romo, the women's 800m runner that he famously cheered on immediately after his landing, before he even celebrated his record jump (she was later to become his first wife, explaining his interest!). Second in that triple jump competition was 1984 Olympic Silver medallist Mike Conley with a leap of 17.71m, the twenty-two-year-old double NCAA triple jump champion from the University of Arkansas very much the coming man in the sport, Banks at 29 at the back end of his career.

Contemporary commentators would describe that triple jump final in Indianapolis as the greatest in history, with Conley's distance of 58ft $1\frac{1}{4}$in (17.71m) the third-furthest of all time and the first time two men had reached 58ft in one competition, Banks later saying he should not have started his victory lap until Conley had finished, so favourable were the conditions that evening. In the post-record television interview, Banks also said, "when you're having fun you can't help but do well" and that was to be the key driver of the remainder of his career. He was never again ranked higher than 7th in the world (in

[437] 'BANKS TRIPLE-JUMPS TO WORLD MARK', Don Pierson, *Chicago Tribune*, 17 June 1985

[438] Cunningham, *op. cit.*

[439] Chuck Debus, long-time track and field coach, most notably for the Los Angeles Track Club; trained nearly 200 athletes onto USA national teams in his career [1945-].

1987 and 1988) after the 1985 season and Conley would be the premier American jumper into the mid 1990's. Banks would claim the IAAF World Cup in Canberra, Australia in 1985, his only major international victory and a Silver in the 1987 Pan American Games, in Indianapolis once more, the Gold going to Conley with a windy 17.31m, before finishing in sixth at the 1988 Olympics in Seoul, as he had in 1984 when so disappointing both himself and his fans.

[440]Injury had affected him in the run up to Seoul, this time to his ankle, an oft-stated desire to finally claim that Olympic Gold medal never realistic despite coming under the tutelage of now legendary track and field coach Randy Huntington[441] who Banks said helped him to "put everything together",[442] but it was an achievement in itself to make the United States triple jump team in 1988, such was the depth of talent, Conley the leading jumper that season, but outside the three qualification places in the trials. In those Olympic Trials, held once again in Indianapolis, Banks became the first man over 18m, registering efforts of 59ft 3in (18.06m) and 59ft $8\frac{1}{2}$in (18.20m) in windy conditions, recorded at +5.2m/s for the latter and whilst this was not recognised as a new World Record, these jumps represented the high point of his career.

---

[440] Willie Banks competing in Seoul 1988 © Ken Hackman, United States Air Force
[441] Randy Huntington, amongst other leading Olympians, he coached Banks to his windy 18.20m in 1988 and Mike Powell to his long jump World Record of 8.95m in 1991, which stands to this day; now head coach of the Chinese Athletics Association track and field program, with 2022 World Champion long jumper Wang Jianan winning China's first world title in a field event [1954-].
[442] Cunningham, *op. cit.*

A serious problem with the Achilles tendon in both legs later that year could not be fixed with surgery and ultimately prevented him from furthering his best distance as he so hoped, "quite a let down from a glorious career"[443] he later recalled. He never jumped over 17m again, but believed he could have reached 60ft under Randy Huntington, if not for that injury he said originated in that event.[444] In Indianapolis he had his 'wow' moment where triple jumping had never felt easier, describing the feeling as, "so fluid and so attuned to your mind and body, you go *wow, did I even do that*",[445] the closest he ever got to the sensation of *flying* that the very best triple jumpers have all described.

Banks would have one last hurrah in attempting to qualify for the Barcelona Olympics in 1992, but it was not to be. By then he was thirty-six-years-old and it was time to fully retire, still the World Record holder after seven years and to competitors like Mike Conley, he was then "the greatest triple jumpers alive who's ever jumped."[446] His impact on his sport far outweighed his major competition success and his world best would outlast the career of a number of the greatest triple jumpers in history, only being beaten in 1995 by the man who holds it to this day. He had added 8cm to de Oliveira's record distance which had stood for four months shy of ten years and in returning it to sea-level – Indianapolis being around 700ft in height, Mexico City over 7,000ft – he had set a mark that demanded total respect, being then expected to stand for some time again.

In retirement, the consummate showman on the track has become one of the elder statesmen of athletics, a global ambassador

---

[443] https://worldathletics.org/news/press-release/willie-banks-world-record-vest-heritage-donat
[444] Cunningham, *op. cit.*
[445] Harvey, *op. cit.*
[446] Pierson, *op. cit.*

whose popularity transcends his sport (when competing, he was already known as 'The Ambassador of Track and Field', such was his impact). He was inducted into the USA Track and Field Hall of Fame in 1999 and the boy who told his mother he dreamed of becoming the President of the United States, instead went on the campaign trail for athletes' rights. In recent years he has led the call for athletes in the United States to be paid a 'living wage' and warned that sporting boycotts should be a last resort, such as the World Athletics decision to ban Russian athletes from the 2022 World Championships in Oregon over the invasion of Ukraine, from his own experience in 1980 being "steadfast that athletes should be able to compete."[447]

This is not an attempt to tell all that Banks' has achieved in life, but since retiring as an athlete he has run his own international sports management and consulting firm that sells sports floors and artificial turf, primarily in Japan, led the effort to include the women's triple jump in the United States national championships, been the Director of Athlete Services at Atlanta 1996 where he introduced the game of laser tag to the Olympic village for 'fun', assisted cities when bidding for competitions like the Olympics, gained various leading positions within athletics, both within the United States and at the global level, including what may well be the pinnacle, currently an elected Individual Member of the World Athletics Council (until August 2023); he also led the organising committee for the inaugural World Beach Games in 2019, so that diversity of experience he sought out as a young man continues into his later years! He is now married to Hitomi, with four grown children and four grandchildren, resident in Carlsbad, California where he grew up, but with those strong business interests in Japan where his wife was born.

---

[447] 'Column: Ban Russian athletes if want, but not because of Ukraine invasion', Mark Zeigler, *The San Diego Union-Tribune,* 19 July 2022

As a jumper he has not completely closed the book, returning to competition in 2001 as a Masters[448] athlete and breaking a number of American and World Records since then. He set the M45 (45-49 years) World Record in his old event the year he returned to competition and latterly set the world best for the high jump in the M65 (65-69 years) in July 2021,[449] from a three-step run up and classic straddle style, without spikes and still relying on the *natural bounce* that he first demonstrated as a hyperactive child, who would not stop jumping then and has still not stopped as he approaches the age of seventy, attributing his incredible longevity as an older athlete to his five times a week Zumba[450] classes, saying "motion is lotion."[451] He continues to both inspire and lead in the sport of athletics and beyond, fundamental parts of his ongoing legacy and his greatest impact may well be yet to come, as an important leader in his sport's governing body, seeking to put power in the hands of the promoters and athletes rather than administrators, so that the sport might continue to grow.[452]

In a narrative such as this, some jumps are more important than others and what Banks achieved that night in Indianapolis when leaping 17.97m has truly stood the test of time as a landmark best. Until João Carlos de Oliveira proved otherwise, the jump-dominated technique had not been considered reliable, but characterised by a distinctive hang action in the final phase, Banks was a prime exponent of a style that was continued by Mike Conley in his later career and then to great effect by Jonathan Edwards, the World Record holder since 1995. His jump phase was the longest of all the World Record

---

[448] Essentially competitive athletics for the over 35's.
[449] https://timesofsandiego.com/sports/2021/07/19/world-record-for-willie-banks-at-65-tokyo-games-official-top-high-jumper/
[450] Latin-inspired dance fitness training.
[451] Harvey, *op. cit.*
[452] https://lopemagazine.com/2020/08/25/willie-banks-world-athletics-council-track-interview-triple-jump-clap/

distances to that date and was 0.25m ahead of the next furthest, that of 'Jumping John' in October 1975 (6.69m to 6.44m). Banks was never to win the Olympic Gold medal he so craved, cruelly robbed of his best chance in 1980 due to the political boycott and he only ever competed in the one World Championships in 1983 (he failed to qualify for the final in 1987), so he does not have the international *palmarès*[453] of many of the great jumpers before him, but his record-breaking career is now defined by a supreme technique that accentuated the jump into some remarkable triple jump distances (and his track side, event saving, hand-clapping antics!).

His World Record was also notable for returning the best mark to sea-level, after many years of high-altitude meetings being exploited and it was to last for ten years, one month and two days until Edwards claimed it in Salamanca in July 1995. His 1985 jump ranks him 7th in the all-time list, with only three Americans jumping further – Kenny Harrison, Will Claye and Christian Taylor – and in the pantheon of great jumpers, his popularising of the event with the now ubiquitous hand-clap likely saved it from falling off athletics schedules in the 1980's. Willie Banks changed the perception of his sport and whilst the chance to be Olympic Champion eluded him – to be considered the best in the world for one day – his enduring impact on athletics in general has even outlasted a World Record that advanced his event and remarkably would stand for a decade itself.

16.06.1985 WR 17.97m (58ft 11$\frac{1}{4}$in) Willie Banks (USA) Indianapolis, USA (+1.5m/s)

---

[453] French word borrowed from Latin, to mean a prize list or list of winners.

FAST AND FLAT – JONATHAN EDWARDS

"I just floated over the ground in '95"[454]

Willie Banks' 1985 triple jump World Record would last for ten years, one month and two days, until Great Britain's Jonathan Edwards claimed it for the first time in the Salamanca sunshine in July 1995. That summer, he had been chasing Banks' record for a month and on 25 June he had made the longest triple jump in history *under any conditions*, reaching 60ft $5\frac{6}{10}$in (18.43m) in the 1995 European Cup, at the *Stadium Nord de Villeneuve d'Ascq*[455] in France, albeit with an illegal tailwind of +2.4m/s. Only two men in history had been further than 18m in the event at that stage, Banks with 18.20m (+5.2m/s) in the 1988 United States Olympic Trials and Mike Conley with a distance of 18.17m (+2.1m/s) when winning Olympic Gold in Barcelona 1992, both startling jumps but paling into comparison with what Edwards managed that day in Lille, backing up that jump with a second attempt at 18.39m (+3.7m/s).

The IAAF measured the toe to heel distance of Edwards' jump at approximately 18.60m and he later recalled in 1996 being, "very disappointed... I think my 18.43m was... certainly worth more than (Banks' then World Record) 17.97m."[456] As the likes of Banks and Conley watched on from afar that summer, Edwards would see his own

---

[454] 'Exclusive Jonathan Edwards interview: A giant leap for mankind – 25 years on, his triple jump world record has stood the test of time', Oliver Brown, *The Telegraph*, 7 August 2020
[455] Now the *Stadium Lille-Métropole*.
[456] https://www.european-athletics.com/news/golden-moments-edwards-giant-leap-the-1995-european-cup

disappointment turn to jubilation in less than a month, the British athlete completely re-writing the triple jump record books and claiming the World Record on 18 July 1995, with a distance that both Americans had coveted, even expected, in their highly successful careers. He would take the record out further in Gothenburg on 7 August 1995 – twice – and his second jump that day was measured at 60ft 0in (18.29m), with the wind being well within the allowable limit. At the time of writing, that distance has not been improved, making the men's triple jump World Record one of *the* longest standing track and field records and Edwards is still regularly hailed as the greatest triple jumper in history, and certainly the furthest.

When Bob Beamon obliterated the long jump record in Mexico City in 1968, his feat was so astonishing that his name has been used ever since as a superlative for spectacular achievements in any sport, not just track and field. Jonathan Edwards was to sensationally break the World Record three times in the summer of 1995, twice in the same competition in consecutive jumps, yet it was an achievement that was never expected to be the generation-defining landmark that it is now, nearly 28 years distant and still counting. He had come from being ranked equal 22nd in the all-time list in the early weeks of his record-breaking season,[457] to being the longest triple jumper in history, with a World Record that has never been truly threatened since. The story of Jonathan Edwards and his *annus mirabilis* in 1995 is intertwined with the other 18m trailblazers in Banks and Conley, and is a story of technique, speed, physiology and the sheer grit and determination of a twenty-nine-year-old Briton to become the first, and only, 60ft jumper in the history of his sport.

---

[457] https://www.european-athletics.com/news/golden-moments-edwards-giant-leap-the-1995-european-cup

We pick up the technical journey of the triple jump at the 1988 Olympics in Seoul, a journey that would go on and see the 'Skipping Stone Style' of Mike Conley perfected when Edwards became the "ultimate skimmer."[458] The leading proponents in the triple jump in the late 1980's were elite athletes and the overall standard in competition had risen markedly since the 1970's, with appearance money and shoe contracts enabling the best to be true professionals. The world number one through 1986-88 was Khristo Markov of Bulgaria and he was to rubber-stamp a notable career with Olympic Gold in Seoul, to go with European and World Championships titles in 1986 and 1987 respectively, landing a career best 58ft $9\frac{1}{12}$in (17.92m) in the latter competition in Rome, in addition to European and World Indoor Championships victories in 1985.

Markov was a top-class triple jumper and his style was best described as being both powerful and unique. It was commonly accepted by then that a successful triple jumper had to be powerful, and Markov may well be the best power jumper in history. Banks was the World Record holder in 1988, but was well beyond his best, qualification for the Seoul Olympics an achievement in itself. Markov won the Gold medal with his first jump of the final, a mark that the three leading Soviet jumpers could not better when finishing in consecutive places behind him, with the medallists each surpassing Viktor Saneyev's 1968 Olympic Record, then long overdue for improvement. The Bulgarian's jumping style was notable for a long hop, but truly characterised by his windmill-style motion. This included an over-the-head movement as he touched the ground in his hop, a pronounced swinging of the arm that really prevented him from jumping further than he did. His victories were based on the terrific

---

458 'The art of triple jump', John Shepherd, *Athletics Weekly*, 16 May 2021

leg power that allowed him to overcome this serious deficiency in technique, which itself caused such a considerable loss in horizontal velocity that it obscured the skill he displayed as a jumper in his final phase.

Markov was to see his career end early due to injuries likely sustained by his unorthodox technique, but that did not stop coaches seeking to imitate the counter, or alternate, arm movement, which had brought him great success in the late 1980's. The 1987 European Record he set in Rome – his fourth – would not be beaten until Edwards broke the World Record for the first time in Salamanca in July 1995 and in an August 2020 interview on the 25th anniversary of his record-breaking feats in Gothenburg,[459] the Briton recalled that until illness caused him to miss the 1994 season, he had for a long time been trying to copy the Bulgarian with his distinctive opposite arm movement and windmill-style motion. His long lay-off would lead him to consider his technical shortcomings and in realizing he was more naturally predisposed to be a speed rather than power jumper like Markov, he switched to watching then world number one, Mike Conley of the United States, who he came to greatly admire.

Conley was a supremely talented jumper, possibly the greatest combined long and triple jumper in history, with a deserved reputation for last round victories. His own rise came as Banks was already at his peak and they enjoyed several years as rivals, until the older American accepted that it was time to retire when failing to qualify for Barcelona 1992. Conley was a star athlete at college, winning nine NCAA outdoor and indoor titles in the two jumping events, then as a professional he was ranked in the top ten an incredible fourteen times for the triple jump and ten times in the long jump. He was triple jump

---

[459] Brown, *op. cit.*

world number one from 1992-94, in what should have been the twilight of his career, having turned thirty in the 1992 season and by 1994 when Edwards began to watch him closely, he had won Olympic Silver in 1984, Gold in 1992 with an incredible wind-assisted 18.17m and was victorious at the 1993 World Athletics Championships, having medalled in the three previous editions dating back to 1983.

The American had undergone his own technical awakening early in his career, having used the single-arm take-off until 1985 and his technique being hop-dominated. The double-arm take-off is commonly said to affect horizontal velocity in the last few strides and when switching from the single-arm method that Banks had found helped him to maintain his own speed, his superior sprint speed and ability as a long jumper carried him to ever greater distances, particularly in his improved jump phase (he was the Bronze medallist in the long jump in the 1983 World Championships). In the 1988 United States Olympic Trials, he had finished outside of the qualification places for the triple jump, when his shorts were controversially ruled to have brushed the sand on his last round jump, costing him around 2in, and thus Barcelona 1992 had an added importance for him, having been heavily favoured throughout his career to improve on the Silver he won in 1984.

Conley was in superb form in Barcelona and his victory on 3 August 1992 would be the largest winning margin in the event since the first modern Olympics in 1896. Now in a bodysuit rather than the loose shorts that had been so costly in the 1988 Trials, his second jump broke Markov's Olympic Record at 17.64m and his final attempt was a new World Record at 59ft $7\frac{4}{10}$in (18.17m), at least for the five minutes it took for the wind reading to be confirmed at +2.1m/s and the 'record' taken from him. He thought he had become the first legal 18m

209

jumper in history, but the tailwind was agonisingly ruled over the allowable limit, the only windy jump of the competition! For a brief moment in time, he had bettered Banks' 1985 record by 20cm – and in commentary, the older American pointedly said, "if the wind..." when his co-commentators initially claimed a new World Record, then took great pains to remind them of his own windy 18.20m in 1988 – but it was still an incredible jump, with barely any conspicuous wind assistance.

Watching Conley's landmark jumps in the 1992 Olympic final, it is noticeable how low to the ground his body remained during the hop phase in particular, allowing him to maintain horizontal velocity through the next two phases, with his ability as an accomplished sprinter – he could post world class 200m times – that marked the technical development Edwards would come to study in his own injury-ravaged 1994 season. It was this lack of height and conserving of horizontal speed that had led to Banks describing Conley's technique in 1985 as a "skipping stone style",[460] the former believing his technique to be slightly superior, but lacking the speed of the younger athlete he was more efficient in jumping as high as possible in each phase and it was only Conley's improvement as a technician that meant he could harness his natural gift as a sprinter in jumping in a low arc.

Conley admitted in a 1996 interview that he had expected that he would have been the first man beyond 60ft, saying "I let years go by assuming it"[461] and the improving 1995 version of Edwards had almost sneaked up on the leading jumpers in that sensational summer. The

---

460 'TRIPLE THREAT: For Conley, Banks and Other Hopefuls, the Record Is a Long Way Out There', Mal Florence, *Los Angeles Times*, 6 June 1985
461 'LEAP OF FAITH ONCE SUNDAYS WERE NO LONGER SACROSANCT, ENGLAND'S JONATHAN EDWARDS EXPLODED INTO THE GREATEST TRIPLE JUMPER IN HISTORY', Tim Layden, *Sports Illustrated*, 13 May 1996

American was a great athlete, but he compensated for his technical flaws with his speed, in much the same way that Banks admitted in 2001 that he got comfortable and never worked on his step,[462] compensating with his superior jump. Banks had seemingly mastered the concept of *bounding* when triple jumping, rather than *landing* he could remain *active* through the three phases in his lower legs, in his own words, essentially "pawing the ground like a horse".[463] Conley famously won an NBA[464] Celebrity Slam Dunk Contest against legendary long jumper Mike Powell in 1992 with the longest recorded dunk[465] in basketball history, a phenomenal demonstration of *jumping* from the former Chicago high school basketball star and father of current NBA player Mike Conley Jr. of the Minnesota Timberwolves, but it was Edwards who would truly show the world how to *float* rather than *bounce* in the triple jump, "who skimmed the ground like a stone skipping across the water..."[466]

[467]**Jonathan David Edwards** was born on 10 May 1966 in Westminster, London, the eldest of three children of the Reverend Andy Edwards, an Anglican Minister and Jill. He grew up in the north Devon seaside town of Ilfracombe, attending the leading fee-paying school in

---

[462] https://theolympians.co/2021/08/02/yulimar-rojas-sets-the-world-record-for-womens-triple-jump-willie-banks-knows-she-can-do-better/

[463] 'STEPPING UP – CORRECTING ERRORS TO IMPROVE THE RESULT', Willie Banks, *Techniques for Track & Field and Cross Country*, Vol. 9/No. 2 November 2015

[464] National Basketball Association, the major professional league in North America and founded in 1946.

[465] A basketball shot where the player jumps in the air and pushes the ball through the net, with one or both hands; Conley dunked from around 2in behind the free-throw line, which is 15ft from the basket!

[466] https://www.reuters.com/article/athletics-idowu-idUKLDE71D1CE20110215

[467] Jonathan Edwards competing in the 1995 World Championships © unknown

the area in West Buckland School. Now he is one of the most notable of the school's former pupils, but at the time he was a useful all-round athlete who enjoyed competing in a multitude of sports, yet never gave a real indication of the huge potential within him. One of his nicknames at school was 'Titch',[468] a youthful observation of his small size compared to his peers and in a theme for the rest of his career, he readily admits he was a late developer, although he stood out enough to be a prefect (a leadership position) and was awarded the school's top medal for sporting and academic excellence in his senior year. His friendship group was focused on the church rather than school – never being 'one of the lads' – and beyond family, religion would prove to be the central tenet of his life, until post-retirement reflection brought about a total loss of faith, that continues to this day.

Edwards had won the triple jump at the English Schools' Athletics Championship[469] in 1984 as an eighteen-year-old, having finished 9th the previous year and whilst this event has been an important grassroots milestone for the overwhelming majority of athletes to later represent Great Britain in the senior ranks, he recalled that his distances were not enough to stand out at a global level, with the leading triple jumper in the age group two years below him actually jumping further.[470] He was not convinced that an athletics career was possible for him, being some way off the world age-bests at the time, but with his father urging him to harness what he said was his God-given ability, he went to Durham University, near Newcastle, to study

---

[468] 'It almost feels like somebody else's life', Adrian Lobb, *The Big Issue*, 23 July 2021
[469] Organised by the English Schools' Athletics Association (ESAA), the leading annual national athletics championships in England for students aged 12-18; held since 1925 and each county in England selects a squad from the leading eligible students in their region.
[470] Lobb, *op. cit.*

Physics and continue with his jumping, although his ambitions in the latter were limited.

As an eighteen-year-old, Edwards had jumped a windy 49ft 3in (15.01m) in the English Schools Championships, remarking on his attitude at the time, "my memory is of not training much"[471] and his father had to push him to stay involved with triple jumping at university, noting Jonathan did not take it seriously at the time. He trained infrequently at university, latterly at Gateshead, near Newcastle, with Carl Johnson,[472] the northeast national coach, yet this was never more than once a week and his Bible study group had a greater prominence in the life of this student-athlete, more focused on the former than the latter. During his time at Durham, Edwards would also attend training weekends at Crystal Palace Stadium, London, as part of the elite squad under John Crotty,[473] national triple jump coach throughout the 1980's and 1990's, but he was not at all dedicated to his sport and middling results in domestic competitions in those years were to Edwards, "no great shakes really".[474]

Nearing graduation in 1987, Edwards came to realise that he belatedly still had a choice to make about focusing on his athletics career. He asked his coach Carl Johnson if he thought he had the talent required to at least give it a go and he told him that he did, Edwards recalling later[475] that Johnson went on in his mid-twenties to say he was

---

[471] Layden, *op. cit.*

[472] Carlton 'Carl' Johnson, British Athletics Federation coach since 1969 with a long association with Loughborough College, coaching 35 athletes to international standard, author, teacher, educator and inducted into the England Athletics Hall of Fame in 2017 [1938-].

[473] John W. Crotty, longtime UK Athletics coach, particularly involved with coach development; national event coach for the triple jump 1981-99 [1948-].

[474] 'A TIME TO JUMP – THE AUTHORISED BIOGRAPHY OF JONATHAN EDWARDS', p. 60, Malcolm Folley, 2000

[475] 'Olympic hero Edwards on new mission', David Kelly, *Belfast Telegraph*, 20 November 2009

as talented as Colin Jackson,[476] the then Olympic Silver medallist in the 110m hurdles from the Seoul Olympics in 1988. From Johnson, Edwards would finally gain the belief that he could become an elite athlete, but in 1988 the twenty-two-year-old was still wrestling with his faith and the restrictions his devout Christianity put on his athletics beyond those naturally imposed by ability, a personal conflict over his longstanding decision not to compete on Sundays – the Sabbath to many faiths, the holiest day of the week set aside for rest and worship – that would rage until the end of 1992 and give rise to countless newspaper headlines in the British press.

He returned to northeast England after graduation in 1987 with a one-way train ticket, having reached the conclusion that God wanted him to be an athlete and he settled in the Newcastle suburb of Heaton, an inner-city area far from the Devon countryside of his youth, from where he could still train at the Gateshead Stadium under Carl Johnson. Heaton was where he had gone to church as a student and after a period of unemployment, he found work in a cytogenetics (the study of chromosomes) laboratory at the Royal Victoria Infirmary in the city. In autumn 1986 his personal best was still only 16.05m, showing how little he had developed whilst at Durham University, with his early lackadaisical approach to training and religious conviction preventing any activity on half of the weekend having stalled his progress as an athlete, and the Jonathan Edwards who came 9th in the 1987 World Student Games final in Zagreb, Croatia, would do so with a jump of only 15.96m.[477]

---

[476] Colin R. Jackson, one of Great Britain's greatest hurdlers, twice World Champion in 1993 & 1999, four-time European Champion and two-time Commonwealth Champion, amongst a host of other major championship medals; now a well-known television personality and athletics commentator [1967-].

[477] First was Charles Simpkins of the United States with 17.16m and second was compatriot Kenny Harrison with 17.07m – more on him competing against Edwards in major finals later!

Edwards' lack of belief in himself in those early years at university would be manifested in various aches and pains, a general reluctance to commit to hard work (in an athletics environment) and a tendency to end training at the first sign of adversity, having succeeded to date on natural talent alone. In Carl Johnson the diffident young man found the perfect foil and they would continue to work together until Edwards sought new ideas, the high point for Johnson being recognised in his own right as the British Coach of the Year 1995 after that record-breaking summer, although they were increasingly distant by that stage. Johnson was astute in realizing that Edwards had no real experience of athletic training – being "athletically rather naïve"[478] – and with one doctor advising him to quit the sport due to the configuration of the bones in his foot suggesting a propensity for recurring injury, Johnson elected to allow the athlete to develop at his own pace, backing off at the point of stress and accepting that his optimum development could be delayed by a year or two, knowing that Edwards would begin to trust both his training methods and his maturing body at his own pace, in developing the elastic strength he would demonstrate to great effect from 1995.

Edwards began to make steady rather than spectacular progress and by summer 1988 he was no longer the novice he had been at university two years prior, when first coming into contact with Johnson, yet he had still drawn little press interest. That summer he had jumped the furthest of any British athlete ahead of the Olympic Trials and had passed the qualifying standard of 16.65m, yet the young athlete was to see his faith gain him nationwide attention, in the most unwelcome manner. He had previously rejected an invitation for England 'A' without any fuss, but in now informing the selectors that

---

[478] Folley, *op. cit.*, pp.57-8

he would not take part in the Trials as they were also on a Sunday and potentially passing up an Olympic place on a point of principle, however important it was to him and his family, he found himself portrayed as a modern-day Eric Liddell of *Chariots of Fire* fame.[479] The comparison was not overly fitting, Edwards being on the cusp of his career and Liddell one of the favourites for 100m Gold in Paris 1924, but the media storm that he found himself in was overwhelming, journalists door-stopping his church in Heaton and place of work.

He was subsequently awarded the third discretionary place and went to Seoul with the intention of gaining much-needed experience. He jumped poorly and did not qualify for the final, finishing in 23rd place with a best jump of 15.88m, but being an Olympian at that stage for the late developer was an achievement in its own right. He became National Champion for the first time in 1989 and his major international breakthrough came when jumping 17.28m in Barcelona on 9 September 1989, ending that season ranked 11th in the world. He was to miss both the 1989 European Cup, held in his adopted home of Gateshead and the 1991 World Championships in Tokyo (won by Kenny Harrison of the United States) with the respective finals being scheduled on a Sunday, and whilst he reported receiving much encouragement from the British public over his beliefs, the pressure on him was growing, both in his own mind and elsewhere. Elite athletes would just not pass up the chance to compete in the World Championships because of the scheduling conflicting with religious conviction...

---

[479] Eric H. Liddell, Scottish sprinter, rugby player and Christian missionary; refused to run in the 100m heats in the 1924 Olympics as they were on a Sunday and instead took part in the 400m, which he unexpectedly won [1902-45]. His exploits and later death in a Japanese internment camp in the Second World War were portrayed in the Oscar-winning 1981 film, *Chariots of Fire*.

He ended the 1991 season ranked eighth in the world and the Barcelona Olympics was looming in August 1992, the question of his participation dependent upon which day of the week the triple jump was to be scheduled. His first major championship medal had been a Silver in Auckland, New Zealand in the 1990 Commonwealth Games and he had some hope of an Olympic medal in 1992, but in choosing to honour God as he had done throughout his career with his devotion, he publicly accepted that he was prepared to miss the Games if the event was scheduled for a Sunday. Fortunately, the qualifying rounds were confirmed for a Saturday and the final on the following Monday, but despite having cleared 17m twice that season, his season best being 17.22m on 10 July at Crystal Palace, he was disappointing in the Olympics once more, missing the final with a best jump of only 15.76m and finishing in a wretched 35th place. Edwards had always placed such belief in God, but his faith was not being repaid in his sporting life and he began to question the longstanding decision not to compete on Sundays.

The end of the 1992 season offered Edwards the chance for some immediate redemption at the IAAF World Cup, held in late September in Havana, Cuba. He was ill at the time, vomiting on the morning of competition, but only seven weeks removed from the failure at the Barcelona Olympics which precipitated his crisis of faith, he claimed the title in some style on 26 September 1992, moving from fourth to first place on his last jump, a season best of 17.34m. This was a glorious way for him to finish a season in which he had largely been disappointing, and it was his most important victory to date, improving from third place in the previous World Cup in Barcelona in 1989. In the winter of 1992, the now twenty-six-year-old Edwards was the leading triple jumper in Great Britain, National Champion in 1989 and 1992, AAA[480] Champion in 1989[481] and regularly exceeded 17m in competition, but to borrow the trope regularly applied to him by British newspaper headline writers when he later became a record-breaker, his biggest *leap of faith* was actually about to come.

The challenges brought about by his faith are intertwined with his story as a professional triple jumper and Edwards had been truly tested in those Barcelona Olympics. He fouled his first jump and made of mess of the other two, in front of his father, with his now wife Alison and mother due to be in the stadium for the final. His performance was even worse than it had been in Seoul, when he was only meant to gain valuable experience and he finished his second Games nearly 2m down on Mike Conley, the new Olympic Record holder at 17.63m who was only denied a new World Record for his 18.17m jump by the slimmest of wind readings. That winter he wrestled with his decision not to compete on Sundays and the decision was essentially made for him; the major competitions of 1993 were all to be held on a Sunday, so in the spring of that year he announced publicly that he had changed his mind. Edwards had gone into athletics to serve God, competition being the stage on which he could demonstrate his Christian witness and despite some real resistance from his parents over his reconsideration, amidst concerns he would be widely labelled a hypocrite, the negative experience in Barcelona had brought him closer to God and even more convinced he could serve him as an athlete.

---

[480] The Amateur Athletic Association (AAA), the oldest national athletics governing body in the world, being established in 1880 and now absorbed into England Athletics. The AAA Championships were considered the national championships from 1880-2006, albeit with a separate UK Athletics Championships running from 1977-97. Both now replaced by the British Athletics Championships since 2007.
[481] He would also be AAA champion in 1994, 1998 & 2001.

218

The highpoint of the 1993 season would prove to be the IAAF World Championships in Stuttgart, Germany on 16 August. His first child, Samuel, was born six days earlier[482] and leaving his wife behind with the newborn, being under pressure as a professional athlete to make a living, he earned his first major championship medal, finishing third with a career best distance of 17.44m, with world number one Mike Conley claiming Gold. This was Edwards' major breakthrough and further good fortune would follow that season, a grant from a foundation in the northeast set up to provide financial assistance to promising local sportsmen enabling him to assuage the nagging concerns over supporting his family and to become a full-time athlete for the first time.

1994 was all set to be the season that Edwards would begin to repay the faith others like Carl Johnson had in his ability. He was to turn 28 that May and by the end of January his coach recorded that he was in the training form of his life.[483] Then he went down with the flu and perhaps buoyed by the encouraging results in his early season training, he continued to push ever harder, electing for once not to listen to his body as he had so diligently when he was a young athlete. The indoor season came and went without any noticeable performances, but he began to have a gnawing feeling that something was not right with his body, lethargic for no obvious reason and a sixth place in the 1994 European Championships in Helsinki in mid-August, was a sign that his level was declining. Later that month he surprised himself in winning Silver in the Commonwealth Games in Victoria, British Columbia, Canada with a jump of 17.00m, yet he knew he was not feeling good. Returning to England, blood tests showed that he

---

[482] Second son Nathan was born in May 1995.
[483] Folley, *op. cit.*, p.92

was suffering from the Epstein-Barr virus and his season was essentially over, rest the only cure.

Amidst concerns over the lingering effects of the virus and training only lightly at the beginning of 1995, Edwards took his family to Tallahassee, Florida to a British Olympic Association funded camp, opened to enable Great Britain athletes to acclimatize for Atlanta 1996 the following year, but giving him a much-needed change of environment and chance to get in shape. The warm-weather training confirmed to Edwards that he needed to hear new ideas and it was in Florida that he first came into contact with esteemed American jumps coach Dennis Nobles,[484] who would continue to be employed by the Briton through his later Olympic successes in 1996 and 2000. He returned home in March 1995 and was soon contemplating changes, "I was at a dead end, so I felt the freedom to experiment."[485]

Edwards later recalled in his biography published in 2000 (*A Time to Jump*, London: HarperCollinsPublishers), that he had begun to drift away from Carl Johnson in the years preceding the 1995 season and the trip to Florida seemed to have opened his eyes to new ideas, Johnson always having favoured a scientific approach to training that eventually espoused a relationship lacking in the dynamism and continual stimulus that Edwards required to perform at his best. He had been lifting weights with a legally blind powerlifter named Norman Anderson[486] for two years by then and he was to become a fatherly figure to Edwards, the increased power he gained from these sessions

---

[484] Dennis A. Nobles, long-time Florida State University coach, recognized as one of the leading horizontal jumps coaches in the United States, with nine of his college athletes going on to become Olympians [c.1959-].

[485] Layden, *op. cit.*

[486] Norman Anderson, a physiotherapist and competitive weightlifter into his 70's, before he met Edwards he had already mentored a number of northeast based athletes to Olympic medals, including Steve Cram, Mike McLeod & Charlie Spedding in 1984 [c.1938-].

allied to a newfound toughness from the harsh environment of the public gymnasium at the Gateshead Stadium, contributing significantly to the success he enjoyed from 1995-2003. He has since regularly remarked how he would not have achieved what he did without the guidance of Anderson, but always took pains to pay his respects to Carl Johnson as well.

The other significant figure to have entered Edwards' orbit ahead of that 1995 season was local jumps coach Peter Stanley. Whereas Anderson was crucial in helping him order his mind – Edwards said "Norman gets rid of what he calls the rat inside my head"[487] – Stanley was to be the central figure in improving his mechanics, and Edwards recalled in 2000 that it was watching film with him that made Conley's action stand out when he was seeking a new approach, in his words "a light bulb had been switched on."[488] The triple jump had seen many technical changes and variations in style to that point, and Edwards was now going to concentrate on emulating the skywards double-arm movement the American made during his last phase jump, particularly in Barcelona 1992 when he had so nearly claimed the World Record, but for a slight gust of wind.

Much as the triple jump is about properly conserving (after first harnessing) momentum, the story of Edwards' historic season is of an athlete in peak fitness in the spring, who combined more days off than he had ever had with the most training jumps of his life. He was then able to gain impetus as the standard of competition grew through the season, until under the late sunshine in Gothenburg on 7 August, he blew away an elite field in the final of the 1995 World

---

[487] 'Norman lit athletic flame; As the Olympic Torch passes through the region, JOANNE BUTCHER meets Jonathan Edwards and the coach who helped him to glory', Joanne Butcher, *The Journal* (Newcastle, England), 16 June 2012
[488] Folley, *op. cit.*, p.97

Championships, with the greatest performance the sport had ever seen. The slightly built, 6ft (182cm), 11st 6lb (73kg) Edwards, who had never been a dominant jumper in his career, known more through the British press for his devotion to God than for his athletics victories, would win all 14 meets he entered in the 1995 season and show that the *skipping stone* could jump further than any of the *bouncing balls* that had come before, shocking his sport to the core.

The march into the record books that would climax in the Scandinavian sunshine in August began in cold and wet weather in England on 11 June. In the Loughborough International Match, Edwards jumped a National Record 57ft $8\frac{9}{10}$in (17.58m), 14cm further than he had ever gone before and more than just confirmation that he had fully recovered from the virus that had wiped out the 1994 season. He had felt like he was in the best shape of his career after his enforced absence and this important domestic landmark jump proved to him that his form was better than ever, even if there only a couple of hundred spectators in attendance and his achievement went unnoticed in the press. He followed up this performance a week later with his second victory of the season, jumping 17.46m in defeating a strong international field in Villeneuve d'Ascq, France, again in wet weather and giving him a growing confidence, although a miserable weights session at the Gateshead Stadium on his return home served to introduce a slight doubt that the virus could yet return.

He returned to Villeneuve d'Ascq on 25 June in blustery conditions and was to assuage any concerns – and the *rat inside his head* – that the virus could afflict him again. The 1995 European Cup would see Edwards become a history-maker in the most surprising display of jumping the sport had ever seen, the man ranked equal 22nd in the world landing the two longest triple jumps in history *under any conditions*.

He opened with a wind-assisted distance of 58ft $8\frac{7}{10}$in (17.90m), only exceeded by five men in history and in his 2000 biography he recalled that he knew the jump to be flawed, with more to come in favourable weather, allied to a fast runway.

[489]His second jump soared to 60ft $5\frac{6}{10}$in (18.43m) and he landed beyond the measuring point set alongside the sandpit, calibrated to just over 18m, which he had very clearly exceeded! Willie Banks' World

Record had stood for nearly ten years at this stage and whilst the wind speed was quickly calculated at an illegal +2.4m/s, Edwards shocked both himself and the world, video showing him smiling away but clutching his head in disbelief. Despite his jump not being a new World Record, he had become the first man over 60ft in reaching a milestone the likes of Banks and Conley had chased for years. And whilst he had achieved it seemingly out of nowhere, his fourth (and final) jump that day went to 18.39m (+3.7m/s) showing that this was no fluke.

An invigorated Edwards returned to England, believing he was in the form to land a legal World Record distance, jumping a windy 18.03m in Gateshead on 2 July 1995 and 17.69m at Crystal Palace five days later. He recalled later in his authorised biography that he was trying too hard at this stage and his technique was getting loose, with a sore ankle suffered at the latter event, the British Championships, causing him to miss the AAA Championships in Birmingham, ostensibly a trial for the World Championships later that year.

---

[489] Screenshot of Edwards celebrating his jump of 18.43m in the 1995 European Cup © BBC Television via YouTube

Edwards' feats that season meant that his qualification for the Worlds was secure, although his close relationship with promoter Andy Norman (see chapter on Banks for more on his impact on another leading triple jumper) led to some suggestions that his withdrawal from the Birmingham meeting was overplayed, when only three days later a fit again Edwards arrived for a provincial meeting in Salamanca, Spain on 18 July 1995.

Norman had arranged for Edwards to compete in Salamanca unannounced and he hoped that a warm evening in a stadium just below the altitude assistance threshold and conducive to landmark jumps – Cuban great Javier Sotomayor had broken the high jump World Record twice in the stadium – would see the Briton claim the triple jump mark he had chased for a month, with increasing desperation and the pressure on him growing. The field was thin, with only Mike Conley to trouble him, the man whose technique he had adopted to great effect in the spring and who Edwards himself considered to be the outstanding triple jumper of all time. In previous competitions the American had always been superior to Edwards, but the latter now had the massive leap in Villeneuve d'Ascq on his resumé and he was on the precipice of the peak of his career.

[490]He mistimed his jump on his first effort and still landed a distance of 17.39m. Edwards certainly did not look like a man about to re-write the history books  at that stage and Conley cannot have been impressed. Yet the Briton knew he had been only one successful phase away from another jump of the type he landed in the European Cup in June and on his second

---

[490] Screenshot of Edwards celebrating his World Record jump on 18 July 1995 in Salamanca, Spain © Eurosport via YouTube

effort went out and uncorked a distance of 58ft 11$\frac{3}{4}$in (17.98m),[491] with a tailwind of +1.8m/s, a quick check of the wind marker leading to tremendous joy. He had claimed the World Record in beating Banks' mark by $\frac{1}{2}$in and the transformation from the good, but not great, triple jumper he had been up to the 1995 season was complete. He now had both the furthest legal distance in the history of his sport and the best under any conditions, but Edwards still had another target before the end of the season, in *needing* to claim his first major championship victory in Gothenburg.

Competitors such as Conley and Brian Wellman[492] of Bermuda were later said to have been energised by Edwards' achievements that summer – the latter said "it's a wake-up call for all of us"[493] – but they were both reduced to being spectators to the greatest individual performance of a triple jumper in a major final in Gothenburg on 7 August 1995. Edwards was now considered an elite athlete after his World Record in July and his profile in the Great Britain team had risen to put him alongside superstars like Linford Christie.[494] He was uncomfortable with being given preferential treatment within the team, but that evening in a World Championships final in Gothenburg he gave the performance of a true great, despite later admitting in a 2021 interview[495] with World Athletics that he was "petrified"!

---

[491] Ratified as such, but more correctly 58ft 11$\frac{9}{10}$in.
[492] Brian Wellman, a rival to Edwards in the 1990's; 1995 World Indoor Champion, Silver medallist in the 1995 World Championships, two-time NCAA Champion at the University of Arkansas and still the Bermudian record holder [1967-].
[493] Layden, *op. cit.*
[494] Linford C. Christie, Great Britain sprinter, the first British athlete to win each of the major competitions open to them, the first European under 10sec in the 100m and the 1992 Olympic 100m champion, amongst a host of major championship medals and records; career ended in 1999 with a disputed drug ban [1960-].
[495] https://www.youtube.com/watch?v=hWIAdOmqJ9E ['Jonathan Edwards reflects on his triple jump world record from Göteborg 1995 – One Moment in Time'].

In Barcelona 1992, Edwards had been the spectator when Conley won Olympic Gold, having failed to qualify for the final and in Gothenburg the roles were almost reversed as the American, the former world number one, was amongst the field of elite athletes to be blown away by Edwards. Triple jumpers had demonstrated many styles over the years, from the power jumpers to the bouncers, the specific phase-dominant to the balanced technique, but one area of relative consistency was in body size. By the 1990's triple jumpers were said to need to be tall men with powerful legs, yet Edwards was now bucking that trend, being fast but slight of build and not especially tall. In front of a primetime television audience back home in Great Britain, the quiet and unassuming son of an Anglican Minister who previously refused to compete on Sundays would sear himself into the consciousness of the British people, his exploits in Gothenburg fondly remembered to this day, even by the most casual observers of athletics.

Edwards had impressively maintained his form over the 1995 season and in Sheffield on 23 July had jumped a windy 18.08m, his second 18m distance of the month and fourth of the summer beyond the allowable following wind. The field in Gothenburg included Conley, Wellman, Jérôme Romain[496] of Dominica and two dangerous Cubans in Yoelbi Quesada and Yoel Garcia.[497] He was favourite for a major title for the first time in his career and after his sensational season he was the man to beat, only three weeks removed from breaking the World Record in Salamanca and many expected him to do so again in Gothenburg, the men's triple jump billed as the marquee event of the championships. Jumping tenth of twelve in the Ullevi Stadium, his

---

[496] Jérôme Romain, Silver medallist in the 1995 Pan American Games and Bronze in the 1995 World Championships; later represented France [1971-].
[497] Yoel Garcia Luis, World Indoor Champion in 1997 and Silver medallist in Sydney 2000 [1973-].

main rivals would all go before him, except Wellman and he was very tense, Edwards himself recalling in the 2021 interview with World Athletics that he had bought darkened sunglasses at the airport so his competitors would not see the fear in his eyes in the changing room!

Yet as was often the case with Edwards, the tension subsided once he made his way to the runway and the time for thinking was over. He had perfected his technique that season, but it was more a triumph of both mind and body, the former clear of doubt at the key moments and the latter managed by an experienced athlete to absolutely peak condition. In watching the video of his jumping in Gothenburg, he had never looked more confident and recalled in the 2021 interview thinking at the time, "I could jump a massive distance here." He was twenty-nine-years-old then and 57 now, but his recollection of that evening is crystal clear, a man still in thrall to what he achieved, as much still in disbelief as well as proud, with a smile never far from his face when discussing those monumental jumps.

Edwards still needed a small piece of fortune and that balmy evening offered it. Here there was to be no chance an excessive wind would cost him another World Record and with an expectant crowd clapping rhythmically, he took off down the Mondotrack[498] like a man on a mission, the surface considered by organisers to be favourable and subsequent biomechanical analysis proved he was much faster that day on his approach than any of his competitors.[499] His speed that day gave his jumps the flat trajectory with which they are synonymous – *fast and flat* being the common description ever since – and seemingly floating over the ground, his first effort was measured at 59ft $6\frac{3}{4}$in

---

[498] A trademarked synthetic rubber track surface made by Mondo.
[499] https://www.european-athletics.com/news/edwards-barrier-breaking-leap-celebrates-another-anniversary

(18.16m),[500] immediately obvious to the 45,000 capacity crowd that he had broken the World Record in clearly exceeding the measuring board set at just over 18m.

[501]He was a relieved man when he broke the World Record on that first jump, adding an incredible 18cm to his former mark. He appeared dazed or even bemused, with the overriding image of him miming to promoter Andy Norman at trackside as to whether his arms were right in that jump! Ushering the photographers out of the way so Wellman could jump next, Edwards was in the zone

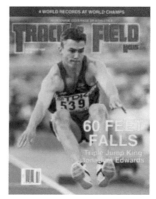

and almost willing his place to come round in the order again, saying later in the 2021 interview that he had, "a feeling of I'm not done yet in this competition." The capacity crowd were in anticipation of what could come next from Edwards, and it was clear to all that they were witnessing one of *the* moments in the history of triple jump, let alone track and field. For his part, Edwards kept himself loose for the fifteen or so minutes between jumps, doing some light bounding and shifting his arms from front to back in the double-arm movement he was in the process of making iconic, an athlete visualizing an ever better jump than he had delivered in the first-round.

A moment of anxiety came before his second jump, when James Beckford[502] of Jamaica, the hugely talented horizontal jumper (at the time just twenty and the best Junior in the world for both disciplines in the year prior), recorded a distance of 17.13m. This was

---

[500] Ratified as such, but essentially 59ft 7in.
[501] *Track & Field News* cover following the World Record jumps, October 1995 © Track & Field News
[502] James Beckford, Olympic long jump Silver medallist in Atlanta 1996 and Silver in both the 1995 & 2003 World Championships for the long jump [1975-].

a modest jump for a man whose personal best was 17.92m from May of that year, but it was the wind speed of +2.5m/s that was notable for Edwards, over the allowable limit for any further World Record distance. His first jump had seen the immense pressure of chasing the record throughout a summer of expectancy lift and the athlete who stood on that runway the second time that evening was now relaxed, even serene. He remarked in a 2020 interview that a big jump in competition would normally see him lose his edge, the adrenalin lost, but in Gothenburg he knew it was "a once-in-a-lifetime opportunity"[503] with perfect conditions and the crowd behind him, so when the wind reading fortunately lowered, he took off on his sprint, thinking to himself, "let's see what you can do here".[504]

Whereas his first jump had seen him *float* over the ground, he really *flew* on his second, pushing his World Record out to 60ft 0in (18.29m).[505] He knew his step had been close to perfect second time and the athlete who rose from the sandpit in disbelief once again knew he had taken his event to a whole new level, the scoreboard showing an almost bewildering distance. He was not just the first man to 18m and then to 60ft in consecutive jumps only twenty minutes apart but had broken both the metric and imperial measurement barriers in the same competition. His achievement would bring parallels to Bob Beamon's World Record long jump in Mexico City in 1968, Edwards making his rivals that day appear even *ordinary* in comparison, the rhythm of his almost effortless jumping as near to poetry as athletics can be. A sensational season had just been taken into the record-breaking equivalent of the stratosphere.

---

[503] https://www.bbc.co.uk/sport/athletics/53661335
[504] https://www.bbc.co.uk/sport/athletics/53661335
[505] Ratified as such, but more correctly 60ft $\frac{1}{10}$in.

Edwards had been very aware that 18.29m was enough to reach the 60ft threshold and the magnitude of that achievement was not lost on him, even amongst the euphoria of the moment. He passed on his third and fourth attempts that night to allow Wellman to concentrate on his own routine without a bundle of photographers in his way and he was always grateful for that show of respect, not least because he secured Silver with a windy 17.62m. Edwards did take his fifth jump as he felt he owed it to the crowd, but he ended his competition after that effort of 17.49m. The best jumps for five of the top seven were all wind-assisted and perhaps his life-long devotion to his faith had been repaid at last with a small favour, as although the wind was not a factor in his jumping, his career-defining efforts could have been denied to him with some unfortunate gusts of wind.

[506]During the medal ceremony, the Gothenburg crowd gave Edwards a standing ovation for the three minutes it took for this modest man to finally motion them all back into their seats. His life had changed irrevocably, and he had proven himself the finest exponent of the triple jump in history. Willie Banks said the following year of Edwards, "he's got the secret... he's figured it out"[507] and it was certainly true that no one before him had been able to demonstrate such balanced or velocity-orientated phases. Edwards had notable speed, posting a 10.48sec personal best in the 100m in 1996 and an indoor 60m best of 6.73sec in 1998, but his record-breaking jumps

---

[506] Screenshot from the televised 1995 World Championships medal presentation © BBC Television via YouTube
[507] Layden, *op. cit.*

were due to the time he spent off the ground, not on it. Banks often speaks of an active landing being key to distance covered in a triple jump and Edwards was able to make his ground contacts as light as possible, the motion that gave rise to the skipping stone analogies he is now associated with. Coach Peter Stanley summed it up best as, "the way his foot strikes the ground is magical... they [his rivals] don't have that."[508]

Edwards thought he would go on to break the World Record again – he had after all jumped further in Lille with the marginally illegal wind – and from 1996 he sought to make himself faster and stronger in pursuit of that, but his technique was never as good as it had been in 1995. He was sage enough to realise in 1993 that his increased speed then was too much for his technique to cope with at the time,[509] leading to the devastating failure in the 1992 Olympics, yet the events of the 1995 season must have dimmed his competitive zeal and he would certainly be plagued by uncertainty as he approached the next Olympics in Atlanta. He had earnt around $400,000 in prize money that season,[510] many times his previous highest and whilst he would remain ranked in the top three in the world until he retired in 2003, being number one in 1995, 1998, 2000-02, the years that followed Gothenburg brought periods of introspection and a sense of claustrophobia, due to expectation and public interest now being so high.

---

[508] Layden, *op. cit.*
[509] 'Athletics: Edwards leaps clear of Sunday obstacle: Mike Rowbottom reports on the British triple-jumper who was inspired by a dream to relax his religious tenet before the World Indoor Championships, starting today', Mike Rowbottom, *The Independent*, 11 March 1993
[510] Folley, *op. cit.*, p.120

[511]The 1996 Olympics saw a further high-profile failure when losing a memorable head-to-head competition with Kenny Harrison of the United States, on the anniversary of the event's introduction at the Games. Edwards went to Atlanta as the youngest of the main contenders at thirty-years-old and was heavily favoured, with 1991 World

Championships winner Harrison a year older and returning from a serious knee injury, an enigmatic athlete remarkably competing in his first Olympics. The Briton struggled in the preliminary round and missed the qualification standard of 17m yet progressed as one of the twelve highest placed jumpers. He opened the final with a jump in excess of 18m, but it was to be one of four foul jumps for Edwards and although his fourth-round jump of 17.88m exceeded the former Olympic Record of Mike Conley, Harrison went further on his first and fourth attempts, claiming Gold with an impressive distance of 59ft $4\frac{1}{5}$in (18.09m), into a headwind of 0.4m/s, the Olympic Record to this day and still the furthest triple jump with a negative wind reading (where an athlete is running or jumping into the wind!). Edwards beat Harrison in five of their seven meetings that season but could not do so in the competition that mattered the most.

Despite missing out on the Olympic title, Edwards was delighted with the Silver medal, after a season in which his record-breaking exploits of 1995 had become a bit of a burden and his family had suffered the trauma of Alison requiring emergency surgery in the

---

[511] Kenny Harrison stepping in the 1996 Olympic triple jump final – his effort obvious!! © unknown

February. Life for Edwards was quieter after Atlanta and the 1997 season brought the opportunity to defend his World Championships title in Athens, Greece. He picked up an injury to his left heel when defending the European Cup on 22 June in a rainy Munich, having jumped 17.74m and the resultant bruised heel – a crucial contact point for a triple jumper – meant that he cleared his calendar for an initial 6-week period of rest after jumping 17.54m in Sheffield at the end of June, besting Olympic Champion Harrison in that final meeting. He would continue to feel the need to protect his ankle that season and withdrew from all competition until Athens.

The 1997 World Championships would see Edwards disappoint in a major final once more and this time he was not satisfied with Silver. Cuban Yoelbi Quesada had put pressure on the Briton early with a second-round 17.85m and Edwards could not respond, a season of limited competition and a tight hamstring restricting him. His 2000 biography speaks of an athlete struggling to align his faith with what he had achieved, a sense of detachment evident in the demotivating factor he sometimes felt as the greatest jumper in history; essentially, he was competing against himself in his mind and he needed to find a new purpose with his profession. He was an athlete requiring frequent stimulus and he did not always get what he now needed from his Gateshead setup, seeking out ideas from other coaches and masseurs in those next few years. This saw him run around Anderson's gym with his arms in strange positions, not without comment from his long-time mentor, and he even tried some training exercises in roller blades, never stopping his search for marginal gains!

Important victories followed in the 1998 season, including the European indoor title in February, jumping 18.01m in Oslo, Norway on 9 July, the first time he had cleared 18m since Gothenburg and he claimed the European Championships title in late August, constantly pushing his body when the mind allowed it. He was still racked with uncertainty over the fear of injury as he had been in 1997 and his left ankle troubled him all season, the pain managed with anti-inflammatories, before he was forced to give in and have surgery in September 1998. Edwards initially feared his career could be over at 32, still with another World Championships and final Olympics in his sights, and a need for redemptive victories in both was to drive him on.

[512]The 1999 World Championships in Seville, Spain came and went with another disappointing result, finishing third behind surprise winner Charles  Friedek[513] of Germany, having struggled to get himself fully fit that season and still showing the technical deficiencies that cost him Gold in the 1996 Olympics. His 2000 biography details how he believed his Olympic dream perished in Seville, with the result so personally devastating, but he would still train as if victory in Sydney 2000 was possible, knowing that only Kenny Harrison could then defeat a fully fit Edwards. The buildup to Sydney was extremely difficult for his family, with Alison's mother seriously ill and when she passed whilst Edwards was already in Australia, his urge was to come home; yet his wife encouraged him to stay and relying on his faith once again to help him make a decision, he remained in Sydney and was to finally claim an Olympic Gold at the fourth time of asking, the oldest champion ever in his event with a third-round 17.71m on 25 September 2000.

---

[512] A victorious Edwards celebrating in the Sydney Olympics © unknown
[513] Charles M. Friedek, World Championships and World Indoor Championships Gold in 1999, with a Silver in the 2002 European Championships [1971-].

In a 2001 interview, Edwards professed he had found some inner peace with victory in the Sydney Olympics and a "feeling of completeness."[514]   On 6 August 2001, he won the World Championships in Edmonton, Canada with a jump of 58ft $9\frac{1}{2}$in (17.92m),[515] the longest jump in the world for three years and it was typical of Edwards that he had to overcome both a poor qualifying round and bad start to the final to claim victory. At thirty-five-years-old he was the model of longevity, the oldest athlete in the competition and it was his last major global title,[516] retirement coming when finishing 12th in the 2003 World Championships in Paris, having been troubled that summer by a serious ankle problem.

Retirement has been kind to Edwards, comfortable financially from his career and for a while he found his niche as a sports presenter, across a variety of sports and platforms, including road cycling. His achievements as an athlete were truly extraordinary and remain so to this day. The three World Record jumps in 1995 were hugely respected at the time and each season that passes without the 18.29m being seriously threatened adds further lustre to his achievement. His 1990's rivals felt that he had opened the door for more *talented* athletes – in their words – to go further, but no one has. Edwards' triple jump record has lasted longer than the fabled long jump record of Bob Beamon and the man who floated over the Gothenburg surface that sunny Scandinavian evening perfected a balance in technique that even he could never replicate in future seasons.

He has always attributed his improvement to the adoption of the double-arm movement of Mike Conley that gave him a better

---

[514] 'Interview: Jonathan Edwards', Duncan Mackay, *The Guardian*, 30 July 2001
[515] Still the men's M35 World Record.
[516] He did also win the 2002 Commonwealth Games title in Manchester, England, but it was not a major global event comparable to the World Championships.

position in his final phase, and the story of Jonathan Edwards is of a gifted athlete who truly fulfilled his potential. His transformation was remarkable and was as much a result of his own dedication, as it was the work of his evolving coaching group, their diversity of ideas and challenging of him providing the potent stimuli to his late career surge. Remarkably, in 2007 he announced that he had lost his faith, no longer believing that God existed and despite some serious conflict from his decision, his family have come to accept his decision. The man who often over-thought his jumping, does not see a gap in his life from the loss of a once very public faith and he is finally comfortable *being* Jonathan Edwards and all he achieved as an athlete. On 7 August 1995, he had stood on that runway in Gothenburg ahead of his second jump, nodded his head, wagged his finger to himself and in the words of Willie Banks, who became a bit of a late career mentor to the man who surpassed his World Record, he went "out there where other guys never even dream of going."[517]

18.07.1995 WR 17.98m (58ft 11$\frac{3}{4}$in) Jonathan Edwards (GBR) Salamanca, Spain (+1.8m/s)

07.08.1995 WR 18.16m (59ft 6$\frac{3}{4}$in) Jonathan Edwards (GBR) Gothenburg, Sweden (+1.3m/s)

07.08.1995 WR 18.29m (60ft 0in) Jonathan Edwards (GBR) Gothenburg, Sweden (+1.3m/s)

---

[517] 'TRACK AND FIELD; For Edwards, 59-0 Was a Leap of Faith', Christopher Clarey, *The New York Times*, 5 August 1995

THE 'GOAT'?

"It eats at me that I'm number two all time"[518]

How should *greatness* in an athlete be defined? The athlete who ran the fastest, jumped the highest, threw the longest or leaped the furthest? Or the champion athlete with the most major victories and global competition medals. Metric measurements (metres, seconds) are used by World Athletics to offer a black and white definition of time, height and distance in track and field events, and World Records offer the clearest examples of the leading exponents in each discipline of all time, even indoors or outdoors. The longest standing of the athletics individual all time bests is the women's 800m mark set by Jarmila Kratochvílová[519] of the Czech Republic (then Czechoslovakia) and in July 2023 it will have been 40 years since she clocked a time of 1:53.28 in Munich. Since that World Record in 1983, only two women have come within a second of it, but it is not considered a 'clean' mark by anti-doping campaigners, with drug testing sporadic in the 1980's and suspicion around Kratochvílová and other record-breaking runners in that era, although she never failed a test. The triple jump World Record of Jonathan Edwards is approaching thirty years itself and has almost become a thing of fable, hugely respected yet a mark so out of reach for so long that it is now considered *historic*, current athletes looking to more recent superstars for their *GOAT*, the Greatest of All Time.

---

[518] https://olympics.com/en/news/christian-taylor-injury-recovery-podcast-interview
[519] Jarmila Kratochvílová, World Champion in the 400m & 800m in 1983, Olympic Silver medallist in the 400m in 1980 and former World Record holder in the 400m, with her indoor 400m record not broken until February 2023 [1951-].

The term 'GOAT', or 'G.O.A.T.', is commonly believed to have originated in September 1992, when the wife of icon Muhammad Ali[520] – a phenomenon remembered for so much more than his boxing pedigree – incorporated the term for her husband's intellectual property purposes. He proclaimed himself "The Greatest" throughout his career, although never used the GOAT acronym and that only gained traction after 2000, with the release of a popular song of the same name.[521] From the 2000's the term has become part of mainstream sporting vocabulary and every sport now has a GOAT, or at least heated debates about it! The younger generations, including active athletes, are so much more dynamic than their parents and with a mass propensity for abbreviation following the rise of social media, modern sporting greats benefit from a strong recency bias that overemphasises recent achievement and are readily labelled as the GOAT, commonly shown on social media via the 🐐 emoji.

The very definition of greatness suggests that it is an honorific title only bestowed on very few, in the case of sport that being great teams or notable individuals. But is it earned over a long career of exceptional results in major competition, having been challenged by elite peers or do moments of greatness confer on an individual that status, by virtue of momentary achievement ahead of those that came before you? Jonathan Edwards retired in 2003 as the World Record holder and with an exceptional overall medal record, yet further great triple jumpers have followed him and the story of the men's triple jump did not end on 7 August 1995 in Gothenburg.

---

[520] Muhammad Ali, born Cassius M. Clay Jr., professional boxer and activist who was one of the most significant sporting and cultural figures of the 20th century [1942-2016].
[521] 'G.O.A.T. (Greatest of All Time)', the eighth studio album of American rapper, LL Cool J, released in 2000 and included a song named 'The G.O.A.T.', debuting as the number one album in the United States.

Watching on in the crowd that day, was a fifteen-year-old programme seller, Gothenburger Christian Olsson.[522] Sitting fifteen rows back from a spectacle he would never forget and amongst the crowd that exploded with joy so vividly that day, he was inspired by Edwards to later make what was seen by Swedes as a surprising switch to the triple jump, having won the European Junior Championships high jump title in 1999 and been convinced to make the change by new coach Yannick Tregaro.[523] In those same championships in Riga, Estonia, he took Silver in the triple jump, having cleared 16m for the first time in the season opener and finished the year with a personal best of 16.30m.[524] He then still considered himself a high jumper, but having failed to qualify for the triple jump final in Sydney 2000, the following season he announced himself with regular world class jumps, narrowly missing reaching 17m for the first time.

By the summer of 2001, he was twenty-one-years-old with a career best triple jump of 17.49m from early July in Greece and had defeated Edwards in Helsinki in late June. He ended that season as the world number two with a Silver medal from the World Championships in Edmonton, having only lost to Edwards all year and even beaten him twice, a metronomic rise to the top level of the sport that he always credits to a friendly rivalry with the Briton. Now a major sporting personality in his native Sweden, the following season he would claim his first European Championships title in Munich – he repeated this in his hometown Gothenburg in 2006 – and with victory in the European Indoor Championships in Vienna, Austria he heralded himself as a

[522] Christian Olsson, 2003 World Champion, 2004 Olympic Champion and World Indoor Champion in both of those years, whose career was later derailed by serious injury; also joint IAAF Golden League jackpot winner in 2006, having won all six events and he took home a prize of $500,000 [1980-].
[523] Yannick Tregaro, Swedish former high jumper, and now leading jumps coach, leading several athletes to World medals, both indoor and outdoor [1978-].
[524] https://worldathletics.org/news/news/christian-olsson-is-for-real

239

major force in the sport, ready to fill the void left by the aging Edwards and a noticeable figure in track and field events with his crop of blonde hair.

Olsson was to claim a clutch of titles in 2003-04, including the 2003 World Championships, when in the neat bookend that only sport seems to provide, he won his first major championship on the day that Edwards retired, the teenager in the 1995 Gothenburg crowd now the world number one and undefeated in fifteen meetings in 2003. The following year, now firmly established as Edwards' successor, he repeated as World Indoor Champion in Budapest on 7 March, a career best jump of 58ft 6in (17.83m) that was ratified as the World Indoor Record. He went to the Athens Olympics in 2004 as the favourite and did not disappoint, winning with a second-round effort of 58ft $4\frac{2}{5}$in (17.79m), a class above the rest of the field and still the Swedish National Record to this day.

But that season was to sadly be the peak for Olsson as the leading triple jumper in the world, a series of injuries that originated with a foot problem – a bone bruise – in the Athens final plaguing him for the rest of his career and surgery could never return him to the level he had so brilliantly demonstrated in 2003-04. He eventually retired in 2012, a second European title in 2006 in Gothenburg giving false hope to the obsessively driven Swede that he could yet make a full recovery and sadly for him after seven surgeries on his ankle, he was never able to challenge the 18m threshold that was to become the benchmark for the truly elite jumpers.

Whereas Olsson was leggy compared to Edwards, 6ft $3\frac{1}{2}$in (1.92m) in height as opposed to 6ft (1.82m), he never had the same ground speed and utilised a more rhythmic style, believing his technique to be superior to that of the Briton and which he expected

240

to take him beyond 18m in time. Persistent injury in 2004-05 would prevent him from returning to full speed in competition until 2006, with that initial return ultimately short-lived and he was never able to fully explore how far his undoubted potential could take him. His was a short but dominant career filled with magnificent moments, World and Olympic titles the stand outs, but the man marked by Edwards as his successor[525] would ultimately prove to end his career ranked some way below the best in his event, now *only* 20th on the all-time list. He has since been usurped on that list by rivals Jadel Gregório[526] and Marian Oprea,[527] joint 10th and joint 18th respectively all-time, and a new generation of athletes would succeed him who would jump beyond 18m like Edwards, headed by the man now contemporaneously called the GOAT, Christian Taylor of the United States.

It could be said that after Edwards there was a race to be the third to clear 18m (Kenny Harrison being the second), but Olsson and Phillips Idowu[528] of Great Britain were the early front-runners, even before the World Record holder was forced into retirement in 2003 by serious injury. We have seen how Edwards and the young Swede had a friendly rivalry, driving Olsson on to improve at break-neck speed, yet the rivalry between the two Great Britain athletes would continue into Edwards' retirement, eventually becoming a feud (that was

[525] https://worldathletics.org/news/news/edwards-simply-a-matter-of-faith
[526] Jadel A. G. Gregório, Brazilian triple jumper who was sixth in the 2008 Olympic final, Silver medallist in the 2007 World Championships and 2007 Pan American Games Champion, being world number one in 2007 [1980-].
[527] Marian Oprea of Romania, the 2000 World Junior Championships winner, Silver medallist in Athens 2004 and World Championships Bronze in 2005; world number one in 2005 [1982-].
[528] Phillips O. Idowu, World Champion in 2009, Olympic Silver medallist in 2008 and Diamond League Champion in 2011, amongst other major championship victories and medals; the second-best triple jumper from Great Britain of all time [1978-].

resolved) and Idowu never really managed to escape the older man's long shadow, despite high profile successes of his own.

Whereas Edwards was the perceptibly ordinary man with extraordinary achievements who never felt comfortable in the limelight, Idowu was an extrovert with an eccentric personality, 6ft 6in (1.97m) tall, powerful and fast, who eventually managed to fall out with the UK Athletics hierarchy ahead of a home Olympics and even his own long-time coach, Aston Moore.[529] The flamboyant dress sense, facial piercings and brightly dyed hair would all serve to sadly detract from the achievements of a supremely talented athlete and if he had been born a few years later and avoided the injury curse that caused him to miss a number of major championships at his peak, then he might well have been the man to challenge Edwards' World Record.

In the 2002 Commonwealth Games in Manchester, England, Idowu would put the then thirty-six-year-old Edwards under serious pressure with a second-round jump of 17.68m and it took great mental fortitude for him to pull out a third-round 17.86m to claim Gold from the upstart, enabling him to hold the World Record, World, Olympic, European and Commonwealth titles at the same time.[530] Idowu would go on to have a career best 58ft $5\frac{1}{5}$in (17.81m) when a commanding performance won the 2010 European Championships in Barcelona and his crowning moment would be victory in the 2009 World Championships in Berlin with a then personal best of 17.73m, although this moment of glory was soured for him by Edwards being asked to present his medal, "on what was supposed to be my (Idowu's)

---

[529] Aston L. Moore, Commonwealth Bronze medallist in the triple jump in 1976 & 1982, now the national event coach for the triple jump, having previously trained leading British jumpers Phillips Idowu and Ashia Hansen [1956-].
[530] Olsson would claim the European title from him in August 2002, when Edwards came third behind 1999 World Champion, Charles Friedek.

occasion."[531] He was doomed always to be remembered as *just* the second best jumper in Great Britain triple jumping, let alone the world, his own notable achievements obscured in comparison to the furthest jumper in history being British and it was to be younger athletes who would prove better able to challenge the World Record holder in the coming years.

The 2005 World Championships in Helsinki would be won by Walter Davis[532] of the United States and the 2007 iteration in Osaka, Japan by Nelson Évora[533] of Portugal. Davis would be ranked only fourth in the world in 2005, despite his World title, but would top the rankings the following year with a jump of 17.71m. Évora would go on to have a remarkable career himself, topped with Olympic Gold in Beijing 2008, a four-time World Championships medallist who could still claim a World indoor Bronze in 2018 and a Silver in the European Indoor Championships the following year, by then aged nearly 35.

But the triple jump was stagnating after the retirement of Edwards and injury struggles of Olsson in particular, more athletes reaching 17.50m than before, yet those at the top someway short of jumping 18m, let alone putting the World Record under threat, with Jadel Gregório's 58ft $8\frac{7}{10}$in (17.90m) in Belém, Brazil on 20 May 2007 the leading distance since 2001. The triple jump was crying out for a new King and whilst Phillips Idowu was enjoying his finest moment in winning the 2009 World Championships in Berlin, the fall of that year would see a freshman phenomenon at the University of Florida

---

[531] 'I'm world champion says Phillips Idowu but I'll never jump out of the shadow of Jonathan Edwards', Ian Stafford, *Mail on Sunday*, 25 October 2009

[532] Walter L. Davis, World Championships Gold in 2005, Bronze in 2007 and World Indoor Champion in 2006; given a one-year ban in 2014 for missing three mandatory drugs tests [1979-].

[533] Nelson Évora, World Champion in 2007, Olympic Champion in 2008 and a host of indoor medals, in both the Worlds and Europeans [1984-].

commencing a journey that would re-write the triple jump history books insomuch that he is now commonly called the GOAT.

[534]Born on 18 June 1990 in Long Island, New York, but raised in Fayetteville, Georgia where his parents Ian and Stephanie moved after his birth, **Christian Taylor** was a sporting standout for as long as anyone can remember. Growing up with a younger sister whom he would race around the house, he played the typical sports of an American childhood, including football (American), basketball, soccer, golf and even karate, but his first love was soccer, with a dream to play in the World Cup. His was an active childhood and in his early teenage years his parents challenged him to try track and field, with the belief that his sporting talent could lead to a college scholarship, as they would not pay for tuition when he was so gifted. The focus began to switch to athletics and it was at Sandy Creek High School in Tyrone, Georgia and as a member of the QuickSilver Track Club in nearby Atlanta from the age of sixteen[535] that the long-limbed Taylor became a nascent sprinting and jumping star.

Having set high school records in the triple jump, long jump and 400m,[536] and won Gold in the triple jump and Bronze in the long jump at the 2007 World Youth Championships in Ostrava, Czech Republic, with a triple jump of 15.98m having just turned seventeen, he was the 2008 Gatorade Athlete of the Year for the state of Georgia. He left high school having won the 2008 National Scholastic Indoor

---

[534] Christian Taylor pictured in 2010 having won the NCAA Outdoor Triple Jump Championship at the University of Florida © unknown

[535] '#56: Christian Taylor, Olympic Gold Medalist and World Champion in the Triple Jump', *Clean Sport Collective Podcast*, hosts Chris McClung & Kara Goucher, 5 July 2020

[536] https://fl.milesplit.com/articles/89240/road-to-london-christian-taylor

Championships for the triple jump, long jump and 400m and with back-to-back team state championships in 2007-08. A teenage phenomenon who was humbled by the year older Teddy Tamgho[537] of France in the World Junior Championships in Poland in July 2008 (more on him later) and then jumped 52ft $6\frac{1}{2}$in (16.01m) in that September, still as a high school senior, he was heavily recruited to the University of Florida (UF) by then assistant field coach Rana Reider.[538] Taylor was courted by other leading colleges such as FSU, but was attracted by the recent high profile national success of UF in other sports, particularly American football.

[539]He enrolled at UF in the fall of 2008, now committed to athletics over his once-favoured soccer and within months took Gold at the NCAA Indoor Championships, the first of consecutive titles and the first steps towards building a legacy at Florida, both as an individual and helping the team to their first national title  in track and field, which they did indoors in the 2010 season under head coach, Mike Holloway.[540] Reider had surprisingly departed before his freshman year and he was latterly coached by jumps guru Dick

[537] Teddy Tamgho, former World Indoor Record holder from 2011-21, World Indoor Champion in 2010 and World Champion in 2013; retired aged only thirty in 2019, having struggled with frequent injury since 2011 and now coach of Hugues Fabrice Zango, the current World Indoor Record holder [1989-].

[538] Rana Reider, renowned sprint and jumps coach, who in addition to Christian Taylor and a period working for UK Athletics, coached Andre de Grasse of Canada to Olympic Gold in the 200m in 2020 amongst a host of other Olympic and World medals; later investigated for sexual misconduct and the athletes in his charge have distanced themselves from him since 2021 [1970-].

[539] Christian Taylor competing for the University of Florida, cover of *Techniques for Track & Field and Cross Country*, Vol. 5/No. 2 November 2011)

[540] Michael 'Mike' D. Holloway, still the head coach of the University of Florida track and field team and has led UF to a number of NCAA titles, including five Division I indoor national championships that included two with Taylor and Claye [c.1959-].

Booth,[541] who in a long-time role at the University of Arkansas prior to a two-year stint at UF in Taylor's sophomore and junior years, worked with the likes of Jérôme Romain, Brian Wellman and most notably Mike Conley, coaching him to that stellar jump of 18.17m (wind-aided) in the Barcelona Olympics in 1992. Booth would take Taylor and fellow UF jumper Will Claye[542] – the 2009 NCAA outdoor triple jump champion who transferred from the University of Oklahoma in 2010 to work with Booth, after injuries had slowed his progress and who would deny Taylor a hat-trick of indoor titles in 2011 – to great success at the collegiate level, pushing each other on a daily basis and culminating in a 1-2 finish in the 2011 NCAA Outdoor Triple Jump Championships in June, in Des Moines, Iowa.

Having elected to turn professional as a college junior and signed with Chinese athletics company Li-Ning, Taylor gave up his remaining year of college eligibility, former UF assistant Rana Reider now his personal coach and he would work with him until 2021, initially as part of a training group back home in Atlanta including leading United States long jumper Dwight Phillips.[543] Taylor had won the NCAA Championships that June with a windy 17.80m and the 1-2 placing for him and Claye in the USA Track & Field (USATF) event in Oregon qualified them both for that year's World Championships in Daegu, South Korea, where Claye would also compete in the long jump. Taylor had improved his triple jumping by almost 1m in the

---

[541] Dick Booth, veteran jumps coach, with around 49 individual NCAA Champions and 11 Olympians having worked under him [c.1945-].
[542] William B. Claye, World Indoor Champion in 2012 & 2018, three-time Olympic medallist in the triple jump and long jump, with four World Championships medals in the triple jump in consecutive competitions from 2011-19; the third furthest man in the triple jump in history [1991-].
[543] Dwight Phillips, 2004 Olympic long jump Gold and World Champion in 2003, 2005, 2009 & 2011 [1977-].

2011 season,[544] and with four NCAA individual titles[545] and a memorable back-and-forth with Claye in that 2011 outdoor final – Claye jumped a wind-assisted 17.62, adding over 8 inches to his best, with Taylor going to 17.80m – Taylor had around two months to prepare for the World Championships as a professional.

A college sensation in three seasons of competition, a ten-time NCAA All-American and the first to reach 58ft in a NCAA event since Mike Conley in 1985, the now leading triple jumper in the United States headed to Europe to begin his professional career. His debut meet was the London Grand Prix in August 2011 and it was to be the first of many career wins in the Diamond League[546] competition, with a personal best 58ft $\frac{1}{10}$in (17.68m). This was good enough for third best in the world season to date and was to place him just outside the then all-time top twenty, so despite being relatively inexperienced on the international stage he had high hopes as he travelled to Daegu, taking comfort from great friend and rival Will Claye competing alongside him, as well as experienced training partner Dwight Phillips, who he would see win Gold in the long jump ahead of his own final.

Taylor was used to winning, particularly so since he seriously got into the triple jump as a fourteen-year-old[547] at middle school and disappointments since then had been few. In upsetting Phillips Idowu in the London Grand Prix, he had served notice that he might well challenge in Daegu, but nobody really expected what was to come at those 2011 World Championships, when he was to jump on the biggest

---

[544] https://worldathletics.org/news/report/mens-triple-jump-final-taylor-sails-1796m
[545] Most online sources credit Taylor with only three NCAA titles, but his fourth was the 2011 outdoor championship.
[546] Inaugurated in 2010, an annual series of elite track and field events which replaced the IAAF Golden League, which had been held since 1998. The Diamond League includes invitational meetings around the world, in addition to the traditional European competitions and is intended to broaden the global appeal of athletics.
[547] McClung & Goucher, *op. cit.*

stage for the first time. In a sign of his unsophistication as an international senior athlete, he allowed his nerves to upset any chance of adjusting his sleep pattern ahead of travelling to South Korea and in misunderstanding his coach's instruction about what to do on the plane, he remained seated the whole time in his compression socks and failed to keep moving, his ankles so swollen on arrival that he could not train for two days![548]

Idowu came into the event as the defending champion and was favoured to become the first athlete to win back-to-back triple jump titles in the World Championships, something even Edwards never managed. Taylor's season in the collegiate ranks had started in January and eight months later he still needed to find a further level yet to challenge the best jumpers in the world, a poor qualifying session seeing him finish outside of the automatic mark and he would only scrape into the Daegu final as the 9th best jumper. It is difficult for an athlete to sustain success over such a prolonged period (the college season starts in January, the professionals do not compete outdoors until around May) and it was Claye, in qualifying third-best for the triple jump final and in also reaching the long jump final, who was to be the American history-maker at that stage, the first since Mike Conley to final in both at the World Championships (he did it in 1983 and 1987).

Teddy Tamgho had beaten Taylor in the 2008 World Junior Championships and made a phenomenal start to life as a young professional. He was the 2010 World Indoor Champion and had broken the seventeen-year-old World Indoor Record in taking the title, extending that distance of 17.90m to 17.91m in February 2011 in the French Championships, and then to 17.92m (twice) on 6 March 2011 in Paris, when winning the European Indoor Championships. Even

---

[548] McClung & Goucher, *op. cit.*

more impressively he had jumped the best outdoor distance for over a decade in the New York Diamond League meeting on 12 June 2010, 58ft 11$\frac{9}{10}$in (17.98m) making him the third-furthest legal triple jumper in history. It was considered that covering 18m was only a matter of time for Tamgho and the World Championships was a target, yet he fractured his right ankle in July 2011 and for a while this was considered a career threatening injury. He would not return fully to competition until March 2013 and in Daegu, the inconsistent Idowu now without a serious rival, would perhaps be vulnerable to the young college tyros from the United States, if they could each find another gear...

The Briton started confidently in the 2011 World Championships final on the evening of 4 September and after three rounds led with a best effort of 17.70m, not far off his personal best of 17.81m set in Barcelona the previous summer. Claye was second at that stage and Taylor third, the latter having jumped 17.40m, and having been pulled aside by fellow American triple jumper Walter Davis after his third-round jump, the 2005 World Champion who had failed to qualify for the 2011 final told Taylor that he had what it took. Davis had been one of the younger man's idols and to be recognised as having the ability to win on this stage – in 2020 Taylor said he "felt like he [Davis] had just handed him the baton"[549] in borrowing a sprint relay term – he resolved to treat the World Championship final as just another competition, no longer uneasy about suddenly finding himself rubbing shoulders with the elite as the youngest jumper in the final at only 21.

Taylor was jumping before Idowu and the latter's third-round 17.70m was not far from being a season best, well clear of Claye's third-round personal best of 17.50m in second (and it was to be good enough

549 McClung & Goucher, *op. cit.*

for Bronze). For the first time in a major competition, Idowu was showing the consistency of performance that had eluded him for years and it would take something special to stop him from defending his title. Yet little did he know that the young American then standing on the runway awaiting his fourth effort, the world number three, an infectious smile on his face, arms aloft in leading the crowd to clap along in time before he took off down the runway with that elite sprinter's speed, was about to begin his own storied journey into the triple jump record books at Idowu's expense.

[550]Taylor landed that jump only slightly short of 18m and left less than 1cm from his left foot to the plasticine on the board, victory all but assured when most were jumping around 17.50m. It was a stunning jump beyond all expectations, despite his pedigree at UF and sustained success as a college athlete, Taylor himself high kneeing away from the pit in disbelief at what he had achieved. It was measured at 58ft 11$\frac{1}{10}$in (17.96m) and was the third furthest jump from an American of all time, into a marginal headwind of 0.1m/s. Taylor had put 28cm on his personal best and it was a picture of technical proficiency, Taylor floating through the phases like Mike Conley, rather than bouncing like Kenny Harrison and his was an overtly jump-dominated style. He was still to fully harness his technique, but the victory in Daegu was no fluke and he had announced himself to the world as a triple jumper of enormous potential,

---

[550] Taylor jumping in the 2011 World Championships in Daegu, South Korea © Erik van Leeuwen

commenting afterwards that the win did not surprise him, but "the distance did... for something like that to happen was just a blessing."[551]

At 21 Taylor had taken himself to a new level in a matter of weeks since turning professional and he would end the 2011 season as the new world number one. Idowu was matter of fact about the defeat in Daegu, content with his performance and remarking in a post-final interview that it "only takes one jump," taking comfort from the way he responded in the fourth round with a season best 17.77m. The problem for him was that Taylor had gone way beyond his own personal best in Daegu and whilst Idowu knew he must kick on to claim a much-coveted Olympic Gold in home-city London the following year, so must Taylor also improve, Daegu being only the beginning. Taylor had shown blazing speed in his first major competition, throughout his later career being one of the fastest jumpers in the last step before take-off, but of the 2011 World Championships finalists he had the second-shortest hop, the horizontal velocity he carried into his step seeing him through to the bigger lengths in the middle and jump phases that secured him the Gold medal, so it was obvious where he could improve.

Idowu started the 2012 season the more impressively of the two, winning the Shanghai leg of the Diamond League in atrocious conditions in May when the rivals met for the first time that year, but thereafter the season was increasingly owned by Taylor, by the London Olympics utilising an extended stride, or leap, in his run-up in the style of the Cubans, in order to increase his acceleration into the board. The American was the winner in the Prefontaine Classic in Eugene, Oregon on 1 June, with a world-leading 17.62m, where Idowu could only jump 17.05m and the Briton was not to compete again until the Olympics in

August, concerns around injury from an awkward landing in Oregon and an ongoing battle with the UK Athletics hierarchy disrupting his preparation. Taylor would win again in the London Grand Prix at Crystal Palace in July, on his way to his first overall Diamond League title at season's end and he was continuing to ride the crest of a wave, his introduction to the professional ranks seeing the success he had enjoyed since high school so far sustained to ever greater heights as a senior athlete.

Taylor had lost out to Will Claye in both the USA Indoor Championships and the World Indoor Championships that spring, but had set an indoor personal best in the latter and at the United States Olympic Trials he beat his rival by 8cm, extending his world-leading mark to 17.63m. He arrived in London as the strong favourite and did not disappoint in qualifying, advancing to the final with his first jump of 17.21m, Claye taking all three attempts to make the standard and scraping through. Idowu had pulled out of the London Grand Prix in mid-July with tightness in his hip and it was clear he was not right in qualifying, a proud athlete desperate to achieve his dream in his home-city Games. The Olympic Stadium was only a stone's throw from where he grew up in Hackney, but he failed to even qualify for the final, a troubled year reaching a desperately sad nadir and the expected showdown between him and Taylor over.

The World Champion came to Britain that summer with such confidence that he felt the World Record was in reach, saying at Crystal Palace in July, "I'm just fine-tuning to go for this World Record."[552] The triple jump has often seen its greatest performances in the biggest events and Taylor had been acutely aware of Edwards' record ever since he was at high school, marking out the distance in training as a

---

[552] 'London 2012: Christian Taylor aims high as Phillips Idowu stays away', Anna Kessel, *The Guardian*, 15 July 2012

constant reminder of how far he needed to go, even when it was well beyond the sandpits he had available to him then! His entry to the sport had been explosive and he was now a more seasoned athlete after a full twelve months in the professional ranks, no one doubting that this talented jumper could well trouble a record that had then lasted for 17 years. He oft stated that the World Record was the goal after winning the title in Daegu and it was just a question of how long it would take him to break it, such was his undoubted talent.

Perhaps Taylor allowed thoughts of that record to obscure his thinking in London, as he fouled on both of his first two attempts in his maiden Olympic final, his second foul in the region of 17.70m.[553] For the first time he carried the burden of expectation in a major final and in recent interviews[554] he has spoken of being motivated at various times of his career by representing UF, the United States, his Church and as a Classroom Champions[555] mentor, so in London he must have felt an enormous weight of pressure as the favourite, later recalling he was anxious.[556] Great athletes deliver when under pressure and he was at risk of elimination from a final he was expected to win easily, his only competition coming from Claye, now the new Olympic Bronze medallist in the long jump and leading the triple jump after two rounds, a distance of 17.54m being 10cm clear of the field. So, when Taylor took off for his third-round effort he had to deliver, with expectant family members in the stadium from both America and Barbados, where his parents were born...

---

[553] https://worldathletics.org/news/report/london-2012-event-report-mens-triple-jump-1

[554] McClung & Goucher, *op. cit.*

[555] An international non-profit charity organization, connecting top athletes with students in high-need schools and academic programmes.

[556] https://worldathletics.org/news/report/london-2012-event-report-mens-triple-jump-1

[557]And deliver he did, beginning a reputation as a clutch performer who came up big in the most dramatic moments. He advanced to the second part of the final with a safe – well behind the board – distance of 17.15m and in the fourth-round won himself the Gold medal with the longest jump of the season at 17.81m, his technique coming together for one big jump under pressure

as it had in Daegu, with none of the leaders improving their marks in the last two rounds. Claye took Silver and became the first jumper to win a medal in the long jump and triple jump in the same Olympics since Naoto Tajima in 1936, with Taylor the first triple jump Gold medallist for the United States since Kenny Harrison in 1996. Taylor had taken another massive step forward in his career as the dominant performer in the triple jump and whilst he never troubled the World Record he had publicly targeted on the quick surface in London, he was the youngest Olympic Champion in the discipline for 100 years.

The times that life seems most settled are often when the strangest of curve balls can be thrown at a person. Comfortable working with his coach, Rana Reider, having enjoyed great success together in two seasons as a professional (Reider had also recruited him to UF before leaving ahead of his freshman year), training in the favourable warm weather of Florida alongside world-class athletes like Claye who would push him each and every day, and with his sister Kaitlyn moving to Jacksonville, Florida to study, only an hour or so away from his Daytona Beach base, Christian Taylor was now very

---

[557] A smiling Taylor posing with his Olympic Gold medal at the Great North CityGames in Gateshead, 15 September 2012 © Stephen Caffull

settled. He was the dominant triple jumper in the world and after the 2012 season he was baptized at his home church in Georgia, ready to begin a new journey with the Lord, searching for true fulfilment outside of his sport, but knowing that his love of track and field was not yet sated. The 2013 season would then demand another trait commonly found in great athletes, that being resilience.

Reider was lured by UK Athletics after London 2012 to work with their elite jumpers and sprinters at the high-performance centre in Loughborough, England, and Taylor was one of a number of United States athletes who chose to move with him, such was their desire to continue working with his group, despite the much-altered circumstances, training dynamics and particularly the wet weather! Taylor took the change in his stride, being able to enjoy skateboarding to training in a relatively sleepy English town and embraced his new surroundings on his way to becoming a true internationalist, but a major hurdle was approaching which was potentially career-ending, noticing that his jumps were starting to shorten in the 2012 season and knee pain was becoming persistent.

Over the winter months knee pain was increasingly causing Taylor to miss training and having consulted with specialists, he was diagnosed with the early stages of patella tendonitis, triple jumping having taken its toll on his knees, with as much as nine times his body weight forced through his joints on his landings. His left knee was significantly affected and with fears that it could blow out if he carried on jumping off that leg, he soldiered on with a World title he was determined to defend in Moscow in early August, frequently afflicted with inflammation and his body no longer able to take the high intensity training required of a triple jumper. The tendonitis impeded him tremendously in the 2013 World Championships and despite qualifying third, he could not repeat that distance in the final, finishing just outside the medals in fourth with a best effort of 17.20m.

A rejuvenated Tamgho took the title with a last round 18.04m, having missed the entire indoor season to prepare for the championships after a 22-month injury layoff and he was the third man legally over 18m in a sensational display of jumping. He had other jumps of similar distance ruled marginal fouls in the final, but his career would peter out after this high, due to a combination of serious injury and an 18-month drugs ban for whereabouts violations. Claye took Bronze behind an impressive up-and-coming Cuban named Pedro Pablo Pichardo,[558] the 2012 World Junior Champion and another serious threat to Taylor's dominance. He knew his jumping was not right and needing points from the final Diamond League meeting in Brussels that September to secure the overall title, his coach encouraged him to jump off his right leg, doing just enough to claim the second place behind Tamgho required to retain the title, but a major decision loomed.

Learning to jump from the other leg is the same as attempting to write with the non-dominant hand or kick a ball with the other foot, essentially training the other side of the brain to operate skills that are already second nature, resetting his career. Willie Banks is the best-known triple jumper to have made the change before Taylor, although his leg switch came about from a basketball injury to his left ankle as a young man and not whilst he was an elite jumper.[559] Taylor knew he had to do it or his career could soon be over and recalling in 2014 "my

---

[558] Pedro P. Pichardo, Cuban-born but representing Portugal since 2017, the 2020 Olympic Champion and 2022 World Champion amongst many other leading honours; world number one since 2021 [1993-].
[559] Harvey, *op. cit.*

256

passion for it [triple jumping] exceeded the doubt,"[560] he made it happen through will and hard work. He demonstrated remarkable resilience and courage in attempting to do so whilst he was at the peak of his sport, with thoughts of claiming the World Record replaced by doubts as to what level he would return to, that first competition jump off his right leg in Zürich being over 1m down from his personal best, although this gave him some encouragement he could be successful.

He returned to competition in the 2014 season some way off his best – his personal best of 17.96m now being from the left leg he was no longer leading off from – and having won only twice all season, a season best 17.51m in the Diamond League final in Zürich, Switzerland in September was enough to win a third consecutive title. The winning jump came from his last effort and demonstrated that in a season of adversity and serial doubt from other coaches and athletes as to whether he would return to the elite level, that the clutch performances which were his trademark were still possible. It is truly remarkable what Taylor achieved in transitioning to lead off with the *other* leg mid-career and he was sustained by his faith, returning with an even deeper love for athletics and belief in himself, for what he had already achieved and still wanted to achieve.

Whereas the 2014 season required repetition, repetition, repetition as he re-trained his body to gain the necessary muscle memory and coordination, 2015 would see him break new ground, his confidence restored and no longer burdened with such persistent knee pain, transferring the weight now to his right knee. The previous season had also seen Taylor embrace the 400m again as he mixed up his training in a year with no major global championships and the restoration of the almost elite sprinting speed from his college days

---

[560] https://edition.cnn.com/2014/09/24/sport/christian-taylor-triple-jump-olympics-athletics/index.html

would propel him to new heights after his leg switch. Coach Reider had told him five years earlier that he could jump further off the other leg based on scientific tests[561] and 2015 would see personal best after personal best, the major decision to switch legs paying off in style, no longer working off the shortened run-up he used in 2014 when he was yet to be fully confident that his right leg could cope with jumping at full speed.

[562]In the first Diamond League meeting of the season in Doha, Qatar on 15 May 2015, Pichardo and then Taylor only minutes later, would both exceed 18m, Pichardo's 59ft 3in (18.06m) being the third-furthest jump in history. Pichardo had opened the season in stunning form and only a week before Doha had broken the Cuban National Record in covering 17.94m in Havana, yet Taylor still appeared slightly stunned when the new Diamond League record was measured over 18m. Conditions in Doha that evening were perfect for jumping – a slight following wind, warm weather and a fast surface – and emboldening his reputation as a clutch performer, Taylor responded on his final effort with a distance of 18.04m, the first time two men had exceeded 18m in the same competition in history. He was only 5cm off Kenny Harrison's American record, a relieved Pichardo seeing the jump measured behind his own, a triple jump history-maker at only 21 and now the most illustrious in a long list of excellent Cuban jumpers in the discipline, the

[561] https://olympics.nbcsports.com/2016/01/11/christian-taylor-triple-jump-track-and-field-olympics/
[562] Christian Taylor jumping in the Doha Diamond League meeting on 15 May 2015 © Mohan, Doha Stadium Plus

first of his countrymen to use a "proper take-off and add the much-needed jump phase at the end"[563] according to Willie Banks.

[564]Taylor had remarked that Doha was a special day for him in going over 18m for the first time and it set up the 2015 season as a duel between these two, with the World Championships in late August expectantly billed as the climax. He had equalled Tamgho's 2013 World Championships winning distance from Moscow to place him 4th all-time, but the talented Frenchman himself departed that event in Doha with an Achilles tendon injury and has never returned to major competition. Pichardo took over as Taylor's most dangerous rival in the following weeks, younger by three years and the world number one in 2014 when the American was resetting his career with the enforced leg switch; that summer his emergence would take the event and Christian Taylor to ever greater distances, hitherto out of reach.

Pichardo remarked after the Doha win that he felt 18.30m was possible for him,[565] the twenty-year-old World Record seemingly attainable once again, especially with the growing rivalry between him and Taylor. He liked to think that he had Edwards' speed on the runway and the jumping power of Harrison and Tamgho, but did acknowledge his "step and jump need some work"[566] and ground speed was the one area where Taylor clearly bettered his rival. Two weeks after Doha, Pichardo pushed his world-leading distance out to 59ft

---

[563] 'STEPPING UP – CORRECTING ERRORS TO IMPROVE THE RESULT', Willie Banks, *Techniques for Track & Field and Cross Country*, Vol. 9/No. 2 November 2015

[564] Pedro Pichardo jumping in the Doha Diamond League meeting on 15 May 2015 © Mohan, Doha Stadium Plus

[565] https://worldathletics.org/news/feature/pichardo-triple-jump

[566] https://worldathletics.org/news/feature/pichardo-triple-jump

$3\frac{4}{5}$in (18.08m) in another meeting in Havana and he had remained unbeaten that season, as the Diamond League went to Lausanne, Switzerland on 9 July 2015, for the long-held *Athletissima* meeting.

In front of a capacity crowd of just over 15,000 appreciative fans, in a historic stadium marked for destruction and old enough to have hosted matches in the 1954 football (soccer) World Cup finals, Pichardo was again the man to beat, taking a half metre lead with a first-round effort of 17.85m in blustery conditions. Taylor closed the gap in the second, before the Cuban was agonizingly short of 18m on his third effort, measured at 17.99m. The American had to respond and spurred on by this exciting new rivalry bringing the discipline some much need attention – 2015 quickly becoming known as the 'year of the triple jump' – he scratched his fourth effort, then in consecutive jumps he finished with distances of 18.02m and finally 18.06m as the heat of the day subsided, matching Pichardo's best from Doha. Afterwards he remarked that he was getting more consistent at the highest level and he joined Jonathan Edwards as the only athletes with two jumps over 18m in one competition, certainly ready for that year's World Championships in Beijing the following month.

Expectations were high that the triple jump final in Beijing could bring about another memorable chapter in the evolving Pichardo-Taylor rivalry. The 2015 version of Christian Taylor seemed reenergised after his 2013 travails and subsequent leg switch, and American journalist Larry Eder, famous for saying Taylor should have a personal best recorded for each leg, remarked that he had "rediscovered his muse with the triple jump... in racing the 400 meters [sic] once again"[567] in the 2014 season. He was certainly improving as

---

[567] https://www.runblogrun.com/2014/12/christian-taylor-to-move-to-netherlands-following-coach-rana-reider.html

a jumper off his right leg and was covering personal best distances, faster than ever on the ground and he now needed to confirm the success of the leg change with a major global title, no straightforward task with Pichardo surging.

The coach-athlete relationship between Taylor and Reider was very close, as much a friendship as it was about training minutiae and in the winter of 2014, he had followed his coach to the Netherlands, when Reider accepted a post with the Dutch national team (they would later return to Jacksonville, Florida in 2019). Taylor was ever ready to broaden his horizons and Reider was known as much for the mental aspects of his coaching, one notable example being when Taylor had scratched his first two efforts in the London Olympics. Taylor admitted to being clouded by doubt and with Reider urging him at trackside to stand and watch David Rudisha[568] make history with a breath-taking World Record performance in the fastest 800m race of all time,[569] the triple jumper would see his negativity subside, self-belief another trait regularly demonstrated by the greatest athletes and by that final he had already cleared 18m three times that season.

In a qualifying session for the 2015 World Championships final high on expectancy and short on quality, only five athletes made the automatic mark of 17m, Taylor needing two attempts and Pichardo all three. 2013 Bronze medallist Will Claye could only finish 19th and missed the final, in a year where he would still be ranked number six in the world and the track and field rivalry of the summer between Taylor and Pichardo was off to a slow burn in Beijing, the new era they had heralded that summer seemingly stalled at its climactic meeting.

---

[568] David L. Rudisha, Kenyan middle-distance runner, specialising in the 800m in which he was Olympic Champion in 2012 & 2016 and World Champion in 2011 & 2015; still the World Record holder after that remarkable run in London 2012 [1988-].
[569] https://olympics.nbcsports.com/2016/01/11/christian-taylor-triple-jump-track-and-field-olympics/

Gothenburg in 1995 had been a special night with Edwards' solo assault on the World Record and despite a nondescript qualifying session, the 2015 World Championships final at the Beijing National Stadium – the famous 'Bird's Nest' from the 2008 Olympics – would yet prove to be another memorable evening in the history of the triple jump, those in attendance witnessing a moment that would define Taylor's career to this day.

Pichardo was again the frontrunner and held a first-round lead with a jump of 17.52m. These rivals had been trading big jumps all summer and Taylor countered the Cuban with an effort of 17.49m in the second-round. In the third, they incredibly both jumped 17.60m, before Taylor edged into the lead in the fourth round with 17.68m. Pichardo responded in the fifth with 17.52m again and as the final round began, Taylor willed himself to one last performance of the night in an attempt to secure a second World title, with Pichardo due to jump after him and 18m from him still being very possible. In 2011, he had remarked after his first World title that he does "this event because it's the closest thing I can get to flying"[570] and in the Bird's Nest on 27 August 2015, Christian Taylor *flew* into the record books...

His final jump that night has been variously described as mighty, massive and monstrous. It was all of those and more, the closest his technique had been to perfect in one glorious jump of 59ft 8$\frac{9}{10}$in (18.21m), the American Record he had been chasing since 2011 now his and it was the second furthest jump of all time, only 8cm down on the World Record, with Jonathan Edwards watching nervously in a commentary box in Beijing as the stunning leap was being measured well beyond 18m. Taylor knew it was a major jump even as he landed

---

[570] https://worldathletics.org/news/feature/inspired-by-dwight-phillips-taylor-flies-to-t

and he looked in disbelief himself, bowing once and briefly hopping away from the pit to be warmly embraced by his coach. He did not over celebrate, as Pichardo still had one jump to go and whilst he did respond with his best effort of the night at 17.73m, Taylor would finish nearly 50cm ahead of his rival and become a two-time World Champion.

[571]Taylor had delivered the jump of his life under immense pressure, on his final effort as he had so often done, early competition nerves long gone by the sixth-round and he

was an athlete able to pull it all together when he needed to, trusting in his technique and not over-thinking. The 6ft 2in (188cm) and 12st 6lbs (79kg) Taylor had been chasing a big jump ever since his leg switch proved successful and despite being very different in body shape to Edwards, he talked afterwards of "the contacts are quick"[572] when a jump does come together like it had that night, achieving the active landings Banks has spoken of and the skimming stone analogy of Edwards' very best efforts. As the second-furthest in history he was now entering the pantheon of triple jump greats and with three major championship victories to his name, he had a chance to look to surpass Edwards in one area at least.

Taylor used the same double-arm method of recent leading proponents Conley and Edwards, and returning to track competition in 2014 had seen his speed nurtured back to its best, but his stunning

[571] Christian Taylor celebrating victory in the 2015 World Championships © Erik van Leeuwen
[572] 'Christian Taylor soars to gold in world championships triple jump', Owen Gibson, *The Guardian*, 27 August 2015

jump of 18.21m was about the details finally coming together, believing in himself and relaxing his mind, crediting his rivals with pushing him to be stronger and even attributing training partner, long jumper Shara Proctor,[573] with helping him to extend his final jump phase.[574] The jump in Beijing had not been perfect and he had left around 11cm on the board, so he felt there was more to come with the World Record in reach now, in the winter of 2015 commenting he "would hate to end my career and be so close and not take it."[575] Edwards was greatly respected by Taylor, but their jumping styles were markedly different, right from how the Briton would sprint from the start of his approach, whereas the American was about accelerating to the board and whilst both relied on *long* jump phases, the double-arm take-off was their main commonality in style.

And Taylor was not shy in declaring his ambition in the 2016 season was to break the World Record with the Rio Olympics specifically targeted, but it would take the right conditions and strong competition to draw out the performance from him, so the record jump could come at any stage in any meeting, such was his confidence after Beijing. He had dominated the triple jump since the 2011 World Championships and was conscious of his position within his event, ever the entertainer and showman in competition, so his public targeting of the World Record was no display of arrogance. He was mindful that the triple jump did not receive the same attention as other field events at the time (the men's high jump had seen near World Record efforts frequently traded by two athletes in 2013-14) and his

---

[573] Shara Proctor, 2015 World Championships Silver in the long jump representing Great Britain and another UF athlete who followed Rana Reider to England and then the Netherlands to keep working with him [1988-].
[574] Gibson, *op. cit.*
[575] https://www.si.com/more-sports/2015/12/14/christian-taylor-triple-jump-world-record-rio-2016-olympics

chasing of Edwards' mark kept him and his event in the public eye, but that was not what motivated him. He wanted to go further than anybody had been before – "drives me every day"[576] he would remark in an interview ahead of competition at the Rio Olympics – and legacy was always an important factor in his make up as an athlete, when he had achieved so much success already at the highest level.

The 2016 season was all about the Olympics and the need Taylor felt to defend his title, to earn his place amongst the triple jumping greats who had done so before him, including the greatest Olympian in their discipline, Viktor Saneyev (Gold in 1968-76, plus Silver in 1980). Even Edwards had never been able to defend his Olympic title, already 34 when he won it in Sydney for the first time and he never went to another Games due to age and injury. Sadly, for Taylor, the 2016 season would prove to be underwhelming ahead of Rio, Pichardo dealing with injury for much of the season and ultimately being scratched from the Games only days before qualifying due to an ankle problem, his main rival a non-factor in competition throughout the year and the American struggled to lift his own performances. Claye was to beat him in the Olympic Trials on 9 July in Eugene, Oregon in an unexpected defeat, Taylor later admitting that he felt the pressure from the high stakes involved, the United States track and field team being so strong that winning a place was no mean feat and one mistake could well cost him his dream.[577]

---

[576] https://eu.usatoday.com/story/sports/olympics/rio-2016/2016/08/10/christian-taylor-triple-jump-gold-medalist/88529144/
[577] https://athleticsweekly.com/featured/christian-taylor-challenge-world-record-london-47310/

[578]The Rio Olympics men's triple jump final on 16 August 2016 unusually took place in a morning session and this may have contributed to the lack of excitement in what followed, the event not being given top billing by organisers. Taylor was the strong favourite after Pichardo's withdrawal and with a world-leading distance of 17.78m from London only weeks before, he was in good form. He qualified first and went out in the final with a season best of 17.86m on his first effort, Claye jumping well later in the order with a personal best 17.76m, but neither was able to go further and they repeated their 1-2 placing from London 2012. Taylor's 17.86m was good enough to have won Gold at each Olympics dating back to 2000 and a number of his fouls were massive jumps, yet there was to be no World Record that day, Jonathan Edwards later tweeting, "he'll get it one day... great champion and a real gentleman."[579] The biggest excitement on the day actually came from Claye climbing into the crowd to ask United States 400m hurdler Queen Harrison[580] to marry him after finishing with the Silver medal. She said yes and they later married in 2018.

Taylor had wanted the World Record but it was not to be in Rio, yet it had still been a glorious jump, winning his second Olympic Gold from a different take-off leg than his first, a remarkable achievement and he was visibly emotional on the podium. The 2017

[578] Christian Taylor preparing to jump in the 2016 Olympics © 'Citizen59'
[579] https://twitter.com/JDE66/status/765559417685377024
[580] Queen Q. Harrison, Gold in the 100m hurdles in the 2015 Pan American Games and fifth in the 2013 World Championships [1988-].

season offered further opportunity with the World Championships due to be held in London and he was still the only man around to have seriously threatened the World Record. He continued to let it be known he was chasing Edwards and no stone was left unturned, having slimmed down since 2015, worn specially designed spikes from his sponsor Nike,[581] changed his sleeping pattern and stopped eating carbohydrates, no detail too small if it would help him close the 8cm gap to the World Record.

In April of that year Pichardo absconded from a Cuban training camp in Germany and re-appeared in Portugal, signing for the *Sport Lisboa e Benfica* club in Lisbon. He would gain citizenship in December 2017, but was not able to compete for Portugal internationally until August 2019, so Taylor would again be without his strongest rival as roads converged on London for the 2017 World Championships. To follow many narratives of the Taylor and Claye relationship – brothers off the field, fierce rivals on it – you can be forgiven for presuming that Claye was the eternal bridesmaid, but in 2017 he ran Taylor very close and provided the rivalry the other man needed in the enforced absence of Pichardo.

Claye was the triple jump Silver medallist in consecutive Olympic Games behind his great friend, but was a phenomenal jumper in his own right and the outright career record between them two of them is only marginally in favour of Taylor. The difference has often been that Taylor has triumphed in the major championships, Claye being the victim on a number of occasions of 'the last-jump steal' from the man with the reputation as a clutch performer. Claye had memorably bested him in the 2016 Olympic Trials, but in the 2017 season he was to prove he belonged right up alongside him in global

---

[581] Nike, Inc. leading American sportswear, clothing, and footwear manufacturer, founded in 1964.

competition, pushing Taylor harder than anybody else since Pedro Pichardo had emerged.

[582]The triple jump highlight of the Diamond League season came at Hayward Field, Eugene, Oregon on 27 May 2017, in the Prefontaine Classic. Having earnt the nickname 'Track Town' for its fast surface, Hayward Field has seen many records in recent years and would be a popular host stadium with athletes for the 2022

World Championships (re-arranged from 2021 due to the COVID-19 pandemic). Back in 2017, Taylor opened with a windy 17.82m, before Claye responded with a legal 17.66m in the third round. In the fourth, Claye also jumped 17.82m, this time wind-legal and took the lead, and with Taylor desperate for Diamond League points to go on and secure a sixth consecutive overall triple jump title, he had to respond. Afterwards he commented how Claye had "pushed me to get out of my comfort zone and jump"[583] and jump he did, soaring to a massive 59ft 5in (18.11m), wind-legal at 0.8m/s. Claye responded with a windy 18.05m himself but Taylor was the victor, the very real challenge from Claye pushing him to go over 18m once again, when only Diamond League points and bragging rights were really on offer.

The 2017 World Championships in London offered Taylor the chance to win back-to-back global titles and become the first in the triple jump to do so (excluding the Olympic Games). In an interesting

---

[582] *Track & Field News* cover following the 18.11m jump in the May 2017 Pre Classic, July 2017 © Track & Field News

[583] https://worldathletics.org/competitions/diamond-league/news/eugene-diamond-league-2017-taylor-triple-jump

coda, the event final on 10 August was Jonathan Edwards' eldest son's birthday and in March he had acknowledged that the record could go that day, a bad birthday present indeed for him and his son![584] Taylor had gone to Beijing in 2015 to win, but in London he wanted the World Record. Edwards had given him some hints on what may help him find the extra distance to the record – the triple jump often has a collegiate feel, jumpers cognisant of the demands the event puts on the body and the time they spend together at trackside between jumps makes some firm friends – and the man who had written '18.30' inside his trainers for some years (more recently they had been specially embroidered by Nike) to remind him daily of his goal, had only one aim in mind when the final commenced.

The story ahead of the London final on 10 August 2017 was about Taylor chasing the World Record, but with a certain sense of inevitability he would be frustrated and there would not even be any last round heroics. He had been well short of 18m since the Pre Classic in Oregon in May and in the World Championships final he could only muster a best jump of 17.68m. The in-form Claye took a round one lead with 17.54m, Taylor took it back in the second with 17.57m, then Claye went out to 17.63m in the third. With Taylor short of his best, some felt that it was Claye's time to claim a major outdoor global title (he was World Indoor Champion in 2012 and again in 2018), but the two-time Olympic and World Champion was able to pull it all together just once that day, a third-round reply of 58ft $\frac{1}{10}$in (17.68m) enough to claim Gold, his prior desperation to claim the World Record now exchanged for relief at securing his third World title when put under such pressure, the first triple jumper to achieve the feat.

---

[584] https://www.eurosport.com/athletics/world-championships/2017/christian-taylor-has-jonathan-edwards-triple-jump-world-record-in-his-sights_sto6275794/story.shtml

Taking pride in his still ground-breaking achievement, Taylor knew he had to learn from the experience and change his mindset back to doing what it took to win, not getting tunnel-vision over what was by now a distance seemingly ever out of reach. The World Record had stood for 22 years by this point and this longevity did the triple jump no favours with the wider public, the progression of the leading mark having stalled for so long and held by a long-retired athlete. On 16 August 2017, Taylor and Claye had travelled to Tignes, France for an event in the Alps, high altitude long having been an advantage for jumpers and the Olympics was unlikely to ever return to high altitude after Mexico City 1968. A €100,000 prize for a World Record in the long jump or triple jump was on offer from organisers, but Taylor would underwhelm again, never being comfortable in the windy conditions or the elevated track surface (similar to indoor events) and he could only cover 16.99m, Claye the winner with a modest best of 17.42m. The long jump record of Mike Powell[585] similarly remained safe and the 2017 season ended later that month, with Taylor claiming his sixth consecutive Diamond League overall.

The 2018 season was billed as a year for Taylor to have fun and re-charge, with no major global championship on the schedule for the only season in the four-year cycle and he elected to concentrate on sprint training (and finally resume the college degree he put on hold when he turned professional in 2011). The triple jump World Record remained agonisingly out of reach, so he wanted to tick off another bucket list item, in running under 45sec in the 400m and in 2014 he had won Gold with the United States in the 4x400m relay at the IAAF World Relays. He was prepared to accept that his triple jumping may

---

[585] Michael 'Mike' A. Powell, long jump World Record holder since 1991, two-time World Champion in 1991 & 1993 and two-time Olympic Silver medallist in 1988 & 1992 [1963-].

270

suffer, but after so many years of serious competition and the often-painful conditioning required to compete at the highest level, he wanted to have fun again, content with what he had achieved. He never managed to break the 45sec barrier, but did run a 45.07 personal best in the Netherlands on 4 June 2018 and despite seeing a rejuvenated – and now Portuguese – Pichardo end his six-year domination of the Diamond League title, he had entered every event despite not being in optimum condition and was still ranked second in the world by season's end, having jumped 17.81m in Doha back in May.

Approaching the age of 29 as the 2019 season opened, all eyes were on Doha once again, for the World Championships in late September. Taylor and his coach always had an eye on the extra details that could propel him ever further, and in retrospect the 'fun' of the 2018 season may have had an ulterior motive, with the sprint training he focussed on all year being an area where even a marginal improvement could be the difference in finding that extra 8cm he required in the triple jump to match Edwards. Diamond League wins came that season in Monaco and Brussels, on his way to equalling French pole vaulter Renaud Lavillenie[586] (2010-16) with seven overall titles, but the real story of the season was Will Claye's number four all-time performance in June, in Long Beach, California of all places.

As Taylor was contending with the culmination of his college studies (he would graduate with a degree in Sports Management in 2019) whilst attempting to re-claim his triple jumping top spot after the semi-hiatus of 2018, Claye was training as hard as he ever had. He was newly married and benefitting from his wife's experience as a fellow elite athlete, his diet had improved and for a world class athlete who

---

[586] Renaud Lavillenie, pole vault Olympic Gold in 2012, Silver in 2016 and World Champion in 2013, amongst a host of major championship medals, including being three-time World Indoor Champion; World Record holder from 2014-20 [1986-].

was also beginning to make waves as a hip-hop recording artist – by then he was already an aspiring star with a platinum[587] selling record – he found his own tunnel-vision in the 2019 season, focusing hard on his athletics, saying that he was in the best *space* of his life, not necessarily the best shape.[588]

[589]Dealing with the recent passing of his beloved grandmother, Claye went to a small meet in Long Beach on 29 June, the Jim Bush Invitational[590] (Bush being one of Willie Banks' coaches at UCLA in the 1970's) and having surprised himself in winning the long jump, he decided to also compete in his favoured event, only his second meeting of the year and his training having only focussed on his speed. Proving that big jumps can come at any time and in any place, Claye put it all together in front of only a handful of spectators and athletes – it was a district meet after all – bounding out to a huge personal best of 59ft 6$\frac{1}{5}$in (18.14m) with next to no wind assistance (+0.4m/s), the longest triple jump on American soil and the fourth furthest jump in history. He was now the third best of all time, behind only Edwards and Taylor, and having had no thoughts about chasing the big jumps of the past when jumping that afternoon, in his own words, "I just let it happen."[591]

Claye had managed to execute the biggest jump of his career in the most non-descript of surroundings (all his others that series were

---

[587] At least one million copies sold.
[588] https://worldathletics.org/spikes/news/will-claye-strength-from-above
[589] Will Claye competing in the 2019 Paris Diamond League meeting, only a matter of weeks after his stunning jump in Long Beach, California; sadly, no photos seem to exist of him jumping that day, just mobile phone footage © Yann Caradec
[590] Doubling as the Southern California USATF Championships.
[591] https://worldathletics.org/spikes/news/will-claye-strength-from-above

fouls, some even further than 18.14m) and gone from 10th to 3rd all-time. Later that summer he covered 18.06m in the Paris Diamond League meeting on 24 August 2019 and the subsequent World Championships in Doha in late September offered a meeting of three all-time top five jumpers, each having exceeded 18m at least once in their career. Claye was in the form of his life, but what could Taylor and Pichardo do in the biggest event of the year, when up against each other...

The 2019 World Championships final would prove to be another back-and-forth competition between Taylor and Claye, Pichardo setting a season best but narrowly missing out on a Bronze medal to Hugues Fabrice Zango[592] of Burkina Faso, coached by a now retired Teddy Tamgho,[593] another of the 18m jumpers. Claye opened the final with a first round 17.61m, then improved to 17.71m in the second and held a comfortable lead after two rounds. Taylor had fouled on his first two attempts and was facing elimination as he had been in the London Olympics, however, yet again he demonstrated remarkable mental fortitude to calm himself down and post a safe third-round distance of 17.42m.

The defending champion then went on to take over the final, going out to 17.86m in the fourth and 17.92m in the fifth, good enough for first and second in the final standings. Claye performed as well as he had in any major championship, finishing with a best jump of 17.74m, but in Taylor he came up against a rival too motivated to both secure a third consecutive World title and put on a show, rumours swirling that the Diamond League was seeking to condense its schedule

---

[592] Hugues F. Zango, 2022 World Championships Silver, 2020 Olympic Bronze medallist and current World Indoor Record holder [1989-].
[593] In March 2023, Tamgho announced on social media that he wanted to compete in the 2024 Olympics in Paris, but it remains to be seen if he can return to that level.

in 2020 and the triple jump was one of the events at risk. Doha had certainly not lacked drama or excitement, and Taylor had added yet another title to an impressive major championships record, with the chance to match Viktor Saneyev with a third consecutive Olympic Gold in Tokyo the following summer.

The COVID-19 pandemic saw the 2020 season cancelled before it could start and the Tokyo Games would eventually be re-scheduled for the summer of 2021. Taylor would play an influential role in seeing the Games re-scheduled, having set up the Athletics Association in late 2019 in response to the planned cuts to events such as the triple jump, 200m and steeplechase from the core meetings of the 2020 Diamond League, and the members of the association (around a thousand athletes) had voted overwhelmingly to push for a postponement to the Tokyo Games, their own preparation adversely affected by the pandemic and it was the first time in history that the Olympics had been re-scheduled rather than cancelled outright (as it had been during the two World Wars).

Taylor now occupied an important position as a figurehead in his sport, the athletes' body he co-founded with steeplechaser Emma Coburn[594] increasingly prominent in discussions around how social issues overlapped with sport and where the human rights of athletes were not properly considered within the rules. In the wake of George Floyd's death,[595] anti-racism stances in sport became prevalent, but Rule 50 of the IOC Charter essentially banned athletes' protest ever since it was created in 1975. Protest in sport has been important to activism for many years, yet modern Olympians have had this right

---

[594] Emma J. Coburn, 2017 World Champion in the 3000m steeplechase, Silver in 2019 and Olympic Bronze medallist in Rio 2016 [1990-].
[595] George Floyd was murdered by Minnesota police officers after an arrest on 25 May 2020 and images of the events leading up to his death resulted in global protests, particularly supporting the Black Lives Matter movement.

denied to them and despite a consultation with the IOC ahead of the re-scheduled Tokyo Olympics in 2021, it is still a work in progress, with the Athletics Association a key partner.

As the athletics season approached in 2021, Taylor was completely focussed on the Tokyo Olympics, although there would be no official spectators in attendance. He was still a strong favourite for Gold, seeking to cement his place in triple jump history with a third Olympic title – a 'three-peat' – and he felt in good form as he went to Ostrava, Czech Republic for the Golden Spike meeting on 19 May. Hugues Fabrice Zango was also due to compete and had claimed the World Indoor Record in Aubière, France on 16 January 2021, going over 18m himself in a jump measured at 59ft $3\frac{1}{4}$in (18.07m),[596] the eighth best triple jump of all time, indoor or outdoor and placing him sixth in the record books. And it was a desire to keep ahead of the next generation of jumpers that were seeking to take his Olympic crown that was on his mind as he ran down that runway in Ostrava, an out of sorts Taylor having only jumped 16.36m[597] that evening and now commencing his fifth-round attempt...

A month out from the re-arranged and much anticipated Tokyo Olympics that was to put the rubberstamp on his career, a thirty-year-old Christian Taylor ruptured the Achilles tendon in his right leg as he took off from the board for that fifth jump. Ostrava had been the scene where his triple jump journey really started in 2007 – the enjoyment he got out of representing his country (and flying internationally) in the World Youth Championships that year sealing his commitment to track and field – and now he faced such a serious

---

[596] Ratified as such, but more correctly 59 ft $3\frac{2}{5}$in.
[597] https://www.insidethegames.biz/articles/1108036/christian-taylor-ruptured-achilles

injury, that the surgeon who operated a few days later asked him if he had considered jumping off his left leg,[598] knowing nothing of the biggest challenge to his career he had already had to overcome in 2013-14! He could not change legs again, but was determined to be fit for the World Championships in Eugene in July 2022, where he and Claye had enjoyed so many memorable moments over the years.

Taylor married Austrian hurdler Beate Schrott[599] in the autumn of 2019 and they had met in the 2011 World Championships, when he had exploded onto the triple jump scene like a supernova (as of 2023 she is now his coach and they are based in Vienna). He looked to embrace the positives from his injury, put his faith in God as always and was a keen but distant spectator of the Tokyo Olympic final as he recovered, watching Pichardo claim the Gold medal in his absence and great friend Will Claye would finish fourth. It came to light that Claye had torn his Achilles in late 2019 and with the pandemic allowing him to keep it private, he rehabbed with few knowing of his injury, most presuming he had taken a sabbatical to focus on his music and other interests, such as fashion. He had reached out to Taylor after his own Achilles injury to share his secret and it was a mark of their friendship that he chose to do so. Claye had been able to return to the elite level for Tokyo and Taylor was determined to do the same, literally counting the days down to the next World Championships (around 400).

He was to return to fitness in the following season and competed in his first triple jump competition on 12 May 2022, covering 15.91m to finish sixth at the Puerto Rico Athletics Classic. He did go to the 2022 World Championships in July, but did not advance past qualifying and finished 19th with a best effort of 16.48m, the first time

---

[598] 'T&FN Interview – Christian Taylor', Sieg Lindstrom, *Track & Field News*, 9 July 2021

[599] Beate Schrott, eighth place in the 100m hurdles in the 2012 Olympics [1988-].

since 2011 that he had not taken part in the final of the competition and Claye was to finish only 11th. A new guard were now dominating the event and whilst Pichardo claimed his second consecutive major global title with a world-leading 17.92m, there is now a new generation of triple jumpers battling for the medals, including World Indoor Record holder Zango, the Chinese jumper Zhu Yaming[600] with a Silver in Tokyo and Bronze in Eugene and a host of talented Cubans, most representing other countries, such as 2022 Diamond League overall winner, Andy Díaz,[601] granted Italian citizenship in February 2023.

Taylor remains determined to win a fourth Olympic Gold in Paris 2024 and as ever he is targeting the World Record. He will be 34 by then and it is increasingly unlikely that he will secure the final item on his bucket list, the extra distance to Jonathan Edwards from his personal best 18.21m as wide now as it ever was. He has always shown Edwards' achievement the greatest of respect and in some ways, there will be an element of sadness for many if he ends his career as *only* the second furthest jumper of all time. He is certainly the greatest triple jumper of his generation and was likely a good enough athlete to have medalled in other events if he had chosen to do so, such was his talent and dedication to training hard. His 2019 World Championships victory took him into conversation about the greatest of all time in his event and whilst he has not exceeded the distance Edwards achieved in Gothenburg back in 1995, he has a global championship medal record that can only be compared to Viktor Saneyev.

Christian Taylor, the current undeniable 'King of the Triple Jump', is never seen without his infectious smile for long, rivals the

---

[600] Zhu Yaming, 6ft 4in and the leading Asian triple jumper at present, with two medals in global competition in 2021 & 2022 [1994-].
[601] Andy Díaz Hernández, Bronze in the 2019 Pan American Games for his native Cuba and ranked third in the world in 2021 & 2022 [1995-].

track and field entertainer-in-chief Usain Bolt with his charisma and truly lives the motto his personal website[602] carries, "Blessed to be a Blessing." He has joked about becoming a comedian in retirement, such is the enjoyment he gets out of making people laugh[603] and whilst he has not surpassed Edwards in distance, perhaps he has surpassed him with his popularity. The Briton was regularly spoken of as being the "nicest guy" in world athletics, hard for rivals to dislike even when he was tearing up the record books, but the American is widely popular and the esteem other athletes hold for him is clear with the response to the union he co-founded in 2019. And anyone who reveals he watches the uplifting 2006 biographical film *The Pursuit of Happyness* before a major competition to remind himself that true happiness in life comes from hard work, is never going to be short of friends in athletics![604]

As a child he recalled always having a spring in his step and as an athlete he has been the same, grateful to have achieved his ambition in winning both his first Olympics and World Championships titles so young, yet willing to continue competing to burnish a legacy, as much for himself as for the sport of triple jump. He wants to be remembered and whilst he almost certainly will not now be a World Record holder, he has been a serial winner and a true great over a long period, something another all-time great American athlete, Michael Johnson,[605] best described as, "record breaking performances are part of the journey but not the objective."[606] Claye often says that he would have

---

602 https://www.taylored2jump.com
603 '#008: The Education of Life – with Christian Taylor', *Athletes: The Other Side Podcast*, host Ben Nichols, 12 November 2020
604 Nichols, *op. cit.*
605 Michael D. Johnson, sprinter specializing in the 200m & 400m, four-time Olympic Gold medallist and eight-time World champion; only male sprinter to win the 200m & 400m in the same Olympics (1996) [1967-].
606 https://twitter.com/MJGold/status/1622698518359191552?lang=en

retired a long time ago if he had Taylor's Gold medals[607] and it is not for us to say that he [Taylor] will not finally claim that World Record. After all, this is an athlete who as recently as 2022 said, "it kills me to be eight centimetres away."[608]   And that's all that it is that stops him from truly being the GOAT...

07.08.1995 WR 18.29m (60ft 0in) Jonathan Edwards (GBR) Gothenburg, Sweden (+1.3m/s)

[607] https://apnews.com/article/8013107225a24e708fe9a19e265351a3
[608] https://olympics.com/en/news/christian-taylor-injury-recovery-podcast-interview

Part 4 – Jump

The final phase of the triple jump has the most in common with the other horizontal jump, the long jump. Many leading triple jumpers, particularly in the early days of both the men's and women's events, began their careers as long jumpers, being able to rely on their fundamentals in the final *Jump* phase to increase the overall distance covered in a triple jump. Correct technique is paramount in achieving a good final phase and many a World Record has been set in the triple jump on the strength of a *long* jump after more balanced hop and step phases; Willie Banks revealed to us his standing long jump (or broad jump) personal best was around 11ft, without any specific training,[609] comparing well to Ray Ewry's 1904 World Record of 3.47m (11ft $4\frac{1}{4}$in) and the current unofficial World Record set by NFL[610] player Byron Jones[611] in 2015 – an incredible 3.73m (12ft $2\frac{3}{4}$in)!

Some will say this is the easiest of the three phases in the triple jump, although both Jonathan Edwards and Yulimar Rojas have used long closing jumps to propel themselves to their respective World Records and a balanced triple jump at the furthest distances requires a technical proficiency that few athletes can reach. The athlete begins this phase with the weaker, or less preferred, foot in contact with the runway and this is driven into the ground to propel themselves forward to the sandpit, with as much residual momentum as they can muster. Once airborne, or in *flight*, the athlete will reach forward with both legs as far as possible and they will be close to 90 degrees to the body, essentially in a 'L' shape. In keeping with the long jump, the athlete

---

[609] Zoom interview with Willie Banks by author Lawrence Harvey, 8 March 2023.

[610] National Football League, the foremost professional American football league, formed in 1920.

[611] Byron P. Jones, drafted by the Dallas Cowboys in 2015 after showcasing his broad jumping skill in particular; had a good career, mostly with the Cowboys, but as of 2023 remains a free agent [1992-].

will hang in the air with their arms extended skywards, then sweep them down past their legs – simultaneously – serving to bring the legs up for the landing. And in the admittedly rather oddly named 'triple jump', more correctly still a hop, step and a jump, at least the three phases finish with a jump technically true to the name!

THE COMING MEN...

All it takes is just one moment in time

The triple jump remains one of the most compelling of the track and field events to watch and the work of Christian Taylor and the Athletics Association in the winter of 2019 saw the Diamond League reverse the decision to remove it from the core meetings of the 2020 season. The 100m may be the marquee event that attracts the majority of the headlines, but it is the jumping disciplines that are characterised by their crowd interaction and to watch a triple jump competition is to behold an event that can ebb and flow in front of your eyes, a sense of jeopardy with every effort and athletes having to balance risk versus reward with how far they push themselves on any attempt. The 100m is over in 9-10sec, yet it can be argued that the triple jump offers so much more in terms of spectacle and whilst athletics fans rightly marvelled at Usain Bolt's sprinting exploits for many years (even Taylor says Bolt's 2009 World Record in the 100m is his favourite sporting moment[612]), he never had last-gasp, anxiety-inducing victories like Christian Taylor did in the 2015 World Championships in Beijing.

The finest triple jumpers have a certain poetry in motion and there are a number of leading protagonists now dominating the major global championships, pressing their own claims to threaten the World Record. There is also a crop of junior athletes, or recent graduates to the senior ranks, who have the potential to go over 18m in the coming seasons and the 2024 Olympics offers the prospect of a very competitive field. Taylor is certainly not ready to retire and whilst 2023 sees him enter year three of his return from the Achilles tear that would

---

[612] Nichols, *op. cit.*

have likely ended his career in former times, Will Claye would be back challenging for the World indoor title in March 2022, finishing fourth and only 2cm from a Bronze medal, a little over two years from his own serious injury.

This chapter is titled 'The Coming Men...' and whilst some such as Pedro Pichardo have been around for a number of years, turning thirty in the 2023 season and approaching veteran status himself, we have selected several triple jumpers at different stages of their respective careers, who we consider have the potential to challenge Edwards' distance of 18.29m. One of these athletes may yet break the World Record and advance the sport again, perhaps under the bright lights of Paris in August 2024 at the Olympics, someone needing it all to come together just once, at any meet in the world, on any day, for their own *moment in time...*

The World Number One

Cuban-born and representing Portugal since 2019, **Pedro Pablo Pichardo** is the leading triple jumper in the world, ranked number one in 2014, 2018, 2021 and 2022. He was the first of his generation to cover 18m and it was his challenge that inspired Christian Taylor to reach the heights he did from 2015-19, the latter saying how Pichardo helped him see that 18m was no longer unattainable.[613] He had some injury difficulties in 2016 and ultimately defected from the Cuban team to Portugal in April 2017, then was ineligible to compete internationally until August 2019, which prevented him from competing for the global honours of that period.

---

[613] https://www.youtube.com/watch?v=lqs__coRhP0 [*Athletics Weekly*, 'Episode 35: 'Ask The Athlete Q&A' with Christian Taylor – Aiming for the world triple jump record'].

Pichardo has been the dominant jumper since the start of the 2021 season and whilst Taylor is unique with a quasi-personal best with each leg, the Cuban-born Portuguese has his own statistical quirk in being the official National Record holder in both countries he has represented, 59ft $3\frac{3}{4}$in (18.08m) for Cuba and 58ft $11\frac{3}{4}$in (17.98m) for Portugal. The first jump came in Doha in May 2015, in that memorable contest with Taylor in a signature year for the triple jump and he is the fifth furthest man in history. His Portuguese record came when winning the Tokyo Olympics in 2021 and it was his first major global title, after Silver medals in the World Championships in 2013 and 2015. He won that Olympic Gold with much to spare and his third-round 17.98m (0.0m/s) ended the final as a contest, a stunning leap that was the third-furthest winning jump in Olympics history, after Mike Conley's windy 18.17m in 1992 and Kenny Harrison's Olympic Record 18.09m in 1996.

Pichardo is the most likely of the current leading jumpers to challenge the World Record and as he continues to refine his technique under his coach (and father) Jorge, he is not backwards in coming forward about his ambitions. He has been European Indoor Champion in 2021 and 2023, European Champion in 2022, Diamond League overall winner in 2018 and 2021, plus the Gold medallist in the 2020 Olympics (in 2021) and 2022 World Championships. There is no question that he is now dominant and only injury or the emergence of a strong rival will stop him from adding further accolades to his résumé. Taylor could be that rival if his recovery from the Achilles tear is fully complete, but even if he does not regain his previous form to challenge Pichardo, the Portuguese still fancies himself to reach 18.40m before his career ends, saying in October 2021, "winning a place in history... that's what I would like to do."[614]

The World Indoor Record Holder

The first Burkinabé athlete to win a medal in the World Championships and the first (and only) from his country to win an Olympic medal in any discipline, **Hugues Fabrice Zango** of Burkina Faso had already secured his place as the greatest triple jumper of all time from Africa, when on 16 January 2021, he broke the World Indoor Record in Aubière, France with a jump of 59ft $3\frac{1}{4}$in (18.07m),[615] the first African to hold a world best in a jumping event. His outdoor personal best of 17.82m was set in a duel with Pichardo in Székesfehérvár, Hungary on 6 July 2021 and he certainly has the pedigree to challenge the World Record in the near future, a high-achiever in all areas of his life and known at home as 'record-man', stating the World Record of Edwards is the most important thing to him in a 2022 interview.[616]

A proud symbol of hope for the youth of Burkina Faso, one of the poorest nations in the world and a UNICEF[617] Goodwill Ambassador for Children's Rights since August 2022, the triple jump had no real history in his country before his striking rise over the last decade. As with many triple jumpers he fell into the sport, scouted in a school competition in 2011, competed internationally for the first time at the 2013 Summer Universiade when finishing sixth with an effort of 15.96m and was coached locally until a move to Paris in 2016

---

[614] https://www.redbull.com/int-en/pedro-pichardo-triple-jump-interview

[615] Ratified as such, but more correctly 59 ft $3\frac{2}{5}$in.

[616] https://olympics.com/en/news/burkina-fasos-hugues-fabrice-zango-creates-history-2022-worlds

[617] The United Nations Children's Fund, responsible for providing aid to children worldwide since 1946.

to link up with Teddy Tamgho,[618] the man whose 2011 World Indoor Record he would better by 15cm ten years later. He has had to climb the professional ranks from the very bottom with little support and his career was not without major low points, fouling out in the 2015 World Championships in Beijing and failing to even qualify for the Olympic final in Rio 2016.

Moments like Rio made the later successes even sweeter – a surprise Bronze in Doha in 2019 and another in the Tokyo Olympics – and now he is a major championships medal contender and famous figure in his home country, Silver in the 2022 World Championships in Eugene a landmark moment, both for him as an athlete and an African. Dr Zango, as he is after completing a PhD in electrical engineering in Lille in 2022, believes he can challenge for Gold in Paris; if he comes up short, his other dream is to become one of the first engineering professors in Burkina Faso, so the future looks bright for him as he turns thirty in 2023, whatever the colour of any further medals he might win.[619]

The Wildcard

In 2014 a teenage Cuban triple jumper had the world at his feet. With the physique of a grown man yet aged only sixteen and a half, **Lázaro Martinez Santray** jumped 17.24m in Havana on 1 February, the first time a youth (U18) athlete had ever cleared 17m in history. He would exceed 17m twice more before April and was already 6ft 3in (1.90m) in height, lanky with natural speed and wiry legs, and he would yet fill out as he entered adulthood. He was the 2013

---

[618] Teddy Tamgho, former World Indoor Record holder from 2011-21, World Indoor Champion in 2010 and World Champion in 2013; retired aged only thirty in 2019, having struggled with frequent injury since 2011 [1989-].
[619] https://olympics.com/en/news/burkina-fasos-hugues-fabrice-zango-creates-history-2022-worlds

World Youth Champion in 2013 when equalling the U18 record with a jump of 16.63m, then twice World Junior (U20) Champion in 2014 and 2016. It seemed like there were no barriers to what Martinez could go on to achieve with his striking mohawk haircut and despite his tender age, he was then being talked of as a future 60ft jumper.

So, what happened then? Seemingly the next in a long line of great Cuban triple jumpers after his success as a junior, he graduated to the senior ranks, finished eighth in Rio 2016 aged only eighteen and was 11th in the 2017 World Championships in London. His was a powerful running style and he relied more on his strength at the time, jumping further than anybody ever had at his age and it was expected that some refinement to his technique, particularly to a short final jump phase, would see him breakthrough to the very top. But a niggling tibia problem would cause him to miss time in 2017, 2018 and 2019, Martinez fearing that it could break at any time and his long recovery stalled his career, almost terminally.

He would train as a Physical Education teacher, Cuban athletes officially forbidden from turning professional and a personal best 17.26m in Camagüey, Cuba in February 2018 was a false dawn. His struggles continued throughout the COVID-19 pandemic in 2020 when he could hardly compete at all and in 2021, he fared little better, eight meets in Havana leading to no jumps beyond 17m.[620] Coached by Yoelbi Quesada,[621] the 1997 World Champion, since 2018, he credits him for never letting him quit after so many years of injury and disappointment, everyone else in Cuba having long given up on him

---

[620] https://oncubanews.com/deportes/atletismo/lazaro-martinez-cielo-abierto-bajo-techo/
[621] Yoelbi L. Quesada Fernández, Olympic Bronze medallist in Atlanta 1996, three-time Pan American Games Champion (1991-99) and World Champion in 1997 with a personal best of 17.85m; the most decorated Cuban triple jumper of all time [1973-].

and Quesada's confidence would be proven well-placed in the 2022 season.

Encouraging Martinez to compete indoors for the first time in his career, victories in France and Spain in the early months of the 2022 season proved to be the start of his resurgence. He was comfortably jumping over 17m once again and with victory in the World Indoor Tour behind him, he qualified for the 2022 World Indoor Championships in Belgrade, Serbia, something that was unthinkable at the turn of the year. All triple jumpers know that it only takes *one jump* and his opening effort in the *Štark Arena* was to be the one that returned his life to the path he seemed destined to take as a youngster, a distance of 17.64m adding 36cm to his personal best and 16th on the all-time indoor list. He jumped 17.62m in the fourth-round and the likes of Tokyo Olympic Champion Pedro Pichardo and reigning World Indoor Champion Will Claye could not get close to him, despite making their longest jumps of the year, Martinez being crowned an unexpected World Champion.

Martinez was still aged only 24 when he won in Belgrade and the thoughts of quitting his sport from the start of 2022 had been banished. Full of confidence, he went to the 2022 World Championships in Eugene, Oregon, where he had been World Junior Champion in 2014, yet sadly could record no mark in the final, having qualified fifth best. He recovered with an outdoor personal best of 17.50m in Lausanne in August 2022 and it is expected he will improve again in the 2023 season, when he turns 25. He remains an athlete with enormous potential, the first Cuban to be an individual youth, junior and senior World Champion in athletics and he is our wildcard to be the next 60ft jumper.

The Cuban-Spanish Hurricane

Cuba has dominated the youth and junior ranks of the triple jump for many years, the event having a long tradition of excellence on the Caribbean island since former World Record holder Pedro Pérez and the list of leading Cuban-born athletes in the discipline, both male and female, is extraordinary. Cuba has the second-highest number of medals (all events) in the Americas at the Olympics, only behind the United States and even casual fans of the Games will be familiar with the blue and red bibs of Cuban hurdlers, jumpers and boxers in particular. Javier Sotomayor[622] was the dominant high jumper of the 1990's and is still the World Record holder, but the nation has not won a Gold in any athletics event at the Olympics since 2008[623] and the country has been in a deepening socio-economic crisis since the COVID-19 pandemic, causing record numbers of their citizens to flee abroad, including many of their leading athletes and sportspersons.

The World Athletics U20 Championships (World Junior Championships until 2015) were won by Pichardo in 2012, Martinez in 2014 and 2016 and a third Cuban, **Jordan Alejandro Díaz Fortún**, in 2018. Jordan Díaz was the reigning World Youth Champion from 2017, where he had set an U18 World Record of 17.30m (+0.6m/s) on 14 July 2017, at altitude in Nairobi, Kenya. He was only sixteen at the time and jumped over 1m further than any other youth athlete that season, a sign of his supreme talent. In June 2018 he furthered the youth record to 17.41m in Havana and Cubans were waiting for him to come of age and return their nation to the senior medal podium.

[622] Javier Sotomayor Sanabria, Olympic high jump champion in 1992 and Silver medallist in 2000; two-time World Champion in 1993 & 1997 amongst a host of major championship victories and still the only man to high jump 8ft (2.44m) [1967-].
[623] Dayron Robles won Gold in Beijing 2008 in the men's 110m hurdles and he was also World Indoor Champion in 2010 [1986-].

Pichardo had left Cuba for Portugal by this time (Díaz had been training alongside him) and Martinez was fading from view with his injury troubles, so Cubans were desperate for Díaz to be the one to claim that elusive Olympic Gold, perhaps in Tokyo 2020, a personal best of 57ft $4\frac{1}{2}$in (17.49m) in Camagüey in July 2019 good enough to see him ranked sixth in the world, aged only eighteen. Perhaps the re-scheduling of the Games played a part, in addition to the chronic lack of funding for athletics in Cuba for many years, but in June 2021 Díaz left his national team whilst in Spain for an Olympic qualifier (one of a number to do so), and lured away by the chance of a lucrative training contract and a better life, he chose to miss the Olympics and pursue Spanish citizenship, breaking many Cuban hearts.

Now training with Cuban-born long jump legend Iván Pedroso[624] in Guadalajara, as part of a training group that includes women's World Record holder Yulimar Rojas[625] of Venezuela and Cubans now representing other nations, such as Alexis Copello[626] of Azerbaijan, Jordan Díaz gained Spanish citizenship in February 2022, in time for him to be able to satisfy the three-year waiting period from his defection in 2021 to just before the Paris Olympics in August 2024. He represents the famous *Futbol Club Barcelona* athletics team and first claimed the Spanish National Record in the same month he was granted citizenship, having since taken that mark to 17.87m (+1.2m/s) on 26 June 2022 in the national championships (he also managed a

---

[624] Iván L. Pedroso Soler, now a leading triple jump coach, long jump Olympic Champion in 2000, four-time World Champion from 1995-2001 and five-time World Indoor Champion; denied the World Record in 1995 when the legal wind reading was ruled invalid [1972-].

[625] More on Yulimar in a later chapter!

[626] Alexis Copello, Cuban-born but competing internationally for Azerbaijan since 2017, recently European Championships Silver medallist in 2018 and European indoor Silver in 2021 [1985-].

wind-assisted 17.93m in the same series), the joint 13th best performance of all time.

Having decided to follow the path that took Pichardo to Olympic and World titles via Portugal, the now Spanish-citizen Díaz is at the forefront of the next generation of triple jumpers, hoping to emulate the Portuguese in becoming Olympic Champion, Pichardo the only former World Junior Champion to do so in their event. Díaz is already a rarity in that he managed to jump further than his age – over 17m as a sixteen-year-old, Pichardo nearly twenty before he cleared that distance for the first time in February 2013 – and with the blessing of his parents to go abroad to reach his dreams, he is working on his runway speed and final landing with Pedroso, in a hurry to get ready for what could be a career-defining moment in the 2024 Olympics. And with Edwards' World Record a possibility in the future, by Paris he may well have broken the Briton's leading mark on Spanish soil of 17.98m...

The Outsiders

China and India are the two most populous nations in the world, each with over 1.4 billion people, yet China would not win a men's Gold medal in track and field until the 2004 Olympics[627] and India would claim it's first and only athletics Gold in 2021,[628] in the re-scheduled Tokyo Games. Both are powerhouses in other sports – table tennis, basketball and badminton in particular for China, cricket undoubtedly for India – and each nation has for many years been described as 'sleeping giants' in the sports they have yet to proliferate.

---

[627] Liu Xiang, men's 110m hurdles Gold in Athens 2004, World Champion in 2007 and World Indoor Champion in 2008; still the Olympic Record holder [1983-].
[628] Neeraj Chopra, first Asian athlete to win Olympic Gold in men's javelin, 2022 World Championships Silver medallist and his 2016 U20 World Record was the first set by an Indian athlete in history [1997-].

China has the better track and field record of the two countries, with a much richer heritage in the triple jump. The country has made significant investment in the development of athletics since before the Beijing Olympics in 2008, broadly similar to that which was so successful for the Soviet Union, but with a more outward looking perspective when it comes to foreign coaching and technical proficiencies. The current leading Chinese triple jumper is **Zhu Yaming**, with a personal best of 17.57m to go with Olympic Silver in Tokyo and World Championships Bronze in Eugene. Turning 29 in the 2023 season, the 6ft 4in athlete has improved considerably working in the international training group of Brazilian horizontal jumping guru Nélio Moura[629] since 2019 – coach of both the men's and women's Olympic long jump champions in Beijing 2008, and he previously worked with triple jumper Jadel Gregório – and it remains to be seen whether he can emulate long jumper Wang Jianan, the 2022 World Championships Gold medallist from China.

India has the much poorer athletics record of these two 'sleeping giants' and has certainly had the longest slumber! Perennial under-achievers in the Olympics, with only ten Gold medallists since their first Summer Games in 1900 and the most recent is current men's javelin champion, Neeraj Chopra. Strangely enough, India has a longer history in the triple jump than China and very nearly claimed a medal in the 1948 Olympics, when nineteen-year-old Henry Rebello[630] was expected to challenge for Gold having cleared 50ft for the first time that year and been tipped by former World Record holder Jack Metcalfe. His first effort in the 1948 Olympic final was interrupted by organisers and failing to warm-up properly when he was allowed to

---

[629] Nélio A. Moura, one of the world's top jumps coaches [c.1971-].
[630] Henry M. Rebello, later a long career in the Indian Air Force [1928-2013].

resume, he injured his hamstring and could not jump at all, his flirtation with sporting immortality so brief.

The triple jump has languished along with athletics in general in India for many years, but 2022 represented a banner year in the men's triple jump. An historic 1-2 finish in the Commonwealth Games for **Eldhose Paul** and Abdulla Aboobacker in August 2022 served notice that India has some talented jumpers in the event, and the former had made history the month before when qualifying for the World Championships final in Eugene, finishing a very creditable 9th overall. His personal best of 17.03m in the Commonwealth Games demonstrates that he deserves to be on the world stage and with the confidence of his World Championships performance behind him (he was coached virtually during the event as his trainer could not get a visa to the United States in time), he will likely progress further in the 2023 season, when he turns 27 at year-end. It is unlikely to be either Zhu Yaming or Eldhose Paul who will challenge the World Record in their careers, but both are creating a legacy in their respective nations that will surely see other (more) talented athletes attracted to the triple jump in the future.

The Wonderkid

Named the 'wonderkid' by Christian Taylor as recently as December 2022[631] and using the tag '@_.wunderkid_' on his own social media, **Jaydon Hibbert** of Jamaica is attracting some serious attention to the junior (U20) triple jump ranks. Having only turned eighteen in January 2023, his potential is extraordinary and at the time of writing in 2023 he is finishing an unbeaten freshman year at the

---

[631] https://www.youtube.com/watch?v=lqs__coRhP0 [*Athletics Weekly*, 'Episode 35: 'Ask The Athlete Q&A' with Christian Taylor – Aiming for the world triple jump record'].

University of Arkansas, the college formerly attended by the likes of Mike Conley and Brian Wellman, a strong rival to the University of Florida (Christian Taylor and Will Claye most recently) as 'Jumps U', the collegiate heartland of horizontal jumping. He also already has the 13th furthest triple jump in history to his name...

Hibbert announced himself internationally with Silver in the 2021 World U20 Championships in Nairobi, with a then personal best of 16.05m as a sixteen-year-old (the winner, Gabriel Wallmark[632] of Sweden was nineteen!). The following season he claimed his first Jamaican *senior* national title in June 2022, aged only seventeen and an even more notable landmark was to come that summer. On 5 August 2022, in his second World U20 Championships, he broke Jordan Díaz's Championship Record with a first-round jump of 56ft $7\frac{9}{10}$in (17.27m) in Cali, Colombia, winning Gold by over 1m, a 2ft improvement (around 61cm) on his former personal best and with no wind assistance. He collapsed to the track in shock when he saw how far he had jumped and remained on the ground whilst it was measured, visibly emotional when the record distance was confirmed.

He remains second to Díaz in the all-time U18 list, but on 11 March 2023 he claimed his first age-group World Record, having already been the youngest ever to 17m. In the NCAA Division I Indoor Championships in Albuquerque, New Mexico, another first-round effort saw him go further than any other U20 athlete in history (indoors or outdoors), a distance of 56ft $6\frac{1}{2}$in (17.54m), in only his third ever indoor meet. This was also the overall collegiate indoor record,

---

[632] Gabriel Wallmark, World and European U20 champion in 2021, the same year in which he claimed Christian Olsson's Swedish junior record, a sign of his own precocious talent [2002-].

breaking Charlie Simpkins'[633] best from 1986 (which was then the unofficial indoor world best) and Hibbert had gone further aged eighteen than Christian Taylor did in winning his two NCAA indoor titles a decade previously; 17.54m would also have won Silver in the 2022 World Indoor Championships in Belgrade!

He managed this first age-group World Record off a short run-up of only 12 strides (around 18 is now normal for men on a full approach) and as his technique improves, surely so will his speed on the runway, with fellow Arkansas great Mike Conley recently saying it took him almost a lifetime to look like Hibbert does as a freshman, proclaiming the Jamaican a "special guy".[634] At the time of writing, he continued his early season form into outdoor competition, a truly landmark jump in the SEC[635] Championships in Baton Rouge, Louisiana on 13 May 2023 earning him widespread acclaim, talk of his potential now spreading throughout the track and field world. A second-round distance of 58ft 7$\frac{1}{2}$in (17.87m) with a tailwind of 1.2m/s saw Hibbert break both the outdoor NCAA record (Keith Connor,[636] 17.57m, 1982) and the outdoor U20 World Record (Volker Mai,[637] 17.50m, 1985) and he was to pass on his four remaining attempts, satisfied with his day's work and still using the short approach. What he is achieving aged only eighteen is unprecedented, not just in the

---

[633] Charles 'Charlie' Simpkins, Olympic Silver medallist in the triple jump in Barcelona 1992 and fifth in Seoul 1988 [1963-].
[634] https://sportsmax.tv/athletics/item/119427-american-triple-jump-legend-mike-conley-sr-describes-jaydon-hibbert-as-special-he-was-born-to-do-it
[635] The Southeastern Conference (SEC), a regional American athletic conference that includes sporting powerhouse institutions such as the University of Arkansas.
[636] Keith L. Connor, Great Britain triple jumper, Olympic Bronze medallist in 1984, European Champion (and record holder) in 1982 and Commonwealth Gold medallist 1978 & 1982; notable NCAA athlete at Southern Methodist University [1957-].
[637] Volker Mai, German triple jumper with best placing of Silver in the 1989 European Indoor Championships; later implicated in the state-sponsored doping prevalent in East Germany in the early 1980's and post-career he has become a microbiology professor in the United States [1966-].

triple jump and he knows it – "I don't think there's any [other] 18-year-old that does the stuff I do".[638]

Jamaica has been a hotbed of talent for sprinters for many years – being commonly known as the 'sprint capital of the world' – and the promise shown by Hibbert is a useful barometer for the health of the triple jump, that a talented young Jamaican is dedicating himself to the event. He is following a well-trodden path from his country to the University of Arkansas, is certainly benefitting from the world-class training facilities on offer as a collegiate athlete in the United States and all the while he is clearly having immense fun – how many of the greatest triple jumpers have we already said that about as well?

He will still be young enough to defend his World U20 title in 2024 and back-to-back wins would see him make further history (Lázaro Martinez is the only other male triple jumper to do so). In the next couple of years, he will likely target James Beckford's National Record of 17.92m and if he can cover that distance, yet more could come on the grandest stages, an early propensity for big first-round jumps already being shown. If greatness is shown by comparison to your peers, then Hibbert is already on another level at U20 level and if he can continue to develop (and avoid injury), he could be some triple jumper indeed...

---

[638] https://www.wholehogsports.com/news/2023/may/14/hibbert-sets-record-as-razorbacks-claim-title/

WOMEN ON THE RISE

"An Olympiad with females would be impractical, uninteresting,
unaesthetic [sic] *and improper"*[639]

The 1995 athletics season belonged to Jonathan Edwards of Great Britain with his breath-taking exploits in the triple jump, particularly in the World Championships in Gothenburg, Sweden. On 7 August 1995, he would set a World Record that stands to this day – 28 years and counting in the year this book is published – and his performance that evening in Gothenburg gave rise to a number of memorable moments, none more so than a stunned Edwards realising what he had achieved in going (considerably) further than any triple jumper in history. He remains *the* iconic figure of the men's event and to many he is the greatest in his sport, but the World Record-breaking exploits of another leading triple jumper in Gothenburg only three days later should have given rise to a further iconic track and field moment. Instead that second World Record in the women's event has long been over-shadowed, by both Edwards' celebrated assault on the men's record-books and the conduct of the protagonist herself, casting a pall on the nascent women's event that would last for over a generation.

That leading women's athlete was Inessa Kravets of Ukraine and her World Record distance of 50ft 10in (15.50m),[640] an incredible 41cm further than any other woman had jumped in history, would last itself for nearly 26 years and be only rarely approached in that time. But whereas Edwards' achievement had been met with universal

---

[639] Comments made by Pierre de Coubertin, father of the modern Olympic Games, in Stockholm in 1912.

[640] Ratified as such, but more correctly 50ft $10\frac{1}{4}$in.

acclaim and has stood so long that it has become fabled, the performance of the immensely talented Kravets was less easily digested, a recent three-month ban for using stimulants in 1993 coming after her first World Record in 1991 meant that her landmark jump was even then considered *problematic*. She would become the first women's Olympic Champion in her event in Atlanta 1996, but a two-year ban for using a performance-enhancing steroid in 2000 would cast further doubt over her World Record and the longer it stood, the larger the shadow Inessa Kravets cast over the women's triple jump.

A number of talented jumpers have followed in her wake, yet it would not be until August 2021 when the 'Queen of the Triple Jump', Yulimar Rojas of Venezuela, would break Kravets' world best from 1995 which had proved so durable. Rojas is now a global superstar, over 1 million followers on her social media demonstrating that the women's event is challenging the men for wider public interest and the longer Edwards' World Record remains unchallenged, the more stagnant the men's event will appear when compared to the women. Rojas is pushing the boundaries of what was thought possible in the women's triple jump and with some technical refinement still expected, we do not yet know how far she will advance the event herself. The next few years look set to be very exciting for the women's triple jump, but our story now goes back to the start of the 20th century, to explore the origins of the event and the trailblazing women that Rojas has followed so brightly.

The involvement of women in sport dates back to the ancient world, with records of female athletes in both the Egyptian and Greek civilisations evidencing that the tradition is long and historically prominent. Yet the first modern Olympics in 1896 specifically excluded women, Victorian-period sensibilities promoting the idea that women were of the 'fairer sex' and could not stand up to the rigours of competitive sport, with a widespread belief that physical activity could affect their reproductive health. This idea was one of many smashed by the trauma of the First World War, when women in Great Britain and France in particular had assisted the war-effort by undertaking work long considered only suitable to men and in a post-war world of increased opportunity for women – voting rights for women had been established for the first time in a limited capacity in Britain from 1918 – there was increased advocacy for the participation of women in competitive sports, especially at international level.

The first Women's World Games were held in Paris in 1922 and included events previously considered to be too strenuous for women, such as the 1000m, 100yds hurdles and (two-handed) shot put. The Games were organised by the *Fédération Sportive Féminine Internationale* (FSFI)[641] and they would be run every four years, before the organisation folded in 1936 with its ambitions mostly unfulfilled, although women's athletics events were introduced to the Olympic Games from 1928. This was a very important step on the pathway to recognising women's rights in sporting terms, but it would not be until a second global conflict ended in 1945 that the Victorian stereotypes would begin to be finally consigned to history, the Soviet Union team in Helsinki 1952 full of women trained to the same standards as the men and with an equally strong will to win. The United States, with the Cold War pervading sport, had to respond and by the 1960 Olympics in Rome their own squad included women beginning to perform at the elite international level.

The journey towards full equality in athletics terms was not swift and despite women around the world increasingly viewing participation in elite sport as an opportunity for betterment, particularly

---

[641] In English, the International Women's Sports Federation.

in newly independent countries in the era of decolonisation in the 1950's and 1960's, the women's marathon was not introduced to the Olympics until 1984, arguments about the effect on women's health still promulgated by experts. The women's high jump had been included in the Olympics since 1928, yet the triple jump would be excluded until 1996, the third of the jumping events to be introduced, after the long jump had been included from 1948. The triple jump suffered with arguments against its inclusion around the number of events already included in the Olympic schedule and the then Olympic Charter itself required a women's sport to be widely practiced in twenty-five countries, on at least two continents in order to be introduced, but following the success of the event in the 1993 World Championships, it was to finally gain true global recognition at the 1996 Olympics, one hundred years after the men's event itself debuted.

The story of the women's triple jump World Record officially dates from 1 January 1990 when the then IAAF formally recognised the event for record purposes and the first ratified World Record was in August of that year. The unofficial record can be dated back to at least 1899, when Mary Ayer[642] jumped 22ft $\frac{1}{2}$in (6.72m) in the hop, skip and jump at Bryn Mawr College, Philadelphia, an elite, historically women's college in the United States, with the distance recorded in her class yearbook, alongside her school records in the hurdles, 'putting the shot' and 230ft dash! The record remained the preserve of American women for many years, with the IAAF claiming that Ellen Hayes[643] of Sweet Briar College, Virginia (another private women's institution) was the first woman over 10m on 7 April 1913, covering 10.49m, whilst other sources widely available online give the accolade to Elizabeth

---

[642] Mary F. Ayer, later a noted diarist of her student life [1878-1954].
[643] Ellen Hayes [n/k].

Stine,[644] an American track athlete who took long jump Silver in the inaugural Women's World Games and is said to have triple jumped 33ft 10$\frac{1}{4}$in (10.32m) earlier that year, on 13 May 1922, in Mamaroneck, New York State.

Stine is commonly held to be the first modern holder of the unofficial record for the triple jump and did claim the second ratified World Record in the high jump in May 1923. The next athlete to advance the record significantly was Kinue Hitomi[645] of Japan and her all-round track and field exploits deserve to be much more widely known. In a similar vein to Australian jumping great Nick Winter, Hitomi could excel in most track and field events, literally participating in the 800m at the 1928 Olympics as a last-minute entry after disappointing in the 100m and going on to claim Silver, despite never having run the distance before in official competition! She would win three Golds in consecutive Women's World Games (plus five other medals) and in the 1920's and 1930's, claimed numerous unofficial world bests, in addition to World Records in the long jump, 100m, 200m and javelin.

Her first unofficial record in the triple jump came whilst she was aged only eighteen, and she took the best mark out twice, latterly to 38ft 11$\frac{1}{2}$in (11.62m) in late 1926, sources differing over the specific date and location, but not the distance. Hitomi was a true pioneer, one of the first Japanese women on an Olympic team and the first woman from her country to claim an Olympic medal (triple jumper Mikio Oda won Japan's first athletics Gold medal in those Games). She was very

---

[644] Elizabeth G. Stine, member of the first United States women's team to compete internationally in 1922 and the national high jump champion in 1925 [1905-1993].
[645] Kinue Hitomi, multiple track and field World Record holder and the first Japanese woman to win an Olympic medal [1907-1931].

tall for a Japanese of either sex at 5ft $6\frac{1}{2}$in (1.69m) – but not compared to the European women she came up against in 1928 for example – and because of this she was frequently asked embarrassing questions about her *true* sex. Despite her success in Europe, she was not warmly welcomed in conservative Japanese society either, ultimately passing away from pneumonia in August 1931 aged only 24, likely contracted whilst competing in Europe the preceding year after the 3rd Women's World Games in Prague.

Hitomi's record would loosely stand for many years, with further marks in 1939 and 1959 largely discounted,[646] before the landmark came under sustained assault in the 1980's, with the event gaining considerable attention at the NCAA level in the United States and the unofficial World Record was broken upwards of fifteen times. The first to definitely beat Hitomi's mark was the most surprising, yet she had some similarity to the Japanese in reaching the elite level of her sport so young. Terri Turner[647] was a high school junior when she set her first world best of 40ft $9\frac{1}{4}$in (12.43m)[648] on 9 May 1981 in the Texas High School State Championships, then extended that mark to 40ft $10\frac{3}{4}$in (12.47m)[649] the following year to claim her third successive state title. She then went to the University of Texas, won the inaugural NCAA title in the event in 1984, having extended the unofficial World Record twice earlier that season, latterly to 43ft 4in (13.21m)[650] on 13

---

[646] The IAAF records include Frances Keddie of Canada covering 11.83m in 1926, but there is no date; Briton Mary Bignal's 12.21m (later famous as Mary Rand who won Olympic Gold in the 1964 long jump) in 1959 was achieved in training, rather than regular competition.

[647] Terri Turner, 2016 inductee to the University of Texas Hall of Honor [1963-].

[648] More correctly 40ft $9\frac{4}{10}$in.

[649] More correctly 40ft $10\frac{9}{10}$in.

[650] More correctly 43ft $4\frac{1}{10}$in

April in Baton Rouge and claimed a second NCAA title in 1986, an integral figure in the establishing of the women's triple jump at the college level in the United States.

The record would be dominated by American-born or United States-based college athletes, until Li Huirong[651] of the People's Republic of China, an athlete of genuine international class, took the mark over 14m on 11 October 1987 in Hamamatsu, Japan, Terri Turner finishing a distant second with a best of 12.81m. Huirong jumped 46ft $\frac{3}{4}$in (14.04m) that day, then would extend the record to 46ft $5\frac{1}{4}$in (14.16m)[652] on 23 April 1988, in Shijiazhuang, China, the late 1980's and early 1990's a heyday for Chinese triple jumpers, with Huirong among the world's best for a couple of years. Galina Chistyakova[653] of the Soviet Union (then Russia and later Slovakia) was a talented horizontal jumper who was already the long jump World Record holder when she twice exceeded Huirong's 1988 mark the following season, her triple jump of 47ft $7\frac{1}{2}$in (14.52m)[654] in Stockholm on 2 July 1989 the final unratified World Record; she had claimed the 1988 Olympic Bronze in the long jump and was the 1989 World Indoor Champion, before injury in late 1990 prevented her from continuing at that level, with her 1988 long jump World Record still unbeaten to this day.

---

[651] Li Huirong, first women to hold the ratified World Record and 1992 IAAF World Cup Champion [1965-].

[652] More correctly 46ft $5\frac{1}{2}$in.

[653] Galina V. Chistyakova, current World Record holder in the long jump, 1988 Olympic Bronze medallist and 1989 World Indoor Champion in the long jump, and the 1990 European Indoor Champion in both the triple jump and long jump; four-time European Indoor Champion in total [1962-].

[654] More correctly 47ft $7\frac{6}{10}$in.

[655]Huirong would come to the fore on 25 August 1990 with the first World Record in the women's triple jump to be ratified by the IAAF. She covered 47ft $8\frac{1}{4}$in (14.54m)[656] in Sapporo, Japan and although the mark would only last a little over 9 months, **Li Huirong** had her place in the triple jump record books. Born on 14 April 1965 in the People's Republic of China, very little is accurately known of her life. She is said to come from Tianjin, a coastal metropolis in northern China and as a girl she concentrated her efforts in the swimming pool. Her physique did not develop as her coaches required and she switched her focus to track and field, finding that her natural talent in sprinting and jumping drew her to the long jump. She quickly developed as a long jumper, becoming National Champion at the age of only sixteen and the following year she took Bronze in the 1982 Asian Games, in New Delhi, India. However, injuries and the challenge of adapting to professional training slowed her progress and ultimately, she returned home.

As with many triple jumpers, the event found her and her subsequent rise coincided with the IAAF promoting the sport in the late 1980's, the Chinese national team then setting up a special training group. In October 1987 she became the first woman to triple jump over 14m and further progression followed, a second unofficial record in 1988 and the first ratified World Record distance in August 1990,

---

[655] Photograph showing Li Huirong competing on an unspecified date, possibly when she set the first ratified World Record in August 1990 © unknown

[656] Ratified as such, but more correctly 47ft $8\frac{4}{10}$in.

fittingly in the Chūhei Nambu Memorial event, held in honour of the great Japanese. The following March, Huirong claimed Silver in the 1991 World Indoor Championships in Seville, Spain, behind the leading jumper of the day in Inessa Kravets, who only three months later would claim her first World Record, although the meet was a non-championship event. Huirong was now an athlete to watch and in July 1991, she claimed her first major international victory in the Summer Universiade in Sheffield, England, again exceeding 14m and helped by Kravets being a late withdrawal.

Huirong was unable to make further progression and with the rise of Kravets, distances of 14.50m were no longer world leading. She was the National Champion from 1990-92 and established the women's event in China, but her personal best would remain the 14.55m (+0.9m/s) she jumped in Sapporo, in July 1992, some 40cm down on the then World Record. Her final triumph was to come later that year in Havana, Cuba, in the first women's triple jump to be held at the IAAF World Cup. She was injured and could only jump off five steps, yet in wet and windy conditions her opening effort of 13.88m would prove sufficient for Gold, competitors struggling to land legal efforts, Chistyakova now representing Russia finishing second with a best effort of 13.67m. After 1992, Huirong was never ranked internationally again and as quickly as she ascended the triple jump heights, she has since completely disappeared. The World Record holder who followed would take the event to ever greater heights, but the cost to the long-term integrity of the sport was disastrous...

25.08.1990 WR 14.54m (47ft 8¼in) Li Huirong (CHN) Sapporo, Japan (+1.1m/s)

CONTROVERSIAL KRAVETS

"Speed, speed and more speed"[657]

[658]How should one consider the merits of an athlete who broke new ground, yet was twice banned for doping offences? Inessa Kravets was the most prominent women's triple jumper of the 1990's and in August 1995, in a golden summer for the sport, she followed Jonathan Edwards' men's world best with the new landmark distance in the women's discipline, landing a jump 41cm further than the former mark of Anna Biryukova. She never expected to hold the World Record for as long as she did – until 2021 – and in the mid-1990's the women's triple jump was a new and exciting event, the expectation of many being that results would continue to grow year on year and the sport as a whole would benefit. Yet the 1995 World Record of Kravets would hang over the women's discipline for many years, if not a black cloud, then a grey one, inviting suspicion from her doping bans and led competitor Yamilé Aldama[659] (of Great Britain), to remark in 2012 on

---

[657] https://www.elespectador.com/deportes/caterine-debe-ser-mas-veloz-para-romper-mi-record-inessa-kravets/

[658] Screenshot of Kravets preparing to long jump in the 1992 Olympic final © BBC Television via YouTube

[659] Yamilé Aldama Pozo, Cuban-born triple jumper, then represented Sudan (2004-10) and Great Britain (from 2011); Silver medallist in the 1999 World Championships and Gold in 2012 World Indoor Championships, then aged 39 [1972-].

the question of drug use in athletics, that "we have an issue in the triple jump too."[660]

Born on 5 October 1966 in Dnipropetrovsk,[661] Ukrainian Soviet Socialist Republic, now modern-day Ukraine, **Inessa Mykolajivna Kravets (née Shulyak)** was a talented long jumper who would win an Olympic Silver medal in 1992 in that event, then went on to worldwide prominence as a triple jumper. She was trained in the Soviet system through the Spartak organisation and was coached by her mother until she was nineteen years old, both of her parents being sports coaches, then made her international debut at the 1988 Olympics, finishing 10th in the long jump. Whilst she continued to progress as a long jumper, having jumped 7.27m in Kyiv in May 1988 with the World Record of 7.52m then set by fellow Soviet Galina Chistyakova the following month, the triple jump became an option for Kravets as the campaign for its inclusion in the IAAF schedule gained momentum in the late 1980's. The Soviet Union looked for talented long jumpers who could adapt their skills to the nascent women's triple jump and a national women's champion was crowned by them for the first time in 1986.

She would win the long jump at the 1990 Goodwill Games[662] in Seattle, United States and followed that with victory in the 1991 Universiade (World University Games) in Sheffield, England, but the latter come off the back of an even more notable World Record in the triple jump on 10 June 1991 in Moscow. In much the same way that Kravets would be forced to navigate the changing landscape of the

---

[660] https://www.theguardian.com/sport/blog/2012/jun/30/london-2012-clean-athletes-drugs
[661] Named Dnipro since 2016.
[662] International sports competition created as a reaction to the political boycotts that so affected the Olympic Games in the 1980's and intended to ease Cold War tensions; first held in Moscow in 1986 and last event was in 2001.

breakup of the Soviet Union, her athletics career would be one defined by a change in course, not necessarily of her own volition, a burning desire to focus on the more-celebrated long jump eventually trumped by the newly included triple jump offering her the clearer pathway to global success.

In Seville, Spain on 9 March 1991 during the World Indoor Championships, Kravets broke the triple jump World Indoor Record three times in an invitational (non-championship) event, taking Chistyakova's 1990 mark of 14.14m, the first ratified indoor record, out to 14.44m (47ft $4\frac{1}{2}$in). On 10 June 1991 in the Brothers Znamensky Memorial event in Moscow, she broke the outdoor World Record of Li Huirong with a soaring leap of 49ft $\frac{1}{2}$in (14.95m) in the early evening sunshine, improving the landmark best by an incredible 41cm. She still saw herself as a long jumper despite now holding both the indoor and outdoor triple jump records, remarking after her victory in the Summer Universiade on 23 July 1991 that, "good results in the long jump are very important to me now."[663] She had arrived too tired to compete in the triple jump earlier in the Sheffield Universiade, but she could not ignore her leading performances in the discipline for much longer.

By now representing the Dynamo club in Kyiv, Kravets would end the 1991 season as the final Soviet Union triple jump champion, to go with long jump titles in 1988 and 1990, and was ranked as the first proper women's world number one in the triple jump. The 1992 season offered the prospect of the Barcelona Olympics in the summer (athletes from the former Soviet states would compete in the 'Unified Team' at the Games) and with the triple jump yet to be introduced to the Olympics for women, Kravets would focus on the long jump. The

---

[663] 'WORLD UNIVERSITY GAMES: United States Wins Water Polo Gold', *Los Angeles Times*, from *Associated Press*, 24 July 1991

European Indoor Championships in Genoa, Italy in February 1992 offered a strong chance to medal in both horizontal events, finishing a disappointing fourth in the long jump, but claiming an important victory in the triple jump, the only athlete over 14m on the day, with a best effort of 14.15m.

In June 1992, Kravets set her personal best in the long jump with a distance of 7.37m in Kyiv, then won the first CIS (Commonwealth of Independent States[664]) long jump championship two weeks later. She went to the Barcelona Olympics in top form and had come to prominence internationally in the preceding two years, yet no one expected her to challenge for the Gold medal as closely as she did. A first-round effort of 7.12m would prove enough for Silver, missing out on Gold by only 2cm, but still a very creditable second place between Gold medallist Heike Drechsler[665] of Germany and Bronze medallist Jackie Joyner-Kersee[666] of the United States, third and second respectively on the long jump all-time list.

Kravets would win triple jump Gold on 14 March at the 1993 World Indoor Championships in Toronto, Canada, the first time in history that athletes from Ukraine had competed under their own flag as an independent nation and she reclaimed her World Indoor Record from Russian Yolanda Chen with that winning jump of 14.47m, bettering the former mark by only 1cm. Kravets was the star of the small Ukraine team in those championships and also took Bronze in

---

[664] Regional intergovernmental organization formed following the breakup of the Soviet Union in 1991; it still exists and athletes from these nations competed in Barcelona 1992 as the 'United Team', before reverting to their individual national identities in the following sporting seasons.

[665] Heike G. Drechsler, two-time Olympic Gold medallist in the long jump amongst a host of major medals and a former World Record holder; dogged by doping allegations like many East German athletes but she never failed a drugs test [1964-].

[666] Jacqueline 'Jackie' Joyner-Kersee, winner of three Golds, one Silver and two Bronze medals in the heptathlon and long jump across four Olympic Games (1984-96), one of the greatest women athletes of all time and holder of the heptathlon World Record since 1988 [1960-].

the long jump, afterwards saying that she had difficulties with the raised wooden runway during the long jump, but that the experience allowed her to perform to her best in the triple jump two days later, when she had prophetically claimed she might break the indoor record![667] In that same interview she mentioned being recently approached for her autograph for the first time and the burgeoning star of Ukrainian women's sport commented that, "the one experience was very surprising but very nice,"[668] yet in the first signs of the enigma that Kravets would increasingly become, her world would soon come crashing down.

Within a few short months, Kravets would go from the metaphorical high of victory in the SkyDome[669] stadium in Toronto, to the dark cloud that a doping sanction invariably brings. She failed a competition test in Lausanne, Switzerland on 7 July 1993 and was found to have the banned stimulant ephedrine in her system, a substance commonly found in cold remedies, but illegal in athletics and many other sports for the affect it has on increasing energy and decreasing the time to exhaustion in particular. She was immediately suspended for three months by her national federation and would miss the 1993 World Championships in Stuttgart, Germany, the first time that the women's event had been held in the Worlds. Kravets was one of three leading Ukraine women athletes to fail drugs tests that July (the other two received multi-year bans for steroid use) and her appeal would be ultimately rejected, use of a cold remedy no excuse for a professional athlete.

---

[667] 'Kravets sets record in triple jump', Nestor Gula, *The Ukrainian Weekly*, 28 March 1993
[668] Gula, *op. cit.*
[669] Now the Rogers Centre.

In one summer, Kravets had gone from the high of being the triple jump World Indoor Champion and holder of both World Records, to seeing both the outdoor (and also absolute) World Record and the first women's triple jump outdoor World title claimed by Russian rivals, along with being sanctioned for the doping offence. Kravets has never really spoken about why she used the banned stimulant which caused her to fail that drugs test in Lausanne and her defence was certainly shaky, but it can be surmised that she perhaps felt under pressure in the summer of 1993, juggling her new-found status as a leading international triple jumper with limited training resources in an independent Ukraine, most of her fellow countrymen and women facing a daily struggle just to feed themselves.   The women's discipline was gaining interest amongst talented women athletes and from Russia the formidable challenge would be manifested in consecutive World Record holders.

[670]The woman to break Kravet's 1991 World Record was **Yolanda Chen**, her Chinese (and French) heritage not in any way making her less Russian than any other athlete who grew up in the Soviet system and she remains fiercely patriotic to this day. Born on 26 July 1961 in Moscow, she was inspired to take up athletics by her father Yevgeniy Chen, an elite triple jumper himself in the 1950's, who cleared 16m in the 1958 season when he also claimed the unofficial indoor World Record and was ranked in the world top ten from 1955-58. Similarly to then Soviet team-mate Inessa Kravets, Chen initially

---

[670] Yolanda Chen competing in the 1994 Stockholm Grand Prix © unknown

made her name as a long jumper, Silver in the 1989 European Indoor Championships, Gold in the 1989 Universiade and fifth place in the 1990 European Championships marking her out as a horizontal jumper of promise, but a personal best of 7.16m from July 1988 suggested that she could not truly challenge the likes of World Record holder Galina Chistyakova.

She switched to the triple jump in 1992 as the new discipline began to gain full acceptance into the major championships and her subsequent rise to the top level was meteoric. She was a 13.72m triple jumper in July 1992, ranked 26th in the world, yet the following February she would claim her first World Indoor Record, a distance of 14.46m in Moscow briefly taking the landmark from Kravets, who would re-claim it by only 1cm in Toronto just over two weeks later, in the 1993 World Indoor Championships. Chen took Silver in those championships, then demonstrating the rich start she had made to her triple jumping career, on 18 June 1993 she would break the outdoor World Record during the Russian Championships in the Lokomotiv Stadium, Moscow, with a distance of 49ft $1\frac{1}{4}$in (14.97m)[671] on her sixth-round jump, nearly 75cm further than any of her other jumps that day. The World Championships that August were set to offer a top-quality triple jump field headed by Kravets and Chen, but the late sanctioning of the Ukrainian for ephedrine use would see the inaugural women's event become a shoot-out between two Russians, Chen and Biryukova.

---

[671] Ratified as such, but more correctly 49ft $1\frac{4}{10}$in.

[672]Born on 27 September 1967 in Sverdlovsk (now Yekaterinberg), the largest city in the Ural Federal District, **Anna Biryukova (née Derevyankina)**[673] was another middling long jumper who switched to the embryonic women's triple jump in the early 1990's. Her athletic talents had been spotted as a fourteen-year-old in one

of the summer, or 'Young Pioneer', camps that provided much enjoyment and recreation to Soviet youth, and she was encouraged to take up the long jump after easily beating the boys in those holiday track and field competitions. Training in Moscow with the *Moskva Trade Union* team prior to the breakup of the Soviet Union, she was ranked as high as 11th in the world in the long jump in 1990, but the switch to the triple jump saw a rise to the top of the sport that has been unrivalled, certainly in the women's event.

Competing in her first season in the triple jump, her first major competition would be the 1993 World Championships in Stuttgart, Germany. Biryukova would fail to qualify for the long jump final with a best effort of 6.36m (Heike Drechsler would win with 7.11m), but it was to be in the triple jump that she would announce herself on the world stage in glorious fashion, ascending a then unexpected peak that she would never manage to return to, although she would challenge for the leading honours in the next two seasons. In the late afternoon sunshine of 21 August 1993, with little wind and favourable humidity in the *Gottlieb-Daimler-Stadion*,[674] the largely unheralded Biryukova

---

[672] An undated photograph of a young Anna Biryukova © unknown
[673] World Athletics maintain separate profiles for Anna Derevyankina & Anna Biryukova, but they are the same athlete.
[674] The *Neckarstadion* until 1993 and now the Mercedes-Benz Arena.

opened the first women's global (outdoor) triple jump final with a distance of 14.62m, a distance that only Russian Champion Chen could even go on to match that day.

[675]In the second round Biryukova improved her personal best to 14.77m (pre-Stuttgart it was 14.27m) and pushing hard in response, Chen fouled on her first and third attempts, barely qualifying for the last three jumps with a second-round 13.78m. She fouled twice more and in the fifth round was a spectator to a moment of history, Biryukova covering 49ft 6in  (15.09m)[676] for a new World Record and the first woman ever to go over 15m in the triple jump, an important milestone in the progression of a sport only afforded full status in 1990. Chen looked to respond as the former World Record holder, but a final-round 14.70m was only good enough for Silver, still nearly 50cm further than any other woman that day. Biryukova's landmark distance heralded her as a rising star of the event and she ended the year as the world number one, the long jump now consigned to her past.

Yet Biryukova would find that back in Moscow there was little in the way of funding on offer, despite her headline-making performance in Stuttgart. The cost of living in Russia was ever rising in the aftermath of the breakup of the Soviet Union and the economic malaise led to the collapse of social services, so there was no chance that a professional athlete would receive any form of monthly allowance. Some of her competitors had already moved abroad to

---

[675] Anna Biryukova competing in the 1993 World Championships in Stuttgart © unknown

[676] Ratified as such, but more correctly 49ft 6$\frac{1}{10}$in.

enable themselves to continue training and earn a living at the same time, when in 1994 she moved with her husband and young son to the Czech Republic, to be supported by a local track and field club in Jablonec nad Nisou.[677] She was to train under Jan Pospisil,[678] coach of the legendary javelin thrower Jan Železný[679] and who also later worked with leading men's triple jumper Jonathan Edwards in the back end of his career, before the advent of an Olympic year in 1996 led to the Russian athletics federation finally providing her with a reasonable monthly allowance.

March 1994 saw Biryukova finish second in Paris in the European Indoor Championships, Gold going to compatriot Inna Lasovskaya[680] who had broken the World Indoor Record three times in the opening weeks of the season; she would go over 15m in 1996 and also claimed a triple jump Silver medal in the Atlanta Olympics that year, but never threatened the outdoor World Record, with a personal best in 1997 of 15.09m, when the leading mark was by then 15.50m. Biryukova would win the European Championships in August 1994, ahead of Lasovskaya and Kravets respectively in a breezy Helsinki, with the latter claiming long jump Silver behind Drechsler and also victorious in the same event in the 1994 World Cup in Crystal Palace, London, the following month.

The 1995 season opened with Chen in peak form, winning the World Indoor Championships in Barcelona with a new indoor record of 15.03m and she would be the Russian Champion again that year, but she was nearly thirty-four-years-old and was clearly on the back end of

---

[677] https://www.rferl.org/a/1080790.html
[678] Jan Pospisil, also coached javelin thrower Steve Backley of Great Britain in his later career and his training group also included a number of hurdlers [n/k].
[679] Jan Železný, widely considered the greatest javelin thrower of all time, three-time Olympic and three-time World Champion, and still holds the World Record [1966-].
[680] Inna A. Lasovskaya, European Indoor Champion in 1995, World Indoor Champion in 1997 and Olympic Silver medallist in Atlanta 1996 [1969-].

her career. She had been that much older than Kravets and Biryukova when she switched to the triple jump, and Biryukova and Lasovskaya were now the leading triple jumpers from Russia. Chen would retire after the 1996 season, posed for the Russian edition of Playboy[681] magazine and has become a respected sports commentator and TV anchor in her home country. She is often to be found making public protestations on the recent controversies around Russian participation in both the Winter and Summer Olympiads, but Chen is no propagandist, a proud Russian, yet first and foremost conscious of the enormous effect any boycott would have on her fellow athletes, encouraging political process that will see her compatriots still able to compete rather than be excluded. In her career she was a prodigious horizontal jumper – still ranked 25th all-time in the long jump – and actively progressed the triple jump after it entered the women's schedule. And anyone old enough to remember early 1990's track and field, will certainly remember her as a glamourous athlete, notable for her big hair and the copious amount of jewellery she would brazenly wear in-competition!

[682]The 1995 World Championships offered the crowning moment of Jonathan Edwards' history-chasing season on 7 August and the women's event was in good health entering their own competition three days later. Biryukova was the defending champion and Lasovskaya was the world number one at the end of 1994, yet it was to be Inessa Kravets who surprised the world with her demolition of Biryukova's World

---

[681] Men's lifestyle and entertainment magazine founded in Chicago in 1953.
[682] Inessa Kravets compering in the 1995 World Championships in Gothenburg © Foto-Library Palyvoda2006

Record in Gothenburg, in a display that no one truly expected. Kravets has given few interviews since, but she arrived in Sweden in August 1995 in good shape (her season best was 14.82m) and despite fouling on her first two attempts in the final, a 2014 interview with a Colombian newspaper recalled that she knew that those jumps had been good, so in her words about what followed in the third-round, "I didn't do anything special."[683]

But it *was* special and the competition that evening in the Ullevi Stadium proved exhilarating. Chen had led in qualifying and was to finish in 11th place in the final, with fellow Russian Biryukova taking the lead on her second-round 14.85m. At this stage Kravets was in trouble after two fouls and she should not have been thinking about the World Record on her third-round effort, problems with the speed of the runway in Gothenburg having led her to increase the length of her run-up third time round. She later credited pictures of Jonathan Edwards' World Record from three days prior in giving her the inspiration for what happened next and despite her always modest demeanour, the twenty-eight-year-old Ukrainian did not play it safe with her jump...

Sometimes lethargic on the runway and often inconsistent in major competition, Kravets approached the board as quick as she had ever done on the hyper-fast surface and took off around 20cm from the plasticine, an enormous spring in her hop followed by an almost scissor-like splitting of her legs in her step, a fast transition through the phases that on replay looks like it has been speeded up! She rose from the sandpit clearly some way over Biryukova's 1993 mark from Stuttgart and following an agonising delay whilst the distance was confirmed, Kravets had the World Record once again. But this was

---

[683] https://www.elespectador.com/deportes/caterine-debe-ser-mas-veloz-para-romper-mi-record-inessa-kravets/

not just any record jump and in advancing the landmark best by 41cm it was a barrier-breaking effort, 15m having been previously considered elite in the women's event. The qualifying session two days before had been affected by blustery conditions, yet there was to be no such trouble on 10 August 1995, the new World Record measured as 50ft 10in (15.50m)[684] and with a legal tailwind (+0.9m/s).

Kravets was now the first woman to triple jump over 50ft and before Gothenburg there had been only one legal jump over 15m (outdoors)! Biryukova responded in the third-round by covering 15.08m, only 1cm behind the previous World Record, but she was clearly disappointed with the distance which would normally have won Gold. Iva Prandzheva[685] of Bulgaria was the third athlete in the competition to exceed 15m in the fifth round, a distance of 15.18m then the second-furthest in history and she made a final round effort of 15.00m. Kravets was now the World Champion and the lasting memory of her achievement that day is of the almost elfin-like excitement of her celebration, a slight, shy smile at the distance when it was announced and a clapping to herself suggesting an innocence that would later be so momentously belied.

The success of the women's triple jump in the 1995 World Championships ensured its inclusion in the Olympics the following year and Kravets' part in that should not be forgotten. Biryukova would end 1995 ranked by some as the world number one, despite Kravets' record leap[686] and it would be Lasovskaya in 1996, but in both years the Ukrainian would make her own indelible mark on history.

---

[684] Ratified as such, but more correctly 50ft $10\frac{1}{4}$in.

[685] Iva Prandzheva, long jump World Junior Champion in 1990 before switching to the triple jump, Silver in the 1995 World Indoor Championships and European Indoor Champion in 1996; banned for life after a second doping offence in 2000, the first seeing her disqualified from her fourth place in Atlanta 1996 [1972-].

[686] The prominent *Track and Field News* rankings are based on relative merit for example, including head-to-head records.

Lasovskaya was the most consistent performer in the 1996 season and one of the favourites for Gold, yet the first women's triple jump final in Olympic history on 31 July 1996 would see Kravets prove that her Gothenburg performance was no fluke, even if the winning jump was another surprise after an underwhelming season to date, although she did have the experience of competing in the previous two Games in the long jump behind her.

The 1996 Olympics triple jump final was a top-quality field and Lasovskaya would lead after four rounds, with a second-round effort of 14.98m, matched by the tall Šárka Kašpárková[687] in the third, but the Russian held the tiebreaker over the Czech Republic athlete, who would be the next World Champion in 1997. Kravets had a best distance of 14.84m in the second round, when in the fifth she produced an incredible leap of 50ft $3\frac{1}{2}$in (15.33m) which would be the Olympic Record until 2008, when beaten by Françoise Mbango Etone[688] of Cameroon in winning her second consecutive Gold medal. Kravets was *the* first Olympic Champion in the women's discipline and Atlanta marked the final peak of her career, the first phase of the grey cloud we spoke of earlier now approaching.

Under pressure in the Olympic final, Kravets had produced the second-longest jump in women's history and it also demonstrated the maturity of the discipline, her step almost reaching the sandpit. The earliest women to take up the triple jump after it was given full status by the IAAF were from a long jumping background and it was natural that those schooled in the Soviet system – whichever Eastern European nation they went on to represent after independence –

---

[687] Šárka Kašpárková, 1997 World Champion and multiple championship medallist between 1996-99, including Olympic Bronze in 1996 [1971-].
[688] Françoise Mbango Etone, Olympic triple jump champion in 2004 & 2008, World Championships Silver in 2001 & 2003; later competed for France from 2010 [1976-].

would commonly use the 'Russian Style', favouring the hop and relying heavily on their speed in the approach to the board. Most were of above average height, the global mean about 5ft 5in (1.65m) at the time, Biryukova being 5ft $8\frac{1}{2}$in (1.74m) and Kravets 5ft 10in (1.78m), but these were not excessively tall women.

Biryukova broke the World Record in 1993 with a hop of 5.57m and watching a replay of that jump shows how elastic her long legs were through the hop and step, a smooth transition through the phases and a middling final jump achieved through the height she gained. Kravets had a similar technique in 1991, but by 1995 she could add 50cm to her final jump with the same distance of step, a sign of the move to the more jump-dominated technique that is common to this day. Biryukova and Lasovskaya enjoyed more consistent results in their respective periods at the top, and in Gothenburg, Kravets recorded a second-best distance of only 14.55m having landed the 15.50m World Record, yet it was her focus on speed *into the board* that allowed her to enjoy the great moments that she did, a boom or bust mentality seemingly at odds with her passive outward demeanour.

Kravets pulled out of the 1997 World Championships in Athens with a serious Achilles injury (she failed to even turn up for qualifying) and in the 1999 edition in Seville she could not qualify for the final, finishing with a best effort of 13.49m when Gold was taken by Paraskevi Tsiamita[689] of Greece with a personal best 15.07m. Biryukova faded after 1995, never again jumping over 15m after Gothenburg and suffering a major injury in the qualifying round in Seville in 1999, rupturing a patella tendon. Lasovskaya would also fade after winning the World Indoor Championships in Paris in March

---

[689] Paraskevi Tsiamita, 1999 World Champion when she had a career day, with no other major global medals and even failed to make the Greece team for the Athens World Championships in 1997 [1972-].

1997, missing the Worlds that year through injury, but she was able to continue competing until 2002. Biryukova retired in 2000, still then managing to jump 14.44m as she approached the age of 33 and little of her post-career life can be confirmed.

In the summer of 2000, a nearly thirty-four-year-old Kravets posted a world-leading long jump of 7.10m in Barcelona on 7 July and this seemed to be a triumphant return to form after her serious Achilles injury, twice requiring surgery. Sadly, that grey cloud we mentioned earlier would descend completely when she received a two-year ban for using performance-enhancing steroids, having failed a drugs test whilst in Barcelona. This should have been the end of her career, but an athlete who was desperate to continue competing even as the light inevitably faded, would return from her ban to win long jump Silver in Birmingham, England, in the World Indoor Championships in March 2003. She failed to show for the long jump qualifying in the 2003 World Championships in Paris and was not selected for the Ukraine Olympic team in 2004, so she then finally retired, in a later interview saying that her "sports ambitions are fulfilled."[690] She now lives quietly in Kyiv with her daughter Darya, was inducted into the Ukrainian Sports Hall of Fame in November 2020 and provided occasional interviews via her national federation, as leading athletes began to threaten a World Record that seemed it would never be broken.

Inessa Kravets would hold the women's triple jump World Record for 25 years, 11 months and 22 days, before Yulimar Rojas of Venezuela finally became the athlete to break it in 2021, having been willed to consign the Ukrainian's mark to history by so many within athletics. It is important to remember that her World Record was never invalidated because of her steroid use, so a generation of triple jumpers

---

[690] https://www.elespectador.com/deportes/caterine-debe-ser-mas-veloz-para-romper-mi-record-inessa-kravets/

have been forced to accept that the leading distance in their discipline is questionable. No one can say with any certainty that she *cheated* when she set a World Record that was so enduring, nor that she used drugs when winning that Olympic Gold in 1996. What is certain is that she triple jumped 15.50m when 15m was seen as the elite standard and she furthered her event, the type of legacy that any athlete can only dream of. The women's triple jump in the mid-1990's was progressing year on year and Kravets put petrol on the fire with her incredible jumps in Gothenburg and Atlanta. She helped ensure its inclusion in the Olympic programme and at face value, an enigmatic athlete with a best distance measured toe to heel by the IAAF in August 1995 as 15.70m and still the second ranked triple jumper of all time,[691] deserves her place in the pantheon of great women jumpers, having given her event its first two truly memorable performances since full global status was granted.

10.06.1991 WR 14.95m (49ft $\frac{1}{2}$in) Inessa Kravets (URS) Moscow, Soviet Union (-0.2m/s)

18.06.1993 WR 14.97m (49ft 1$\frac{1}{4}$in) Yolanda Chen (RUS) Moscow, Russia (+0.9m/s)

21.08.1993 WR 15.09m (49ft 6in) Anna Biryukova (RUS) Stuttgart, Germany (+0.5m/s)

10.08.1995 WR 15.50m (50ft 10in) Inessa Kravets (UKR) Gothenburg, Sweden (+0.9m/s)

---

[691] Also, the 7th ranked long jumper of all time.

RISING ROJAS

"Estoy en llamas (I'm on fire)"[692]

The turn of the century would see the women's triple jump in full bloom, a decade after finally being afforded full status. Tereza Marinova[693] of Bulgaria would win Gold at the Sydney Olympics in 2000 with a personal best 15.20m, ahead of Tatyana Lebedeva's[694] jump of 15.00m, she by now the leading Russian, but hindered by deteriorating weather conditions that evening. Marinova had been the World Junior (now World U20) Champion in 1996 and her winning jump that year of 14.62m – also in Sydney – remains the age-group record to this day. Marinova and Lebedeva would duel for the major honours in subsequent seasons, trading world number one rankings, yet it was Lebedeva who would end up as one of the most decorated women athletes in the horizontal jumps, starting with victory in the 2001 World Championships in Edmonton, Canada.

Marinova was coached by the great triple jumper Khristo Markov, one of the original male proponents of the single (or opposite) arm take off method that is now prevalent amongst women jumpers, but an Achilles tendon injury in 2002 would see her miss a season of competition and she never regained the heights of 2000-01, retiring before the 2008 Olympics. The powerful Lebedeva was noted for the very high speed of her approach and it was this that carried her to the many medals that followed, including triple jump World titles in 2001

692

https://as.com/juegos_olimpicos/2021/07/31/noticias/1627712545_069637.html

693 Tereza M. Marinova, Olympic Champion in Sydney 2000, World Indoor Champion in 2001 and Bronze in the 2001 Worlds [1977-]

694 Tatyana R. Lebedeva, one Olympic medal of each colour, three-time World and World Indoor Champion across the horizontal jumps but sanctioned by the IOC in 2017 for doping which took away two Silvers from the 2008 Games [1976-].

and 2003, and World Silver in 2007, when she also won Gold in the long jump. The women's discipline was in rude health, with an increasing number of jumps over 15m in the major championship finals, but collectively the technique of the leading jumpers still had room for improvement, small steps in many of the bigger jumps showing that it was still being used as a *link* phase, rather than a separate bound to be exploited for maximum overall distance.

Lebedeva won the 2001 World Championships by an incredible margin of 65cm, ahead of Françoise Mbango Etone[695] of Cameroon in second place and Marinova in third. Speed-oriented jumpers were common as the event matured and power jumpers were rare in the women's ranks, physiological differences in bone, muscle, hormones and testosterone[696] meaning that the technique for each sex remains distinct from the other. Women athletes also have to contend with the natural desire for reproduction and Lebedeva would have her first child in 2002, whilst rival Marinova was injured. The Russian would return to competition successfully in 2003, highlighted by victory in the World Championships in Paris and 15m jumps from her would become frequent, three World Records in the 2004 World Indoor Championships in Budapest in March, amidst an undefeated indoor season, seeing her set a mark (15.36m) that would not be beaten until 2020.[697]

---

[695] Françoise Mbango Etone, Olympic triple jump champion in 2004 & 2008, World Championships Silver in 2001 & 2003; later competed for France from 2010 [1976-].
[696] For more information on the physical differences between men and women jumpers: https://coachesinsider.com/track-x-country/triple-jumpers-the-different-characteristics-of-male-and-female-jumpers/
[697] Chen's World Indoor Record mark of 15.03m had been beaten by Ashia Hansen of Great Britain on 28.02.1998 in Valencia, Spain with a jump of 15.16m; she was twice World Indoor Champion in 1999 & 2003, European Champion in 2002, European Indoor Champion in 1998, Commonwealth Games Champion in 1998 and still the National Record holder indoors and outdoors [1971-].

The livewire Lebedeva looked the real deal and her return to the elite level after pregnancy in 2002 (and again in 2012 after her second child was born in 2011) made her achievements even more impressive, even if her only Olympic Gold came in her less favoured long jump and she cynically passed the 2005 World Championships final[698] to preserve her fitness for the $1,000,000 jackpot on offer in the Golden League that season (which she would win). She would finally retire in 2013 with an envious major championship record and was the golden girl of Russian athletics, later taking an executive role in her national federation when it was increasingly embattled and then became a senator in the Russian Parliament, such was her profile beyond sport (she had been a Lieutenant Colonel in the Russian Army whilst she was an athlete too).

[699]Mbango Etone would be the first women's Olympic Champion in the event to successfully defend her title in Beijing 2008, being also the first athlete from Cameroon to win an Olympic Gold in 2004. She would also take time out in her career, missing around three years in total to study in the United States and due to a series of disputes with her national federation, before giving birth to her first child in 2006, only returning to competition in the 2008 season. Her performance in Beijing was all the more remarkable because of the extended hiatus she had been on and in a final that saw six women go over 15m, she set an Olympic Record of 15.39m that would last until the re-arranged Tokyo Games, in August 2021.

---

[698] Won by Trecia-Kaye Smith of Jamaica with a world-leading 15.11m, seven-time NCAA Champion at the University of Pittsburgh and two-time Commonwealth Games Champion in 2006 & 2010 [1975-].
[699] Mbango Etone competing in the 2008 Olympic triple jump final © Xinhua

This was the era of multiple champions in the women's event, but in a portent of the shadow over the sport that what would come later, the double Olympic Silver medallist from Athens and Beijing, Hrysopiyi Devetzi[700] of Greece, with an awkward record of often jumping further in qualification than in major finals, was banned for two years in 2009 for failing to submit to a doping test. In 2016, samples of hers from August 2007 were re-tested and they revealed anabolic steroid use, her subsequent results from the sample date being annulled by the IOC, costing her a World Championships Bronze from 2007, Silver from the World Indoor Championships in 2008 and that second Olympic Silver in 2008.[701] Lebedeva would then be sanctioned in January 2017 for steroid use after samples of hers from 2008 were re-tested and she would be stripped of her long jump and triple jump Silver medals from the Beijing Games, when her appeal was finally rejected in 2018.[702] There had been suspicions over her 2004 samples, with the Russians who finished second and third behind her in the Olympic long jump final later both sanctioned, but the samples were never re-tested before being destroyed in 2014, so her results before 2008 were never annulled.

It was not known in 2009 that this re-testing would take place when later scientific advances meant certain substances could now be traced in frozen samples, but the then ban for Devetzi raised serious questions on its own given her status as a leading jumper and subsequent events would confirm that the women's triple jump had historic concerns in this period, although it was not exclusive to just

---

[700] Hrysopiyi Devetzi, regular horizontal jumps medallist from 2004-08, but discredited by later bans and annulling of medals from sample re-testing; National Record holder since 2004 [1976-].

[701] https://olympics.com/ioc/news/ioc-sanctions-16-athletes-for-failing-anti-doping-tests-at-beijing-2008

[702] https://olympics.com/ioc/news/ioc-sanctions-two-athletes-for-failing-anti-doping-test-at-beijing-2008

that event. The thirty-one-year-old Mbango Etone sprinkled her own stardust on the event in 2008, wearing a skirt in the Olympic final rather than shorts or skin-tight garments as was common, a personal desire to wear something "more feminine and sexy but not too open",[703] yet new heroes would be required to take the sport on again, even more so than the 'Wonder Woman'[704] type ability and character shown by the Cameroonian with springs in her heels.

Yargelis Savigne[705] of Cuba would add her name to the growing list of double global triple jump champions in this period, winning back-to-back World Championships in 2007-09, but her personal best would be 15.28m in 2007 and the longer the seasons passed from Kravets' 1995 World Record, the greater the burden it became, both in terms of her doping bans and the effect on an event as a whole that does not advance in statistical terms. The 2011 World Championships were won by Olha Saladukha[706] of Ukraine (a career resurgence after childbirth in 2009) although the overall standard was as disappointing as it had been in the 2009 edition in Berlin. In 2009, Savigne had been the only jumper over 14.70m and in Daegu, South Korea in 2011, Saladukha's 14.94m was as close as any woman got to 15m, in admittedly windy conditions. The 2013 World Championships in Moscow were won by Caterine Ibargüen[707] with a world-leading

---

[703] https://worldathletics.org/news/news/mbango-etone-makes-history-as-she-becomes-fir

[704] Fictional female superhero from the DC Comics universe; noted for being warrior born, fiercely competitive, opinionated yet compassionate and caring.

[705] Yargelis Savigne Herrera, two-time World Champion in 2007 & 2009, also World Indoor Champion in 2008; along with numerous other medals, including Olympic Bronze in 2008 [1984-].

[706] Olha Saladukha, World Champion in 2011, World Championship Bronze in 2013 and Olympic Bronze in 2012; three-time European Champion in 2010-14 and in 2019, elected to the Ukrainian Parliament [1983-].

[707] Caterine Ibargüen Mena, 2016 Olympic Champion, Silver medallist in 2012 and two-time World Champion in 2013 & 2015, amongst a host of major championship medals, including podiums in the long jump and high jump in continental competitions [1984-].

14.85m, with subsequent 2014 World Indoor Champion Ekaterina Koneva[708] a close second with 14.81m, but the overall standard was again not high and the competition was essentially over after the second attempt, no woman able to threaten the marks of the Colombian and the Russian in the that round.

It was widely believed that Ibargüen could be the athlete to finally break Kravets' World Record when she became so dominant between 2012-2016, winning an incredible 34 competition finals in a row[709] and she would also be the overall women's triple jump Diamond League winner five times. She had missed out on Gold in the 2012 Olympics to Olga Rypakova[710] of Kazakhstan and it was Rypakova who had finally broken that unbeaten run in July 2016 in Birmingham, England. They had become great rivals in that period, but Ibargüen returned to form a month after that defeat, in the Rio Olympics, winning her first Gold after taking Silver in London 2012, the only woman over 15m in the 2016 Olympic final at 15.17m.

[711]The very popular Ibargüen – a genuine superstar in Colombia – was an outstanding all-round athlete, who started as a high jumper and first went to the Olympics in that discipline in 2004, only committing to the triple jump aged 26. In a career high on notable achievement (over twenty championship medals, including continental competitions), she was triple jump World Champion in 2013 and 2015, with five World and two Olympic medals

---

[708] Ekaterina Koneva, 2014 World Indoor Champion in the triple jump who began her career as a sprinter; received two-year ban in 2007 for excess testosterone [1988-].
[709] https://worldathletics.org/news/report/idl-rome-ibarguen-van-niekirk
[710] Olga Rypakova, 2012 Olympic Champion and World Indoor Champion in 2010; three-time Olympic and World medallist in the triple jump [1984-].
[711] Caterine Ibargüen on her way to Gold in the 2015 World Championships © Erik van Leeuwen

in total and was world number one five times, reigning from 2013-16 and then again in 2018. In a 2014 interview with a Colombian newspaper, she was picked by Kravets as having the potential to break her record,[712] but that never came to pass, a jump of 50ft $2\frac{3}{4}$in (15.31m) in the Monaco Diamond League meeting in July 2014 remaining her personal best and most of her victories came with distances below 15m.

Ibargüen had been a 13.91m triple jumper in 2006 and had only improved to 14.29m in 2010, yet thereafter she would reach a level where she *dominated* the sport and put herself into the conversation for the greatest women's triple jumper of all time. She retired in 2021 – the first full season since 2011 where she did not win a single event – after finishing 10th in the re-arranged Tokyo Olympics and would remark, "I've done more than I ever dreamt",[713] the first Olympic Gold medallist in track and field from Colombia. Kravets' World Record remained in the books however, the shadow it cast ever lengthening and it was the rookie athlete who had claimed Silver behind Ibargüen in the Rio Olympics that has gone on to become the star of the women's discipline after the Colombian. The triple jump was slowly coming out of hibernation with distances progressing again and it was Yulimar Rojas who went into the Tokyo Olympics in 2021 as the hottest favourite in the whole of track and field, but with other matters on her mind beyond the Gold medal...

Born on 21 October 1995 in Caracas, Venezuela, **Yulimar del Valle Rojas Rodríguez**, the future 'Queen of the Triple Jump' would grow up in a rickety house, generously described as a 'shack' or 'ranchito' in her home country, the common accommodation in the

---

[712] https://www.elespectador.com/deportes/caterine-debe-ser-mas-veloz-para-romper-mi-record-inessa-kravets/

[713] https://world-track.org/2021/08/rio-olympic-champion-caterine-ibarguen-retires-37/

port city of Puerto La Cruz where she grew up with her six siblings in one of the poorest neighbourhoods. Her upbringing was humble, with her mother and stepfather having little money, and this restless but happy child would quickly find an outlet in sports, her natural ability clear from an early age and her stepfather (a former professional boxer who fostered her love of sport) recalled a strong interest in street games starting when she was around seven[714] and she would eventually go to a specialist sports school. She fell in love with volleyball when the Venezuelan men's and women's teams qualified for the Olympics for the first time in 2008,[715] with the sport widely popular in Latin America and a teenage Rojas was already set to be very tall, a distinct advantage in volleyball! Yet, as we have seen with many other leading jumpers in this discipline, particularly in the Americas, the triple jump was to find her.

[716]Taken by her parents to the *Simón Bolívar Sports Complex* a mile from her home when she first took an interest in volleyball, there were no coaches or a team, so it was at the *Salvador de la Plaza* athletics centre within the complex that she would take the first steps towards greatness, her later achievements memorialised there now with a mural. The athletics track only has six lanes rather than the standard eight and the complex itself has been allowed to completely degrade since construction in 2007, through a lack of maintenance and regular theft (said to be everything at some

---

[714] https://viewsfromtheconcourse.com/2021/07/29/yulimar-rojas-venezuelas-first-athletics-gold-medallist/

[715] https://www.archysport.com/2021/08/tokyo-2020-athletics-yulimar-rojas-the-girl-from-the-ranch-who-could-with-inessa-kravets/

[716] Rojas pictured at the Paris Diamond League meeting on 24 August 2019, which she would win with a leap of 15.05m © Yann Caradec

stage bar the track!), but Rojas' special talent was quickly noticed. More importantly, she also had the physique to match her ability – she was 5ft 11in (1.80m) tall aged only 14[717] – and she switched from volleyball to athletics at the urging of her soon to be first coach, Jesús Velásquez.[718]

Velásquez would become a father figure to the teenage Rojas and with athletics requiring little to no equipment (the training group even had to dig their first sandpit), she won her first athletics event in the shot put, excelled as a sprinter before focussing on the high jump. The training conditions were severely limited, but no less adverse than the surroundings she was growing up in (the shack would later be washed away by poor weather) and she would only be given her first pair of athletics spikes after a maiden competitive victory in the high jump, in the 2011 South American Junior (U20) Championships in Medellín, Colombia. Her estranged father had refused to allow her permission to travel to international events as a minor before this competition and overcoming such adversity in her youth was to be the fire that has made her later senior career burn so brightly.

Her coach had challenged the Venezuelan Athletics Federation to support Rojas if she won in Medellín and the gifted spikes were their first move. Success in the continental U20 competition one month shy of her sixteenth birthday marked her out as an athlete to watch and she was to claim Bronze in the 2012 South American Under-23 Championships in the September, then disappointed in the South American Youth (U18) Championships the following month, when coming 4th. She had come 6th in the 2012 Ibero-American Championships in June and she was already

---

[717] https://cronica.uno/en-la-cuna-de-preparacion-de-la-medallista-olimpica-yulimar-rojas-reinan-la-desidia-y-el-abandono/
[718] Jesús Velásquez [c.1953-].

demonstrating a flair for performing better when up against quality opposition, beyond those of her own age-group.

In 2013 she improved her personal best in the high jump – setting the then South American junior record – and clocked 11.94sec in the 100m,[719] a sign of the ever-improving ground speed that was to serve her well as a triple jumper. In August she took Silver in the 2013 Pan American Junior Championships, losing Gold on a countback (a system to break a tie in high jump, using the fewest misses at the tie height) and at the Bolivarian Games in November in Peru, she competed in the long jump for the first time, finishing sixth. She quickly improved in this event and whilst she was to win high jump Gold in the 2014 South American Games the following March, against the top-level senior athletes in the region and later calling this one of her "best experiences",[720] her coach was soon forced to seriously consider that another discipline in track and field could well prove to be her best.

Spring 2014 would deliver the chance encounter that would change the course of Rojas' sporting life. By now one of the best junior athletes in the world, she went along to a triple jump practice in Puerto La Cruz with other athletes coached by Velásquez and without any training in the event whatsoever, covered 12m.[721] It could be said that these 12m were the most important she travelled in her life and convincing her sceptical coach to let her try the triple jump in a local meeting in Barquisimeto, on 26 April 2014 she jumped 13.57m on her event debut. She had not expected to jump that far – a national U20 record – and "after that, I became more and more motivated by the

---

[719] 'Yulimar Rojas' quantum leap', Paul Halford, *Athletics Weekly*, 4 May 2016
[720] Halford, *op. cit.*
[721] https://www.france24.com/en/live-news/20210802-sky-s-the-limit-for-venezuela-s-olympic-champion-rojas

triple jump,"[722] extending the U20 record to 13.65m in September 2014 and the national federation was convinced by her potential in the discipline, despite Rojas not yet doing a proper step.[723]

Rojas would compete in both horizontal jumps in the 2014 World Junior Championships in Eugene, Oregon, United States in July, finishing 11th in the long jump and 17th in the triple jump, disappointed to not qualify for the final. Despite that, she would compete in the high jump only once more, finishing fourth at the 2015 Military World Games[724] in South Korea, when she also claimed Silver in the triple jump. By the end of the 2015 season, she held the National Record in both of the horizontal jumps at only twenty-years-old and was clearly now a triple jump specialist. She won triple jump Gold in the South American Championships in June 2015 and in July she set her personal best of 14.20m when finishing fourth at the Pan American Games in Toronto, Gold going to a thirty-one-year-old Caterine Ibargüen in clearing 15m, but she was soon to find the young Venezuelan rivalling her for the major global titles.

Velásquez has frequently said that others thought he was crazy to allow Rojas to change to the triple jump, but with her height, sprinting speed and all-round power, she had all the tools. Today she stands at around 6ft 4in (1.92m) and would be amongst the tallest in the men's discipline, let alone the women, towering over her current rivals by around 12in (30cm) and there has never been an elite women's triple jumper with her height. Being tall in the triple jump is not necessarily a ready advantage, as that much mass comes with greater weight, but long legs (and high hips) certainly help horizontal jumpers,

---

[722] Halford, *op. cit.*
[723] Halford, *op. cit.*
[724] It is not known how long she served in the National Bolivarian Armed Forces of Venezuela, but registering for military service is mandatory at 18 and she likely enjoyed much needed assistance with her training.

and she has both. A bigger body can still be trained to produce more explosive power, Brazilian Jadel Gregório being the closest comparison in the history of the men's event, 6ft 8in (2.03m) himself and 10th in the all-time list. Rojas had demonstrated in the 2013 season that she could approach the distance of the furthest jumps in her age-group without a technical background and for all the talk of the competitive advantage that her size provided, the formative period of her career as a triple jumper started with a speculative connection on Facebook, the online social networking website with its clever algorithms that determine what content a user sees when they login.[725]

Rojas had done well in the Toronto Pan American Games in July 2015 with a new personal best of 14.20m only 15 months after her debut in the event, but returning home with joint pains and not being able to recover in time, she passed on the World Championships that August in Beijing. Ibargüen retained her title with a season best 14.90m and watching at home, the Venezuelan knew now that she could compete with the elite group, if not yet the very best such as the Colombian world number one or Olympic Champion Olga Rypakova. Her coach knew that she required specialist training to reach the next level and also needed the type of support that was not available to elite athletes in Venezuela, mired in poverty after years of failed economic policies. He later remarked, "she has a lot of will, she has speed and a lot of strength, but the three potatoes (meals) and the necessary medical care were not going to happen in Venezuela,"[726] being convinced that her later success would not have happened if she had stayed at home. So, against this background, Yulimar Rojas wrote a message to a

[725] 'Rojas thanks Facebook algorithm after making history in triple jump', Sean Ingle, *The Guardian*, 1 August 2021
[726] 'Yulimar Rojas' first jumps', Florantonia Singer, *El País*, 18 August 2020

leading jumping coach in Europe, with Facebook having suggested that they connect...

That spur of the moment message after the Pan American Games, sent without hesitation, would tell Cuban-born long jump legend Iván Pedroso that it was her dream to train with him. To her surprise, the ten-time global champion responded, saying that he had been following her progress "because he felt that I was very talented"[727] and he invited her to come to Spain, to join his multinational training group in Guadalajara. In a progressive move in a country shaped by the Bolivarian Revolution[728] since 1998, with its loosely socialist ideals and tight control of its citizens, the national athletics federation agreed that she could move to Spain to further her career and she left in October 2015,[729] leaving behind the *barrio*[730] and her Education degree to become a full-time athlete, with a promise to buy her mother a better home.

Rojas later recalled of connecting with Pedroso via Facebook, "it was destiny"[731] and her career took off in Spain as if it was predestined, later signing with the *Futbol Club Barcelona* athletics team, the affiliate of the soccer team she had long supported. Within a matter of months of arriving in Europe and off the back of an unbeaten indoor season in Spain, Rojas went to the World Indoor Championships in Portland, Oregon, United States, in March 2016. Incredibly, after only a few months of hard work with Pedroso to first focus on improving her strength, she went to Portland as the favourite

---

[727] Halford, *op. cit.*

[728] The political process in Venezuela, essentially a popular democracy, that enacted a serious of social reforms and is defined by its nationalism and state-led economy. Named after Simón Bolívar, an early 19th century Venezuelan revolutionary leader, who achieved independence for most of northern South America, fighting Spanish rule.

[729] https://worldathletics.org/news/feature/portland-2016-rojas-triple-jump

[730] Neighbourhood in Spanish-speaking countries.

[731] Ingle, *op. cit.*

for Gold, with a world-leading jump of 14.69m in Madrid in January that was also the South American Indoor Record. She was still a relative newcomer on the global championship stage, but she had learnt from her disappointing performance at the World Junior Championships in 2014 when she was not able to peak at the right time and the psychological work of Pedroso had been critical in helping her to manage the pressures of a world class event.

In a sign of the inconsistent jumper that she still was – Pedroso noted that her technique was off due to a bouncy runway[732] – she fouled on five of her six attempts, but a second-round 14.41m proved enough for Gold and she was a World Indoor Champion, the first from Venezuela. She was still only twenty, yet her historic performance in Portland marked the moment where an athlete long considered the great hope of Venezuelan athletics had now arrived. Henceforth she would perform with the expectation of an entire nation on her shoulders, something this self-assured young woman would bear with ease, newly confident in her ability and ominously for her rivals, remarking afterwards, "my potential has no limits."[733]

Returning to Guadalajara to work with Pedroso on her technique before the outdoor season began, her coach saying in Portland that being very tall meant that work on improving her strength took longer than with other athletes,[734] Rojas would enjoy a breakout season, including competing in the high-profile Diamond League for the first time. In a meeting in Madrid on 23 June 2016, she covered 49ft $3\frac{3}{10}$in (15.02m), achieved despite a marginal headwind of 0.4m/s and it was her first time over 15m, then in the Monaco Diamond League meet on 15 July she jumped 14.64m. Pedroso

---

[732] https://worldathletics.org/news/feature/portland-2016-rojas-triple-jump
[733] https://worldathletics.org/news/feature/portland-2016-rojas-triple-jump
[734] https://worldathletics.org/news/feature/portland-2016-rojas-triple-jump

preached to her that she had to be patient with her progress and she was a willing student, recognising that this was just the start and not the goal, Portland being the first meeting in that indoor season that he had allowed her to jump off a longer eleven step run-up, rather than the nine steps used in previous competitions,[735] but those outdoor jumps that summer showed she was ready to rival Ibargüen in the Rio Olympics.

[736]Rypakova had finally defeated the Colombian in Birmingham in June 2016, to end her long unbeaten streak and was also the defending Olympic Champion, but it was Rojas who had joined Ibargüen as the only other woman to go over 15m that season and the Gold medal appeared destined for a South American country. The Venezuelan had to improve further to challenge the Colombian and in a generally disappointing qualifying round, she made the final with a best distance of only 14.21m, the automatic mark being 14.30m. She opened the final with a leap of 14.32m, but then fouled in the second, where Ibargüen went over 15m. The Colombian went to 15.17m in the fourth round and although the young challenger from Venezuela landed jumps of 14.98m in the fourth and 14.95m in the sixth to finish in second, with Rypakova third, it was Ibargüen who would ensure her near unbeaten four-year cycle was crowned with the Olympic Gold.

Rojas has regularly stated that Asnoldo Devonish,[737] the 1952 Olympic Bronze medallist in the men's triple jump from Venezuela, was her inspiration as an athlete – "a great motivation in my career"[738]

[735] Halford, *op. cit.*

[736] A youthful looking Rojas jumping in the 2016 Olympics in Rio de Janeiro, when she was the triple jump Silver medallist © unknown

[737] Asnoldo V. Devonish Romero [1932-97].

[738] https://worldathletics.org/news/feature/portland-2016-rojas-triple-jump

– and she joined him as the only Venezuelans with track and field Olympic medals in history, Rojas being the first woman from her country with an Olympic Silver in *any* event.[739] She was a history-maker once again and was over-joyed with her medal, recognising the progress she had made in the short time since her move to Europe to become a full-time athlete. She was also trumpeted by the President of Venezuela, Nicolás Maduro,[740] as a part of the nation's 'Golden Generation', those who came of age or were born after Maduro's predecessor Hugo Chávez[741] came to power in 1999, in a period of prosperity (primarily from oil revenues) under the early promise of the Bolivarian Revolution, but long since faded as the country plunged into a severe humanitarian emergency.

The Venezuelan government had recognised the extraordinary potential the youthful Rojas held and she had received support with travel to competitions for example, with her mother also being given a new home in 2014, when the shack Rojas had grown up in was washed away in poor weather. As the policies of *Chavismo*, the left-wing political ideology of Chávez and now Maduro, had taken the country into the worst economic crisis in their history, the situation led to mass emigration from the country, with anti-government protests since 2014 resulting in thousands being arrested and Maduro rules to this day with absolute power. Against this backdrop, Rojas regularly thanks the President for his support and her triumphs are heartily congratulated by Maduro, with her stance inviting criticism from those who oppose the government, both at home and abroad. But those critics must recognise the unique position of *soft power* she holds herself, a proud

---

[739] Bronze medals had been won by women in taekwondo in 2004 & 2008.
[740] Nicolás Maduro Moros, President of Venezuela since 2013 [1962-].
[741] Hugo Rafael Chávez Frías, President of Venezuela from 1999 until his death [1954-2013].

Venezuelan with a truly global platform, who receives the public backing of a government known for human rights abuses, yet is the first sportswoman in her country to identify with the LGBTQ[742] movement and is brave enough to be open about her own sexuality...

In Spanish, Rojas is commonly called *la reina del triple salto*, the queen of the triple jump, but she also occupies a prominent position as an activist for LGBTQ rights in Venezuela and is openly lesbian herself. Rojas has 1 million followers on Instagram[743] alone, proudly displaying a rainbow emoji in her profile and her global popularity transcends track and field, a natural entertainer approaching a level not seen since Usain Bolt. She is massively popular at home, drawing thousands to personal appearances when she returns to Venezuela, but this is a country "that is institutionally hostile to her community"[744] and "the attitude... has been of total denial"[745] in terms of not mentioning her skin colour, sexual orientation and even her gender when speaking of her achievements. Venezuela has a multitude of human rights issues and an athlete should never be expected to change the ills of a malignant political leadership, yet despite criticism from within the country about her open sexuality, a sign of progress is that same-sex activity in the Armed Forces was decriminalised in March 2023,[746] and a superstar like Rojas, supportive of the President whilst continuing to promote her own message, can be a powerful force for change.

Ibargüen's excellent leap in Rio had secured the Gold medal she so desired and she went on to claim the Diamond League overall

---

[742] An initialism covering those who are lesbian, gay, bisexual, transgender or queer/questioning.
[743] Photo and video sharing social networking website.
[744] 'When Will the IOC Finally Take a Stand and Protect Its Athletes?', Michael Rosenberg, *Sports Illustrated*, 2 August 2021
[745] Rosenberg, *op. cit.*
[746] https://www.batimes.com.ar/news/latin-america/venezuelas-supreme-court-decriminalises-homosexuality-in-armed-forces.phtml

triple jump title at the end of the 2016 season, her fourth title in the leading annual athletics series. The Colombian had been able to build on a near four-year dominance in the lead up to the Rio Olympics, but the young challenger from neighbouring Venezuela had pushed her in the Olympic final, despite never truly challenging for the Gold. The summer of 2017 offered the prospect of the World Championships in London, with the emerging rivalry between these two re-energising an event that had been dominated by one athlete for too long and Rojas started the season well, jumping what would be a world-leading 14.96m in Andújar, Spain on 2 June.

The 2017 World Championships final on 7 August has been described as "monumental"[747] by leading British track and field journalist Mike Rowbottom and it would see Ibargüen dethroned as the queen of the triple jump. In warm and relatively calm conditions, the lead switched between them in the opening two rounds, before Ibargüen landed a season best 14.89m in the third to take the lead once again. Rojas responded with a fifth-round 14.91m (+0.4m/s) and when Ibargüen could only reach 14.88m on her last effort, the title was going to the 2016 Olympic Silver medallist who had finally beaten the Colombian, almost ever-present in major competition since 2012 and Rojas was said to have "turned into a jumping jack"[748] such was her exuberance at the achievement.

---

[747] https://www.insidethegames.biz/articles/1053801/rojas-topples-ibarguen-to-earn-venezuelas-first-ever-world-gold
[748] https://www.insidethegames.biz/articles/1053801/rojas-topples-ibarguen-to-earn-venezuelas-first-ever-world-gold

[749]Her technique that evening was excellent, defined by her speed through the phases, horizontal velocity transitioning to sufficient vertical velocity to jump a last phase 5.86m nearly 50cm further than Ibargüen's own jump, despite a smaller hop than most women in that final and a short step that suggested where  improvement could still be made with her superior all-round strength obvious. Later that month in Birmingham at the Diamond League meeting on 20 August, the new World Champion finished in 7th, not even clearing 14m, yet this would be the last time since that date that she has failed to make the podium in *any* competition...

The opening of 2018 season would see Rojas defend her World Indoor Championships title in Birmingham, a fifth-round (and world-leading) 14.63m enough to take victory, in a final of much higher quality than it had been in 2016. She had just won her third consecutive global World title, but having notably overcome such adversity in her rise to the top, injury to both her ankles would rob her of the remainder of the 2018 season in what would prove to be an 11-month hiatus, before she was able to fully return in the indoor season at the start of 2019. She would later reveal that the injury lay-off had been difficult – an athlete unable to compete lacks that essential purpose – yet she said she had "learned to be patient... and [the injuries] helped me become stronger mentally."[750] Ibargüen had been unbeatable in her absence, but the 'Queen of the Triple Jump' was first able to prove to herself that he was back, a South American Indoor Record distance of 14.92m in Madrid on 8 February 2019 a sign that her long absence had left her ability undimmed and that summer, she was to prove to everyone else that she was increasingly untouchable as a triple jumper.

The 2019 season would be long, with the women's triple jump final in the World Championships in Doha scheduled for early October and Rojas would continue working on her technique with Pedroso, ensuring her body was strengthened to stay injury-free. She split victory in the early season Diamond League clashes with Ibargüen and Rojas demonstrated that she was also in good form, consistently jumping around the 15m mark with a new personal best of 15.06m in Huelva, Spain on 20 June. Ibargüen would not enter the triple jump at the Pan American Games in Lima that August, injured in the long jump, but with the competition the source of much regional pride in South America, the Venezuelan took Gold with a Championship Record distance of 49ft $6\frac{9}{10}$in (15.11m), breaking the mark of the Colombian in competing against herself, such was the gulf in class, the psychological work of Pedroso having established a mindset of, "my fiercest rival is myself."[751]

An even more notable milestone was to follow on her return to Spain and she was starting to add in-competition consistency to her armoury. In Andújar on 6 September 2019, she jumped 15.03m in the third round, then after two huge fouls followed on her sixth attempt with a massive distance of 15.41m, the best jump since 2008 when Mbango Etone had covered 15.39m in the Olympic final in Beijing and the first time Rojas had cleared 50ft. This was the women's number two jump of all time and nearly 50cm further than the second ranked jumper that season, Shanieka Ricketts[752] of Jamaica, the Silver medallist

---

[751] https://worldathletics.org/news/feature/yulimar-rojas-triple-jump-venezuela
[752] Shanieka Ricketts, World Championships Silver medallist in 2019 & 2022 and Commonwealth Games Champion in 2022 [1992-]

behind Rojas in the 2019 Pan American Games and talk was beginning about the potential for the World Record going in Doha that season.

Ibargüen had surgery for a plantar fasciitis injury in the summer, yet aged 35 she was now setting Masters records and having not gone over 15m since 2016, she was not expected to challenge Rojas. The Venezuelan had won seven of nine competitions in 2019 – having only lost to Ibargüen in early July and Ricketts in late August – and she was in strong form as the World Championships final came round on 5 October. Putting talk of the World Record behind her with regular protestations of it will come at *some point*, she opened the final strongly with a distance of 14.87m. Ricketts started well herself in covering 14.81m and would jump a consistent series, but Rojas took over in the second round, a distance of 15.37m an emphatic way of sealing her place in history as a double World Champion, after Savigne, Lebedeva and Ibargüen, the latter showing her mettle as a long-time champion in battling for a well-deserved Bronze medal behind the Jamaican. Rojas had also jumped 15.13m in the fourth round and she was now entering a level of consistency in a season not seen since Lebedeva. Ibargüen only registered three career jumps over 15m despite all her accolades and Rojas had managed *six* in the 2019 season alone!

As early as October 2019, Rojas was saying to the Venezuelan press that she would be the first woman to jump 16m,[753] talk born of confidence and an awareness that Pedroso had yet to exploit her full potential, rather than any hint of arrogance or over-confidence. The injury issues in 2018 had caused her to double down on her commitment to training and with Pedroso she had been working four hours a day in 2019, particularly strengthening her legs and abdomen,

---

[753] https://www.liderendeportes.com/noticias/mas-deportes/sere-la-primera-mujer-en-saltar-16-metros/

in that same interview quoting her coach as saying, "success is drunk in the cup of effort." She was maturing as an athlete, despite being only twenty-four-years-old as 2019 closed, with the Tokyo Olympics in the summer of 2020 offering her the chance to become a two-time Olympic Champion. She was "red-hot"[754] and the future was very bright.

Rojas has been quoted on her admiration for Tatyana Lebedeva and she was certainly one of the greatest horizontal jumpers in women's track and field history. The Russian never failed a drugs test whilst competing, but with her samples from the 2008 Olympics re-tested after her retirement and retrospective sanctions applied, she *is* a convicted doper, bringing her career achievements as a whole into question. Rojas has mentioned that she "is a jumper...[I] respect a lot... [having] tried to imitate her technique to improve mine"[755] and whilst some leading athletes are more vocal in their anti-doping stances than others, there is still much to admire in the way that the turbo-charged Russian jumped. At the point she retired, she was in the conversation as the greatest women's triple jumper in history, with Kravets already discredited by her doping ban and characterised by her inconsistency, despite the enduring World Record. Rojas is free to admire the athletes she chooses – it is for World Athletics to invalidate previous marks if necessary – and as the current torchbearer of her sport, she went about moving the conversation along from Lebedeva in the only way she could, by removing her from the record books...

21 February 2020 is a minor footnote in the history of the women's triple jump, yet it marks the start of Rojas' time as a World

---

[754] 'Yulimar Rojas red-hot in the triple jump', Jason Henderson, *Athletics Weekly*, 5 October 2019

[755] https://www.liderendeportes.com/noticias/mas-deportes/sere-la-primera-mujer-en-saltar-16-metros/

Record holder. The women's World Indoor Record had stood since March 2004 and Lebedeva's mark had been close to untouchable. Rojas had started the 2020 indoor season in good form and on 9 February in Metz, France she has jumped an indoor personal best of 15.03m. Twelve days later, she went to the World Athletics Indoor Tour final at the *Polideportivo Gallur* arena in Madrid, the city only an hour from her training base in Guadalajara and the site of a number of important milestones in her career, including that first jump (outdoors) over 15m in 2016. She went to Madrid this time with the expectant words of her coach in her ears, "don't miss this chance"[756] and she would not.

[757]Rojas followed a big first-round foul with a second jump that would have been good enough for victory, even if she was not in the mood that she was that day. Pedroso  had put much effort into improving her mental strength, particularly her approach in-competition and she was clearly focussed on a specific target in Madrid, beyond the title. She fouled again in the third, then soared to an indoor personal best 15.29m in the fourth, the second-best indoor distance of all time and a distance she afterwards said came easily. Having two more attempts to make history, she fouled again in the fifth, then following a long conversation with herself and a round of vigorous finger pointing, she took off to a half-hearted rhythmic clap from the crowd unaware of what was about to happen and bounded into history.

---

[756] https://worldathletics.org/competitions/olympic-games/news/yulimar-rojas-venezuela-triple-jump-world-ind
[757] A picture of determination, Yulimar Rojas lands a new World Indoor Record in Madrid © unknown

She rose from the pit full of adrenaline at what she knew to be a record jump and paced the track with her hands on the back of her head until the distance was confirmed – a new World Indoor Record of 50ft $7\frac{1}{2}$in (15.43m), 7cm further than the former mark and the hug from her coach was that of a man whose determination that it was going to be a big day for her had been proven correct. This was another major step forwards for an athlete who was now a leading figure in track and field, let alone the triple jump and in a sign of her emotion at the achievement, she commented afterwards, "I want to get home and cry."[758] This jump was 2cm beyond her personal best from September 2019 and was the second best of all time, either indoor or outdoor. Then within a month, the COVID-19 pandemic would see her march towards greatness halted and the Tokyo Olympics would eventually be re-scheduled to the summer of 2021, primarily in the interests of the athletes that were due to take part.

The 2020 season was essentially written off that March, with only a few meetings at the back end of the summer and many were unsure how 2021 would unfold, the highlight being the delayed Tokyo Olympics, but it would not be a 'normal' Games, with no public spectators for the first time in history. Despite this, Rojas returned in even better form from the enforced hiatus, jumping 15.14m in Ibiza on 8 May and in every meet she entered ahead of the Olympics, she went over 15m, going to Tokyo as the hottest favourite for a Gold medal throughout track and field. She was an athlete on a mission and for a number of years had deflected talk of the expected World Record by saying it was part of the process and would come, but this was a

---

[758] https://www.insidethegames.biz/articles/1090896/world-triple-jump-record-for-rojas

self-declared *new* Yulimar and a sign of her confidence was the statement she made on the eve of the Games – "I'm on fire."[759]

The preparation for the Tokyo Olympics had been long, an extra year added to the normal four-year cycle by the re-scheduling, yet Rojas had used it as an opportunity, focussing on improving her nutrition in particular. She had enhanced all facets of her triple jumping, developing her long jumping so much that she had hoped to enter both horizonal jumps in Tokyo, but the same day scheduling had put a hold on that ambition. A windy personal best of 7.27m (+2.7m/s) in the Spanish Club Championships on 13 June 2021 was a sign of her progress in the long jump, suggested to her by *Futbol Club Barcelona* and henceforth to be an event she would hold close to her heart, appreciative of the complementary benefits it had on her triple jumping and publicly aiming to medal at a major championship.

The women's triple jump final at the Tokyo Olympics took place on the evening of 1 August 2021 at the Japan National Stadium, a newly built stadium with a very fast and springy track, both factors that had to be managed by the athletes, but offering a positive 'return' to those that could adapt themselves to the conditions, so it did not affect their take off and their contacts with a surface that could *rebound* upwards. In front of a sparse crowd of teammates and officials, but still with a reasonable atmosphere, Rojas jumped second in the final and despite an ungainly take off, having had to cut her final stride short to ensure she did not foul, she bounded out to a new Olympic Record of 15.41m (+1.1m/s), breaking Mbango Etone's mark from 2008 by 2cm. The competition had effectively been settled on her first attempt and the athlete who recalled afterwards that she had woken up that day

[759] https://as.com/juegos_olimpicos/2021/07/31/noticias/1627712545_069637.html

knowing "it was going to be a great day,"[760] was exactly where she and her coach wanted her to be.

[761]Their strategy had been to win the Gold on her first jump and that had been achieved in some style. Thereafter she pushed hard for the World Record, a third-round jump that she believed was a new record only to be flagged as a foul, before a huge fifth-round effort that looked to be well over 16m, before again being red flagged. In post-competition interviews she memorably stated she knew she had the distance in her legs that day, [762] but her technique was letting her down as she chased the dream and she became increasingly angry with herself. It came down to a final attempt – a jump against herself with the competition long decided – and with one final attempt to rouse the crowd with a clap, some pointed words of self-encouragement and audible support from training partner, Ana Peleteiro[763] of Spain, she took off down the runway in Tokyo and bounded into the record books, the woman to finally go beyond Inessa Kravets...

Rojas gave everything in that last attempt and was rewarded with a jump for the ages as she finally surpassed the 1995 mark. It only takes one effort for it all to come together in the jumping events in particular and when she landed, she knew that it was a *good* jump. She bounded from the sandpit and when it was announced, the usually joyous and exuberant Venezuelan was visibly emotional. She had

---

[760] https://www.insidethegames.biz/articles/1111094/yulimar-rojas-triple-jump-world-record
[761] Rojas jumping in the Tokyo Olympics final © unknown
[762] Ingle, *op. cit.*
[763] Ana Peleteiro Brión, Spanish National Record holder, Olympic Bronze in 2020, World Indoor Bronze in 2018 and European Indoor Champion in 2019; World Junior Champion in 2012, aged only seventeen [1995-].

covered 51ft $4\frac{3}{4}$in[764] (15.67m), with only a slight tailwind of 0.7m/s, a smooth display of triple jumping, her long legs barely off the ground in the step with her free arms and leg guiding her body ever forwards, before her high hips saw her stretch into the pit. Her jump phase in particular was incredible, measured at 5.99m and this World Record was achieved in spite of a modest step that was the smallest of the eight finalists in Tokyo.

She had been chasing the record all summer and the 15.43m in Andújar (yet again) in May, had confirmed she was in the right form as the Olympics approached. The greatest sportsmen and women have long been considered able to write their own scripts and a last-round World Record, in an Olympic final and with no serious rival, was almost too good to be true, a perfectly choreographed moment that went down as one of the 'wow' points of the Tokyo Games, the former, longstanding best smashed by 17cm. Her approach speed on the record jump was 10% faster than the next fastest athlete in that final and the top speed that day in her final strides was elite sprinting.

Despite the dominance of Rojas, the Tokyo Olympics final was high on quality, Silver going to Patrícia Mamona[765] of Portugal and Bronze to Peleteiro, both with National Records and the Portuguese also went over 15m, the first woman other than the Venezuelan to do so since Ibargüen in June 2016. Rojas would go on to end 2021 with the eight leading seasonal marks in the women's triple jump and she was also re-writing the all-time list, a jump of 15.52m in Lausanne on 26 August the second furthest in history (she also jumped 15.56m with an illegal wind of +3.5m/s). She was the first female Olympic Gold

---

[764] Ratified as such, but correctly 51ft $4\frac{9}{10}$in.

[765] Patrícia M. B. Mamona, Olympics Silver in 2020, European Champion in 2016 and European Indoor Champion in 2021; Portuguese National Record holder and two-time NCAA Champion at Clemson University in 2010 & 2011 [1988-].

medallist from Venezuela, the first of either sex to win an athletics Gold and her popularity at home would increase yet further after her exploits in Japan. Basketball and baseball are the leading sports in Venezuela, but Rojas had a nation on tenterhooks as she chased that World Record in the Olympic final and having arrived in Tokyo as the best in the world, she left as the best in history.

Kravets had identified Rojas as far back as 2017 as the woman who could finally threaten her World Record, remaining surprised that it had lasted so long when the women's event was progressing at such a pace in the 1990's. In that 2017 interview with a Venezuelan newspaper,[766] Kravets said that Rojas needed to improve the speed of her transition from horizontal to vertical movement in order to challenge the record and the Ukrainian suggested she watched video of Jonathan Edwards, essentially needing to be able to "run the board, not take off from there."[767] Rojas was the new World Champion at the time and had not even been born when Kravets set her long-time World Record in August 1995, but in another interview in 2019 on the eve of the Doha World Championships, she spoke of her admiration of the Ukrainian – "she was such a great athlete"[768] – and the longer that record had lasted, the greater the respect the distance demanded from those still attempting to beat it, despite the shadow of her late-career sanction for steroid use.

The 2022 season would see Rojas answer the question about what would come next after her own World Record performance. She

[766] https://versionfinal.com.ve/deportes/inessa-kravets-yulimar-puede-batir-mi-record/
[767] https://versionfinal.com.ve/deportes/inessa-kravets-yulimar-puede-batir-mi-record/
[768]
https://webcache.googleusercontent.com/search?q=cache:U0BK_TAoF10J:https://iaafworldathleticschamps.com/doha2019/kravets-believes-its-time-for-her-triple-jump-world-record-to-fall/&cd=15&hl=en&ct=clnk&gl=uk&client=safari

had been expected to break Kravets' record for a number of years and now she was the history-maker she had appeared predestined to become when she announced herself in Portland in March 2016. But she was not satiated by the achievement and Pedroso would never allow her to be so, constantly preaching the need for humility. Her focus at the end of 2021 explicitly switched to reaching 16m (as well as focussing on training for the long jump to a greater degree) and that began to move closer to becoming a possibility in Belgrade, Serbia on 20 March 2022, at the World Athletics Indoor Championships, when she took her event another major bound forwards.

[769]In the *Štark Arena* that morning, Rojas would again put on a masterclass in triple jumping, going over 15m four times and saving her best for her last attempt  as she had in Tokyo. In a display of individual brilliance far superior to the level of her competitors, Rojas would essentially secure the Gold with a first-round 15.19m, a safe jump by her own standards, before then chasing after another record. She had been expected to challenge her World Indoor Record after the fireworks in Tokyo the previous summer, but what came on her final attempt in Belgrade was not expected or anticipated by anyone but Rojas and Pedroso, certainly not by the near 15,000 spectators in attendance who were momentarily silenced by what followed.

---

[769] Yulimar Rojas lands her final triple jump attempt to overtake her own absolute world record © Erik van Leeuwen

In a quite astonishing moment, Rojas bounded out to 51ft 7$\frac{1}{2}$in[770] (15.74m) and shattered her own *absolute*[771] World Record, easily surpassing her former World Indoor Record set in 2020 and significantly beyond the mark of 14.63m she posted in Birmingham in 2018, when winning her second World Indoor Championships. She knew as soon as she landed that it was a new World Record and the Belgrade crowd were quickly on their feet to give her a standing ovation, her sixth jump 1m ahead of the rest in the field that day! Kravets' former mark had lasted for nearly 26 years, but Rojas' 2021 world best had been improved again in just over seven months and the women's triple jump was major athletics news once again, the shadow cast by the Ukrainian long gone and the Venezuelan had gone further than any woman triple jumper in history under any conditions, legal or otherwise.

The remainder of the 2022 season would see Rojas continue her dominance and she capped it off with a third consecutive victory in the World Championships in Oregon, the first woman to do so in the triple jump and her sixth global World title. She had started the outdoor season slower than in 2021, yet to go over 15m (outside) and Ricketts of Jamaica seemingly put her under pressure with a world-leading 14.89m in the first round, before the Venezuelan settled another major global competition with an early massive leap, a second-round 15.47m enough for Gold by over 50cm and followed by two further attempts beyond 15m for good measure. The Jamaican would claim Silver and Tori Franklin[772] of the United States took Bronze, the

---

[770] Ratified as such, but more correctly 51ft 7$\frac{7}{10}$in.
[771] Indoor records have been accepted as absolute records since 2000, but the women's triple jump is one of very few to have been affected thus far.
[772] Tori Franklin, National Record holder since 2018 and Bronze in the 2022 World Championships [1992-].

first American woman to medal in the discipline at the World Championships.

At the time of writing, Rojas is aiming for a seventh consecutive World crown in the 2023 World Championships in Budapest, Hungary in August. She is the overwhelming favourite for Gold once more and despite her dalliance with the long jump – her qualifying mark for Oregon would have been good enough for Silver in the 2019 World Championships, but was invalidated as she used the wrong shoes – she remains committed to the triple jump and at twenty-seven-years-old, her best years should be ahead of her, barring injury or a catastrophic loss of form. Her dominance of the event has grown considerably since the 2021-22 seasons and shows no sign of abating, that World Record in Belgrade as close as she has come to technical perfection to date. It was defined by a much longer step (less flat than in Tokyo) and a massive kick action from her free leg visibly propelled her final jump into the sandpit, but almost certainly more is to come as she develops her technique, even with her style now more balanced and less obviously jump-dominated.

The Yulimar Rojas story is not even close to being complete, nor that of the women's triple jump, but our narrative must close with her as the current World Record holder. The widely popular athlete with the huge social media following and 🏃 in her profile, is already the publicly considered 🐐 of the women's discipline and is expected to add further accolades in the coming seasons. She owns seven of the ten best jumps in the all-time list and is an iconoclastic figure in her sport, already a historical great in the triple jump and with a growing handful of performances that will magnify over time, already on the pathway to an enduring sporting *greatness*. It has long been considered impossible for a woman to triple jump 16m, yet she is confident that she will reach that target – "I was born to jump 16m"[773] – and everything about her speaks of smashing boundaries, whether that be in terms of the LGBTQ rights movement she vocally supports in Venezuela or the advancement of her chosen sport, her talent commanding attention for the discipline she now stands astride, the leading woman triple jumper by some distance.

Observers had long considered her step to be modest, her first-round Olympic Record in Tokyo having a noticeably bigger second phase than her eventual World Record that evening and the great Willie Banks, who admits he never worked on his step, wants Rojas to get the middle phase right and in his inimitable style, "to blast past 16m."[774] But perhaps Rojas has been successful through breaking the mould, women jumpers not normally of her height, or with her strength and speed. She is who she is – she makes no apologies and with her bright and frequently changing hair colour, she is not shy – and is a certainly a trailblazer in her sport and beyond. After the lengthening shadow of a World Record from a convicted doper hung over the event for a generation, it needed to be dragged into the 21st century, both statistically and metaphorically. The triple jump needed a hero and got a *SUPER*hero, Yulimar Rojas, the 'Wonder Woman'[775] of track and field who is not finished re-writing what was long thought impossible.

01.08.2021 WR 15.67m (51ft 4$\frac{3}{4}$in) Yulimar Rojas (VEN) Tokyo, Japan (+0.7m/s)

20.03.2022 WR 15.74m (51ft 7$\frac{1}{2}$in) Yulimar Rojas (VEN) Belgrade, Serbia (indoor)

---

[773] https://worldathletics.org/competitions/world-athletics-indoor-championships/world-athletics-indoor-championships-7138985/news/feature/rojas-adds-to-legend-world-record-belgrade

[774] https://theolympians.co/2021/08/02/yulimar-rojas-sets-the-world-record-for-womens-triple-jump-willie-banks-knows-she-can-do-better/

[775] Rojas has referred to feeling like Wonder Woman and proclaimed herself a warrior, an important part of the character of the fictional superhero – https://olympics.com/en/video/yulimar-rojas-wonder-woman-superhero.

Part 5 – Landing

We said that the jump was the final phase, but the **Landing** can impact the maximum jump length in a much more obvious way, athletes being measured from the board to the closest point their body (or clothing) touches the sand; Mike Conley famously missed out on a place at the 1988 Olympics due to his baggy shorts brushing the sand! In flight from the step, the athlete keeps their chin up, eyes looking to the other side of the sandpit and the legs are held forward, having been swung into position by the arms, until the heels (ideally!) hit the sand, when the knees will bend, the hips rise and the athlete lands in the sand.

The athlete wants to land with their feet as far forward of their centre of mass as they can, with timing crucial so that their buttocks and body slide past the hole made by their feet, a long jump phase fundamental that is now common amongst triple jumpers. It was only in the 1968 Olympics that athletes such as Guiseppe Gentile, then a World Record holder for the briefest of periods, would still regularly land on their feet and this is one area of obvious improvement when watching the leading jumpers of today, no one now landing upright unless their technique fails. Jonathan Edwards' 1995 World Record included a 7.02m jump phase and the clean landings of Yulimar Rojas in her 2021 and 2022 World Records show how important the final contact with the sand can be to the overall jump length, her own distances suggesting that World Athletics may yet have to consider increasing the prescribed distance of the take-off board from the sandpit for the women, such is the ground she is covering in her hop and step phases...

THE HARVEY-BENNS METHOD

One of the things that many people love about athletics is that it is a broadly binary sport through the annals of time – especially when it is simply shown as listed results or rankings. You cannot bluff a successful career in athletics as you sometimes can in team sports; many have won medals when playing in successful teams that included great athletes and their own career is skewed by the confirmation bias that on-field success breeds. Team sport medals indicate collective success and it can be very satisfying to achieve a championship as part of a squad or team, but those medals do not necessarily make a sportsman or woman great in their own right. In athletics this just is not possible; the stopwatch tells you how fast you are, the tape measure tells you how far you have jumped! How *good* or even *great* you are as an athlete, is completely objective in this way.

Many athletes live for the comparison that such crude results produce – it allows athletes and coaches to plot progress, compare, contrast and set goals. You would think therefore that the system of times and measurements in athletics would do away with the need for debate, World Records even showing who was the best ever in their sport in terms of those metrics, *the athlete* being *the whole*, as many coaches would attest, even if their own contribution can be significant! However, life is not a binary system and neither is athletics. We think that athletics is a greater meritocracy than many sports due to the objective nature of results and rankings, but history and scientific advancements play a big factor when comparing athletes through the ages, as does competitive performance in major events, the improvement over time in runway and equipment specifications, and, in the case of the triple jump, even rule changes!

358

Many *great* athletes in the triple jump in particular have not broken the World Record and Christian Taylor is a prime example. He is undoubtedly one of the greatest triple jumpers in history, has multiple global titles and sits 2nd on the all-time list for distance, but he has never broken the World Record. This does not diminish his achievements, but in seeking to move a scoring method away from subjectivity into a more meritocratic system, we have to consider how World Records can be adjudged across the years and how and where to place Taylor against a record-breaker from the 1930's. Józef Szmidt broke the men's World Record in 1960 then held it for over eight years and his achievement reflected the sport at that time. If he had been born 50 years earlier it would have been unlikely that he would have surpassed 17m as he did in 1960, yet if he was born in the late 1990's and competed with the benefit of scientific advances in surfaces and shoes made in the interim, what distance could he then jump?

Szmidt *achieved* what he did – the record books confirm it – and it is important for us to fairly appraise all triple jumpers through the history of time, thereby ranking athletes based on what they achieved in 'their moment of history', not merely the binary assessment of 'who jumped furthest'. From the first official men's triple jump World Record in 1911, it has advanced 2.77m with an average improvement rate per year of only 0.2%, having stalled noticeably since 1995 and few athletes have come close to threatening it since, but there has never been a greater depth of active 18m jumpers (currently four). The women's World Record has improved by 1.20m since the first mark was ratified in 1990 and with World Records in 2021 and 2022 it is in a very good moment, but we recognise the importance of subjective context-setting when appraising the history of the event and that was the challenge we set ourselves.

As part of our journey in writing this book, we began to develop a new scoring system to determine how we can rank the legendary triple jumpers throughout the history of the sport. That system has been debated at length and we are now ready to share the results with you the reader, a new system that we believe can be applied to any event in track and field and which will stand up to rigorous testing, without the subjectivity common with many opinion-led all-time lists. We have started with the triple jump being on this journey already, but it has been tested with other events. The triple jump World Record for both sexes is *the* counterpoint where athletic performance and sporting greatness combine, a harmonious interdependence of two, at times, independent strands of the triple jump story and it is this difference that underpins our method... **The Harvey-Benns Method** ® of unique athletics appraisal!

THE HARVEY-BENNS METHOD

Purpose: *"to fairly and objectively appraise individual track & field disciplines / events through the lens of greatest historical impact and achievement; thus determining a simple, meritocratic ranking order of all-time global greatness"*

World Record
(blended score: number of records, growth & longevity)

Olympic & World Championship Medals

Elite Competitive Longevity

We feel The Harvey-Benns Method (HBM) is the first of its kind – a fully objective track and field scoring system that balances the passing of time with numeric factors accounting for the subjective elements. We were inspired by other scoring systems, but disliked their often overly subjective weighting (sometimes with no scoring method at all!), and whilst there is a place for the subjective, the problem is that 'rose-tinted glasses' often kick-in from the experiences during a person's own lifetime; worse still, recency bias in modern sports culture tends to disregard the great legacy feats of the distant (or even not so distant past), even though in their day, the achievements may have been every bit as good (if not better) relatively to anything that came after! Plus, past achievements paved the way for what then came, in the case of athletics, professionalism, global competition, science in sport and so on – we therefore favoured the type of approach that Duckworth, Lewis & Stern applied to cricket instead, effectively applying scores to objective facts, fully appraised in the context of their moment in history.[776]

The stated purpose of The Harvey-Benns Method is: *"to fairly and objectively appraise individual track & field disciplines / events through the lens of greatest historical impact and achievement; thus determining a meritocratic ranking order of all-time global greatness"*. Given this bold ambition, we want to reassure you that in this age of (social) media shock and awe, we have not set out to make the results sensationalist. Nor have we tried to manufacture its output to suit our narrative – the results are what they are. We have worked

---

[776] The Duckworth-Lewis-Stern method (DLS) is a mathematical formulation designed to calculate the target score (number of runs needed to win) for the team batting second in a limited overs cricket match interrupted by weather or other circumstances. The method was first devised by two English statisticians, Frank Duckworth and Tony Lewis, and was formerly known as the Duckworth-Lewis method (D/L).

tirelessly to make our method as objective as we could, with strong justification for each measurement aggregating the total score for each athlete and their final HBM Ranking throughout the history of triple jump (since the start of the modern Olympic Games era).

This final point is key – right from the outset of writing this book and creating HBM, we felt a strong duty to athletes, past and present, to fairly and accurately tell their stories and celebrate their contributions in athletics, in comparison to the more familiar stars still competing or more recently remembered. We hope that HBM will ensure that the landmark performances (not just World Records) of all track and field athletes, from across all disciplines, shall not be forgotten when the *greatest* are being debated.

The detailed points allocations and algorithms that fuel HBM are our secret sauce – much like the well-known secret 'Original Recipe' for fried chicken! This is for no other reason than to protect the formula we have spent some many hours perfecting over the past couple of years. In essence, our method has several objective achievement input feeds, with the heaviest weighting being on the achievement of a World Record, which has been the thread throughout the narrative told in this book. This potentially controversial emphasis was much debated, but is essentially a rooted logic in our method's overall purpose; there is no greater impact than progressing the event's best ever performance than via a World Record. This may appear clinical, but is a key 'Darwinistic'[777] evolutionary concept in all sport, as it is in life.

Notwithstanding the heavy World Record weighting, performance in global competitions is also strongly rewarded in

---

[777] Relating to Darwinism, the theory of evolution by natural, or biological, selection. Named after Charles R. Darwin, the famed Englishman commonly considered one of the most influential figures in human history [1809-82].

recognition of the ability to time peak performance and mental preparation with the physical edge necessary to achieve success when it matters most, against those who are equally focussed on achieving the same goal. For this, the sport's ultimate performance pinnacle is the Olympic Games – it therefore has the highest weighted factor for the achievement of a medal (sliding scale for Gold vs. Silver vs. Bronze), followed by a lower rating for medals in the IAAF/World Athletics World Championships,[778] whilst still recognising its global competition and achievement status.

We have consciously ruled out any Area Championships (e.g. Commonwealth Games, European Championships, Pan American Games etc.). This is not to take away from the achievement of athletes medalling in these championships, but a stern reality point is that these types of events are not open to the 'world' and are sometimes skipped by leading athletes; our ambition is to achieve a measurement of "all-time *global* greatness" and we will not deviate from that aim.

More difficult was coming to a decision to not include major indoor competitions – the *issue* with indoor athletics is complex. You have a sterile environment (no wind and largely unaffected by extreme temperatures) in which a great many athletic disciplines are not represented and because the timetable is typically out-of-season, the calibre of athletics is typically less good; since its inception, the average World Indoor Championships winning distance in the triple jump is around 33cm less than the outdoor World Championships. In addition, the very fact that since 2000 any World Record achieved indoors is ratified as the overall, or absolute, World Record, simply

---

[778] The inaugural IAAF World Championships was in 1983 and occur every two years; twice the frequency of the Olympics, so whilst prestigious, they are not in the same league as the Olympic Games (the inaugural IAAF World Indoor Championships was effectively in 1985 and as per the IAAF World Championships, occur every two years with much less emphasis than outdoor/summer athletic competition).

undermines the credibility of separate 'World Record' status for indoor marks going forward – these marks are probably still better described as 'World Best Indoor Marks'.

Longevity is also heavily rewarded in recognition that generational impact over many years is extremely rare. Originally we recognised this by noting the years between an athlete's first global medal and their last – however, those competing pre-1983 (the introduction of the IAAF World Championships) were at a distinct disadvantage that would have been much more difficult to balance through upweighted scoring – to demonstrate the point, an athlete competing prior to 1983 only had the Olympics as a major global competition every four years, whereas since 1983 athletes have had both the World Championships and the Olympics.

In the intervening years, nearly 50% of athletes winning an Olympic medal also won a World Championship medal (upweighting an actual medal achieved is one thing, but trying to forecast and allocate points for the specific time in between when an athlete *may* have won another medal, would have been guess work, which we did not favour). Consistency of excellence and peak human performance is therefore a key component – in our method this is recognised through 'performance consistency' in the world rankings (based on legally recorded distances). This is especially important for those athletes who *only* ever jumped far, but not quite to a World Record, possibly did not compete or excel in major global competitions (e.g., due to injury or country boycotts etc.), but undeniably left a mark on the event through great historical jumping distance(s).

Lastly, whilst outwardly mathematical, our method is rooted in simplicity by design and avoids the subjectiveness of the *Track & Field News* rankings which have been around since 1947 and are commonly replied upon – they ranked Kravets second in the world in

1995, on a relative merit system that included head-to-head records, despite the Ukrainian having broken the World Record![779] It was extremely important to us that it could be easily explained and understood by *anyone* – if and when we ever do reveal our secret formula in full! Rooted in our ambition was that HBM needed to give fair recognition through a scoring system that could be used universally across all individual athletic disciplines, which it can, even to the point of being able to create a best-of-the-best in athletics history across all events!

---

[779] https://trackandfieldnews.com/wp-content/uploads/2023/04/17-wTJRank.pdf

HARVEY-BENNS METHOD RANKINGS

The men's triple jump was a fascinating choice as the inaugural event to be considered for HBM – the top five have all got there through such different means; it demonstrated the versatility of *greatness* in track and field, testing the logic of *best performance ever*, versus most competitively successful in the global competitions (in the era the athlete competed in, against peers in major competition). Plus, longevity truly matters. This is quite rare in sport and therefore more precious in a scoring system, with track and field principally a young person's *game*; human bodies that are battle-worn and tired tend not to perform quite so well once we enter our late 30's, particularly so in the triple jump with the stresses the event demands on ankles and legs. HBM had to work out a way to reward athletes who have competed at the elite level the longest and we believe it has…

In 5th place is **Christian Taylor**. Of our top five, only he is still a competitive athlete, so his score may well increase, notwithstanding his recent major injury which he continues to battle back from and which denied him the chance of a third Olympic Gold. His achievements were a fascinating test for our model – he is the second furthest triple jumper in history, but never a holder of the World Record (short by 8cm). However, his major championships titles and competitive longevity is remarkable, dating back to 2011 (two Olympic Games Gold / four World Championships Gold) and no triple jumper has ever (yet) won that many World Championships.

By contrast, **Józef Szmidt** was the first man to jump over 17m – in doing so he became a World Record breaker and later winner of two Olympic Games Gold medals. These ground-breaking feats rightly catapult Szmidt to the top places of our HBM leaderboard, where he is ranked as the 4th greatest men's triple jumper. The gap between the top three could not have been closer – a prolific World Record breaker versus the most decorated Olympic Games triple jumper in history versus the furthest triple jumper to ever live!

In 3rd place, is a man who broke the triple jump World Record more times than anyone else in history, notwithstanding the event then being a rapidly maturing sport and not yet saturated by elite athletes. At the time he was active in the 1950's, improvements of the World Record were becoming more frequent, this rapid growth of the event following mass adoption of sport around the globe after the Second World War. **Adhemar da Silva** was also every bit the major championships competitor too, as proven by his Gold medals in the Olympics in both 1952 and 1956, and he single-handedly made the event popular in his home country, with other Brazilian triple jump greats following in his wake.

In 2nd place, narrowly pipped to the top spot, is **Viktor Saneyev**. Amongst athletics aficionados, Saneyev has for a long time been regarded as the triple jump standard bearer for his longevity, his multiple World Records, and most uniquely, his four Olympic medals over 12 years (three of which were Gold in consecutive Games)! In conversation with Willie Banks, he remarked that Saneyev was his GOAT, saying "he set the path for us all"[780] – very high praise indeed. It should also be noted, had we written our book just a year earlier, Saneyev would have been ranked 1st through HBM – an extra year of holding the World Record has accrued the crucial ranking points for whom many consider the greatest triple jumper to ever live...

---

[780] Zoom interview with Willie Banks by author Lawrence Harvey, 8 March 2023.

Unsurprisingly, that man is **Jonathan Edwards**. He is an iconic athlete in track and field – his status is assured even if his World Record is broken in the next couple of years – and he is quite simply the greatest men's triple jumper of all time. He literally won everything he could win on the major stage – Olympic Champion, World Champion, Commonwealth Champion and European Champion – and briefly held all four titles at the same time! He was the first man to legally jump over 18m, the first to surpass 60ft and his longstanding World Record of 18.29m is the longest period any triple jump World Record has ever stood. HBM has confirmed that Edwards is the greatest men's triple jumper in history and few could disagree.

It is worth re-stating that Edwards broke the World Record three times, including twice on the same day in the 1995 World Championships. In addition, he went further than any man in history with his 18.43m earlier that year in Lille, often forgotten due to the marginally illegal wind recording, yet this was a remarkably balanced display of triple jumping and his most technically proficient jump. Like all the top 5, Edwards has a dedicated chapter in our book – his boyish *everyman* appearance, coupled with his once strong faith and mythical tales of strength in the weights room, seem only to have added to the intrigue of an athlete who redefined speed on the triple jump runway. It is perhaps fitting that the man who put triple jumping back on the map during the 1990's and early 2000's should take our top spot – we created HBM to fairly appraise triple jumpers throughout the history of time and in our minds, Edwards' status as the greatest triple jumper to have ever lived is beyond doubt!

The Harvey-Benns Method - Men's Triple Jump All-Time Top 20

ALL-TIME RANKING	ATHLETE	TRIPLE JUMP PB (METRES)	NUMBER OF WORLD RECORDS	WORLD RECORD HOLDER YEARS	OLYMPIC & WORLD MEDALS (EX. INDOORS)	YEARS RANKED WORLD #1	YEARS RANKED IN THE WORLD TOP 10
1	Jonathan Edwards (GBR)	18.29	3	27	7	5	13
2	Viktor Saneyev (URS)	17.44	3	3	4	5	14
3	Adhemar da Silva (BRA)	16.56	5	6	2	6	11
4	Jozef Szmidt (POL)	17.03	1	8	2	6	12
5	Christian Taylor (USA)	18.21	0	0	6	6	10
6	Dan Ahearn (USA)	15.73	1	20	0	6	10
7	João Carlos de Oliveira (BRA)	17.89	1	10	2	4	7
8	Vilho Tuulos (FIN)	15.48	0	0	3	4	14
9	Naoto Tajima (JPN)	16.00	1	15	1	1	3
10	Pedro Pichardo (POR)	18.08	0	0	4	4	9
11	Mikio Oda (JPN)	15.58	1	1	0	4	9
12	Mike Conley (USA)	17.87	0	0	5	3	12
13	Nick Winter (AUS)	15.52	1	7	1	2	10
14	Chuhei Nambu (JPN)	15.72	1	3	1	1	4
15	Christian Olsson (SWE)	17.83i	0	0	3	2	8
16	Willie Banks (USA)	17.97	1	10	0	2	10
17	Khristo Markov (BUL)	17.92	0	0	2	3	6
18	Kenny Harrison (USA)	18.09	0	0	2	3	6
19	Myer Prinstein (USA)	14.47	0	0	2	0	2
20	Leonid Shcherbakov (URS)	16.46	1	2	1	1	10

---

781 Correct as at end of 2022. World rankings based on the data shared at the 'Track and Field Statistics' website available at http://trackfield.brinkster.net/Main.asp?P=F and number one ranking is based on longest legal distance in any given season, avoiding the subjectiveness of the *Track & Field News* rankings in particular.

The women's triple jump would prove to be much more contentious when we were finalising the scoring method for HBM. It is widely considered that Yulimar Rojas, *la reina del triple salto*, is the greatest the women's discipline has ever seen and we have no doubt that she is the true 'Queen of the Triple Jump'. Barring injury or a catastrophic loss of form, either of which would cheat the track and field world of an era-defining athlete in her peak years, Rojas will add further global titles in the coming seasons. Yet her career is still *in progress* and a fair and objective appraisal of her status against the other greats in her sport can only be based on achievements to date. We are comfortable that HBM provides a fully objective track and field scoring system and in doing so we did not seek to make the results suit our own narrative, told in full in this book...

In 5th place is **Françoise Mbango Etone**. She never came close to breaking the World Record, yet in Beijing 2008 became the first women's Olympic Champion in the event to defend her title and in 2004 had been the first athlete from Cameroon to win an Olympic Gold. Her Olympic Record in 2008 was remarkable, coming after a near three-year hiatus in her career and it would stand until the re-arranged Tokyo Games in August 2021. She would only be ranked world number one twice and ranked in the top ten six times, yet her global medal record and major championship pedigree have propelled this talented jumper from West Africa into a deserved top-five all-time ranking.

Coming in ahead of her in 4th, is the model of longevity and consistent success in women's triple jump, **Caterine Ibargüen**. She claimed one Olympic title and two Worlds in a career haul of seven global outdoor medals and it was never in doubt that she would be ranked so high! Ibargüen was in and around the major medals for so long – she won 34 competition finals in a row in 2012-16 – that she was the benchmark in her sport throughout that period, despite never threatening the World Record. She was a great athlete, not just in the horizontal jumps and holds the most World Championship medals of any woman in history (five, with two of them Golds).

3rd place brings us our first woman with a doping sanction in **Tatyana Lebedeva**. The Russian is probably the most talented combined triple and long jumper in the history of women's track and field, with medals in both events at the Olympics, World Championships and World Indoor Championships, and she still has more jumps of 15m+ than any other woman, even Yulimar Rojas. Her late career doping sanction has clouded her reputation and it saw her lose her unique horizontal jumps double Silver from the Beijing Olympics in 2008, but before the truth was known about her serious violation, she was an incredible athlete to watch, being ranked in the world top ten in eleven seasons.

We gave the game away in the introduction, but we have not diminished the integrity of the HBM with the final *career* rankings. **Yulimar Rojas** is now the furthest women's triple jumper but she still has some way to go to overtake **Inessa Kravets** in the HBM rankings, in 1st place. Each has two World Records to their name and enviable global championship medal records, particularly Rojas with one Olympic Gold and three World titles, but Kravets edges the Venezuelan by virtue of her comparable *career* ranking allied to an incredible 28 years in total as a World Record holder. It is difficult to now talk of Kravets being the *greatest* after her two doping bans, but the HBM scoring has an integrity that she perhaps lacked.

The Harvey-Benns Method - Women's Triple Jump All-Time Top 20

ALL-TIME RANKING	ATHLETE	TRIPLE JUMP PB (METRES)	NUMBER OF WORLD RECORDS	WORLD RECORD HOLDER YEARS	OLYMPIC & WORLD MEDALS (EX. INDOORS)	YEARS RANKED WORLD #1	YEARS RANKED IN THE WORLD TOP 10
1	Inessa Kravets (UKR)	15.50	2	28	2	3	7
2	Yulimar Rojas (VEN)	15.74i	2	2	5	5	6
3	Tatyana Lebedeva (RUS)	15.36i	0	0	5	5	11
4	Caterine Ibarguen (COL)	15.31	0	0	7	3	9
5	Francoise Mbango Etone (CMR)	15.39	0	0	4	2	6
6	Olga Rypakova (KAZ)	15.25	0	0	6	1	10
7	Yargelis Savigne (CUB)	15.28	0	0	4	2	7
8	Anna Biryukova (RUS)	15.09	1	2	2	1	5
9	Olha Saladukha (UKR)	14.99	0	1	3	2	9
10	Li Huirong (CHN)	14.55	1	1	0	1	4
11	Tereza Marinova (BUL)	15.20	0	0	2	0	4
12	Sarka Kasparkova (CZE)	15.20	0	0	2	1	4
13	Ekaterina Koneva (RUS)	15.04	0	0	1	1	6
14	Iva Prandzheva (BUL)	15.18	0	0	2	1	5
15	Galina Chistyakova (URS)	14.76	0	0	0	2	5
16	Paraskevi Tsiamita (GRE)	15.07	0	0	0	1	1
17	Yolanda Chen (RUS)	15.03i	1	0	1	0	3
18	Hrysopiyi Devetzi (GRE)	15.32	0	0	1	0	5
19	Trecia Smith (JAM)	15.16	0	0	1	0	3
20	Inna Lasovskaya (RUS)	15.09	0	0	1	0	8

782 Correct as at end of 2022. World rankings based on the data shared at the 'Track and Field Statistics' website available at http://trackfield.brinkster.net/Main.asp?P=F and number one ranking is based on longest legal distance in any given season, avoiding the subjectiveness of the *Track & Field News* rankings in particular.

MEN'S HISTORIC PROGRESSION

Triple jumping has evolved greatly over the past century; from standing jumps, double hops and cinder tracks, to the professionalism of modern athletics, the age of science in sport, synthetic tracks, and mass media. Competition is as intense now as it has ever been – statistics and analysis have played a key part in the evolution of the event, progression that has seen humans soar past first 15m, then 50ft, then 16m, 17m, 18m and most recently over 60ft! We are still waiting for the next milestone to be reached...

'Most recently' is an interesting phrase, *recent* in the history of man, but perhaps less recent by modern athletics standards given the triple jump World Record is now in its 28th year and has not been really threatened since Christian Taylor jumped 18.21m in 2015. The milestones mentioned above are amongst significant progressions in other track and field events over the past few decades, to the extent that around 70% of the current World Records were set in the last twenty years. Interestingly, when Jonathan Edwards leapt beyond first 18m and then 60ft in consecutive jumps in Gothenburg in 1995, he was alone as the first man beyond that latter metric landmark – since then, five other men have surpassed 18m, but none have gone beyond 60ft. It is rare for such stagnation in modern athletics, which makes the World Record of Edwards even more remarkable, the overall depth of performance so much higher, but none yet able to truly challenge the all-time best set way back in 1995.

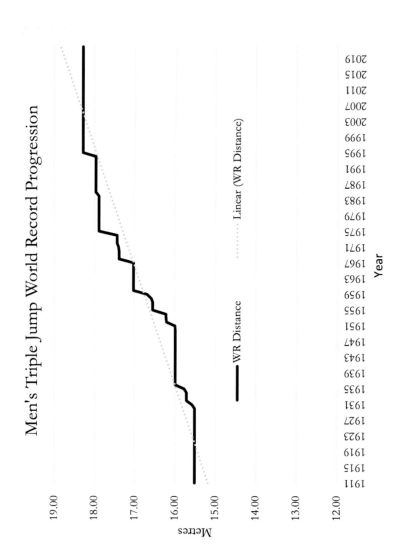

Men's Triple Jump World Record Progression

─────────────────────────

783 The first official IAAF World Record was set in 1911 (Ahearn, 15.52m); prior to this point all previous best recorded distances were noted as 'unofficial World Records' or better known as the 'best marks' of the time. Note that graph does not show additional World Records in years such as 1968.

374

Men's Triple Jump World Record Progression:[784]

1. 30.05.1911 WR 15.52m (50ft 11in) Daniel Ahearn (USA) New York, USA (NWI)
2. 12.07.1924 WR 15.52m (50ft $11\frac{1}{4}$in) Nick Winter (AUS) Paris, France (NWI)
3. 27.10.1931 WR 15.58m (51ft $1\frac{1}{4}$in) Mikio Oda (JPN) Tokyo, Japan (NWI)
4. 14.08.1932 WR 15.72m (51ft $6\frac{3}{4}$in) Chūhei Nambu (JPN) Los Angeles, USA (NWI)
5. 14.12.1935 WR 15.78m (51ft $9\frac{1}{4}$in) Jack Metcalfe (AUS) Sydney, Australia (NWI)
6. 06.08.1936 WR 16.00m (52ft $5\frac{3}{4}$in) Naoto Tajima (JPN) Berlin, Germany (+0.6m/s)
7. 03.12.1950 WR 16.00m (52ft $5\frac{3}{4}$in) Adhemar da Silva (BRA) São Paulo, Brazil (+1.6m/s)
8. 30.09.1951 WR 16.01m (52ft $6\frac{1}{4}$in) Adhemar da Silva (BRA) Rio de Janeiro, Brazil (+1.2m/s)
9. 23.07.1952 WR 16.12m (52ft $10\frac{1}{2}$in) Adhemar da Silva (BRA) Helsinki, Finland (NWI)
10. 23.07.1952 WR 16.22m (53ft $2\frac{1}{4}$in) Adhemar da Silva (BRA) Helsinki, Finland (NWI)
11. 19.07.1953 WR 16.23m (53ft $2\frac{3}{4}$in) Leonid Shcherbakov (URS) Moscow, Soviet Union (+1.5m/s)
12. 16.03.1955 WR(A) 16.56m (54ft $3\frac{1}{4}$in) Adhemar da Silva (BRA) Mexico City, Mexico (+0.2m/s)
13. 28.07.1958 WR 16.59m (54ft 5in) Oleg Ryakhovskiy (URS) Moscow, Soviet Union (+1.0m/s)
14. 03.05.1959 WR 16.70m (54ft $9\frac{1}{4}$in) Oleg Fedoseyev (URS) Nalchik, Soviet Union (0.0m/s)
15. 05.08.1960 WR 17.03m (55ft $10\frac{1}{4}$in) Józef Szmidt (POL) Olsztyn, Poland (+1.0m/s)
16. 16.10.1968 WR(A) 17.10m (56ft 1in) Guiseppe Gentile (ITA) Mexico City, Mexico (0.0m/s)
17. 17.10.1968 WR(A) 17.22m (56ft $5\frac{3}{4}$in) Guiseppe Gentile (ITA) Mexico City, Mexico (0.0m/s)
18. 17.10.1968 WR(A) 17.23m (56ft $6\frac{1}{4}$in) Viktor Saneyev (URS) Mexico City, Mexico (+2.0m/s)
19. 17.10.1968 WR(A) 17.27m (56ft $7\frac{3}{4}$in) Nelson Prudêncio (BRA) Mexico City, Mexico (+2.0m/s)
20. 17.10.1968 WR(A) 17.39m (57ft $1\frac{1}{2}$in) Viktor Saneyev (URS) Mexico City, Mexico (+2.0m/s)
21. 05.08.1971 WR(A) 17.40m (57ft 1in) Pedro Pérez (CUB) Cali, Colombia (+0.4m/s)
22. 17.10.1972 WR 17.44m (57ft $2\frac{1}{2}$in) Viktor Saneyev (URS) Sokhumi, Soviet Union (-0.5m/s)
23. 15.10.1975 WR(A) 17.89m (58ft $8\frac{1}{4}$in) João Carlos de Oliveira (BRA) Mexico City, Mexico (0.0m/s)
24. 16.06.1985 WR 17.97m (58ft $11\frac{1}{4}$in) Willie Banks (USA) Indianapolis, USA (+1.5m/s)
25. 18.07.1995 WR 17.98m (58ft $11\frac{3}{4}$in) Jonathan Edwards (GBR) Salamanca, Spain (+1.8m/s)
26. 07.08.1995 WR 18.16m (59ft $6\frac{3}{4}$in) Jonathan Edwards (GBR) Gothenburg, Sweden (+1.3m/s)
27. 07.08.1995 WR 18.29m (60ft 0in) Jonathan Edwards (GBR) Gothenburg, Sweden (+1.3m/s)

Men's Triple Jump All-Time Top 10 Performances (best by athlete):[785]

1. 18.29m (60ft 0in) 07.08.1995 Jonathan Edwards (GBR) Gothenburg, Sweden (+1.3m/s)
2. 18.21m (59ft $8\frac{3}{4}$in) 27.08.2015 Christian Taylor (USA) Beijing, China (+0.2m/s)
3. 18.14m (59ft 6in) 29.06.2019 Will Claye (USA) Long Beach, USA (+0.4m/s)
4. 18.09m (59ft 4in) 27.07.1996 Kenny Harrison (USA) Atlanta USA (-0.4m/s)
5. 18.08m (59ft $3\frac{3}{4}$in) 28.05.2015 Pedro Pichardo (CUB) Havana, Cuba (0.0m/s)
6. 18.07m (59ft $3\frac{1}{4}$in) 16.01.2021 Hugues Fabrice Zango (BUR) Aubière, France (indoor)
7. 18.04m (59ft 2in) 18.08.2013 Teddy Tamgho (FRA) Moscow, Russia (+0.3m/s)
8. 17.97m (58ft $11\frac{1}{4}$in) 16.06.1985 Willie Banks (USA) Indianapolis, USA (+1.5m/s)
9. 17.92m (58ft $9\frac{1}{2}$in) 31.08.1987 Khristo Markov (BUL) Rome, Italy (+1.6m/s)
   17.92m (58ft $9\frac{1}{2}$in) 20.05.1995 James Beckford (JAM) Odessa, USA (+1.9m/s)

---

[784] Official IAAF/World Athletics progression since 1912.
[785] We have included both outdoor and indoor performances in our all-time list.

Men's Triple Jump Olympic Medallists:

- 1896 (Athens, GRE)
  - ○ **Gold = James Connolly (USA): 13.71m OR**
  - ○ Silver = Alexandre Tufferi (FRA): 12.70m
  - ○ Bronze = Ioannis Persakis (GRE): 12.52m
- 1900 (Paris, FRA)
  - ○ **Gold = Myer Prinstein (USA): 14.47m OR**
  - ○ Silver = James Connolly (USA): 13.97m
  - ○ Bronze = Lewis Sheldon (USA): 13.64m
- 1900 (Paris, FRA) *Standing Triple Jump*
  - ○ **Gold = Ray Ewry (USA): 10.58m OR**
  - ○ Silver = Irving Baxter (USA): 9.95m
  - ○ Bronze = Robert Garrett (USA): 9.50m
- 1904 (St. Louis, USA)
  - ○ **Gold = Myer Prinstein (USA): 14.32m**
  - ○ Silver = Fred Engelhardt (USA): 13.90m
  - ○ Bronze = Robert Stangland (USA): 13.36m
- 1904 (St. Louis, USA) *Standing Triple Jump*
  - ○ **Gold = Ray Ewry (USA): 10.54m**
  - ○ Silver = Charles King (USA): 10.16m
  - ○ Bronze = Joseph Stadler (USA): 9.60m
- 1908 (London, GBR)
  - ○ **Gold = Tim Ahearne (GBR): 14.92m OR**
  - ○ Silver = Garfield MacDonald (CAN): 14.76m
  - ○ Bronze = Edvard Larsen (NOR): 14.39m
- 1912 (Stockholm, SWE)
  - ○ **Gold = Gustav Lindblom (SWE): 14.76m**
  - ○ Silver = Georg Åberg (SWE): 14.51m
  - ○ Bronze = Erik Almlöf (SWE): 14.17m
- 1920 (Antwerp, BEL)
  - ○ **Gold = Vilho Tuulos (FIN): 14.50m**
  - ○ Silver = Folke Jansson (SWE): 14.48m
  - ○ Bronze = Erik Almlöf (SWE): 14.27m
- 1924 (Paris, FRA)
  - ○ **Gold = Nick Winter (AUS): 15.52m WR**
  - ○ Silver = Luis Brunetto (ARG): 15.42m
  - ○ Bronze = Vilho Tuulos (FIN): 15.37m
- 1928 (Amsterdam, NED)
  - ○ **Gold = Mikio Oda (JPN): 15.21m**
  - ○ Silver = Lee Casey (USA): 15.17m
  - ○ Bronze = Vilho Tuulos (FIN): 15.11m
- 1932 (Los Angeles, USA)
  - ○ **Gold = Chūhei Nambu (JPN): 15.72m WR**
  - ○ Silver = Eric Svensson (SWE): 15.32m
  - ○ Bronze = Kenkichi Oshima (JPN): 15.12m
- 1936 (Berlin, GER)
  - ○ **Gold = Naoto Tajima (JPN): 16.00m WR**
  - ○ Silver = Masao Harada (JPN): 15.66m
  - ○ Bronze = Jack Metcalfe (AUS): 15.50m
- 1948 (London, GBR)
  - ○ **Gold = Arne Åhman (SWE): 15.40m**
  - ○ Silver = George Avery (AUS): 15.36m
  - ○ Bronze = Ruhi Sarıalp (TUR): 15.02m
- 1952 (Helsinki, FIN)
  - ○ **Gold = Adhemar da Silva (BRA): 16.22m WR**
  - ○ Silver = Leonid Shcherbakov (URS): 15.98m
  - ○ Bronze = Asnoldo Devonish (VEN): 15.52m
- 1956 (Melbourne, AUS)
  - ○ **Gold = Adhemar da Silva (BRA): 16.35m OR**
  - ○ Silver = Vilhjálmur Einarsson (ISL): 16.26m
  - ○ Bronze = Vitold Kreyer (URS): 16.02m
- 1960 (Rome, ITA)
  - ○ **Gold = Józef Szmidt (POL): 16.81m OR**
  - ○ Silver = Vladimir Goryaev (URS): 16.63m
  - ○ Bronze = Vitold Kreyer (URS): 16.43m
- 1964 (Tokyo, JPN)
  - ○ **Gold = Józef Szmidt (POL): 16.85m OR**
  - ○ Silver = Oleg Fedoseyev (URS): 16.58m
  - ○ Bronze = Viktor Kravchenko (URS): 16.57m
- 1968 (Mexico City, MEX)
  - ○ **Gold = Viktor Saneyev (URS): 17.39m WR**
  - ○ Silver = Nelson Prudêncio (BRA): 17.27m

- o   Bronze = Giuseppe Gentile (ITA): 17.22m
- 1972 (Munich, GER)
  - o   **Gold = Viktor Saneyev (URS): 17.35m**
  - o   Silver = Jörg Drehmel (GDR): 17.31m
  - o   Bronze = Nelson Prudêncio (BRA): 17.05m
- 1976 (Montreal, CAN)
  - o   **Gold = Viktor Saneyev (URS): 17.29m**
  - o   Silver = James Butts (USA): 17.18m
  - o   Bronze = João Carlos de Oliveira (BRA): 16.90m
- 1980 (Moscow, URS)
  - o   **Gold = Jaak Uudmäe (URS): 17.35m**
  - o   Silver = Viktor Saneyev (URS): 17.24m
  - o   Bronze = João Carlos de Oliveira (BRA): 17.22m
- 1984 (Los Angeles, USA)
  - o   **Gold = Al Joyner (USA): 17.26m**
  - o   Silver = Mike Conley Sr. (USA): 17.18m
  - o   Bronze = Keith Connor (GBR): 16.87m
- 1988 (Seoul, KOR)
  - o   **Gold = Khristo Markov (BUL): 17.61m OR**
  - o   Silver = Igor Lapshin (URS): 17.52m
  - o   Bronze = Aleksandr Kovalenko (URS): 17.42m
- 1992 (Barcelona, ESP)
  - o   **Gold = Mike Conley Sr. (USA): 18.17m**
  - o   Silver = Charlie Simpkins (USA): 17.60m
  - o   Bronze = Frank Rutherford (BAH): 17.36m
- 1996 (Atlanta, USA)
  - o   **Gold = Kenny Harrison (USA): 18.09m OR**
  - o   Silver = Jonathan Edwards (GBR): 17.88m
  - o   Bronze = Yoelbi Quesada (CUB): 17.44m
- 2000 (Sydney, AUS)
  - o   **Gold = Jonathan Edwards (GBR): 17.71m**
  - o   Silver = Yoel Garcia (CUB): 17.47m
  - o   Bronze = Denis Kapustin (RUS): 17.46m
- 2004 (Athens, GRE)
  - o   **Gold = Christian Olsson (SWE): 17.79m**
  - o   Silver = Marian Oprea (ROM): 17.55m
  - o   Bronze = Daniil Burkenya (RUS): 17.48m
- 2008 (Beijing, CHN)
  - o   **Gold = Nelson Évora (POR): 17.67m**
  - o   Silver = Phillips Idowu (GBR): 17.62m
  - o   Bronze = Leevan Sands (BAH): 17.59m
- 2012 (London, GBR)
  - o   **Gold = Christian Taylor (USA): 17.81m**
  - o   Silver = Will Claye (USA): 17.62m
  - o   Bronze = Fabrizio Donato (ITA): 17.48m
- 2016 (Rio de Janeiro, BRA)
  - o   **Gold = Christian Taylor (USA): 17.86m**
  - o   Silver = Will Claye (USA): 17.76m
  - o   Bronze = Dong Bin (CHN): 17.58m
- 2020 (Tokyo, JPN)
  - o   **Gold = Pedro Pichardo (POR): 17.98m**
  - o   Silver = Zhu Yaming (CHN): 17.57m
  - o   Bronze = Hugues Fabrice Zango (BUR): 17.47m

Men's Triple Jump World Athletics Championships Medallists:

- 1983 (Helsinki, FIN)
  - **Gold = Zdzisław Hoffmann (POL): 17.42m CR**
  - Silver = Willie Banks (USA): 17.18m
  - Bronze = Ajayi Agbebaku (NGR): 17.18m

- 1987 (Rome, ITA)
  - **Gold = Khristo Markov (BUL): 17.92m CR**
  - Silver = Mike Conley Sr. (USA): 17.67m
  - Bronze = Oleg Sakirkin (URS): 17.43m

- 1991 (Tokyo, JPN)
  - **Gold = Kenny Harrison (USA): 17.78m**
  - Silver = Leonid Voloshin (URS): 17.75m
  - Bronze = Mike Conley Sr. (USA): 17.62m

- 1993 (Stuttgart, GER)
  - **Gold = Mike Conley Sr. (USA): 17.86m**
  - Silver = Leonid Voloshin (RUS): 17.65m
  - Bronze = Jonathan Edwards (GBR): 17.44m

- 1995 (Gothenburg, SWE)
  - **Gold = Jonathan Edwards (GBR): 18.29m WR**
  - Silver = Brian Wellman (BER): 17.62m
  - Bronze = Jérôme Romain (DMA): 17.59m

- 1997 (Athens, GRE)
  - **Gold = Yoelbi Quesada (CUB): 17.85m**
  - Silver = Jonathan Edwards (GBR): 17.69m
  - Bronze = Aliecer Urrutia (CUB): 17.64m

- 1999 (Seville, ESP)
  - **Gold = Charles Friedek (GER): 17.59m**
  - Silver = Rostislav Dimitrov (BUL): 17.49m
  - Bronze = Jonathan Edwards (GBR): 17.48m

- 2001 (Edmonton, CAN)
  - **Gold = Jonathan Edwards (GBR): 17.92m**
  - Silver = Christian Olsson (SWE): 17.47m
  - Bronze = Igor Spasovkhodskiy (RUS): 17.44m

- 2003 (Paris, FRA)
  - **Gold = Christian Olsson (SWE): 17.72m**
  - Silver = Yoandri Betanzos (CUB): 17.28m
  - Bronze = Leevan Sands (BAH): 17.26m

- 2005 (Helsinki, FIN)
  - **Gold = Walter Davis (USA): 17.57m**
  - Silver = Yoandri Betanzos (CUB): 17.42m
  - Bronze = Marian Oprea (ROM): 17.40m

- 2007 (Osaka, JPN)
  - **Gold = Nelson Évora (POR): 17.74m**
  - Silver = Jadel Gregório (BRA): 17.59m
  - Bronze = Walter Davis (USA): 17.33m

- 2009 (Berlin, GER)
  - **Gold = Phillips Idowu (GBR): 17.73m**
  - Silver = Nelson Évora (POR): 17.55m
  - Bronze = Alexis Copello (CUB): 17.36m

- 2011 (Daegu, KOR)
  - **Gold = Christian Taylor (USA): 17.96m**
  - Silver = Phillips Idowu (GBR): 17.77m
  - Bronze = Will Claye (USA): 17.50m

- 2013 (Moscow, RUS)
  - **Gold = Teddy Tamgho (FRA): 18.04m**
  - Silver = Pedro Pichardo (CUB): 17.68m
  - Bronze = Will Claye (USA): 17.52m

- 2015 (Beijing, CHN)
  - **Gold = Christian Taylor (USA): 18.21m**
  - Silver = Pedro Pichardo (CUB): 17.73m
  - Bronze = Nelson Évora (POR): 17.52m

- 2017 (London, GBR)
  - **Gold = Christian Taylor (USA): 17.68m**
  - Silver = Will Claye (USA): 17.63m
  - Bronze = Nelson Évora (POR): 17.19m

- 2019 (Doha, QAT)
  - **Gold = Christian Taylor (USA): 17.92m**
  - Silver = Will Claye (USA): 17.74m
  - Bronze = Hugues Fabrice Zango (BUR): 17.66m

- 2022 (Oregon, USA)
  - **Gold = Pedro Pichardo (POR): 17.95m**
  - Silver = Hugues Fabrice Zango (BUR): 17.55m
  - Bronze = Zhu Yaming (CHN): 17.31m

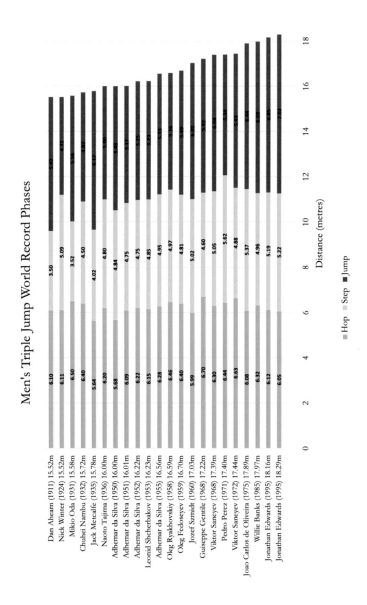

Men's Triple Jump World Record Phases

786 This breakdown of World Record phases includes only those where they have been published by IAAF/World Athletics; the other three World Records in the 1968 Mexico City Olympics were either not recorded (Gentile 17.10m) or excluded here (Saneyev 17.23m & Prudêncio 17.27m) as the IAAF measured those jumps from take-off to landing, rather than from the board. We are also missing the breakdown for da Silva 16.12m & Edwards 17.98m.

Men's Triple Jump World Record & Notable Jump Phases (%)

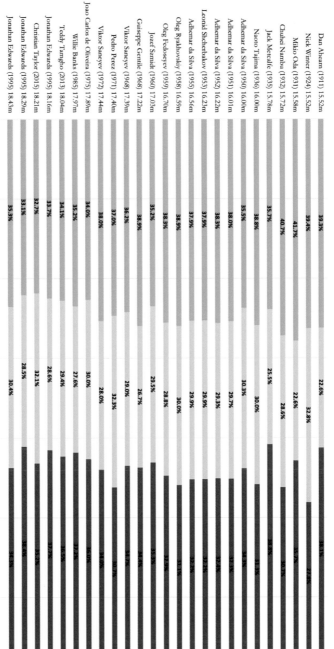

Legend: Hop · Step · Jump

Athlete	Hop	Step	Jump
Dan Ahearn (1911) 15.52m	39.3%	22.6%	38.1%
Nick Winter (1924) 15.52m	39.4%	32.8%	27.8%
Mikio Oda (1931) 15.58m	41.7%	22.6%	35.7%
Chuhei Nambu (1932) 15.72m	40.7%	28.6%	30.7%
Jack Metcalfe (1935) 15.78m	35.7%	25.5%	38.8%
Naoto Tajima (1936) 16.00m	38.8%	30.0%	31.3%
Adhemar da Silva (1950) 16.00m	35.5%	30.3%	34.1%
Adhemar da Silva (1951) 16.01m	38.0%	29.7%	32.3%
Adhemar da Silva (1952) 16.22m	38.3%	29.3%	32.4%
Leonid Shcherbakov (1953) 16.23m	37.9%	29.9%	32.2%
Adhemar da Silva (1955) 16.56m	37.9%	29.9%	32.2%
Oleg Ryakhovskiy (1958) 16.59m	38.9%	30.0%	31.1%
Oleg Fedoseyev (1959) 16.70m	38.3%	28.8%	32.9%
Jozef Szmidt (1960) 17.03m	35.2%	29.5%	35.3%
Guiseppe Gentile (1968) 17.22m	38.9%	26.7%	34.4%
Viktor Saneyev (1968) 17.39m	36.2%	29.0%	34.8%
Pedro Perez (1971) 17.40m	37.0%	32.3%	30.7%
Viktor Saneyev (1972) 17.44m	38.0%	28.0%	34.0%
Joao Carlos de Oliveira (1975) 17.89m	34.0%	30.0%	36.0%
Willie Banks (1985) 17.97m	35.2%	27.6%	37.4%
Teddy Tamgho (2013) 18.04m	34.1%	29.4%	36.5%
Jonathan Edwards (1995) 18.16m	33.7%	28.6%	37.7%
Christian Taylor (2015) 18.21m	32.7%	32.1%	35.2%
Jonathan Edwards (1995) 18.29m	33.1%	28.5%	38.4%
Jonathan Edwards (1995) 18.43m	35.3%	30.4%	34.3%

The men's event has a much longer 'official' history than that of the women and this provides us with a much deeper dataset when considering how both the discipline and leading protagonists have evolved. The world is now very different from how it was in 1912 when the first IAAF World Record was ratified in the event (for a 1911 performance) and the triple jump is no exception to the widespread change in the intervening century, particularly in relation to the advent of professionalism of sport and the evolution of sports science, with all its many obvious benefits, to both athlete's bodies and equipment (notably spikes in the triple jump world). Yet, the progression of the men's triple jump has stunted in absolute terms, i.e., the advancing of the World Record after 1995, and we find this fascinating.

We remain convinced that the World Record will be broken, but the progression curve for the absolute best performance mark in the event has fallen far below what would have been forecast from the progression of the landmark jumps back to 1911. From a purely statistical perspective we would have 'expected' the World Record to have been broken around 2005-10, some 10-15 years after Jonathan Edwards landed in the Gothenburg sandpit, especially when considering the distance required to be world number one for the most part has been on an ever-upwards trajectory. There has still been some stagnation in since 1995, but upwards progress resumed from the mid-2010's and has only slowed in recent years, likely due to the effects of the hiatus on competition in 2020 from the COVID-19 pandemic.

Our best and most balanced analysis came from overlaying the progression of the world number one ranking performance – in terms of furthest distance jumped in each year since 1891 – with the mean average of the number one ranked distance over each. To the data we added a tracer on the progression of the World Record and have used the world number one ranking performance as a proxy for the overall standard of the event at that time. We contemplated using the mean average of the top 3 distances, the top 10 and even the top 100 distances, but ultimately, we were most interested in the absolute best performances each year, alongside the incumbent World Record mark.

This was especially helpful given that if we only assessed the event's progression through the most absolute measure of the World Record, the underlying progress evident in the 2010's would be lost; our assessment suggests that Edwards' World Record is (statistically) on borrowed time, as only twice before in the history of the event has a decade mean average been so close to the World Record (the mean average world number one ranking performance in 2010-2019 was a historical record-high of 17.98m). In the 2010's, the mean average performance was to within 1.7% of the World Record, with Christian Taylor's 18.21m in 2015, the closest at 0.4% (8cm) from the incumbent World Record. On the two previous occasions the mean decade average and the number one ranked individual performance were so close to the World Record (in the 1920's & 1980's), a new landmark soon followed...

- *1920's #1 Mean Average Distance =* **15.28m** *vs. WR (15.52m) =* **-1.57%**
- *1930's #1 Mean Average Distance =* **15.65m** *vs. WR (16.00m) =* **-2.24%**
- *1940's #1 Mean Average Distance =* **15.51m** *vs. WR (16.00m) =* **-3.16%**
- *1950's #1 Mean Average Distance =* **16.33m** *vs. WR (16.70m) =* **-2.27%**
- *1960's #1 Mean Average Distance =* **16.92m** *vs. WR (17.39m) =* **-2.78%**
- *1970's #1 Mean Average Distance =* **17.38m** *vs. WR (17.89m) =* **-2.93%**
- *1980's #1 Mean Average Distance =* **17.66m** *vs. WR (17.97m) =* **-1.76%**
- *1990's #1 Mean Average Distance =* **17.88m** *vs. WR (18.29m) =* **-2.29%**
- *2000's #1 Mean Average Distance =* **17.79m** *vs. WR (18.29m) =* **-2.81%**
- *2010's #1 Mean Average Distance =* **17.98m** *vs. WR (18.29m) =* **-1.72%**

787

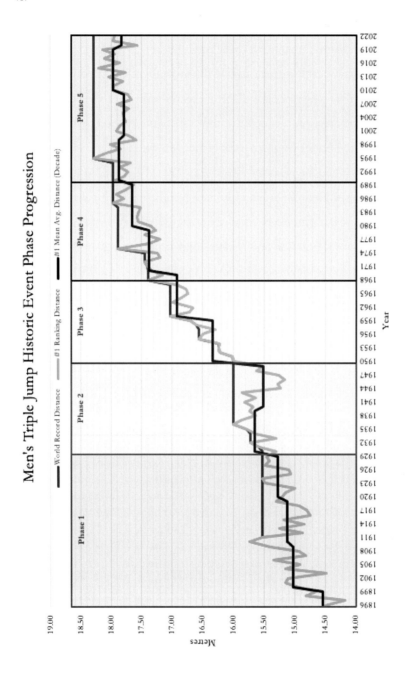

787 Correct as at end of 2022. World rankings based on the data shared at the 'Track and Field Statistics' website available at http://trackfield.brinkster.net/Main.asp?P=F.

Phase 1 = The Early Development Phase & Olympic Introduction Phase (Steady Growth) – *a period starting during the event's formative years (1896), encompassing both the triple jump's introduction to the modern Olympic Games and the formal recognition of the first World Record; this period spanned 34 years as the event was formally established and saw an average improvement in the World #1 Ranking performance of +0.15% per annum.*

Phase 2 = The Discovery & Experimentation Phase (Stalled by War) – *this phase started in 1930 and peaked at 16.00m in 1936, before the Second World War saw international sport suffer from an enforced hiatus; this period spanned 20 long years and saw a long stagnation in the average #1 Ranking performance, improving by only 0.08% per annum.*

Phase 3 = The Post-War, Mass Adoption Phase (Global Conscious & Rapid Growth) – *this phase started in 1950, and whilst brief, it would witness the World Record beginning to be progressed significantly – in a post-war world, the mass adoption of sport came on a new wave of human hope and optimism; this period spanned 18 years and saw the greatest period of improvement in the World #1 Ranking performance at +0.51% per annum.*

Phase 4 = The Race for Perfection Phase (Country Status & Ideological Emphasis) – *this phase started in 1968, the year of those historic Olympic Games in Mexico City where a number of track & field World Records were progressed beyond that which many thought possible; in addition, sport became a pawn in the Cold War and performance levels soared in the name of ideological success and political point-scoring; this phase lasted for 22 years, and even as maturity approached, pushed the average improvement of the World #1 Ranking performance to a further +0.20% per annum.*

Phase 5 = The Mature Phase (Mass Sports Science & Information Sharing + Performance Refinement & Marginal Gains) – *the final phase started in 1990 and continues as the progress of sports science and information-sharing through the digital age has enhanced performances further, in spite of the long maturation of the event; this phase is 33 years and counting… yet the World #1 Ranking performance has stalled once more, with only a slight improvement in the average #1 Ranking performance of 0.03% per annum.*

WOMEN'S HISTORIC PROGRESSION

As with the men's event, the women's triple jump continues to evolve.

It is less *mature* than then men's event, not being recognised by the IAAF until 1990 and was not included in the Olympic Games until 1996. The World Record until very recently was as stagnant as the men's best, but since 2021 Yulimar Rojas is taking her discipline to new heights and interest in the women's event has surpassed that of the men. Inessa Kravet's previous World Record of 15.50m (50ft 10in) had stood for a remarkable 26 years, but it remained a questionable mark with her two doping bans. Rojas has already broken her World Record again in 2022 – this time indoors – and she is on a very public quest to be the first ever woman over 16m, a milestone believed for many years to be beyond women.

The World Athletics Scoring System[788] dates back to 1979 and remains the most popular ranking system in athletics – HBM will hopefully be the challenger in 2023! In the words of World Athletics, "athletes score points based on a combination of result and place depending on the level of the competition in which the result is achieved" and it is equitable in attempting to standardise a ranking system across events. Rojas' 2022 World Record gives her a best score of 1297 points and Edwards' 1995 landmark is 1303 points; Usain Bolt's 2009 100m World Record was scored at 1352, Mondo Duplantis' 2023 pole vault World Record at 1328 and Galina Chistyakova's 1988 women's long jump World Record at 1333 – this ranking system certainly suggests there is more to come in the triple jump, particularly from the red-hot Rojas...

---

[788] https://worldathletics.org/world-rankings/introduction

789

Metres

Year

Women's Triple Jump World Record Progression

WR Distance

Linear (WR Distance)

The first official IAAF World Record was set in 1990 (Huirong, 14.54m); prior to this point all previous best recorded distances were noted as 'unofficial World Records' or better known as the 'best marks' of the time. Note that graph does not show the additional World Record in 1993 (Chen, 14.97m).

Women's Triple Jump World Record Progression:[790]

1. 25.08.1990 WR 14.54m (47ft $8\frac{1}{4}$in) Li Huirong (CHN) Sapporo, Japan (+1.1m/s)
2. 10.06.1991 WR 14.95m (49ft $\frac{1}{2}$in) Inessa Kravets (URS) Moscow, Soviet Union (-0.2m/s)
3. 18.06.1993 WR 14.97m (49ft $1\frac{1}{4}$in) Yolanda Chen (RUS) Moscow, Russia (+0.9m/s)
4. 21.08.1993 WR 15.09m (49ft 6in) Anna Biryukova (RUS) Stuttgart, Germany (+0.5m/s)
5. 10.08.1995 WR 15.50m (50ft 10in) Inessa Kravets (UKR) Gothenburg, Sweden (+0.9m/s)
6. 01.08.2021 WR 15.67m (51ft $4\frac{3}{4}$in) Yulimar Rojas (VEN) Tokyo, Japan (+0.7m/s)
7. 20.03.2022 WR 15.74m (51ft $7\frac{1}{2}$in) Yulimar Rojas (VEN) Belgrade, Serbia (indoor)

Women's Triple Jump All-Time Top 10 Performances (best by athlete):[791]

1. 15.74m (51ft $7\frac{1}{2}$in) 20.03.2022 Yulimar Rojas (VEN) Belgrade, Serbia (indoor)
2. 15.50m (50ft 10in) 10.08.1995 Inessa Kravets (UKR) Gothenburg, Sweden (+0.9m/s)
3. 15.39m (50ft $5\frac{3}{4}$in) 17.08.2008 Françoise Mbango Etone (CMR) Beijing, China (+0.5m/s)
4. 15.36m (50ft $4\frac{1}{2}$in) 06.03.2004 Tatyana Lebedeva (RUS) Budapest, Hungary (indoor)
5. 15.32m (50ft 3in) 21.08.2004 Hrysopiyi Devetzi (GRE) Athens, Greece (+0.9m/s)
6. 15.31m (50ft $2\frac{3}{4}$in) 18.07.2014 Caterine Ibargüen (COL) Monaco, France (0.0m/s)
7. 15.29m (50ft $1\frac{3}{4}$in) 11.07.2003 Yamilé Aldama (CUB) Rome, Italy (+0.3m/s)
8. 15.28m (50ft $1\frac{1}{2}$in) 31.08.2007 Yargelis Savigne (CUB) Osaka, Japan (+0.9m/s)
9. 15.25m (50ft $\frac{1}{4}$in) 04.09.2010 Olga Rypakova (KAZ) Split, Croatia (+1.7m/s)
10. 15.20m (49ft $10\frac{1}{4}$in) 04.08.1997 Šárka Kašpárková (CZE) Athens, Greece (0.0m/s)
    15.20m (49ft $10\frac{1}{4}$in) 24.09.2000 Tereza Marinova (BUL) Sydney, Australia (-0.3m/s)

---

[790] Official IAAF/World Athletics progression since 1990.
[791] We have included both outdoor and indoor performances in our all-time list.

Women's Triple Jump Olympic Medallists:

- 1996 (Atlanta, USA)
  - **Gold = Inessa Kravets (UKR): 15.33m OR**
  - Silver = Inna Lasovskaya (RUS): 14.98m
  - Bronze = Šárka Kašpárková (CZE): 14.98m
- 2000 (Sydney, AUS)
  - **Gold = Tereza Marinova (BUL): 15.20m**
  - Silver = Tatyana Lebedeva (RUS): 15.00m
  - Bronze = Olena Hovorova (UKR): 14.96m
- 2004 (Athens, GRE)
  - **Gold = Françoise Etone Mbango (CMR): 15.30m**
  - Silver = Hrysopiyi Devetzi (GRE): 15.25m
  - Bronze = Tatyana Lebedeva (RUS): 15.14m
- 2008 (Beijing, CHN)
  - **Gold = Françoise Etone Mbango (CMR): 15.39m OR**
  - Silver = Olga Rypakova (KAZ): 15.11m
  - Bronze = Yargelis Savigne (CUB): 15.05m
- 2012 (London, GBR)
  - **Gold = Olga Rypakova (KAZ): 14.98m**
  - Silver = Caterine Ibargüen (COL): 14.80m
  - Bronze = Olha Saladukha (UKR): 14.79m
- 2016 (Rio de Janeiro, BRA)
  - **Gold = Caterine Ibargüen (COL): 15.17m**
  - Silver = Yulimar Rojas (VEN): 14.98m
  - Bronze = Olga Rypakova (KAZ): 14.74m
- 2020 (Tokyo, JPN)
  - **Gold = Yulimar Rojas (VEN): 15.67m WR**
  - Silver = Patrícia Mamona (POR): 15.01m
  - Bronze = Ana Peleteiro (ESP): 14.87m

Women's Triple Jump World Athletics Championships Medallists:

- 1993 (Stuttgart, GER)
- Gold = Anna Biryukova (RUS): 15.09m WR
- Silver = Yolanda Chen (RUS): 14.70m
- Bronze = Iva Prandzheva (BUL): 14.23m

- 1995 (Gothenburg, SWE)
- Gold = Inessa Kravets (UKR): 15.50m WR
- Silver = Iva Prandzheva (BUL): 15.18m
- Bronze = Anna Biryukova (RUS): 15.08m

- 1997 (Athens, GRE)
- Gold = Šárka Kašpárková (CZE): 15.20m
- Silver = Rodica Mateescu (ROU): 15.16m
- Bronze = Olena Hovorova (UKR): 14.67m

- 1999 (Seville, ESP)
- Gold = Paraskevi Tsiamita (GRE): 14.88m
- Silver = Yamilé Aldama (CUB): 14.61m
- Bronze = Olga Vasdeki (GRE): 14.61m

- 2001 (Edmonton, CAN)
- Gold = Tatyana Lebedeva (RUS): 15.25m
- Silver = Françoise Etone Mbango (CMR): 14.60m
- Bronze = Tereza Marinova (BUL): 14.58m

- 2003 (Paris, FRA)
- Gold = Tatyana Lebedeva (RUS): 15.18m
- Silver = Françoise Etone Mbango (CMR): 15.05m
- Bronze = Magdelín Martínez (ITA): 14.90m

- 2005 (Helsinki, FIN)
- Gold = Trecia Smith (JAM): 15.11m
- Silver = Yargelis Savigne (CUB): 14.82m
- Bronze = Anna Pyatykh (RUS): 14.78m

- 2007 (Osaka, JPN)
- Gold = Yargelis Savigne (CUB): 15.28m
- Silver = Tatyana Lebedeva (RUS): 15.07m
- Bronze = Marija Šestak (SLO): 14.72m

- 2009 (Berlin, GER)
- Gold = Yargelis Savigne (CUB): 14.95m
- Silver = Mabel Gay (CUB): 14.61m
- Bronze = Anna Pyatykh (CUB): 14.58m

- 2011 (Daegu, KOR)
- Gold = Olha Saladukha (UKR): 14.94m
- Silver = Olga Rypakova (KAZ): 14.89m
- Bronze = Caterine Ibargüen (COL): 14.84m

- 2013 (Moscow, RUS)
- Gold = Caterine Ibargüen (COL): 14.85m
- Silver = Ekaterina Koneva (RUS): 14.81m
- Bronze = Olha Saladukha (UKR): 14.65m

- 2015 (Beijing, CHN)
- Gold = Caterine Ibargüen (COL): 14.90m
- Silver = Hanna Knyazyeva-Minenko (ISR): 14.78m
- Bronze = Olga Rypakova (KAZ): 14.77m

- 2017 (London, GBR)
- Gold = Yulimar Rojas (VEN): 14.91m
- Silver = Caterine Ibargüen (COL): 14.89m
- Bronze = Olga Rypakova (KAZ): 14.77m

- 2019 (Doha, QAT)
- Gold = Yulimar Rojas (VEN): 15.37m
- Silver = Shanieka Ricketts (JAM): 14.92m
- Bronze = Caterine Ibargüen (COL): 14.73m

- 2022 (Oregon, USA)
- Gold = Yulimar Rojas (VEN): 15.47m
- Silver = Shanieka Ricketts (JAM): 14.89m
- Bronze = Tori Franklin (USA): 14.72m

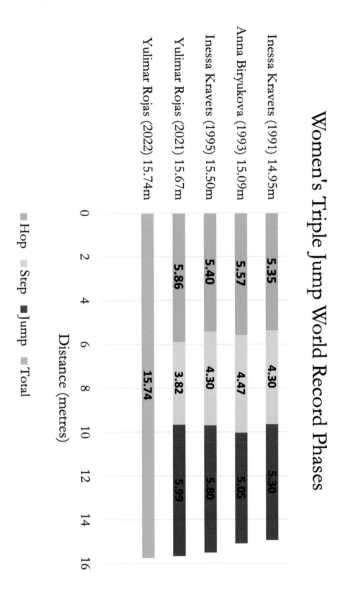

Women's Triple Jump World Record Phases

792 This breakdown of World Record phases includes only those where they have been published by IAAF/World Athletics and Rojas 15.74m has been included as the incumbent World Record, despite no breakdown being yet available. We are also missing the breakdown for Huirong 14.54m & Chen 14.97m.

Women's Triple Jump World Record Phases (%)

Athlete	Hop	Step	Jump
Inessa Kravets (1991) 14.95m	35.8%	28.8%	35.5%
Anna Biryukova (1993) 15.09m	36.9%	29.6%	33.5%
Inessa Kravets (1995) 15.50m	34.8%	27.7%	37.4%
Yulimar Rojas (2021) 15.67m	37.4%	24.4%	38.2%

Hop ■ Step ■ Jump

The women's event does not lend itself to the same long-term analysis as the men's does, with a ratified World Record dating back to 1911 for the men and only 1990 for the women. The women's triple jump has been (and continues to be) on an ever-evolving journey and whilst it is much less mature than the men's event, the progression of the World Record until 2021 has been every bit as static. Even in 2023 women can still experience much discrimination but in the sport of the triple jump it is the women who are leading the way, and not just the era-defining performances of the leading protagonist, Yulimar Rojas. Until a true rival emerges – Caterine Ibargüen was the last triple jumper to regular beat an admittedly youthful Rojas – she will continue to dominate the event as she has since the 2017 World Championships.

The quest is on for the first woman to exceed the 16m milestone and we see only one realistic candidate in the stupendously talented Venezuelan. We cannot attempt an historic phase progression chart as we did with the men's event as there is just not the depth of data available, but we have included two graphs that may be of interest to readers – at the start of this section we overlaid the individual women's World Record distances with a tracer on the trajectory of the record distance; this suggests that (statistically) the current World Record, as brilliant as it is, lags behind the long-term data point for the best... on the following page we have also included data on the progression of the world number one distance each year from 1989; the impact of Kravets in 1995, the multi-champions who followed such as Ibargüen who dominated from 2012-16 and the upwards trend since Rojas burst onto the scene are clear to see, but the peak of the Venezuelan is so far ahead of the tracer in the same way she is bounds ahead of her competitors...

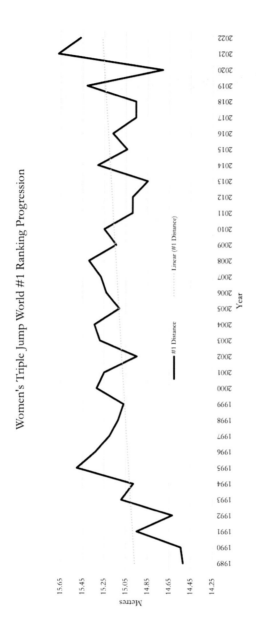

[793] Note that Yulimar Rojas' best outdoor distance of 15.47m has been used for 2022, rather than her World Record of 15.74m, the absolute mark both indoors and outdoors. This is to be consistent with the previous ranking data used in the graph.

394

WINDY DAYS

Willie Banks became the first triple jumper over 18m in July 1988 in Indianapolis, but a tailwind of 5.2m/s meant it was not ratified as a World Record, being well over the allowable limit of +2.0m/s. The IAAF first introduced a 'wind rule' in 1936, having commissioned a study on the impact of wind on sprint times in particular. This study had established that wind speeds in excess of +1.0m/s provided an advantage to sprinters, prompting the 1936 agreement to only ratify records where the wind was 2.0m/s or below. Since 1977, the IAAF have required that hand timings for records are fully automatic, but the wind rule has been retained as it was, enabling the fairest comparison of performances, notwithstanding its imperfections (some have argued over the years for a reconciliation of sprint times that are adjusted up or down to account for the respective tailwind assistance or headwind).

The triple jump is equally affected by this rule, given the importance of horizontal speed to generating jumping distance. Determining the positive or negative impact to the centimetre of performances benefitting from wind assistance has not (to our knowledge) been modelled, given the greater number of variables in a triple jump than in a sprint race. However, the assistance of wind over 2.0m/s is undeniable to the overall jumping distance achieved and the unpredictable element of the wind has given a number of leading triple jumpers their personal best performance, hence we have included this section entitled 'Windy Days'.

Dan Ahearn had a number of leading marks in 1911 that were never accepted as World Records as we covered in the chapter titled 'Irish Trailblazers'. He was reported to have jumped 51ft $4\frac{1}{2}$in (15.66m) in New York on 4 June 1911, but this was never accepted as a World

Record, either unofficial or otherwise. World Athletics to this day include this distance in their list of triple jump records in the IAAF era, yet it was never ratified and we suspect it was discounted due to the wind conditions in Celtic Park that afternoon; if it had, this would have been the first ratified World Record instead of his distance of 15.52m from May 1911 and would have stood until Chūhei Nambu covered 15.72m in August 1932, erasing Nick Winter and Mikio Oda from their respective places in the record books!

Nambu was one of three Japanese to hold the World Record in 1930's and this was a golden era for the country in the triple jump. That era could have been burnished further if the jump of 15.82m from Kenkichi Oshima in Osaka on 16 September 1934 had been accepted as a World Record. World Athletics record now that it was discounted due to a wind reading of +2.2m/s,[794] although this was two years before the 1936 Congress of the IAAF agreed an official wind rule and it was recognised at the time as the new National Record; fellow Japanese Masao Harada also exceeded the former World Record that day with a distance of 15.75m himself.

The most well-known example of a triple jumper *losing* a World Record due to wind was Mike Conley in the 1992 Olympics in Barcelona. He landed an incredible jump of 18.17, but a marginally illegal tailwind of 2.1m/s denied him the record, although an Olympic Gold medal will have been some comfort! Jonathan Edwards was later to become the first man to legally break the 18m barrier in Gothenburg, Sweden in August 1995, but his distance of 18.43m (+2.4m/s) in Villeneuve d'Ascq, France in June 1995 remains the *furthest* triple jump in history, under any conditions; that wind-aided jump is probably the

---

[794] Also Quercetani, *op. cit.*, p.262.

closest any triple jumper has come to perfection in the eyes of many athletics observers and was notable for how balanced his phases were.

A women's triple jump World Record has only been ratified since 1990 and the stunning improvements to it made by Yulimar Rojas in 2021 and 2022, have ensured that the leading legal mark for the women is also the furthest under *any* conditions, unusually so in events like the triple jump that can benefit from wind and altitude assistance in particular. The unofficial record changed hands even more frequently than it did with the men before official recognition for record purposes came in 1990, yet since then there have only been seven World Records, a sign of the fast maturity of the event in the early 1990's and long period of stagnation that followed, at least in terms of statistical advancement of the leading mark. There have been few wind-aided distances of note when compared to the incumbent women's World Record, with the 15.56m (+3.5m/s) that Rojas covered in Lausanne on 26 August 2021 the only jump close to troubling the absolute record at the time, that being her first World Record of 15.67m set only about three weeks before in the re-scheduled Tokyo Olympics.

Men's Triple Jump Wind-Assisted All-Time Top 10 Performances (best by athlete):

1. 18.43m (60ft 5$\frac{1}{2}$in) 25.06.1995 Jonathan Edwards (GBR) Villeneuve-d'Ascq, France (+2.4m/s)
2. 18.20m (59ft 8$\frac{1}{2}$in) 16.07.1988 Willie Banks (USA) Indianapolis, USA (+5.2m/s)
3. 18.17m (59ft 7$\frac{1}{2}$in) 03.08.1992 Mike Conley (USA) Barcelona, Spain (+2.1m/s)
4. 18.05m (59ft 2$\frac{1}{2}$in) 27.05.2017 Will Claye (USA) Eugene, USA (+2.4m/s)
5. 18.01m (59ft 1in) 15.06.1996 Kenny Harrison (USA) Atlanta, USA (+3.7m/s)
6. 17.97m (58ft 11$\frac{1}{2}$in) 20.06.1995 Yoelbi Quesada (CUB) Madrid, Spain (+7.5m/s)
7. 17.93m (58ft 10in) 16.07.1988 Charlie Simpkins (USA) Indianapolis, USA (+5.2m/s)
   17.93m (58ft 10in) 09.07.2019 Christian Taylor (USA) Székesfehérvár, Hungary (+3.4m/s)
   17.93m (58ft 10in) 13.07.2003 Jordan Díaz (CUB) Nerja, Spain (+2.5m/s)
10. 17.92m (58ft 9$\frac{1}{2}$in) 13.06.2003 Christian Olsson (SWE) Gateshead, United Kingdom (+3.4 m/s)

Women's Triple Jump Wind-Assisted All-Time Top 10 Performances (best by athlete):

1. 15.56m (51ft) 26.08.2021 Yulimar Rojas (VEN) Lausanne, Switzerland (+3.5m/s)
2. 15.24m(A) (50ft) 01.08.2004 Magdelín Martínez (ITA) Sestriere, Italy (+4.2m/s)
3. 15.18m (49ft 9$\frac{1}{2}$in) 30.05.2015 Caterine Ibargüen (COL) Eugene, USA (+2.1m/s)
4. 15.17m (49ft 9$\frac{1}{2}$in) 03.07.2006 Anna Pyatykh (RUS) Athens, Greece (+2.4m/s)
5. 15.10m (49ft 6$\frac{1}{2}$in) 06.05.2007 Keila Costa (BRA) Uberlandia, Brazil (+2.7m/s)
6. 15.07m (49ft 5$\frac{1}{2}$in) 10.06.2000 Tereza Marinova (BUL) Rethymno, Greece (+2.5m/s)
7. 15.06m (49ft 4$\frac{1}{2}$in) 29.07.2011 Olha Saladukha (UKR) Stockholm, Sweden (+2.3m/s)
8. 15.05m (49ft 4$\frac{1}{4}$in) 03.06.1995 Inna Lasovskaya (RUS) Seville, Spain (+2.7m/s)
   15.05m (49ft 4$\frac{1}{4}$in) 08.03.2019 Liadagmis Povea (CUB) Havana, Cuba (+3.1m/s)
10. 15.02m (49ft 3$\frac{1}{4}$in) 26.08.2021 Shanieka Ricketts (JAM) Lausanne, Switzerland (+2.7m/s)

EXCLUSIVE Q&A WITH JONATHAN EDWARDS
TRIPLE JUMP WORLD RECORD HOLDER

We were very fortunate to meet with Jonathan Edwards on a number of occasions and here we have compiled excerpts from our exclusive Q&A sessions with him in June 2023. We are extremely grateful that he so willingly gave of his time and we hope that these answers reveal a little more about the greatest men's triple jumper in history, a man who so modestly – and frequently – has decried his achievements as "it's only jumping into a sandpit" – yet by this stage of the book you will know that it took a whole lot more than that to reach the pinnacle of his sport, where he still stands today, aged 57 and the men's World Record holder for nearly 28 years as we go to print...

There's a question that I've never seen asked of you... who was your inspiration growing up, sporting or otherwise?

Someone I always wanted to do well though was John McEnroe,[795] some sort of alter-ego thing! I've always loved the aesthetics of sport as much as the performance, I like to see someone do it with a bit of panache and to do it beautifully. I used to love watching Carl Lewis[796] run for example, because he was fast but it was also beautiful, and there was an artistry about McEnroe and I think I loved his passion. In terms of triple jumping, [Khristo] Markov and [Mike] Conley, more Markov then and Conley later on. I styled my initial technique on Markov's big

---

[795] John P. McEnroe Jr., famous American tennis player with seven Grand Slam singles titles in a storied career, now working as a television commentator [1959-].

[796] Frederick 'Carl' C. Lewis, dominant sprinter and long jumper from the United States, one of only six Olympians to win a Gold medal in the same individual event in four consecutive Games, nine-time Olympic Gold medallist and eight-time World Champion in sprints, relays and long jump; regularly voted as *the* athlete of the 20th century [1961-].

windmill-type motion, which didn't suit me particularly well as it turned out, but he was the best at the time. I wasn't that sort of big, muscular jumper like he was and was a bit quicker. He really did have something about him, with the big hair and long socks, and would have been a superstar if he was around these days.

Did you ever consider the long jump?

I never did much long jumping and would have loved to have done the hitch kick that [Carl] Lewis did, but could never master that. He was something else. I had one off-season trying a bit of long jumping, but it's interesting, I don't know if it's the power, the timing, to just do that one effort, what I was good at was rebounding. My standing jump isn't that good, I couldn't dunk a basketball, my strength was my horizontal speed and being able to then rebound and spend as little time on the ground.

On short approach I was OK but not great, some of the other guys their short approach jumping was fabulous, because they weren't so speed dependent, they had better plyometric ability. Standing long jump [PB] was probably not much over 3m, standing triple jump I couldn't remember, I was always struck by Conley, who used to do that pro-celebrity slam dunk thing, he could slam dunk from the free-throw line! I couldn't dream of doing that, I remember him saying in an interview he could never be as quick through the phases as I was. The speed of my contacts... I didn't jump, I rebounded, I had very rigid ankles, I don't know what it is you would call it, but I could just bounce and maintain my speed.

I honestly think a lot of people will take heart from that. I actually saw you do a standing long jump the year you won BBC Sports Personality of the Year[797] [1995] and you got beaten by a rugby league star, Martin Offiah![798]

I was very fast. Over 30m, from my blocks,[799] I was quick and very strong. Interestingly my clean snatches were very good, probably pound for pound stronger than anybody, Colin Jackson[800] was similar, my basic static jumping ability was not brilliant. My best absolute lift was 150kg at 75kg [in weight], 72kg was my jumping weight and I probably would have done 145-147kg, hang snatch [often seen in Olympic weightlifting] I think I did 115kg. Sprinting, a lot of working out of blocks, not masses of plyometrics, but my clean and my snatch were very good. I was strong, my technique was good, but it was the quickness of my movement. I used to love the Olympic lifting, getting the feeling when you got it absolutely right and just caught it, I really enjoyed it [*big smile from Jonathan at this point of the interview!*].

I remember seeing you jump live at Crystal Palace in 2000, the year you won the Olympics, your speed on the runway, you went like a cannon over 18 strides and would run clean off the board...

I went like I was going out of the blocks [Jonathan later told us he trained in Tallahassee, Florida in 1996 with Namibian sprinter Frankie

---

[797] Annual award given by the BBC, the public service broadcaster in Great Britain, to a leading sportsperson judged by a public vote.
[798] Martin N. Offiah, British former professional rugby player, inducted into the Rugby League Hall of Fame in 2013 and much loved by rugby fans; noted for his blazing speed and try-scoring exploits [1965-].
[799] Device used by sprinters to brace their feet and prevent slipping as they start a race.
[800] Colin R. Jackson, one of Great Britain's greatest hurdlers, twice World Champion in 1993 & 1999 [1967-].

Fredericks[801] ahead of the Atlanta Olympics and was as fast as him out of the blocks over 30m; Fredericks would go on to claim the Silver in both the 100m and 200m in those Games!] One year I experimented with the jogging, Cuban-type style, but you don't get the same speed. My philosophy with the run-up was to go as hard as you could, which meant there was less room for error and the board would happen to be under my foot as I took off. I remember [Brian] Wellman would run his first ten strides with his head down and not even look at the board, to just establish his rhythm and his speed without any reference to the board at all, and then it was just an automatic pilot. Again, your stride length is your stride length and even running flat out, you should be within 5cm of the same mark every time. The triple jump take-off is very different from the long jump, there's not much modification going on, running off the board and having my leg out in front of me, so my centre of gravity is not too far forward, to stop the over-rotation. My sprinting was influenced by my strength and my power, but my jumping was all about the rebound, having so little time to exert forces. I would never run over 60m after the first month of preparation in training and I always thought it slightly odd that Christian Taylor wanted to continue doing a few 400m races, he's fantastic but I don't think running 400m much helps you triple jump!

Now that you're some distance from your career, when you look back, what do you think was your greatest moment?

There was nothing like the feeling of Lille and 18.43m [*furthest triple jump of all time under any conditions, on 25 June 1995*]. My best jump before then

---

[801] Frank 'Frankie' Fredericks, 100m & 200m Olympic Silver medallist in both 1992 & 1996, and World Champion in 1993 over 200m, amongst many major championship podiums; later a World Athletics Council member [1967-].

was 17.70m windy at Meadowbank I think in 1993 [Edinburgh, 2 July 1993], but very windy and I'd jumped 17.50m, I think I broke the British record at Loughborough a couple of weeks beforehand [17.58m, 11 June 1995] and in the first round I jumped 17.90m without a step, it was crazy! But 18.43m, with just marginal wind, had that been [a legal] +1.9m/s it was still 18.43m. I never jumped like that again, it was just phenomenal, everything was just brilliant. I remember all the guys there I was jumping against, looking at me, thinking "what has happened there, this is Edwards we've been jumping against him for four years and he's a 17.20m, 17.30m jumper and he's just jumped 18.50m". 18.29m was obviously amazing, and the circumstances of being in the World Championships made it even more special, but already I'd jumped further than that and that was the moment I broke through. So, there was nothing like the 18.43m.

What did it actually feel like, you were in the air for so long?

The whole thing was seamless, the rhythm, the fluidity of movement, it was like flying. It was absolutely like flying, it was just staggering. And you can't find it anywhere on YouTube, but I jumped 18.37m in the fourth round [in Lille]. For the emotional impact it was still the most amazing jump [18.43m compared to subsequent World Record 18.29m]. The 18.29m was still great and I knew it was a record when I landed as it was better than the previous one and there was a moment in the step, where I just had to pause, because it was a better transition from hop to step, that little feathering of the front leg, and when I landed I stood up and sort of shrugged my shoulders, as if to say, that's another World Record. Because it was, I knew it was better.

403

At what moment going into the 1995 season, did you know the World Record was on?

I was training well, but I was uncertain after the Epstein-Barr virus. My training had been very on-off in the lead up to the 1995 season, I was doing a bit of jumping in training and I was jumping well. But I don't really know what I'm going to do until I go into competition and I never jumped off full approach in training, nor got close to what I can do in competition in training. I jumped 17.58m in Loughborough, it was cold, it was wet and Malcolm Arnold[802] came up to me afterwards and said, "you can break the World Record", or maybe he told Andy Norman[803] who was my agent, whoever it was, they were just like "wow, it looks phenomenal".

Then I went to Lille and jumped 17.46m into a headwind and then went back for the European Cup [*where he covered the windy 18.43m*]. I thought I could jump 17.90m, maybe towards 18m, I knew I could mix it with the best guys, but thought that Conley was unbeatable, I thought he was just a different level. I didn't think I was going to have the season that I had, I thought I was going to have a good season. You go back to [Józef] Szmidt in the 1960's jumping 17m, so you'd lived with decades of 17m triple jumps, with just the odd wind-assisted 18m. That was the currency everybody worked with, so I didn't think of myself as somebody who was going to re-write the record-books. And I don't think anybody else thought I would do that as well, even now they probably think "how did he do that!"

---

[802] Malcolm Arnold, longtime athletics coach in Great Britain, coaching teams to 13 Olympics and athletes to 70 major medals in a near 50-year career [1940-].
[803] Andrew 'Andy' J. Norman, sports administrator, and agent [1943-2007].

The authors (Lawrence left and Andy right), with Jonathan Edwards in June 2023. We are so grateful to Jonathan for inviting us into his home and sharing his time so willingly.

Jonathan was kind enough to show us his IAAF World Record commemorative plaque during our visit. What a unique privilege it was as track and field fans to handle one of these rare items! How many readers even knew these existed...?

What did you say to yourself on the runway, when getting ready in those big competitions?

Nothing much more than run fast and jump far! Before the 18.29m in Gothenburg, there was a real sense of wanting to enjoy the moment, because I was very scared. I wouldn't say I necessarily enjoyed competing until I got a jump out and I settled into a competition. But yeah, there was no particular psychology.

How do you contextualise the achievement of beating your peers when the competition matters most, compared to your distances, which remain unrivalled?

I guess one of the best measures of that is how many times I have watched my Olympic winning jump compared to how many times I have watched my World Record jump; and the answer is, there's no comparison. I get a lot more pleasure and satisfaction out of the World Record for sure. Now, had it lasted less time, maybe that wouldn't be the case and I would look back, if I had no World Record, I'd say, well that was the Olympics you know, when it mattered and all of that. Given how long it has stood and even if it was now broken, it has still stood for nearly three decades, not many records have done that in the history of track and field. So, if you ask what makes me stand out as an athlete, it would be the World Record and not an Olympic medal.

It takes me back to school, we had the AAA awards system on the changing room notice board and it was all about how fast you ran and how far you jumped, that was athletics, the wonder of the tape measure being pulled out. It was nice to win something, but it was all about jumping my best and breaking my best. That for me has always been the magic of athletics, maybe that's why athletics has not held its own as a sport within the hyper professional era we are in now. That's because it is more about pure performance than the entertainment value; Bolt runs 9.58sec and its visually arresting, so people watch, but are they bothered that it's 9.58sec? I don't think they are, it's just that emotional impact that it creates.

And hence competition and drama, plays out better in today's market than just pure performance. Mondo Duplantis[804] is a great example of that. You go back in the day and everybody loved [Sergey] Bubka,[805] and it's 1cm at a time [*when he was frequently breaking the World Record*]. What Duplantis is doing is phenomenal, he's staggering, I mean he's flying over that bar by 20cm and setting World Records, and nobody knows him, really.

Who do you think could threaten your World Record?

I don't think [Pedro] Pichardo will, but he could, he along with this new Jamaican kid [Jaydon Hibbert] are probably the most likely, he [Hibbert] really is quite something, even off a short approach. The speed thing made a huge difference for me, and I said mine wasn't about jumping ability. So, depending on what type of jumper you are, just by running faster it's not necessarily going to make you jump further, because you may not be able to exert the same power in a shorter period of time.

---

[804] Armand 'Mondo' G. Duplantis, Swedish pole vaulter and current World Record holder, being Olympic Champion in 2021 and World Champion in 2022; still only aged 23! [1999-].

[805] Sergey N. Bubka, Ukrainian pole vaulter, six-time World Champion, Olympic Champion in 1988 and three-time World Indoor Champion amongst a host of major medals; broke the men's World Record 35 times and an inaugural inductee to the IAAF Hall of Fame in 2012 [1963-].

Anything else you would like to achieve in this lifetime, with the benefit of distance from your record-breaking career?

No, not really. I like to do interesting things and enjoy my life, but I do feel sated in terms of achievements. I never thought I would achieve what I achieved as an athlete and I couldn't have asked for more. What I did was so far ahead of what I thought I could do...

How do you wish to be remembered?

I hope people think fondly of me one way or the other, but when I'm gone, I'm gone! All the standard stuff, a nice guy, good family man, if people look back and think my athletics career was good, then that's a nice thing too.

Jonathan Edwards, June 2023

BIBLIOGRAPHY

Academia/Books/Podcasts/Publications

Aherne, Tom, *Ahearne men leapt to glory on world stage* (Limerick Leader, 10 September 2016)

Anon, *UNFORGETTABLE MOMENTS* (Soviet Life, No. 10, October 1980)

Associated Press, *WORLD UNIVERSITY GAMES: United States Wins Water Polo Gold* (Los Angeles Times, 24 July 1991)

Associated Press, *World Record Is Set In The Triple Jump* (The New York Times, 19 July 1995)

Banks, Willie, *STEPPING UP – CORRECTING ERRORS TO IMPROVE THE RESULT* (Techniques for Track & Field and Cross Country, Vol. 9/No. 2 November 2015)

Brown, Oliver, *Exclusive Jonathan Edwards interview: A giant leap for mankind – 25 years on, his triple jump world record has stood the test of time* (The Telegraph, 7 August 2020)

Butcher, Joanne, *Norman lit athletic flame; As the Olympic Torch passes through the region, JOANNE BUTCHER meets Jonathan Edwards and the coach who helped him to glory* (The Journal [Newcastle, England], 16 June 2012)

de Carvalho, George, *THE TRIPLE JUMPER FROM BRAZIL* (Sports Illustrated, 31 August 1959)

Clarey, Christopher, *TRACK AND FIELD; For Edwards, 59-0 Was a Leap of Faith* (The New York Times, 5 August 1995)

Cooke, Jerry, *SPORTS IN THE U.S.S.R.* (Sports Illustrated, 2 December 1957)

Cunningham, Mike (hosted by), *#63: Willie Banks-world record holder, Olympian, Triple Jump KING* (The Gill Athletics Track and Field Connections Podcast, 10 August 2020)

Drake, Dick, *Olympic Games Issue* (Track & Field News, Oct./Nov. 1968)

Fachet, Robert, *After the Tears, Banks Aimed for World Record* (The Washington Post, 18 June 1985)

410

Florence, Mal, *TRIPLE THREAT: For Conley, Banks and Other Hopefuls, the Record Is a Long Way Out There* (Los Angeles Times, 6 June 1985)

Folley, Malcolm, *A TIME TO JUMP – THE AUTHORISED BIOGRAPHY OF JONATHAN EDWARDS* (London: HarperCollinsPublishers, 2000)

Gleason, David, *WILLIE BANKS* (Track & Field News, November 1980 – 13)

Halford, Paul, *Yulimar Rojas' quantum leap* (Athletics Weekly, 4 May 2016)

Hay, James G., *The biomechanics of the triple jump: A review* (Journal of Sports Sciences – 10:4, 343-378, 1992)

Hay, James G. & Miller, John A., *Kinematics of a World Record and Other World-Class Performances in the Triple Jump* (International Journal of Sport Biomechanics – 2, 272-288, 1986)

Hymans, Richard (edited by), *Progression of World Athletics Records* (World Athletics, 2020)

Ingle, Sean, *Rojas thanks Facebook algorithm after making history in triple jump* (The Guardian, 1 August 2021)

Gibson, Owen, *Christian Taylor soars to gold in world championships triple jump* (The Guardian, 27 August 2015)

Guiney, David, *A hop, skip and jump into history* (Irish Times, 6 April 1996)

Gula, Nestor, *Kravets sets record in triple jump* (The Ukrainian Weekly, 28 March 1993)

Henderson, Jason, *Yulimar Rojas red-hot in the triple jump* (Athletics Weekly, 5 October 2019)

Kelly, David, *Olympic hero Edwards on new mission* (Belfast Telegraph, 20 November 2009)

Kessel, Anna, *London 2012: Christian Taylor aims high as Phillips Idowu stays away* (The Guardian, 15 July 2012)

Kluge, Volker, *Adhemar da Silva and the "little uncle", Rio Special* (ISOH, Journal of Olympic History – Vol. 24/No. 2, 2016)

Lane, Tim, *Cheating the only conclusion you can jump to* (Sydney Morning Herald, 18 August 2013)

Larkins, Clifford, *The optimal contribution of the phase distances in the triple jump: novices versus elites* (Doctoral research, University of Michigan, USA, 1987)

Layden, Tim, *LEAP OF FAITH ONCE SUNDAYS WERE NO LONGER SACROSANCT, ENGLAND'S JONATHAN EDWARDS EXPLODED INTO THE GREATEST TRIPLE JUMPER IN HISTORY* (Sports Illustrated, 13 May 1996)

Lindstrom, Sieg, *T&FN Interview – Christian Taylor* (Track & Field News, 9 July 2021)

Lobb, Adrian, *It almost feels like somebody else's life* (The Big Issue, 23 July 2021)

Mackay, Duncan, *Interview: Jonathan Edwards* (The Guardian, 30 July 2001)

Marshall, Joe, *NOT QUITE AS HIGH, BUT A BIT MIGHTIER* (Sports Illustrated, 17 July 1978)

Maule, Tex, *POWER VERSUS PERFECTION: THE U.S.-EUROPE TRACK MEETS* (Sports Illustrated, 17 July 1961)

McNally, Frank, *Great leaps forward – An Irishman's Diary about our supposed national talent for long-jumping* (Irish Times, 12 April 2018)

McClung, Chris & Goucher, Kara (hosted by), *#56: Christian Taylor, Olympic Gold Medalist and World Champion in the Triple Jump* (Clean Sport Collective Podcast, 5 July 2020)

Newman, Nick, *The Horizontal Jumps – Planning for Long Term Development* (Long Beach, United States: JumPR Publishing, 2012)

Nichols, Ben (hosted by), *#008: The Education of Life – with Christian Taylor* (Athletes: The Other Side Podcast, 12 November 2020)

Nielsen, Erik, *Sport and the British World, 1900-1930, Amateurism and National Identity in Australasia and Beyond* (London: Palgrave Macmillan UK, 2014)

Ó Ceallaigh, Séamus, *Great Limerick Athletes, (No. 11) – DAN AHEARNE of Athea* (Limerick Leader, abt. 1950's)

Quercetani, Roberto L., *A World History of Track and Field Athletics 1864-1964* (London, United Kingdom: Oxford University Press, 1964)

Phinizy, Coles, *THE UNBELIEVABLE MOMENT* (Sports Illustrated, 23 December 1968)

412

Pierson, Don, *BANKS TRIPLE-JUMPS TO WORLD MARK* (Chicago Tribune, 17 June 1985)

Rosenberg, Michael, *When Will the IOC Finally Take a Stand and Protect Its Athletes?* (Sports Illustrated, 2 August 2021)

Rowbottom, Mike, *Athletics: Edwards leaps clear of Sunday obstacle: Mike Rowbottom reports on the British triple-jumper who was inspired by a dream to relax his religious tenet before the World Indoor Championships, starting today* (The Independent, 11 March 1993)

Shepherd, John, *The art of triple jump* (Athletics Weekly, 16 May 2021)

Singer, Florantonia, *Yulimar Rojas' first jumps* (El Pais, 18 August 2020)

Sotomayor, Antonio & Torres, Cesar R., *Olimpismo: The Olympic Movement in the Making of Latin America and the Caribbean* (Fayetville, United States: University of Arkansas Press, 2020)

Srebnitsky, Alexei, *VICTOR SANEYEV APPROACHES THE 60-FOOT MARK* (Soviet Life, No. 6, June 1973)

Stafford, Ian, *I'm world champion says Phillips Idowu but I'll never jump out of the shadow of Jonathan Edwards* (Mail on Sunday, 25 October 2009)

Verschoth, Anita, *THE BOUNDING BARRISTER* (Sports Illustrated, 17 May 1982)

White, Lonnie, *LEAP OF FAITH* (Los Angeles Times, 26 April 2005)

Wind, Herbert W., *AROUND THE MULBERRY BUSH* (Sports Illustrated, 3 March 1958)

Zeigler, Mark, *Column: Ban Russian athletes if want, but not because of Ukraine invasion* (The San Diego Union-Tribune, 19 July 2022)

Internet

Preface
https://usopm.org/james-connolly-was-an-unlikely-u-s-olympic-hero/
https://olympics.nbcsports.com/2020/04/06/james-connolly-first-olympic-champion/
https://olympics.com/en/news/connolly-takes-a-leap-into-the-history-books

Irish Trailblazers
https://www.limerickpost.ie/2020/04/08/the-athea-brothers-who-took-on-the-world-and-won/?fbclid=IwAR0DQZ2VmQ6D1nr2z1MxyNSS0LPQPUp74vVib8h0R ZR6qjCitwcU0WChB7E
http://www.limerickcity.ie/Library/LocalStudies/SeamusOCeallaighsGreat LimerickSportsmen/
https://www.irishtimes.com/opinion/great-leaps-forward-an-irishman-s-diary-about-our-supposed-national-talent-for-long-jumping-1.3458384
https://www.independent.ie/sport/other-sports/flying-26878664.html
http://homepages.rootsweb.com/~aherns/danahern.htm
https://localstudies.limerick.ie/Library/LocalStudies/LocalStudiesFiles/S/S portsPeople/

From the Bush to Paris
http://isoh.org/wp-content/uploads/2015/04/7.pdf
https://adb.anu.edu.au/biography/winter-anthony-william-9156
https://www.athletics.com.au/hall-of-fame-directory/anthony-nick-winter/
https://sahof.org.au/hall-of-fame-member/nick-winter/

The Jumping Sons of Japan
https://worldathletics.org/news/news/interview-with-mikio-oda-first-japanese-olymp
https://www.insidethegames.biz/articles/1107749/japans-first-olympic-champion-blog
https://yab.yomiuri.co.jp/adv/wol/dy/culture/140326.html
https://abcnews.go.com/Sports/wireStory/era-oda-wins-japans-olympic-gold-1928-64432127
https://olympics.com/en/news/oda-jumps-for-joy
https://theolympians.co/2017/02/22/naoto-tajima-part-1-the-last-japanese-star-at-the-end-of-japans-track-and-field-golden-age/
http://www.athleticsasia.org/legends-of-asia-naoto-tajima/
https://sahof.org.au/hall-of-fame-member/jack-metcalfe/
https://theolympians.co/2017/02/23/naoto-tajima-part-2-the-last-japanese-star-at-the-end-of-japans-track-and-field-golden-age/

Death from Brazil
https://www.insidethegames.biz/articles/1040623/adhemar-ferreira-da-silva-the-brazilian-sporting-legend-forgotten-by-rio-2016

https://worldathletics.org/news/news/brazilian-olympic-champion-adhemar-ferreira-d
https://www.worldathletics.org/heritage/plaque/list/dietrich-gerner
https://www.insidethegames.biz/articles/1040623/adhemar-ferreira-da-silva-the-brazilian-sporting-legend-forgotten-by-rio-2016

The Eastern Bloc Arrives
https://www.linkedin.com/pulse/depth-jump-shock-method-common-misconceptions-valeri-stoimenov/

17 Metre József
https://katowice.wyborcza.pl/katowice/7,35024,26185414,mija-60-lat-od-rekordu swiata-jozefa-szmidta-byl-pierwszym.html?disableRedirects=true [in Polish]
https://sport.onet.pl/igrzyska/historia/jozef-schmidt/lmvxr [in Polish]
https://www.olsztyn24.com/news/10300-jak-bdquoslaski-kangurrdquo-honorowe-obywatelstwo-olsztyna-odbieral.html [in Polish]
https://sport.tvp.pl/49738697/kangur-z-polski-jak-jozef-szmidt-zostawal-mistrzem-olimpijskim [in Polish]

Milestones in Mexico City
https://www.lagazzettadelmezzogiorno.it/news/sport/1128790/olimpiadi-citta-del-messico-1968-gentile-e-la-medaglia-spezzata.html [in Italian]
http://www.sportolimpico.it/index.php?option=com_content&view=article&id=2553:saro-greve-luigi-rosati-maestro-amico-e-fratello&catid=1:focus [in Italian]
https://www.gazzetta.it/Atletica/17-10-2018/messico1968-olimpiadi-300740440534.shtml [in Italian]
http://www.sienanews.it/sport/panathlon-club-siena-conviviale-di-marzo-con-giuseppe-gentile/ [in Italian]

Golden Viktor
https://www.pbs.org/stealinghome/sport/diamond.html
http://www.cubadebate.cu/noticias/2018/07/19/pedro-perez-duenas-reivindicacion-de-un-hombre-record/ [in Spanish]

Mischief in Moscow
https://www.uol.com.br/esporte/reportagens-especiais/a-morte-tripla-de-joao-do-pulo/#page7
[in Portuguese]
https://terceirotempo.uol.com.br/que-fim-levou/joao-do-pulo-1679 [in Portuguese]
https://www.geledes.org.br/a-historia-de-joao-do-pulo-um-icones-do-esporte-brasileiro/ [in Portuguese]
https://www.cbat.org.br/atletas/nelson.asp [in Portuguese]
https://www.smh.com.au/sport/athletics/cheating-the-only-conclusion-you-can-jump-to-20130817-2s3q6.html
https://www.theguardian.com/sport/blog/2013/aug/07/ian-campbell-triple-jumper-moscow-olympics

https://www.theguardian.com/news/1999/jun/16/guardianobituaries.duncanmackay
https://uk.sports.yahoo.com/news/robbed-at-the-1980-olympics-123321307.html
https://chernayakobra.ru/i-wanted-to-sell-medals-i-served-pizza-zigzags-of-fate-for-champion-saneev/
https://www.insidethegames.biz/articles/1096450/phil-barker-big-read-moscow-1980-forty

Hand-Clapping Willie
https://www.presstelegram.com/2009/05/01/former-ucla-leaper-still-gets-a-hand/
https://www.latimes.com/archives/la-xpm-2005-apr-26-sp-uclatrack26-story.html
https://ca.milesplit.com/articles/244151/legends-of-the-sport-the-impact-of-willie-banks
https://timesofsandiego.com/sports/2021/07/19/world-record-for-willie-banks-at-65-tokyo-games-official-top-high-jumper/
https://lopemagazine.com/2020/08/25/willie-banks-world-athletics-council-track-interview-triple-jump-clap/
https://worldathletics.org/news/press-release/willie-banks-world-record-vest-heritage-donat

Fast and Flat – Jonathan Edwards
https://www.european-athletics.com/news/golden-moments-edwards-giant-leap-the-1995-european-cup
https://theolympians.co/2021/08/02/yulimar-rojas-sets-the-world-record-for-womens-triple-jump-willie-banks-knows-she-can-do-better/
https://www.reuters.com/article/athletics-idowu-idUKLDE71D1CE20110215
https://www.european-athletics.com/news/edwards-barrier-breaking-leap-celebrates-another-anniversary
https://worldathletics.org/heritage/news/jonathan-edwards-world-record-triple-jump
https://worldathletics.org/news/feature/jonathan-edwards-world-record-triple-jump
https://www.bbc.co.uk/sport/athletics/53661335

The GOAT?
https://olympics.com/en/news/christian-taylor-injury-recovery-podcast-interview
https://worldathletics.org/news/news/christian-olsson-is-for-real
https://worldathletics.org/news/news/edwards-simply-a-matter-of-faith
https://worldathletics.org/news/report/mens-triple-jump-final-taylor-sails-1796m
https://athleticsweekly.com/featured/a-quantum-leap-for-christian-taylor-34816/
https://worldathletics.org/news/report/london-2012-event-report-mens-triple-jump-1

https://edition.cnn.com/2014/09/24/sport/christian-taylor-triple-jump-olympics-athletics/index.html
https://olympics.nbcsports.com/2016/01/11/christian-taylor-triple-jump-track-and-field-olympics/
https://worldathletics.org/news/series/christian-taylor-usa-triple-jump-challenge
https://www.worldathletics.org/news/report/doha-2015-diamond-league-pichardo-taylor
https://worldathletics.org/news/feature/pichardo-triple-jump
https://www.insidethegames.biz/articles/1028638/how-the-iaafs-lausanne-diamond-league-pointed-the-way-to-future-successful-meetings-no-dull-world-record-attempts
https://www.runblogrun.com/2014/12/christian-taylor-to-move-to-netherlands-following-coach-rana-reider.html
https://www.si.com/more-sports/2015/12/14/christian-taylor-triple-jump-world-record-rio-2016-olympics
https://eu.usatoday.com/story/sports/olympics/rio-2016/2016/08/10/christian-taylor-triple-jump-gold-medalist/88529144/
https://athleticsweekly.com/featured/christian-taylor-challenge-world-record-london-47310/
https://sportsworld.nbcsports.com/christian-taylor-world-record-olympics/
https://worldathletics.org/competitions/diamond-league/news/eugene-diamond-league-2017-taylor-triple-jump
https://www.eurosport.com/athletics/world-championships/2017/christian-taylor-has-jonathan-edwards-triple-jump-world-record-in-his-sights_sto6275794/story.shtml
https://worldathletics.org/spikes/news/will-claye-strength-from-above
https://www.insidethegames.biz/articles/1135636/tamgho-seeks-return-at-paris-2024
https://www.insidethegames.biz/articles/1108036/christian-taylor-ruptured-achilles
https://apnews.com/article/8013107225a24e708fe9a19e265351a3

The Coming Men...
https://www.worldathletics.org/spikes/news/ato-boldon-speaks-to-pedro-pablo-pichardo
https://www.redbull.com/int-en/pedro-pichardo-triple-jump-interview
https://olympics.com/en/news/burkina-fasos-hugues-fabrice-zango-creates-history-2022-worlds
https://www.insidethegames.biz/articles/1092625/fisu-legend-hugues-fabrice-zango
https://worldathletics.org/competitions/world-athletics-indoor-championships/world-athletics-indoor-championships-7138985/news/feature/triple-jump-comeback-lazaro-martinez-belgrade
https://oncubanews.com/deportes/atletismo/lazaro-martinez-cielo-abierto-bajo-techo/ [in Spanish]
https://worldathletics.org/competitions/world-athletics-indoor-championships/world-athletics-indoor-championships-7138985/news/report/belgrade-22-men-triple-jump-report

https://worldathletics.org/news/feature/world-u18-champs-nairobi-2017-jordan-diaz-tri
https://morningexpress.in/jordan-diaz-the-athlete-who-changed-cuba-for-spain-my-parents-told-me-you-have-to-leave-if-you-want-to-be-great/
https://www.tribunaavila.com/noticias/296262/el-salto-de-jonathan-edwards-en-salamanca-resiste-por-11-centimetros-al-huracan-jordan-diaz [in Spanish]
https://www.elespanol.com/deportes/otros-deportes/20220203/jordan-diaz-atletismo-escondio-zaragoza-espana-nacionalizado/647185486_0.html [in Spanish]
https://worldathletics.org/competitions/world-athletics-u20-championships/world-athletics-u20-championships-7163112/news/report/wu20-cali-22-day-five-afternoon-field-hibbert
https://sportsmax.tv/athletics/item/119427-american-triple-jump-legend-mike-conley-sr-describes-jaydon-hibbert-as-special-he-was-born-to-do-it
https://www.wholehogsports.com/news/2023/may/14/hibbert-sets-record-as-razorbacks-claim-title/

Women On The Rise
https://www.smithsonianmag.com/science-nature/rise-modern-sportswoman-180960174/
https://www.sportanddev.org/latest/news/tracing-challenging-history-women's-participation-sport
https://repository.brynmawr.edu/cgi/viewcontent.cgi?referer=&httpsredir=1&article=1001&context=bmc_yearbooks
https://www.theguardian.com/sport/blog/2012/jun/30/london-2012-clean-athletes-drugs

Controversial Kravets
https://www.elespectador.com/deportes/caterine-debe-ser-mas-veloz-para-romper-mi-record-inessa-kravets/ [in Spanish]
https://www.ukrweekly.com/archive/1993/The_Ukrainian_Weekly_1993-13.pdf

Rising Rojas
https://as.com/juegos_olimpicos/2021/07/31/noticias/1627712545_069637.html [in Spanish]
https://olympics.com/ioc/news/ioc-sanctions-16-athletes-for-failing-anti-doping-tests-at-beijing-2008
https://athleticsweekly.com/featured/triple-jumper-hrysopiyi-devetzi-set-to-be-stripped-of-olympic-bronze-51962/
https://worldathletics.org/news/news/mbango-etone-makes-history-as-she-becomes-fir
https://olympics.com/ioc/news/ioc-sanctions-two-athletes-for-failing-anti-doping-test-at-beijing-2008
https://coachesinsider.com/track-x-country/triple-jumpers-the-different-characteristics-of-male-and-female-jumpers/
https://worldathletics.org/news/report/idl-rome-ibarguen-van-niekirk

https://world-track.org/2021/08/rio-olympic-champion-caterine-ibarguen-retires-37/
https://viewsfromtheconcourse.com/2021/07/29/yulimar-rojas-venezuelas-first-athletics-gold-medallist/
https://www.archysport.com/2021/08/tokyo-2020-athletics-yulimar-rojas-the-girl-from-the-ranch-who-could-with-inessa-kravets/
https://cronica.uno/en-la-cuna-de-preparacion-de-la-medallista-olimpica-yulimar-rojas-reinan-la-desidia-y-el-abandono/ [in Spanish]
https://www.france24.com/en/live-news/20210802-sky-s-the-limit-for-venezuela-s-olympic-champion-rojas
https://worldathletics.org/news/feature/portland-2016-rojas-triple-jump
https://www.caracaschronicles.com/2019/09/14/yulimar-rojas-historical-jump/
https://worldathletics.org/news/report/rio-2016-olympic-games-women-triple-jump-fina
https://www.batimes.com.ar/news/latin-america/venezuelas-supreme-court-decriminalises-homosexuality-in-armed-forces.phtml
https://www.insidethegames.biz/articles/1053801/rojas-topples-ibarguen-to-earn-venezuelas-first-ever-world-gold
https://worldathletics.org/news/feature/yulimar-rojas-triple-jump-venezuela
https://www.liderendeportes.com/noticias/mas-deportes/sere-la-primera-mujer-en-saltar-16-metros/ [in Spanish]
https://worldathletics.org/competitions/olympic-games/news/yulimar-rojas-venezuela-triple-jump-world-ind
https://www.insidethegames.biz/articles/1090896/world-triple-jump-record-for-rojas
https://worldathletics.org/news/report/indoor-tour-madrid-2020-world-record-triple-j
https://www.insidethegames.biz/articles/1111094/yulimar-rojas-triple-jump-world-record
https://versionfinal.com.ve/deportes/inessa-kravets-yulimar-puede-batir-mi-record/
https://webcache.googleusercontent.com/search?q=cache:U0BK_TAoF10J:https://iaafworldathleticschamps.com/doha2019/kravets-believes-its-time-for-her-triple-jump-world-record-to-fall/&cd=15&hl=en&ct=clnk&gl=uk&client=safari
https://worldathletics.org/competitions/world-athletics-championships/budapest23/news/news/the-superhero-who-jumped-from-poverty-to-the-top-of-the-world
https://theolympians.co/2021/08/02/yulimar-rojas-sets-the-world-record-for-womens-triple-jump-willie-banks-knows-she-can-do-better/
https://olympics.com/en/video/yulimar-rojas-wonder-woman-superhero

Finally, we hope that you have enjoyed journeying through the history of the triple jump with us... reviews will help to spread the word so if you are minded, please leave a review on either Amazon or The Great British Bookshop.

Andy & Lawrence

www.harveybennsmethod.com

BS - #0013 - 121223 - C64 - 234/156/19 - PB - 9781739474959 - Gloss Lamination